REFORMING THE MORAL SUBJECT

REFORMING
THE MORAL SUBJECT

Ethics and Sexuality in Central Europe,
1890–1930

TRACIE MATYSIK

CORNELL UNIVERSITY PRESS
ITHACA AND LONDON

Publication of this book was made possible, in part, by a University Co-operative Society Subvention Grant awarded by The University of Texas at Austin.

First published 2008 by Cornell University Press

Printed in the United States of America

Library of Congress Cataloging-in-Publication Data

Matysik, Tracie.
    Reforming the moral subject : ethics and sexuality in Central Europe, 1890–1930 / Tracie Matysik.
        p. cm.
    Includes bibliographical references and index.
    ISBN 978-0–8014–4712–9 (cloth : alk. paper)
    1. Ethical culture movement—Europe, Central—History—19th century.
2. Ethical culture movement—Europe, Central—History—20th century.
3. Sexual ethics—Europe, Central—History—19th century. 4. Sexual ethics—Europe, Central—History—20th century. 5. Ethics, Modern—19th century. 6. Ethics, Modern—20th century. 7. Europe, Central—Intellectual life—19th century. 8. Europe, Central—Intellectual life—20th century. 9. Europe, Central—Moral conditions. I. Title.

    BJ10.E8M33 2008
    170.943'09034—dc22
                                                                    2008033583

Cloth printing   10   9   8   7   6   5   4   3   2   1

Until now nobody has examined the *value* of that most famous of all medicines, that so-called morality: the first step would be—for once to question it. Well then, precisely this is our task.

FRIEDRICH NIETZSCHE

CONTENTS

Acknowledgments

In his book *Given Time,* Jacques Derrida described the gift as "the impossible"—as something that intrinsically demands repayment on the part of the recipient even as its very definition *as gift* prohibits such reciprocity. Whereas Derrida reflected on the gift and its impossibility in relationship to time and being, I have come to a much more personal understanding of it while writing this book, as I have accumulated a series of insurmountable debts along the way. Faced with the impossibility of ever repaying those myriad debts directly, I want at least to hint at my gratitude to the friends, colleagues, and institutions that have made this book possible.

I begin with my mentors. I owe most to Dominick LaCapra, who oversaw this project at its earliest stage and who has offered unswerving support for more than a decade. More important, he has modeled for me the value of "intellectual citizenship" as the openness to and engagement with new ideas. Isabel Hull has also been an invaluable mentor. She patiently guided me as I slowly acquired the skills of a historian, challenging me to find my own voice. I thank Biddy Martin not only for her always smart and kind mentorship but also for the thematic inspiration for this book. Neither she nor I understood the path she was sending me down by giving me her old photocopies of texts by Helene Stöcker and Ellen Key. My debts go back even further, to the Program in the Comparative History of Ideas at the University of Washington. John Toews and Jim Clowes sparked my intellectual interests and gave me the confidence to pursue them. John's friendship has been a personal treasure, and his teaching and research an inspiration. Sadly, Jim died before he could see this book, but I hope he understood the important influence he had on my life and work.

Andrew Zimmerman graciously offered to read my entire manuscript when it was near completion, encouraging me to send it to a publisher. Many others generously took the time to read this work in its entirety. Kathleen Canning's remarks on the penultimate version were invaluable, as were the comments of an anonymous reader for Cornell University Press. My colleagues at the University of Texas—David Crew, Joan Neuberger, and Bob Abzug—all labored through a slightly less polished version of the manuscript, giving me encouragement and helpful suggestions. Many people at Cornell University read all or parts of the manuscript, including Chris Bilodeau, Marlene Briggs, Ben Brower, Vicki Caron, Peter Dear, Federico Finchelstein, Mary Gayne, Peter Holquist, Steve Kaplan, Eleanor Kaufman, Anna Märker, Mary Miles, Anna Parkinson, Rachel Weil, Richard Schaefer, Brook Stanton, Michael Steinberg, Suzanne Stewart-Steinberg, Judith Surkis, Gary Tsifrin, and Adelheid Voskuhl. Friends and colleagues outside Cornell read and offered feedback on specific chapters. For their helpful insights, I thank Geoff Eley, Ben Hett, Jennifer Jordan, Brent Maner, John David Smith, John Toews, and Todd Weir.

I have presented several chapters or parts of chapters at conferences and colloquia over the years. I thank the organizers and participants of the European History Colloquium at Cornell University, of the Institute for German Culture Studies Colloquium at Cornell University, and of the Visiting Scholar Colloquium at the Center for European Studies at Harvard University. I am grateful to Carl Caldwell of Rice University for giving me the chance to present chapter 3 to a diverse range of scholars, and Linda Henderson for organizing the Modernist Studies Colloquium at the University of Texas, where I was able to get still further feedback. Richard Wetzell and Edward Ross Dickinson deserve thanks for allowing me to present chapter 5 to the Conference on the History of Sexuality at the German Historical Institute in Washington, D.C. I am grateful to Ludger Hermanns, who runs the Forum für die Geschichte der Psychoanalyse in Berlin, not only for allowing me to participate in that organization's monthly colloquium while I was living in Berlin but also for giving me a chance to present chapter 7. I also thank Edward Ross Dickinson, Geoff Eley, and Jennifer Jenkins for organizing the "Rethinking German Modernities" workshops, at which I was able to try out several small pieces of the book as well as reflect on the significance of my overall argument.

Over the years important conversations with individuals have helped me to think through this book and its orientation. I am especially grateful to Charles Maier, Andreas Daum, Kristin McGuire, and David Blackbourn for their time and insight.

Many institutions funded my work on this book. I thank the History Department, the Center for European Studies, and the Center for Feminist, Gender, and Sexuality Studies, all at Cornell University; the Deutscher Akademischer Austausch Dienst; and the Andrew W. Mellon Foundation for fellowships. The Andrew W. Mellon Foundation, together with the Department of German Studies and the Society for the Humanities at Cornell, provided a postdoctoral fellowship, giving me the chance to rethink the general argument. Likewise, a James Bryant Conant fellowship from the Minda de Gunzburg Center for European Studies at Harvard University provided me with time and resources for further research. The University of Texas subsequently offered a friendly home at which to finish this book. I am grateful for its extension of resources, including a Summer Research Assignment, a Dean's Fellowship, and many smaller research grants. I thank the Universität Erfurt and the Forschungsbibliothek Gotha, which together provided me the resources and welcoming environment to finish the last revisions. I am also indebted to the Stiftung Weimarer Klassik and the Kolleg-Friedrich-Nietzsche, as well as the Kolleg's director, Rüdiger Schmidt-Grépály, for a pleasant month at that institution in 2006, during which time I was able to double-check many citations and collect a last few documents.

Countless libraries and archives in Germany, the United States, Austria, and France provided assistance. I begin with my "home" libraries, first at Cornell University (Olin and Kroch libraries), then at Harvard University (Widener Library as well as the Divinity School's precious collections), and finally at the Perry-Castañeda Library at the University of Texas, where the interlibrary loan staff performed nothing short of miracles. Many institutions provided more temporary research homes, including the Rockefeller Library at Brown University, the Waidener-Spahr Library at Dickinson College, the Staatsbibliothek zu Berlin, the libraries at the Humboldt and Free universities in Berlin, and the Bibliothèque Nationale in Paris. The staffs at the Forschungsbibliothek Gotha in the beautiful Schloss Friedenstein and at the Herzogin-Anna-Amalia-Bibliothek in Weimar deserve special mention. Many archives also made their special collections available. For sharing their time and knowledge, I am grateful to Wendy Chmielewski and the staff at the Swarthmore Peace Collection in Pennsylvania, Reinhard Fabian and Jutta Valent and the archival staff at the Forschungsstelle und Dokumentationszentrum für Österreichische Philosophie in Graz, Thomas Bach at the Ernst-Haeckel-Archiv in Jena, Kornelia Küchmeister and the staff at the Schleswig-Holsteinsche Landesbibliothek in Kiel, Evelyn Liepsch at the Goethe- und Schiller-Archiv in Weimar, and the staffs at the Kungliga Biblioteket in Stockholm, the Landesarchiv Berlin, and the Rare Book and Manuscript Collection at Columbia University. I thank Dorothee Pfeiffer of the Lou Andreas-Salomé-Archiv in Göttingen for granting me brief reading privileges of correspondence between Salomé and Ellen Key. I am also grateful to the Ehrenfels family for permission to see and reference the personal papers of Christian von Ehrenfels.

I have had the good fortune to work with two gracious and excellent editors at Cornell University Press: Alison Kalett and John Ackerman. Alison offered insightful comments on both the macro- and microscopic levels—as well as much-needed encouragement—during the last months of writing. John used his expert editorial skills to help me see the project in a broader and more reader-friendly perspective. Kim Vivier did a masterful job with the copyediting. I thank these three and the entire staff at Cornell University Press—especially Teresa Jesionowski—for their work on this book. I also thank Carol Blosser Fanning for her assistance with the index.

On a personal note, I thank my family for their years of support as they tried to grasp my devotion to this project and this career. The number of friends who have provided encouragement over the last several years is too long to list. I mention only Susan Boettcher, Carolyn Eastman, Loril Gossett, Taylor Martin, Al Martinez, and Karl Miller, who together have provided an infallible support network at the University of Texas since I arrived in 2003.

Chris Bilodeau has stood by my side throughout the highs and lows of this endeavor. He has read or listened to almost every word of this book and has offered refuge when I needed a break. Most important, he has somehow remained my friend all these years, even when my anxiety and obsessions would have tried the patience of any other saint. To him I dedicate this book.

TRACIE MATYSIK

Austin, Texas

Reforming the Moral Subject

Introduction

CRITICAL ETHICS, OR THE SUBJECT OF REFORM

"All thinking persons can see that ideas about upstanding morality upheld by the religions and laws of the occident are experiencing in our time a radical reorganization."[1] Thus opened *Love and Marriage,* the 1905 manifesto of the Swedish feminist activist Ellen Key, who toured Europe in search of like-minded reformers committed to "a life-enhancing use of the sexual powers both for the individual and for the race."[2] It was no coincidence, however, that, in the words of the British sexologist Havelock Ellis, "it is in Germany that her fame has been made."[3] Indeed, when Key's book appeared in German translation, arguing for the deregulation of sexual relations as the key to a human future, it found a climate primed for

1. Ellen Key, *Über Liebe und Ehe,* trans. from Swedish to German by Francis Maro (Berlin, 1905), 1. All translations into English are my own unless otherwise indicated.
2. Ibid., 4.
3. Havelock Ellis, Introduction to *Love and Marriage,* by Ellen Key, trans. from Swedish to English by Arthur G. Chater (New York, 1912), xiii.

debate. Heated public discussions among intellectuals were already taking place about the role of ethics in modern life, about the relationship of ethics to inherited custom, religion, and law, and about the place of sexuality in ethics and the makeup of the moral subject. That is, it landed in a climate ready for cultural reorientation or, in the words of the Central European interlocutors, for "ethics reform."

Ethics reform (*ethische Reform*), sometimes also referred to as the ethics movement (*ethische Bewegung*), was a broad and protean movement concentrated in Germany but extending into the Austrian Empire and Switzerland and in dialogue with individuals and groups throughout Europe and North America. It consisted of intellectuals and activists primarily from free-thinker or religious dissident orientation—including sexual liberationists, moral philosophers, pedagogy reformers, eugenicists, socialists, psychoanalysts, and many others. These participants were joined by two common sentiments: first, that *ethics mattered,* that is, that ethics was a crucial topic of public consideration with implications for all dimensions of social organization; and second, that ethics needed to be rethought for an explicitly modern context.

But why did participants in ethics reform come to see ethics as a privileged category of social organization and reform? To answer this question, it is helpful to consider the macroscopic context. In Germany in particular, significant social transformations were under way in the last years of the nineteenth century, opening up basic questions about social life. Germany had unified in 1871 and shortly thereafter had undergone a rapid process of industrialization at a pace unmatched in Europe. With industrialization came an unprecedented population growth of 60 percent between unification in 1871 and the outbreak of World War I in 1914. Moreover, industrialization and population expansion combined to produce equally rapid urbanization. Cities such as Berlin, where the ethics reform movement had its greatest concentration, more than doubled in size between 1871 and 1910, while other cities whose growth centered on industry had much more dramatic population increases.[4] Something similar was happening in the multinational Austrian Empire, as residents from the Austrian

---

4. Numbers quoted in David Blackbourn, *The Long Nineteenth Century: A History of Germany, 1780–1918* (Oxford, 1998), 200, 351. See also Thomas Nipperdey, *Deutsche Geschichte, 1866–1918* (Munich, 1990), 37.

countryside flooded into Vienna. This urban migration meant that a large number of individuals now lived in new social contexts, a circumstance that involved, as the women's activist Marianne Weber observed, "the social uprooting of the individual from earlier groups and forms of community" and a corresponding "disruption of inherited, self-evident norms and religious traditions." For Weber, the new social circumstances meant that "the moral question today is not only a question of individual character building, but a social question for which we all are responsible in the highest measure."[5]

If dramatic social change brought with it a certain anxiety about lost traditions, as Weber's lament illustrates, it entailed as well the sense that everything was possible—that society could be made anew. From efforts at education reform to innovations in social welfare, from nudism to vegetarianism to nature preservation, Germany and Central Europe were awash with ideas of social, cultural, and political reform at the turn of the century. And much of this effort at reform took place outside channels of government or political parties. To be sure, Kaiser Wilhelm II's ascendancy to the throne in Germany in 1890 and his announcement of a "New Course" brought with it optimism about political reform, especially on the "social question." And efforts at political and governmental reform continued from 1890 until 1914 and the outbreak of World War I. But in this period, reform in civil society that often included but was not limited to lobbying for governmental action was even more common, especially as discussions of reform in civil society traveled easily across political borders.[6]

In this regard, the ethics movement was typical of reform movements. Its participants tended to view the changing social circumstances less as crisis than as opportunity and a worthy challenge—and as one to be addressed

5. Marianne Weber, "Sexual-ethische Prinzipienfragen" (1907), in *Frauenfragen und Frauengedanken: Gesammelte Aufsätze* (Tübingen, 1919), 46. On urbanization in Europe, see Andrew Lees, *Cities Perceived: Urban Society in European and American Thought, 1820–1940* (Manchester, 1985).

6. On the role of the "New Course" in triggering social reform, see Kevin Repp, *Reformers, Critics, and the Paths of German Modernity: Anti-politics and the Search for Alternatives, 1890–1914* (Cambridge, Mass., 2000), 19–37. On political reform in the *Kaiserreich*, see Geoff Eley and James Retallack, eds., *Wilhelminism and Its Legacies: German Modernities, Imperialism, and the Meanings of Reform, 1890–1930* (New York, 2003); and Rüdiger vom Bruch, ed., *Weder Kommunismus noch Kapitalismus: Bürgerliche Sozialreform in Deutschland vom Vormärz bis zur Ära Adenauer* (Munich, 1985).

largely in the realm of civil society. But its spokespersons also claimed for ethics reform a special role as the most fundamental of all categories of reform because it offered them a way to rethink what makes social life possible in a modern context. By approaching social problems from the standpoint of ethics, reformers could ask in abstract terms how individuals relate to society, to tradition, to family, to nation, to law. They could ask what exactly constitutes a moral subject, where moral conscience or sentiment originates, and how intimate relations inform moral subjectivity. And they could ask what constitutes a community of moral responsibility: should it be defined as coterminous with the *Volk* or the nation, or instead be defined as universal humanity—or, more disturbingly, as the "white race"? In an explicitly critical vein, discussions of ethics were a way to question the moral foundation of existing definitions of state, citizen, and subject—to ask how and why an individual is supposed to feel a special moral loyalty to a particular community or nation. Moreover, these discussions were a way to ask such questions not just about currently existing relations and institutions but also about the kinds of relations and institutions that *should* exist. In this sense, ethics—rather than law, social contract, constitutions—proved the most critical category of interrogation because it was said to belong properly to no existing institutions: not to the state, not to the church, not to the law.

In its critical function, ethics reform represented a culture of intellectual liberalism, though not in the sense of a political party, or in the sense of an economic or political doctrine, or even in the sense of unlimited freedom of expression. Rather, it represented intellectual liberalism in its commitment to cultural activism, or to a context in which private individuals and organizations could voice opinion, debate the most basic dimensions of social life, and lobby accordingly for political and social change.[7]

For the ethics reform movement, terminology was of utmost importance from the outset. In their efforts to open up the language of ethics

7. Alternatively, ethics reform could be said to represent an "age of Enlightenment," in the sense that Immanuel Kant famously used the term in his essay "An Answer to the Question: 'What Is Enlightenment?'" in *Kant: Political Writings,* ed. Hans Reiss, trans. H. B. Nisbet (Cambridge, 1970), 54–60. Ethics reform also suggests a more vibrant public sphere at the end of the nineteenth century than Jürgen Habermas credited to the period in his *Strukturwandel der Öffentlichkeit: Untersuchungen zu einer Kategorie der bürgerlichen Gesellschaft* (Neuwied, 1962).

for critical interrogation, ethics reformers regularly distinguished between *Ethik* (ethics) as a critical mode of interrogation and *Sittlichkeit* (morality) as a set of inherited norms that many reformers found ill-equipped for modernity. The Austrian philosopher Friedrich Jodl, for example, outlining the goals of one of the major ethics reform organizations, explained why he and his colleagues had chosen to talk about ethics rather than morality:

> The words *"sittlich"* [moral] and *"moralisch"* [moralistic] are somewhat hackneyed phrases in German usage; a certain pedantic trait clings to *"moralisch,"* and *"sittlich"* has taken on a specific meaning in recent times. I think only of the German *Sittlichkeits-Vereine* [morality leagues] that have just the tiniest bit to do with what we describe as our aims. *"Ethik,"* however, is the name of that academic discipline that seeks to derive the rules of reasonable organization of life for the individual and for the whole from thoughtful observation of people and society.[8]

Not all reformers endorsed Jodl's platform, but the sentiment that *Ethik* stands in critical relationship to *Sittlichkeit* and the conviction that it was necessary to rethink ethics altogether were the chief characteristics of "ethics reform" as a movement, however broad and various. Some reformers sought simply to draw attention to uncritical presuppositions behind specific moral claims made by public officials or luminaries; others insistently mobilized new definitions of ethics. Arguments flared as universalists confronted historicists, and rationalists faced off against biological primitivists. One strain of reformers took cues from Immanuel Kant, another from the utilitarianism of Jeremy Bentham; many sexual liberationists found promise in Friedrich Nietzsche's thought, while some left-liberal and socialist thinkers took their talking points from Karl Marx. The vigor of the ethics movement thus consisted not in the mobilization of a particular conception of ethics but rather in the disagreements that fed into the ethics debates. In seeking to reproduce the vitality of those disagreements, this book does not define ethics in advance, preferring rather to chronicle how the idea of ethics functioned as a historically contingent site of contestation.

8. Friedrich Jodl, *Wesen und Ziele der ethischen Bewegung in Deutschland* (Frankfurt am Main, 1893), 4.

Approaching ethics from often irreconcilable stances, intellectuals and activists nevertheless found several important points of agreement. First, they agreed that the definition of ethics and the makeup of the moral subject were not mere academic topics but pressing matters of public and political concern central to all considerations of social order—from law to politics to private intimacy. Further, while disagreeing fervently about the hows and the whys, interlocutors also found common ground with the assumption that sexuality must somehow be central to any discussion of ethics. Some viewed the moral entity as that being that could suppress sexual drives; others saw sexual drives and sexual autonomy as the source of moral energy and sentiment, the very grounds of the moral command to "love thy neighbor." Despite such differences, however, a consensus gradually emerged that sexuality was somehow constitutive of the moral subject. Finally, in their shared assumption that ethics and sexuality were urgent topics for public discussion, participants in the ethics debates succeeded in taking the seemingly private matters of sexuality and moral conscience out of the private domain and making them matters of public relevance.

Not surprisingly, sexuality came to inflect considerations of ethics at the fin de siècle, as it came to inflect almost all aspects of the era's public life. Not only did sexology establish itself as a recognized field of study during those years, but Darwinism and its social Darwinist offshoots put issues of sexual selection squarely on the cultural map. Things took a eugenical turn after 1895, as Germany's birth rate began to decline and "population politics" erupted in public and state discourse.[9] At the same time, the women's movement blossomed, and with it grew discussions of gender roles that gave way by the turn of the century to more explicit discussions of sexuality and sexual roles. As some bourgeois groups mobilized for public decency and others sought to educate working-class women in "proper" sexual behavior, the more radical middle-class branch of the women's movement dared to speak of women's sexual enjoyment and reproductive freedom. If smaller in numbers, the homosexual emancipation movement was also gaining strength by the century's turn. Furthermore, none of these developments was ever far removed from general *Lebensreform* (life reform)

9. James Woycke, *Birth Control in Germany, 1871–1933* (New York, 1988), 1.

efforts, some coupling abstinence with vegetarianism and ideas of a healthy body, others combining a return to nature with healthy sex lives.

So broad was the growing rhetoric about sexual matters that it seems impossible that ethics discussions could have failed to join in. But if the ethics discussions were bound to be sexualized, they were not bound to take that sexualization in any particular direction. Certainly some voices argued for explicit social and self-regulation of sexual behaviors and desires, and hence for the strengthening of a moral conscience, while others clung to humanist models of centered, autonomous subjects. Yet these voices were matched by those that mobilized the sexualized moral subject in ways that confounded categorization and eluded regulation and stable identity formation. The latter might even be seen to have anticipated the stylizing of the self that Michel Foucault articulated in the last years of his life.[10] Indeed, precisely the association of sexuality with a wide and

10. In books such as *Discipline and Punish* and *The History of Sexuality, Volume 1,* Foucault emphasized how social-scientific, humanist, and social-reform discourses produced the modern subject of discipline. Over the years, many avenues of departure have evolved from and against this Foucauldean critique of the subject. Feminist theory long contested the adequacy of the Foucauldean framework, drawing attention to the kinds of subjects—or the dimensions of the subject—that elude categorization and discipline. Psychoanalytic theory, too, especially in its Lacanian bent, asked whether Foucault's account of subject-formation adequately accounted for the "subject of desire," the subject as that which falls out of, or fails in, language. According to Joan Copjec, for instance, the "historicist" paradigm, as she calls it, reduces subjectivity entirely to discourse; the Lacanian paradigm, conversely, considers the crucial moment of subject-formation to be the construction of a desire that is pushed out of the realm of representation. In the last years of his life, however, Foucault himself began to supplement his portrayal of the subject of discipline with inquiries into the "aesthetics of existence" and the "care of the self." In this shift, he did not renounce his earlier understanding of the self as a product of discursive disciplinary networks. Rather, he simply shifted emphasis from the passive subject as the entity on which those disciplinary mechanisms work, or which they produce, to the active subject who reflects on and negotiates those mechanisms. Insisting on a rhetoric of freedom rather than liberation, Foucault emphasized that the active subject—again, still a product of discursive mechanisms—can nevertheless make choices about how the self will situate itself in relation to any particular disciplinary practice. This book follows none of these theoretical frameworks but rather is indebted to them all in its effort to reconstruct the fin-de-siècle debates on subject formation. On feminist counters to Foucault, see, for instance, Dianna Taylor and Karen Vintges, eds., *Feminism and the Final Foucault* (Urbana, Ill., 2004); Caroline Ramazanoğlu, ed., *Up against Foucault: Explorations of Some Tensions between Foucault and Feminism* (New York, 1993); Jana Sawicki, *Disciplining Foucault: Feminism, Power, and the Body* (New York, 1991); and Biddy Martin, "Feminism, Criticism, and Foucault," in *Knowing Women: Feminism and Knowledge,* ed.

variegated discussion of ethics made the sexualized moral subject an open concept that could not be fully regulated, confined, or conflated with national identity.

It is tempting to assume that this public interest in the sexuality of the moral subject implied a heightened social regulation of the private individual. Indeed, even the most enthusiastic celebrators of European liberalism and its supposed protection of the individual's private life and conscience had long feared that both political and cultural democratization exposed that lone individual to ever greater social scrutiny and control, subject not just to the distant sovereign's law but to the autonomous neighbors' scrutinizing norms.[11] Yet attention to public intellectual discussion of ethics and sexuality in fin-de-siècle Central Europe suggests a different picture. If intellectual and activist interest in ethics could lend itself at times to social regulation of the individual's most private domain, it could also work in the opposite direction. That is, many participants in the debates sought to open up the related categories of ethics and sexuality to ask how the seemingly private phenomena of individual moral conscience and sexuality might challenge the contours of the public. Moreover, they often defined the sexualized moral subject in ways that posed critical questions to and even eluded social discipline. Altogether the conjoined attention to ethics and sexuality

---

Helen Crowley and Susan Himmelweit (Cambridge, Mass., 1992). Joan Copjec provides the best statement of the Lacanian challenge to Foucault in her *Read My Desire: Lacan against the Historicists* (Cambridge, Mass., 1994). Although Judith Butler remains much more indebted to the Foucauldean tradition, her own work, *The Psychic Life of Power: Theories in Subjection* (Palo Alto, Calif., 1997), can also be seen to pose questions about the adequacy of a Foucauldean model of constructed subjects. For Foucault's disciplinary period, see *Discipline and Punish: The Birth of the Prison*, trans. Alan Sheridan (New York, 1979); and *The History of Sexuality, Vol. 1*, trans. Robert Hurley (New York, 1990). For his late self-critiques, see *The History of Sexuality, Vol. 2: The Use of Pleasure*, trans. Robert Hurley (New York, 1990); "An Aesthetics of Existence" and "The Art of Telling the Truth," trans. Alan Sheridan, in *Michel Foucault: Politics, Philosophy, Culture; Interviews and Other Writings, 1977–1984*, ed. Lawrence Kritzman (New York, 1990); and "The Ethic of Care for the Self as a Practice of Freedom," trans. J. D. Gauthier, *Philosophy and Social Criticism* 2 (1987): 112–131.

11. See, for instance, Alexis de Tocqueville's concerns about the "tyranny of the majority" or John Stuart Mill's anxiety about the "social tyranny" that is "more formidable than many kinds of political oppression" because "it leaves fewer means of escape, penetrating much more deeply into the details of life, and enslaving the soul itself." In Alexis de Tocqueville (quoting James Madison), *Democracy in America,* trans. George Lawrence (New York, 1988), 246–276; and John Stuart Mill, *On Liberty* (Indianapolis, Ind., 1978), 4.

suggests neither a social regulation that infringed ever more on the private lives of individuals nor an ever-expanding realm of individual liberties; rather, it reveals a vibrant, multifaceted, sustained engagement with the very terms by which the self and the social, the public and the private—in other words, the building blocks of liberalism—might be understood.

The first task of this book is thus to reconstruct the climate in which definitions of ethics and of the moral subject were vital concerns of public inquiry in Central Europe at the turn of the nineteenth to the twentieth century. It concentrates especially on ethics reformers, those who explicitly sought to update and modernize the language of ethics, but it treats as well their many critics and the heated arguments reformers and their critics waged with one another. Second, the book depicts the prevalent but highly diverse assumption that sexuality was somehow central to any consideration of ethics and to the makeup of the moral subject. Finally, it uncovers the many and diverse meanings that the sexualization of the moral subject implied for his and especially her political, legal, national, and supranational status. Considerable ambiguity—and hence considerable debate—surrounded the relationship of femininity to ethics. In fact, because women did not enjoy full citizenship rights, the concepts of feminine morality and of a feminine subject of ethics were easily mobilized by reformers in their search for alternatives to an understanding of morality as equivalent with (and limited to) loyalty to the nation. This book follows reformers in its attention to the troubled relationship of ethics to femininity, but it suggests as well that the tension around the feminine subject of ethics is only a more obvious case of the general tension between moral subjecthood and either citizenship or national affiliation that ethics reformers highlighted.[12]

12. For complementary inquiries into the relationship between sexuality and the moral subject in Europe, see Judith Surkis, *Sexing the Citizen: Morality and Masculinity in France, 1870–1920* (Ithaca, N.Y., 2006); Richard Weikart, *From Darwin to Hitler: Evolutionary Ethics, Eugenics, and Racism in Germany* (New York, 2004); Andrew Lees, *Cities, Sin, and Social Reform in Imperial Germany* (Ann Arbor, Mich., 2002); Alan Hunt, *Governing Morals: A Social History of Moral Regulation* (New York, 1999); Lieselotte Steinbrügge, *The Moral Sex: Woman's Nature in the French Enlightenment,* trans. Pamela Selwyn (New York, 1995); and Kristin McGuire, "Activism, Intimacy, and the Politics of Selfhood: The Gendered Terms of Citizenship in Poland and Germany, 1890–1919" (Ph.D. diss., University of Michigan, 2004). My work builds especially on Ann Taylor Allen, *Feminism and Motherhood in Germany, 1800–1914* (New Brunswick, N.J., 1991), which addresses the gendering of ethics more so than the production of sexualized moral subjects.

Chronologically, this book begins with the late nineteenth century, with intellectuals who took up the challenges that Marx, Darwin, Nietzsche, and other materialist thinkers of the nineteenth century had brought to traditional ideas of moral norms. It ends with the politicization of ethics reform and its legacies in the seemingly nonpolitical but intellectually important psychoanalytic movement. The book does not, however, take Nietzsche, Darwin, Marx, or Freud as its specific focus. Rather, it seeks fundamentally to re-create the public intellectual discussion about ethics in the decades surrounding the turn of the century—debates that resonated insofar as they played out *as* public discussion and simultaneously sought to reshape the manner in which individuals understood the ethical relationship of their private lives to the public sphere. It is an intellectual history, but not one of a specific individual or a discrete intellectual movement. Rather, it is an intellectual history of a public discussion that was made up of conflicts and contradictions but that revolved around the shared theme of ethics. And it suggests that the interaction of ideas in the public is as complicated and requires as close a reading as that in the philosophy classroom.

With its emphasis on the public, the project of ethics reform tended to blur social boundaries. To be sure, the majority of discussants were middle class, highly educated, and of Protestant or Jewish descent. Yet beyond this generalization, the interests of participants in the discussions were broad. If led in part by university-based intellectuals who sought to make the academic philosophy of ethics relevant to nonacademic concerns, ethics reform was equally the project of writers without academic positions who nevertheless borrowed from and revised the language of the academy. Many of the female participants, for example, were among the first generation of university-educated women in Europe. In ethics reform, these women turned their intellectual training not to purely academic concerns but rather to public activist purposes. At times the discussions also cut across class lines. Although the majority of the leaders of the ethics reform movement

---

On the expansion of citizenship as a category of historical analysis, see Kathleen Canning, "Class vs. Citizenship: Keywords in German Gender History," *Central European History* 37, no. 2 (2004): 225–244; Canning and Sonja Rose, eds., *Gender, Citizenships, and Subjectivities* (Ames, Iowa, 2002); Aihwa Ong, *Flexible Citizenship: The Cultural Logics of Transnationality* (Durham, N.C., 1999); Pnina Werbner and Nira Yuval-Davis, eds., *Women, Citizenship, and Difference* (London, 1999); Bryan Turner, ed., *Citizenship and Social Theory* (London, 1993); and T. H. Marshall and Tom Bottomore, *Citizenship and Social Class, and Other Essays* (London, 1992).

came from the *Bildungsbürgertum* (educated middle class), representatives from both German and Austrian Social Democracy also participated in the debates, especially as they pertained to materialism and the possibilities of a materialist ethics. In this context, social activists and university philosophers, both men and women, found themselves on a common playing field.

It is important at the outset to establish how and why ethics mattered to contemporaries at the turn of the century and what implications ethics discussions seemed to carry. The first part of the book thus explores the politics of ethics reform as approached from two radically different but complementary angles. The opening chapter provides a panorama of the range of concerns beyond sexuality that discussions of ethics elicited in the last decade of the nineteenth century. It follows the controversy that surrounded the founding of the German Society for Ethical Culture in 1892, as intellectuals and activists from all parts of Central Europe offered up their opinions on the idea of ethics as a category of social organization. The second chapter explores the challenges ethics reform could pose to the liberal and nationally defined citizen as moral subject. It tracks the controversy that surrounded the Nietzsche-inspired sexual-liberationist "New Ethic" that Helene Stöcker developed in the 1890s and institutionalized in her League for the Protection of Mothers in 1905. The controversy itself highlights the tensions between the sexually autonomous moral subject Stöcker advocated and the conceptions of the liberal subject she called into question. Together the two chapters illustrate the social and intellectual breadth of conflict that discussions of ethics could elicit.

Part II consists of three chapters that witness the complex, multifaceted meaning of sexualized ethics and the sexed moral subject. Chapter 3 follows the fallout in the relatively staid German Society for Ethical Culture when it became institutionally allied with Stöcker's League for the Protection of Mothers. It highlights how opposing parties on matters of religion and secularism came to accept that an individual's ethical capacity necessarily derives from sexual drives in some form or other, disagreeing only about the implications of that sexualized moral subject for the meaning of ethics, of modern religion and secularism, and of subjectivity. Of course, the ethics debates took place against the background of European imperialism and a heightened rhetoric of race. Chapter 4 thus examines how the context of globalizing empire and race science inflected ethics debates. It takes as its focus three responses to ethics reform that struggled with ethics as a category operating on the border between culture and biology, and the prominent role that sexuality served in ethicists' related efforts to come to terms with matters of universalism and cultural difference. Chapter 5 examines the controversy that arose when, in 1909, the German government circulated a proposal for a new Criminal Code that would have criminalized female homosexuality. The discussions around the proposed Criminal Code reveal the difficulty of matching the sexual subject clearly to moral and legal definitions of subjecthood. This legal focus provides a glimpse of the effects of the multiple ways of viewing the sexualized moral subject in the reform context.

The final section of the book moves beyond ethics reform to examine resonances and resistances in adjacent political and cultural arenas. It turns to Social Democracy on the one hand and psychoanalysis on the other to see how the very movements that posed the most fundamental challenges to ethics reform as a movement also revealed the reach of its influence. Conventionally, the divide between bourgeois and worker movements is said to have been the deepest divide in German society during the *Kaiserreich*. Accordingly, one would expect Social Democracy to have demonstrated little interest in the largely bourgeois ethics reform movement. Chapter 6, however, examines the sustained dialogue between leaders of Social Democracy and ethics reformers, and the refracted ways in which Social Democracy at once resisted ethics reform while refashioning the language of ethics on its own historical materialist terms. With the onset of World War I, pressing debates of moral subject formation gave way to more immediate concerns, whether the politics of nationalism, pacifism, revolution, or democracy building. Yet the intellectual interest in the relationship of sexuality to ethics did not die, and psychoanalysis stepped in to fill the breach. On the one hand, psychoanalysis took a step away from the reform movement when it began to formulate conceptions of the conflicted moral subject that made ethics less open to reform. On the other hand, the "femininity debates" of the 1920s gave psychoanalysis an opportunity to consider its challenge to ethics within the terms of sexual differentiation in ways resonant with several strains of ethics reform. Focusing especially on Lou Andreas-Salomé and highlighting biographical and intellectual lines of connection between ethics reform and the psychoanalytic movement, chapter 7 depicts the ambivalent legacy of ethics reform and of the sexualized moral subject in psychoanalysis.

By the time psychoanalysis dove into its femininity debates, however, the legal and political situation had changed, and women had full citizenship rights in Germany and Austria. Accordingly, if the mobilization of a distinctively feminine ethics could play certain critical roles in the prewar era when women did not have full citizenship rights, it remains to ponder what role it played afterward. Did the articulation of woman's unique moral subject position now undermine her legal and political equality? Or did it suggest that despite legal citizenship something was still missing in women's social and cultural standing? Or did it continue simply to pose the kind of radical critique of citizenship that it once did, albeit from a different vantage point? These questions, which emerge out of chapter 7, serve as the springboard to a short afterword on the relationship of moral citizenship to legal and political rights. The afterword provides an opportunity to reflect on the lasting legacies of the critical approach to ethics by reformers at the turn of the nineteenth to the twentieth century. It asks whether challenges that were often posed in the name of sexually differentiated ethics were circumscribed by the era of heightened nationalism and empire or whether they are also relevant—if in new formations—in an even more globalized era.

With their mixed aims and outcomes, the ethics discussions as a whole indicate a climate much more publicly and politically dynamic than historians once portrayed.[13] The ethics controversies suggest an intellectual culture that eagerly explored both the promises and limits of liberalism, a culture that *practiced* liberalism through sustained public debate. The debates that brought together sexuality and moral conscience did so not to retreat from the public and the political but to ask how those dimensions of the self that had been relegated to the private might energize and reshape the public sphere.[14]

In his cultural history of the German imperial era, Matthew Jefferies laments that no historian has successfully presented a synthetic interpretation

13. The most important histories that pictured the decline of liberalism in bourgeois intellectual circles were George Mosse, *The Crisis of German Ideology: Intellectual Origins of the Third Reich* (New York, 1964); Fritz Stern, *The Politics of Cultural Despair: A Study in the Rise of the Germanic Ideology* (Berkeley, Calif., 1961); and Fritz Ringer, *Decline of the German Mandarins: The German Academic Community, 1890–1933* (Cambridge, Mass., 1969). On Austria, see Carl Schorske, *Fin-de-Siècle Vienna: Politics and Culture* (New York, 1981); and William McGrath, *Dionysian Art and Populist Politics in Austria* (New Haven, Conn., 1974).

14. Crucial for overturning a historiographical paradigm that viewed Germany as antimodern was David Blackbourn and Geoff Eley, *The Peculiarities of German History: Bourgeois Society and Politics in Nineteenth-Century Germany* (New York, 1984).

of the culture of reform.[15] Yet the importance of ethics reform as a movement lay precisely in its resistance to synthesis—in the contradictions, dis-
putes, and misunderstandings it displayed. This book thus attends much
more to the movement's points of dispute than to its points of agreement,
engaging sets of tensions that reveal the breadth of cultural issues that were
treated by ethics reform. Moreover, the book makes no effort to explain a
singular "underlying cause" of the ethics debates or their sexualization—
that is, to say that the talk about ethics and sexuality was "really about" class,
religion, bourgeois anxiety, imperialism, or some other singular causal factor. If ethics, sexuality, and religion/secularism were an interlocking triad
of concerns, they were equally informed by urbanization, industrialization, imperialism, the growing popularity of science, and much more. By
attending to those points of discord and disruption, we gain insight not just
into the meanings of ethics, sexuality, and subjectivity that congealed over
time, but also into the multiplicity of voices that debated the first principles
of social organization and the numerous forces that fed into and in turn
were shaped by those debates.

If there is a methodological assumption in this book, it is thus that
meaning in language and human interaction is always unstable, and that
seemingly stable meanings are only condensed repetitions in time. Accordingly, the book aims to resurrect the instability of the most basic terms
of social order over which contemporaries worried themselves: the uncertainty about the meaning of the "individual" or the "social," the private, the
public, ethics, sexuality, and citizenship. The book's governing practice is
to pay close attention to textual and intertextual tensions that arose during
the public discussions, reading with equal attention to detail both philosophical treatises on ethics and activist pamphlets regarding moral and
legal regulation. The aim behind this method is not to recast the Central
European fin de siècle as the era of "crisis"—whether the crisis of subjectivity, of liberalism, of "meaning," of the social. Rather, the book seeks to
resurrect the instability of social categories in order to depict the productivity of that instability and the hard thought and constant argumentation it elicited from contemporaries as they navigated their way from the
nineteenth century into the twentieth.

15. Matthew Jefferies, *Imperial Culture in Germany, 1871–1918* (New York, 2003), 192.

PART I

Ethics Reform

1

An Ethics of *Gesellschaft*

What can help us? The ethical movement answers as follows: an inversion or
at least the clarification of the public spirit, and this is only possible if a new
ideal, the thought of social duty, emerges in the individual.

FRIEDRICH JODL

At the initial meeting of the Deutsche Gesellschaft für ethische Kultur (German Society for Ethical Culture; henceforth DGEK) in October
1892, the presiding chairperson, Georg von Gizycki, noted how happy he
was that participants so strongly disagreed with one another, adding his
hope that new participants and new objections would lead "to ever new
quarrels."[1] Such early infighting would hardly seem a likely start for a
successful association that would persist in one form or another for more
than forty years. But discord and disagreement were precisely what the
founders sought. They wanted to stir up public discussion around a topic
that many might take for granted: the place of ethics in modern life. Moreover, they wanted to carry out this discussion without adherence to any
particular religious, political, or philosophical framework. Thus they set
out to provide a forum in which individuals, "independent of all religious

---

1. *Mitteilungen der Deutschen Gesellschaft für ethische Kultur,* vol. 1, ed. Georg von
Gizycki (Berlin, 1892), 2.

and political persuasions," could participate in the discussion.[2] They published a biweekly periodical, *Ethische Kultur (Ethical Culture),* as well as numerous books and pamphlets, and they promoted public presentations to be followed by lively conversation. The founders chose not to define "ethics" but rather to encourage debate among their contemporaries about competing interpretations of the concept. The only limitation on participants was the commitment to a vaguely humanist definition of "ethical culture" as "a condition in which justice and truth, humanity and mutual respect reign."[3]

Not surprisingly, contemporaries found the DGEK's project frustratingly vague. Ernst Haeckel, for instance, the outspoken Darwinist in Germany and a vocal critic of the organization, ridiculed its aim as "so general that anyone could support it."[4] Likewise, the Social Democrat Eduard Bernstein disparaged the phrases of the DGEK as "absolutely empty," noting that even the most extreme reactionaries could agree with them.[5] Neither "ethics" nor "ethical culture," it seemed, were at all obvious categories for reform to contemporaries of the DGEK. According to the organization's founders, however, critics such as Haeckel and Bernstein merely failed to grasp the simplicity and novelty of "ethics reform." "One understands the founding of a new political group," noted Friedrich Jodl, a Prague-based philosopher and charter member of the DGEK,[6] and "one also understands the founding of a new religious sect." But, Jodl insisted, a society for ethical culture belonged properly to neither of those categories. Likewise, it was not a typical reform organization that advocated for a

2. Georg von Gizycki, introduction to *Ethische Kultur* 1, no. 1 (1893): 1.

3. §1 of the "Satzungen der Deutschen Gesellschaft für ethische Kultur," in *Einführung in die Grundgedanken der ethischen Bewegung: Zur Ausbreitung des Wirkens der Deutschen Gesellschaft für ethische Kultur,* ed. Friedrich Wilhelm Foerster (Berlin, 1894), 3. See also Gizycki, introduction to *Ethische Kultur,* 1; Friedrich Jodl, "Was heißt 'ethische Kultur'?" *Ethische Kultur* 1, no. 1 (1893): 2.

4. Ernst Haeckel, "Ethik und Weltanschauung," *Die Zukunft* 1 (1892): 310.

5. Eduard Bernstein, "Moralische und unmoralische Spaziergänge," *Die Neue Zeit* 12, pt. 1, no. 1 (1893): 6–7.

6. Friedrich Jodl is usually identified as a Vienna-based philosopher, but he was working in Prague at the time of the founding of the DGEK. On Jodl's life and work, see Wilhelm Börner, *Friedrich Jodl: Eine Studie* (Stuttgart, 1911); and Margarete Jodl, *Friedrich Jodl: Sein Leben und Wirken* (Stuttgart, 1920). On Jodl's work, see also *Ego und Alterego: Wilhelm Bolin und Friedrich Jodl im Kampf um die Aufklärung,* ed. Georg Gimpl (Frankfurt am Main, 1996).

specific social cause. As Jodl explained, it did not fight "anti-Semitism or alcoholism," nor did it "make demands for people's kitchens, kindergartens, or vacation colonies." Rather, the DGEK set out to address something it considered much more fundamental, something that transcended the limits of any particular political, religious, or social reform organization. It set out to address "the matter of humanity as such," Jodl explained. To discuss ethics, he added, would be "an apprenticeship in human desires and acts within a community."[7]

The DGEK came into being in a tense climate regarding matters of religion and political affiliation. Far from sensing that religion was on the decline around them, members saw both confessional identities and confessional conflicts flourishing. They had seen Catholicism thrive in the wake of anti-Catholic persecution during the *Kulturkampf,* and they had seen anti-Semitism find a political footing. They had also seen efforts— indeed, some members of the DGEK had participated in these efforts—to make Protestantism the de facto national religion.[8] In this context, neither members of the DGEK nor their contemporaries could assume that anything like secularization—in the form of the decline of religious belief and practice or in terms of the separation of church and state—was happening in public life. Although they lobbied for secularism, it was unclear what they really sought. Was secularism to be a concrete social movement, and

7. Friedrich Jodl, "Die ethische Bewegung in Deutschland," *Neue freie Presse,* August 23, 1893; reprinted in Foerster, *Einführung in die Grundgedanken der ethischen Bewegung,* 6.

8. Recent literature on the perpetuation and modernization of confessional conflicts in Germany includes Michael Geyer and Hartmut Lehmann, eds., *Religion und Nation, Nation und Religion: Beiträge zu einer unbewältigten Geschichte* (Göttingen, 2004); Helmut Walser Smith, ed., *Protestants, Catholics, and Jews in Germany, 1800–1914* (New York, 2001); Olaf Blaschke, "Das 19. Jahrhundert: Ein Zweites Konfessionelles Zeitalter?" *Geschichte und Gesellschaft* 26 (2000): 38–75; Hartmut Lehmann, ed., *Säkularisierung, Dechristianisierung, Rechristianisierung im neuzeitlichen Europa* (Göttingen, 1997); and Dagmar Herzog, *Intimacy and Exclusion: Religious Politics in Pre-Revolutionary Baden* (Princeton, N.J., 1996). On Protestantism, see Friedrich Wilhelm Graf and Hans Martin Müller, eds., *Der Deutsche Protestantismus um 1900* (Gütersloh, 1996); and Gangolf Hübinger, *Kulturprotestantismus und Politik: Zum Verhältnis von Liberalismus und Protestantismus im wilhelminischen Deutschland* (Tübingen, 1994). On Catholicism and its persecution, see Margaret Lavinia Anderson, "The Limits of Secularization: On the Problem of the Catholic Revival in Nineteenth-Century Germany," *Historical Journal* 38, no. 3 (1995): 647–670; David Blackbourn, *Marpingen: Apparitions of the Virgin Mary in Nineteenth-Century Germany* (New York, 1994); and Jonathan Sperber, *Popular Catholicism in Nineteenth-Century Germany* (Princeton, N.J., 1984).

if so, what form should it take? Should it provide an explicit alternative to religion, a substitute religion, something like a "fourth confession"?[9] Must it offer a comprehensive and unified *Weltanschauung?* Or could it work in a more open fashion? Did modern secularism mean religious tolerance or anti-religion? And what was the relationship of secularism to rationalism, to materialism, and to scientific practice and belief?[10]

Against this background, the DGEK adopted a unique strategy. As a fundamentally critical organization, it did not start out with answers to any of these questions about secularism or about the content of ethics. Rather, it took these questions as intellectual problems to consider and discuss. In its strategy, the DGEK could be seen as acting on a project that Ferdinand Tönnies, a founding member, had suggested in his sociological study *Gemeinschaft und Gesellschaft (Community and Civil Society)* just five years earlier.[11] Often regarded as the seminal text of German sociology, Tönnies's 1887 book had traced the shift from the organic model of community, which he labeled *Gemeinschaft,* to the inorganic model of society, which he called *Gesellschaft.* In one strain of the argument, Tönnies proposed that a shift to modern *Gesellschaft* forces religious belief to give way to scientific and rational inquiry.[12] This strain of the argument was not so different from what Max Weber would suggest three decades later with his notion of "disenchantment" in the modern age.[13] Alongside this relatively straightforward depiction of secularization as disenchantment or loss, however, Tönnies offered another narrative, one in which the homogeneity of belief in *Gemeinschaft* gives way to a contest for public opinion

9. Todd Weir, "The Fourth Confession: Atheism, Monism, and Politics in the Freigeistig Movement in Berlin, 1859–1924" (Ph.D. diss., Columbia University, 2005).

10. Recent theoretical discussions of secularism as a complex and dynamic phenomenon include Talal Asad, *Formations of the Secular: Christianity, Islam, Modernity* (Palo Alto, Calif., 2003); Rajeev Bhargava, ed., *Secularism and Its Critics* (New York, 1998); Friedrich Wilhelm Graf, " 'Dechristianisierung': Zur Problemgeschichte eines kulturpolitischen Topos," in Lehman, *Säkularisierung, Dechristianisierung, Rechristianisierung,* 32–66; and Hermann Lübbe, *Säkularisierung: Geschichte eines ideenpolitischen Begriffs* (Freiburg, 1965).

11. See Ferdinand Tönnies, *Gemeinschaft und Gesellschaft: Abhandlung des Communismus und des Socialismus als empirischer Culturformen* (Leipzig, 1887).

12. Ibid., 182.

13. Max Weber, "Wissenschaft als Beruf," *Gesammelte Aufsätze zur Wissenschaftslehre* (Tübingen, 1922), 536 ff.; reprinted as "Science as a Vocation," in *From Max Weber: Essays in Sociology,* ed. and trans. H. H. Gerth and C. Wright Mills (New York, 1946), 139 ff.

(*öffentliche Meinung*) in *Gesellschaft*.[14] In this second narrative, Tönnies presented public opinion as the moral voice of society, standing above the state, ready to judge the rightness or wrongness of the state's actions. Intrinsically, it is a site of contestation, but one that always seeks homogeneity or monopoly. In a rare break from a staunchly scientist tone, Tönnies stated that public opinion in the 1880s could act as a vital force in society when it involves personal interaction and demands participation from individuals. But when dominated by the mass media—as he felt public opinion then was—it becomes depersonalized, looming as just one more alienating force over the lone individual of *Gesellschaft*.[15]

Using Tönnies's terms, it is fair to say that the DGEK sought to revitalize public opinion throughout German-speaking Europe in the 1890s. To be sure, there were many individuals—both members and critics of the DGEK—who sought to salvage a comprehensive *Weltanschauung* through the organization or in reaction to it. Some stood for traditional religions; others pushed for removal of all religion from public life; still others argued for ethics *as* a new religion. None of these individual stances, however, characterized the novelty of the DGEK experiment, which was fundamentally to provide a forum for the discussion of ethics and related issues, a forum in which the contest for public opinion could play itself out. In other words, what was unique about the DGEK is that it emphasized *form* over *content:* the *form* of critical discussion over the *content* of any particular approach to ethics or the articulation of a comprehensive *Weltanschauung.* By motivating opponents to engage in discussion and to lay bare their assumptions and claims about the constitution of the moral individual and the community of moral responsibility, the DGEK achieved its aim, in the process carving out a unique and illuminating role in the public discussion of religion and secularism at the end of the nineteenth century. It is this discussion itself—and not any one voice within it—that indicates the DGEK's role in the "culture wars" of the late nineteenth century.[16]

---

14. For Tönnies's mature reflections on the problem of public opinion, see *Kritik der öffentlichen Meinung* (Berlin, 1922).

15. Tönnies, *Gemeinschaft und Gesellschaft,* 247, 268. The parallels between Tönnies's view of public opinion and that of Jürgen Habermas are striking. See Habermas, *Strukturwandel der Öffentlichkeit.*

16. For alternative treatments of the DGEK as a movement related to the *freigeistige Bewegung,* see Frank Simon-Ritz, *Die Organisation einer Weltanschauung: Die freigeistige*

If contemporaries could not easily place the abstract project of the DGEK or the notion of "ethics reform" that it was advocating, they nonetheless had no trouble commenting on it. Thus Gizycki, who had celebrated the arguments that ensued at the founding of the organization, also trumpeted the fact that opponents would find "new opportunities to mock" the project, as it meant those opponents would be participating in critical discussion.[17] Indeed, because contemporaries were somewhat bewildered by the DGEK, they responded to it as they might to a Rorschach test, wherein the meaning of "ethics" varied according to the viewer. Some understood ethics to be a product of universal rationality; others took it to be the historical embodiment of a distinct culture; and still others saw it as an intrinsic product of religious belief and practice. None of these perspectives would understand ethics as a category that could be reformed: if ethics is universal or historically entrenched, it can't be changed quickly. What, then, did it mean to make ethics a category for reform? If the DGEK gave its own answers to that question, the controversies that surrounded its founding are equally important. That founding elicited a wide variety of voices across Central Europe, all of which chimed in on the meaning of ethics as a topic of public controversy at the end of the nineteenth century, and on its social, cultural, and political relevance. Consequently, the founding of the DGEK serves as an especially wide lens through which to see what role contemporaries thought ethics might have in modern individual and social life, and what they thought was its relationship to social and cultural reform in Germany and Central Europe.

Founding of the DGEK

Modeled after U.S. and British efforts, the DGEK came into existence in October 1892. In Britain, several ethics reform organizations had arisen in

---

Bewegung im wilhelminischen Deutschland (Gütersloh, 1997); Horst Groschopp, *Dissidenten: Freidenkerei und Kultur in Deutschland* (Berlin, 1997); Weir, "Fourth Confession"; and Lübbe, *Säkularisierung,* 44–49. On the nineteenth century as a period of "culture wars," see Christopher Clark and Wolfram Kaiser, eds., *Culture Wars: Secular-Catholic Conflict in Nineteenth-Century Europe* (Cambridge, 2003); and Lisa Swartout, "Culture Wars: Protestant, Catholic, and Jewish Students at German Universities, 1890–1914," in Geyer and Lehman, *Religion und Nation,* 157–175.

17. Gizycki, *Mitteilungen,* 2.

the late nineteenth century, each more or less devoted to a particular school of moral philosophy.[18] It was primarily the work of the philosophically more ecumenical Felix Adler, however, a German-born moral philosopher at Columbia University and founder of Ethical Culture in New York, that influenced the founders of the DGEK. Adler had started Ethical Culture in the United States largely as a secular Jewish organization in 1876. Worried that Judaism and other organized religions had lost their ability to provide moral guidelines for both individual and social life, he sought an organization that could fill the void.[19] Ethical Culture thus came about as a forum in which to debate in nonreligious terms the pressing moral problems that its members confronted in a rapidly changing world.[20]

A visit by Adler to Berlin in the spring of 1892 encouraged the founders of the German Society for Ethical Culture to organize. Added to his visit were ongoing local concerns regarding public school reform in Prussia.[21] Elementary education in Prussia had been a political and social source of concern for decades, largely because of an outdated funding structure that few deemed equitable.[22] Although a school-reform bill had been on the agenda since 1850, when the Prussian constitution had promised a school law, little progress was made until the 1890s. Otto von Bismarck had resisted reform because any restructuring would surely mean an increased tax burden on the landed nobility, whom he had no wish to alienate. With Bismarck's resignation in March 1890, several deputies in the Prussian Landtag (parliament) tried to restart education reform. In addition to the issue of funding, however, was the question of the confessional

18. On British variants of ethics reform, see Gustav Spiller, *The Ethical Movement in Great Britain: A Documentary History* (London, 1934); and Ian Duncan MacKillop, *The British Ethical Societies* (Cambridge, 1986).

19. Howard B. Radest, *Felix Adler: An Ethical Culture* (New York, 1998), 10. See also James F. Hornback, "The Philosophic Sources and Sanctions of the Founders of Ethical Culture" (Ph.D. diss., Columbia University, 1983); Horace L. Friess, *Felix Adler and Ethical Culture: Memories and Studies,* ed. Fannia Weingartner (New York, 1981); and Benny Kraut, *From Reform Judaism to Ethical Culture: The Religious Evolution of Felix Adler* (Cincinnati, 1979).

20. Friess, *Felix Adler,* 49. Adopted from one of Adler's early speeches, the motto of the organization was "Diversity in the Creed, unanimity in the deed."

21. "Schlusswort," in *Die ethische Bewegung in Deutschland: Vorbereitende Mitteilungen eines Kreises gleichgesinnter Männer und Frauen zu Berlin* (Berlin, 1892), 27; Max Henning, *Handbuch der freigeistigen Bewegung Deutschlands, Österreichs und der Schweiz (Jahrbuch des Weimarer Kartells: 1914)* (Frankfurt am Main, 1914), 35.

22. Marjorie Lamberti, *State, Society, and the Elementary School in Imperial Germany* (New York, 1989), 155.

or interconfessional status of the schools, that is, their particular relationship to the three recognized confessions: Catholicism, Protestantism, and
Judaism. Confessional conflict killed the first effort, an 1890 bill that in
the eyes of both Catholics and orthodox Protestants did not guarantee
enough influence for the churches in religious and moral instruction.[23]
In its wake, the newly appointed minister of culture, Robert von Zedlitz-
Trützschler, sponsored a revised education bill in October 1981 that would
provide much more insurance for the Protestant and Catholic influence in
the schools, even allowing church participation in examining teachers for
licensure.[24] This bill would also largely have eliminated interconfessional
schools, as it sought to guarantee that students be taught by teachers of
their own faith.[25] Although the bill ultimately failed to pass the Landtag,
it mobilized many who wanted to defend interconfessionalism in public and state institutions. The initial concern with an educational matter
brought many pedagogy specialists into the early ranks of the DGEK, and
education remained an important issue within the organization throughout its existence. This issue even led in 1906 to a spinoff organization,
the German League for Secular Schools and Moral Education (Deutsche
Bund für weltliche Schule und Moralunterricht).[26] Yet if the Zedlitz-
Trützschler bill prompted the founders of the DGEK to organize, it was
really the threat that the state might grant a monopoly on moral life to
the churches more generally that proved the crucial motivation for the
founders.

Against the background of the late nineteenth-century culture wars
around religion and secularism, the DGEK cut a unique figure. Although
the society was made up largely of liberal Protestants-turned-secular-
activists, and could at times exhibit a strong anti-Catholic tendency, it was
particularly proud also to list many Jews as members and to foreground

23. Ibid., 157–160.

24. Ibid., 160–163.

25. Marjorie Lamberti, *Jewish Activism in Imperial Germany* (New Haven, Conn., 1978),
126–127. For an argument against the bill on the grounds that it privileged students from
"recognized religions," and thus persecuted children of nonconfessional or "dissident" orientation, see "Wir Dissidenten und der neue Volksschulgesetzes-Entwurf," *Freireligiöses
Familien-Blatt* 1, no. 3 (1892), 17–18.

26. Rudolph Penzig, introductory article in *Deutsche Liga für weltliche Schule und
Moralunterricht* 1, no. 1 (1906): 1–4; Henning, *Handbuch der freigeistigen Bewegung,* 73–78.

accordingly its interconfessional membership rolls.[27] Nevertheless, the membership of the DGEK was never very large. It reached its apex at the outset, when there were more than 2,000 members in Berlin in 1893 and anywhere between 30 and 200 members in branch societies in other cities across Germany, Switzerland, and the Austrian Empire. The numbers progressively declined thereafter, falling off to roughly 850 members by 1914.[28]

What brought attention—and opposition—to the DGEK was not its size but both its interconfessional composition and the luminary quality of the intellectuals and activists who supported its cause. Many of the prominent young intellectuals of the period participated in the founding of the society, including the esteemed Berlin astronomer Wilhelm Foerster as first president, the Kiel sociologist Ferdinand Tönnies, the Marburg neo-Kantian philosopher Hermann Cohen, the Berlin-based socialist-feminist activist Lily Kretschmann (later Lily von Gizycki, then Lily Braun), and the philosopher Alois Riehl from Freiburg.[29] The Berlin-based moral philosopher, Gizycki, served as the first editor of the DGEK's biweekly periodical, *Ethische Kultur,* succeeded in 1895 by Friedrich Wilhelm Foerster, Wilhelm Foerster's son and a pedagogy specialist and future peace activist.[30] At the outset, *Ethische Kultur* maintained a loose relationship with the DGEK, supported by the organization and charged with the task of providing a forum for the publication of ideas about ethics, coming under formal aegis of the organization only in 1897.[31]

The attendees at the founding meeting were largely but not exclusively based in Berlin, but the publication of *Ethische Kultur* helped extend the organization's reach to urban centers across German-speaking Europe.

27. See, for example, Wilhelm Foerster, *Zur Ethik des Nationalismus und der Judenfrage: Vortrag gehalten am 23. November 1892 zu Berlin in der Deutschen Gesellschaft für ethische Kultur* (Berlin, 1893), 13–14.

28. Henning, *Handbuch der freigeistigen Bewegung,* 34–37.

29. For a complete listing of the original membership, see Groschopp, *Dissidenten,* 128–133.

30. Foerster edited the periodical with Lily von Gizycki from May to October 1895, when the collaboration fell apart over a dispute regarding Social Democracy. See Lily von Gizycki's letter to the readers explaining her departure from the periodical in "An die Leser," *Ethische Kultur* 3, no. 42 (1895): 369–370. Foerster left behind a rich array of letters to his father from the year 1892, speaking mostly to his anticipation of the founding of the DGEK. He was based in Freiburg in 1892–1893 and was in close contact with Riehl, whose enthusiasm he shared. See Handschriften Abteilung, Staatsbibliothek zu Berlin, Preussischer Kulturbesitz, Nachlass Foerster, Teil Nachlass Friedrich Wilhelm Foerster, Box 25, Mp. 7.

31. Henning, *Handbuch der freigeistigen Bewegung,* 38.

The first installment, for instance, featured an article on Viennese political culture by Bertha von Suttner, the Vienna-based founder of the German-speaking pacifist movement; an article on the meaning of "ethical culture" by Jodl, the philosopher then teaching in Prague; and a piece from the Berlin-based neo-Kantian philosopher Friedrich Paulsen titled "Independent Morality and Its Churchly Judge."[32]

The DGEK understood its own realm of activity precisely at the intersection of these three writers and their articles, that is, between philosophic contemplation and cultural and political activism. Comprised largely of university professors and social activists, members explained time and again that the society's mission was "to provide a way to work between academic ethics and real life."[33] While their debates engaged pressing social concerns, academic philosophy was supposed to provide an intellectual rigor as resistance to popular fantasies and swings of public opinion. Explaining the project of the DGEK in a publicity statement, Gizycki noted, "We in Germany very much need a place to pursue the knowledge of good and bad through common work by people of all orientations and all social relations; in our times, however, it is often harder to recognize what is good than it is to do that which is already recognized as good."[34] In other words, it was necessary to reevaluate what the good itself is taken to be. In a similar vein, Adler had commented in his pre-inaugural address that the "language of speculative philosophy speaks in one way, the language of dogma and tradition speaks in another, and the language of subjective religious sentiment a third."[35] The DGEK sought to facilitate communication and translation between these competing domains. The premise was, in short, that unbiased public discussion (1) could take place; (2) would be the means to subject unquestioned moral norms and predisposition to rational interrogation; and (3) would enable critical revision of moral values.

32. Bertha von Suttner, "Groß-Wien"; Jodl, "Was heißt ethische Kultur?"; and Friedrich Paulsen, "Die unabhängige Moral und ihre kirchlichen Richter—Thesen über Religion und Moral," all in *Ethische Kultur* 1, no. 1 (1893): 2–5.

33. Wilhelm Börner, *Die ethische Bewegung in Deutschland* (Gautzsch bei Leipzig, 1912), 2.

34. Georg von Gizycki, "In Sachen der Deutschen Gesellschaft für ethische Kultur," *Vorwärts: Berliner Volksblatt,* October 5, 1892.

35. Felix Adler, "Rede, gehalten in einer Versammlung im Victoria-Lyceum zu Berlin am 7. Mai 1892," in *Die ethische Bewegung in Deutschland,* 16.

Although the DGEK insisted on political and religious autonomy, it exhibited certain leanings in its early formation, leanings that were significant in terms of the initial public response to its project. Many of the initial founders, for instance, were very sympathetic to the Social Democratic cause. Gizycki went so far as to pose the DGEK as an autonomous entity that nonetheless would be aligned with the Social Democratic movement and would work to find an ethics appropriate to Social Democracy.[36] In keeping with the sympathy for Social Democracy, the founders were also profoundly critical of chauvinistic nationalism and understood the pursuit of a new ethics as something that pertained intrinsically to the whole of humanity.[37] The first of many meetings of the International Union of Ethical Societies took place in Zurich in 1896, signaling a sustained interest in international correspondence with Ethical Culture societies in other countries.[38] Although this first meeting consisted almost exclusively of participants from Germany, Britain, and the United States, chapters eventually grew not only in other European countries but in Japan, India, and New Zealand as well.[39]

With time the political leanings of the DGEK shifted. In the first decade of the twentieth century, its stance on religious tolerance became unsustainable, as positions polarized and hardened around questions of sexuality and its role in the constitution of the moral subject. In the years just before the war, the society eventually joined the Weimarer Kartell (Weimar Cartel), a coalition of organizations from the *freigeistige Bewegung* (freethinkers' movement) consisting of groups such as Ernst Haeckel's Monistenbund (Monist League) and Helene Stöcker's Bund für Mutterschutz (League for

36. Georg von Gizycki, "In Sachen der Deutschen Gesellschaft," 3. On the DGEK and Social Democracy, see Georg Gimpl, "Ethisch oder sozial? Zur missglückten Synthese der Ethischen Bewegung," in *Vernetzungen: Friedrich Jodl und sein Kampf um die Aufklärung* (Oulu, 1990), 58–100.

37. See §2 of the organization's *Leitsätze,* cited in F. W. Foerster, *Einführung in die Grundgedanken der ethischen Bewegung,* 3; W. Foerster, *Zur Ethik des Nationalismus;* Adler, "Rede, gehalten in einer Versammlung," 16.

38. On the international reach of Ethical Culture, see Börner, *Die ethische Bewegung,* 9–12.

39. See Spiller, *Ethical Movement in Great Britain,* 186–195; Felix Adler, "The International Ethical Congress," *Ethical Addresses* 3 (1896): 133–150; Börner, *Die ethische Bewegung,* 11–12.

the Protection of Mothers).[40] After World War I, the DGEK's profile declined somewhat, but the organization held together. Then, in 1933, *Ethische Kultur* was briefly co-opted by the Nazis, finally folding in 1936.[41] Its origins, however, rather than its gradual decline, prove most compelling in terms of the effort to articulate a project of *Anti-Weltanschauung* and the controversy the group elicited.

On the whole, the responses to the DGEK can be sorted into three categories. In addition to responses pertaining to the DGEK's relationship to Social Democracy—a realm so significant that it deserves a chapter of its own (chapter 6)—these categories were, roughly, considerations about confession or lack thereof, and considerations about materialism and science. Opposition on both fronts circled largely around the question of the autonomy of ethics and the makeup of the community of moral consideration, but the second, more secularly oriented critique forced as well a question about the makeup of the community out of which the individual emerges as an autonomous moral entity.

Ethics and Religion

The DGEK's opposition to enforced confession in public schools earned the most hostility from those who viewed the organization as explicitly antireligious. The most direct, if brief, response in this vein came from Adolf Stöcker, the former Prussian court preacher and a high-profile representative of the orthodox strain of Protestantism in Germany. This strain understood Protestantism as the basis of Prussian "greatness" and generally opposed any trends that seemed to remove religion from the public

40. The other organizations in the Weimarer Kartell were the Deutscher Monistenbund, the Deutscher Freidenkerbund, the Jungdeutscher Kulturbund, the Bund für weltliche Schule und Moralunterricht, der Bund für persönliche Religion, the Kartell der freiheitlichen Vereine Münchens, the Freie ethische Gesellschaft, the Berliner Kartell, the Kartell der freiheitlichen Vereine, and the Bund für Mutterschutz. See Henning, *Handbuch der freigeistigen Bewegung,* 22–23. I treat Helene Stöcker and the League for the Protection of Mothers in detail in chapter 2.

41. One can see the process of *Gleichschaltung* (National Socialist "coordination") already taking over the organization's journal, *Ethische Kultur,* in May 1933. See in particular Ernst Falk, "Kultur der Zeit," *Ethische Kultur* 41, no. 9 (1933): 140–142, an article that takes up the language of the DGEK but applies it to the National Socialist project.

domain.[42] Stöcker had also been a leader of post-unification anti-Semitism in Germany, founding the Christian Social Workers Party, through which he voiced his expressly anti-Semitic sentiments.[43] His anti-Semitism was less explicitly racial than it was religious, although the two variants could easily be blurred.[44] Stöcker decided that it was the Jews of Germany who were leading the nation away from Protestantism and toward secularism.[45] In his response to the DGEK, he expressed his antisecular anti-Semitism, charging that it was only the "Jewish press" that celebrated the DGEK and its nonconfessional aims. He mocked a claim that the DGEK was supposed to be a benefit to the "people," countering that the "people" remain on the whole very devout.[46] Moreover, he identified all opposition to the school-reform bill as a form of hatred toward Christianity.[47] To be sure, Stöcker represented an extreme position, not representative of all orthodox Protestants. But his stance demonstrates how vociferous the debates around ethics became and how clearly linked they were for many to the issue of whether German modernity would be predominantly confessional, inter-confessional, or neither of the two.

If critics such as Stöcker objected *tout court* to the slightest hint of secularism, however, others began to ask more subtle questions about the relationship of individual morality to a shared religious outlook or *Weltanschauung*. Like Stöcker, the Budapest-based philosopher and librarian

---

42. See, for example, Adolf Stöcker, "Das Volksschulgesetz und die Generalsynode," *Deutsche Evangelische Kirchenzeitung* 6, no. 5 (1892): 45; and "Das Volksschulgesetz und seine Gegner," *Deutsche evangelische Kirchenzeitung* 6, no. 7 (1892): 61–62. In both cases Stöcker campaigns enthusiastically for Protestant religious education in public schools.

43. On Adolf Stöcker, see John Fout, "Adolf Stöcker's Rationale for Anti-Semitism," *Journal of Church and State* 17, no. 1 (1975): 48; D. A. Jeremy Telman, "Adolf Stöcker: Anti-Semite with a Christian Mission," *Jewish History* 9, no. 2 (1995): 93–112; and Günter Brakelmann, Martin Greschat, and Werner Jochmann, eds., *Protestantismus und Politik: Werk und Wirkung Adolf Stöckers* (Hamburg, 1982).

44. On how religious anti-Semitism could bleed into racial anti-Semitism, see Werner Bergmann, "Völkischer Antisemitismus," in *Handbuch zur "völkischen Bewegung," 1871– 1918,* ed. Uwe Puschner, Walter Schmitz, and Justus H. Ulbricht (Munich, 1996), 449–463; and Telman, "Adolf Stöcker," 93–112.

45. Adolf Stöcker, *Reden im Reichstag: Amtlicher Vorlaut,* ed. Reinhard Mumm (Schwerin, 1914), 65, cited in Fout, "Adolf Stöcker's Rationale," 52.

46. Adolf Stöcker, "Vereine und Kongresse," *Deutsche Evangelische Kirchenzeitung* 6, no. 44 (1892): 428–429.

47. Stöcker, "Das Volksschulgesetz und seine Gegner," 61–62.

Eugen Heinrich Schmitt questioned just how nonreligious the populace really was.[48] More urgently, however, Schmitt expressed his fear that something like the DGEK only worked to create a breach between individual morality on the one hand and a religious *Weltanschauung* that could be shared by the "community" on the other. Schmitt was heavily influenced by a strain of Hegelian thought that holds that human freedom is fully realized only when the legal and moral circumstances of a society reflect, and are reflected in, individual morality as dictated by reason.[49] Although Schmitt placed far less emphasis on the rational component than did his Hegelian precursors, he adhered to the premise that social discord thrives when individual and social morality do not coincide. A few "morally robust individuals" may be able to steer themselves along an individually defined morality, he suggested, but "humanity in its totality" is not capable of such a challenging task. Schmitt maintained that a split between individual ethics and a socially shared *Weltanschauung* would thus lead to inevitable cultural decline, degenerating into chaos. To avoid such chaos, he advocated that either the church or the state act as a moral authority. Whether that moral authority was secular or religious was not the issue— though he privileged a Christian religious authority—so long as it was in the position to prevent the spread of "untruths" that might lead wayward individuals astray and have a "corrosive effect on society." Insofar as the DGEK seemed not to herald any particular authority—and even seemed to resist the idea that either the state or a church might be viewed as such an authority—Schmitt feared the DGEK was only going to facilitate a descent into social chaos.[50]

Although Schmitt was concerned primarily with the relationship of individual to social morality, his argument raised a closely related question about the autonomy of ethics. For Schmitt, it was important that ethics

48. Eugen Heinrich Schmitt, *Warum ist eine religiöse Bewegung Notwendigkeit? Ein Wort an die "Gesellschaften für ethische Kultur"* (Leipzig, 1894), 6.

49. See especially G. W. F. Hegel's introduction to *Vorlesungen über die Geschichte der Philosophie,* vols. 18–20 of Hegel, *Werke,* ed. Eva Moldenhauer and Karl Markus Michel (Frankfurt am Main, 1970); translated into English by Robert Brown as *Lectures on the Philosophy of History,* 3 vols. (Berkeley, Calif., 1990). To see Schmitt's efforts to adapt Hegelianism to his own "new gnosticism," see Eugen Heinrich Schmitt, *Die Gnosis: Grundlagen der Weltanschauung einer edleren Kultur,* 2 vols. (Leipzig, 1903–1907).

50. Schmitt, *Warum ist eine religiöse Bewegung Notwendigkeit?* 3–4.

remain subordinate to religious faith—or to an equivalent *Weltanschauung*—working solely as a tool of that faith. This resistance to the autonomy of ethics, however, was not necessary to a defense of Christianity. Friedrich Paulsen, a moral philosopher in Berlin who did not sign onto the project of the DGEK, nevertheless defended the organization on just this point. Writing in *Ethische Kultur* but marking his nonaffiliation with the DGEK, he informed readers that the much esteemed Immanuel Kant had already attempted almost a century ago to found ethics on autonomous ground, that is, on the basis of individual freedom. The Kantian categorical imperative, which held that one should act "that the maxim of your will could always hold at the same time as a principle in a giving of universal law," presupposed that the moral law has no a priori content.[51] That is, it does not rely on any preestablished "good," whether a moral, religious, or political good. If it did, the moral agent would be subservient to that preestablished good, and hence not free. Moreover, when making a moral decision, the individual must rely on no external laws or social norms, as these too would infringe on moral autonomy. It was only the individual's own use of reason that could determine the outcome of any moral question—and the categorical imperative was the tool with which to determine that outcome. In one of his last works, *Religion within the Limits of Reason Alone,* Kant had set out to rebuild religious faith on the basis of autonomous ethics. The moral agent, he argued, gets a glimpse into what a perfect or divine being would be when he or she contemplates a moral act, because in doing so he or she intuits how a perfect being would behave. In this way Kant had not severed ethics from religion; he had just inverted the order. Rather than derive ethics from religion, Kant understood religion as a necessary consequence of ethics.[52] For Paulsen, Kant's argument worked to allow ethics to be at once autonomous and compatible with religious belief.

Paulsen treated the issue of ethics and autonomy as more of a philosophical concern than a social one. However, for Wilhelm Bousset, an evangelical theologian and religious historian in Göttingen, the notion of autonomous

51. Immanuel Kant, *Critique of Practical Reason,* trans. and ed. Mary Gregor (Cambridge, 1997), §7, p. 28, sec. 5:31. See also Immanuel Kant, *Foundations of the Metaphysics of Morals,* trans. Lewis White Beck (New York, 1959); *The Metaphysics of Morals,* trans. and ed. Mary Gregor (Cambridge, 1996).

52. Immanuel Kant, *Religion within the Boundaries of Mere Reason,* trans. and ed. Allen Wood and George Di Giovanni (Cambridge, 1998).

ethics spoke first and foremost to the issue of the moral community. Like Paulsen, Bousset was sympathetic to the autonomy of ethics; he understood the soundness of Kant's arguments too well to object to the DGEK on that ground.[53] He also shared with the DGEK founders the view that "religions are no longer a community-building [*gemeinschaftbildendes*] element of human society," that is, they no longer provide the glue that makes societies cohesive. But he worried nonetheless: if the DGEK were to replace religion with ethics—ethics either as a new religion or as some other, less direct form of substitute—then it needed to have a unified moral theory. And such a unified moral theory, Bousset lamented, the DGEK did not have.[54] This matter returned Bousset to the question Schmitt had raised, namely, the relationship of ethics to community. However, where Schmitt had been concerned primarily about whether or not a community had a shared moral framework that could provide moral orientation for the individual, Bousset was concerned more about the definition or expanse of community, and about how assumptions regarding ethics shaped that definition.

With this concern in mind, Bousset identified two competing tendencies in the DGEK. On one side, he suggested, was a utilitarian strain that emphasized the idea of the greatest good for the greatest number. On the other side was a "scientific" strain holding that only a scientifically grounded ethics could apply to the whole of humanity.[55] And this assessment by Bousset was apt. Gizycki had written his *Moralphilosophie gemeinverständlich dargestellt (Moral Philosophy: A Popular Presentation)* largely as a utilitarian tract, and both Gizycki and Wilhelm Foerster were much indebted to Anglo-American utilitarians, especially Stanton Coit, William Mackintire Salter, and, more indirectly, Jeremy Bentham, the father of modern utilitarianism.[56] At the same time, Tönnies and Jodl routinely referred to the quest to put ethics on a scientific grounding—to approach ethics, Jodl suggested,

53. Wilhelm Bousset, "Die Gesellschaften für ethische Kultur," *Die Christliche Welt* (1895): 6.

54. Ibid., 7.

55. Ibid., 8–9.

56. Georg von Gizycki, *Moralphilosophie gemeinverständlich dargestellt* (Leipzig, 1888). The English translation is *A Students' Manual of Ethical Philosophy*, trans. Stanton Coit (London, 1889). Gizycki translated some of Salter's lectures into German. See, for instance, William Mackintire Salter, *Die Religion der Moral: Vorträge, gehalten in der Gesellschaft für moralische Kultur, in Chicago*, ed. and trans. Georg von Gizycki (Leipzig, 1885).

in the same way that the "practical chemist, the electrotechnician, the engineer does the great problems of chemistry, physics, and mechanics."[57]

Where the founders happily entertained multiple views on ethics, however, Bousset found an irresolvable conflict. For Bousset, the utilitarian logic took into account a specific, local community, whereas the notion of a "scientific" ethics implied an ethics appropriate to all of humanity. Bousset sympathized with an ethics that privileged care for the immediate neighbor, an ethics that he believed mirrored the Christian "love for the individual person."[58] He expressed his deep skepticism, however, about an ethics based on what he called the "abstraction" of humanity—something that could never motivate the passions in the way that concern for the immediate neighbor supposedly could.[59] The conflict for Bousset thus resided in the definition of the "community" that one made the object of moral consideration. Although he was not specific about the delineations or boundaries of a local community, and he certainly did not equate the local community with the national community, his reservations expressed a clear preference for a community of moral consideration that would be considerably less than the whole of humanity.

In contrast to Bousset's claim, however, the utilitarian strain of the DGEK understood "community" to exceed all boundaries in order to include the entirety of humanity, just as it did for the more scientific strain. Though no stance was definitive for the DGEK, Gizycki's argument on the expansiveness of "community" set the tone for the organization. His *Moralphilosophie* began with the idea that ethics are not universal but rather evolve over time.[60] The long historical process of ethics, according to Gizycki, was one in which raw affect slowly gave way to sublimated reason. Following a Benthamite utilitarian logic, he held that value judgments of good and bad derived originally from experiences of pleasure and pain. Societal discord in this framework is a source of considerable discomfort.

---

57. Jodl, "Die ethische Bewegung in Deutschland," in F. W. Foerster, *Einführung*, 7. See also Ferdinand Tönnies, who describes the DGEK as "a weak beginning of an attempt to translate into life philosophical thought that is today saturated with lively science," in *"Ethische Cultur" und ihr Geleite: 1) Nietzsche-Narren [in der "Zukunft" und in der "Gegenwart"]; and 2) Wölfe in Fuchspelzen* (Berlin, 1893), 11.

58. Bousset, "Die Gesellschaften für ethische Kultur," 80.

59. Ibid.

60. Gizycki, *Moralphilosophie*, 21.

It is thus in the individual's interest to pursue not only his or her own personal happiness but also the greatest happiness for the group. Given that discord among groups as well leads to unhappiness, the ultimate moral ambition must be "in harmony with the welfare of mankind."[61] If at first the object of moral consideration is "the tribe [or] the nation," it will ultimately become "mankind [and] all sentient beings."[62] The goal is thus to conceive of universal humanity as the community of moral consideration.

Interlude on the Limits of Universalism

If most early members of the DGEK shared the commitment to universal humanity in theory, they often confronted the limits to universalism in practice. An early episode regarding animal protection (*Tierschutz*) and anti-Semitism illustrates this problem. In April 1893, the Berlin chapter of the DGEK held a meeting at which Hans Beringer gave a talk titled "Animal Protection: An Important Moral Question,"[63] interrogating the inclusivity of the DGEK's conception of community. Building largely on the philosophy of Arthur Schopenhauer, whose 1819 magnum opus *The World as Will and Representation* earned many followers in the second half of the century, especially in the vegetarian and animal-protection movements, Beringer suggested that not only humans but animals too should be considered the object of moral consideration.[64] In short, universal humanity was not extensive enough. In *The World as Will and Representation,* Schopenhauer presented the world as a combination of one indivisible will and endless individuated representations of that will. Because individuated entities—animals, humans, and plants alike—do not recognize that they are all individuated representations of the one indivisible will, they conflict with one another in ceaseless efforts for individual power and self-preservation. The result is a cauldron of suffering. Only

61. Ibid., 19.
62. Ibid., 9.
63. The entirety of the discussion was reported in "Deutsche Gesellschaft für ethische Kultur (Abteilung Berlin)," *Ethische Kultur* 1, no. 17 (1893): 136–138.
64. For a particularly illustrative example of Schopenhauer's influence on animal protectionists in Germany, see the masthead of the animal-rights periodical *Ethische Rundschau,* which featured a portrait of Schopenhauer and Richard Wagner.

when individual entities learn to deny the self and to practice sympathy for other beings can they ethically overcome this turmoil of suffering. With Schopenhauer as his guide, Beringer advocated an ethics of sympathy that would take into account not only human-human relations but also human-animal relations. Children in particular, he argued, might learn the art of sympathy rather than mere egoism if they were taught to respect animals from the earliest age. Beringer then proceeded to inform the audience about the many cruelties entailed in modern meat preparation and called on the DGEK to support the program of the Animal Protection League (Tierschutz-Verein) to eliminate inhumane forms of animal slaughter.

While making his plea in the name of an expanded universalism that includes all sentient beings, however, Beringer also erected new divisions. He linked his general appeal for animal protection with the contemporary campaign against shehitah (*Schächte*), the kosher Jewish method of slaughtering animals, therein attaching it to a favorite theme of anti-Semitism. Since 1886, the National Association of Animal Protection Societies (Verband der Thierschutzvereine des Deutschen Reiches), the umbrella organization for the various German animal-protection leagues, had been lobbying representatives in the Reichstag to introduce a law to ban Jewish kosher slaughter.[65] The animal-protection argument maintained that livestock should be stunned with a quick shot to the head before slaughter, a practice that would violate the Jewish law prohibiting damage to the brain in the slaughtering process. When the bill was finally introduced in 1893, it found support primarily from anti-Semitic and conservative representatives in the Reichstag.[66] To be sure, there were Jewish animal

65. For an analysis of the ensuing debates, including the fundamental question of the right of the state to intervene in traditional trades, religious practices, and everyday lives of citizens, see Dorothee Brantz, "Stunning Bodies: Animal Slaughter, Judaism, and the Meaning of Humanity in Imperial Germany," *Central European History* 35, no. 2 (2002): 167–194. A comprehensive account of such debates throughout the nineteenth century is Robin Judd, *Contested Rituals: Circumcision, Kosher Butchering, and Jewish Political Life in Germany, 1843–1933* (Ithaca, N.Y., 2007). See also Miriam Zerbel, *Tierschutz im Kaiserreich: Ein Beitrag zur Geschichte des Vereinswesens* (Frankfurt am Main, 1993). On animal rights, dietary laws, and Judaism, see Elijah Schochet, *Animal Life in Jewish Tradition: Attitudes and Relationships* (New York, 1994), 47–51, 157–165.

66. Miriam Zerbel, "Tierschutzbewegung," in Puschner et al., *Handbuch zur "Völkischen Bewegung,"* 552.

protectionists, and it was quite possible in principle to support animal protection—or to object to shehitah—while not participating in anti-Semitic politics.[67] Moreover, outside anti-Semitic circles, there existed little consensus on whether stunning was or was not a particularly humane way to slaughter animals, or whether shehitah was in any way particularly cruel.[68] But animal protection had a back-to-nature, antimodern slant that was typical of *völkisch* movements. Moreover, in a manner very similar to Adolf Stöcker's anti-Semitism, it had a tendency to equate Judaism with the forces of progress and urbanism that caused humans to lose sight of their tie to the natural animal world.[69] Although Beringer insisted that his presentation did not "in any way approach the Jewish question, but rather had to do with the reform of slaughter practices generally," he treated she-hitah as the particular practice against which ethicists should concentrate their energies, and his audience was quick to make the connection.[70]

The mixed response to Beringer at the DGEK meeting illustrates the diverse challenges of the organization's liberal universalism in the face of particularist interests. The first respondent praised Beringer for his talk but objected "passionately" to the fact that Beringer had raised the "Jewish question" in conjunction with animal protection. Another, claiming to speak "in the name of many Jews," said she had no choice but to share Beringer's perspective, noting that the failure of orthodox religions to adapt to modern technologies must be a primary area of concern for ethics reform. Still another Jewish attendee agreed with the previous speaker but thought the occasion drew attention to an even more pressing problem: that the Jewish community as a whole did not have a periodical similar to *Ethische Kultur* in which to discuss matters of concern particular to that community. Still more agitated, yet another Jewish attendee warned against "oppressing the conscience of the Jewish members," predicting that full endorsement of Beringer's proposal to protest shehitah would force "numerous other Jewish members to resign from the society."[71] The evening's moderator, Wilhelm Foerster, had already made clear months

67. Ibid.

68. Brantz, "Stunning Bodies," 174, 180–182.

69. On vegetarianism, see Wolfgang R. Krabbe, *Gesellschaftsveränderung durch Lebens-reform* (Göttingen, 1974), 50–78.

70. "Deutsche Gesellschaft für ethische Kultur," 137.

71. Ibid., 137–138.

before that his hard line against orthodox religiosity of all types made no exception in the case of Judaism, despite the minority status of Jews in Germany and their vulnerability to persecution.[72] Though he had initially applauded Beringer's presentation, he concluded the evening by emphasizing that the DGEK sought in no way to pressure any of its members in matters of conscience and by noting how important the Jewish members of the DGEK were to the organization and to its non-Jewish members.

In sum, the brief animal-protection controversy in the DGEK arose as a question about the limits of the society's appeal to universal humanity as the community of moral responsibility. For Beringer, it was not inclusive enough in that it did not include nonhuman animals. But when he tried to extend the community of moral responsibility to nonhuman animals, he managed to fracture the notion of humanity itself, inserting a divide between Jews and non-Jews. If this splitting was not a logically necessary consequence of the extension of the community of moral responsibility beyond universal humanity, the historically contingent circumstances in which it was legible to all participants exemplifies the difficulties the DGEK confronted in maintaining its operating premise of tolerance and inclusiveness. Not insignificantly, when the question of vegetarianism arose again eighteen months later, Gizycki quickly insisted that although he applauded vegetarianism insofar as it may benefit human health, one should not lose sight of the fact that "human existence is more valuable than animal existence."[73] Even if he had stated in his *Moralphilosophie* that the community of moral responsibility logically includes all sentient beings, the political contingencies that linked animal protection to a divisive politics necessitated a retreat to the safer grounds of the universality of humanity—without the animals.

This small controversy illuminates how complex reform culture could be at the end of the century, as progressive and reactionary, *völkisch* and modern tendencies did not necessarily separate themselves neatly but rather wove themselves into a historically and logically intricate fabric. On this front it is important to note that Beringer presented his anti-Semitic agenda

---

72. See *Zur Ethik des Nationalismus,* in which Foerster denounces nationalism of all forms, including Jewish nationalism.

73. Georg von Gizycki, in response to B. Lindner, "Ethik und Vegetarismus," *Ethische Kultur* 2, no. 39 (1894): 306.

not as reactionary but as progressive, aiming only to expand a rhetoric of rights to all sentient beings. In this way the controversy looks less like a conflict between progressive and reactionary forces than a conflict about the shape of modern liberalism and its rhetoric of rights and about the bearers of those rights. It also provides an informative example of why the DGEK insisted on the autonomy of ethics and how this work dovetailed with its own expansive notion of community. There was nothing inherently anti-Semitic about an ethics derived from sympathy. Indeed, such an ethics would logically imply an expansive conception of the object of moral consideration, in that the suffering of any being would imply the suffering of the self and of all, if all are really representations of the single will. Only the *contingent* political alliance between animal protection and anti-Semitism prevented an ethics of sympathy from applying to the inclusive notion of community that an ethics of sympathy might logically entail. In order to reestablish ethics as a critical category—and, we might add, as a *humanist* category—the DGEK thus aimed to free all models of ethics from precisely this kind of political alliance.

Materialism, Monism, and *Ersatzreligionen*

Just as confessional identities thrived in the nineteenth century, the sciences underwent a dramatic process of popularization.[74] Even as they evolved into professionalized areas of academic knowledge, with experts in specific fields, the physical sciences emerged as the metaphors of progress and liberalism for the nonspecialist. Popular science lectures and mass publications with charts, diagrams, and medical drawings informed the public of the advances being made in scientific research. Such advances seemed to take up the promise of the Enlightenment to procure a better future. As Paul Weindling puts it, the belief was common that "mass education would purge societies of ignorance, privilege and superstition."[75]

74. See especially Andreas Daum, *Wissenschaftspopularisierung im 19. Jahrhundert: Bürgerliche Kultur, naturwissenschaftliche Bildung und die deutsche Öffentlichkeit, 1848–1914* (Munich, 2002).

75. Paul Weindling, *Health, Race, and German Politics between National Unification and Nazism, 1870–1945* (New York, 1989), 3; on the more illiberal tendencies in German

Moreover, as the sciences and scientific thinking became ever more popular, they emerged as the touchstone against which progressive attitudes were measured.

Accompanying the developments in science was a materialist explanation of the world.[76] Although there existed a wide variety of materialist theories, they tended to share the fundamental notion that matter was the primary and true element of existence. Many held as well that science might consequently be able to provide a complete account of all phenomena in the world.[77] In early nineteenth-century materialism, Hegelian speculative philosophy provided an especially popular target, insofar as it had presented the material world as a product of the rational ideal that would reveal itself in history. Even more provocative to future practitioners of science was the *Naturphilosophie* (natural philosophy) of Friedrich Wilhelm Joseph von Schelling, which sought to discover the inner ideal of the natural and objective world as the counterpart to the ideal of thought. Confronting the Christian religious paradigm explicitly, Ludwig Feuerbach's *The Essence of Christianity (Das Wesen des Christentums)* inverted the Hegelian system to present a real material world that was filled with suffering, and that consequently created Christianity as a projection of an ideal world without suffering.[78] Karl Marx's material understanding of social relations and his critique of religion as a product of human alienation from its own material production was greatly indebted to Feuerbach's work.[79] By midcentury the works of Karl Vogt, Jakob Moleschott, and Ludwig Büchner typified the materialist approach to science and philosophy, Büchner's 1855 book

---

science's popularity, see Anne Harrington, *Re-enchanted Science: Holism in German Culture from Wilhelm II to Hitler* (Princeton, N.J., 1996).

76. The most thorough discussion is Frederick Gregory, *Scientific Materialism in Nineteenth Century Germany* (Dordrecht, 1977).

77. J. W. Burrow, *The Crisis of Reason: European Thought, 1848–1914* (New Haven, Conn., 2000), 35. See also Sir William Cecil Dampier, *A History of Science and Its Relations with Philosophy and Religion,* 4th rev. ed. (New York, 1949), 202.

78. Ludwig Feuerbach, *Das Wesen des Christentums* (Leipzig, 1841).

79. See especially Karl Marx and Friedrich Engels, "Die deutsche Ideologie: Kritik der neuesten deutschen Philosophie in ihren Repräsentanten Feuerbach, B. Bauer und Stirner, und des deutschen Sozialismus in seinen verschiedenen Propheten," and Karl Marx, "Marx über Feuerbach [generally known as the "Theses on Feuerbach" in English]," both in *Karl Marx, Friedrich Engels: Werke,* vol. 3, ed. Institut für Marxismus-Leninismus (Berlin, 1961–1974).

Force and Matter (Kraft und Stoff) serving as the primer for nineteenth-century German materialism.[80] Usually seen as the popularizer rather than the originator of the materialist paradigm, Büchner drew on empirical scientific discoveries about the operation of the human body and the natural world to counter *Naturphilosophie* directly.[81] Particularly provocative was Büchner's argument that, like all activity, the activity of thought was just another physical process, a matter of chemical and biological movements.[82] Interested in social politics as much as scientific thought, Büchner was also instrumental in the development of atheism (*Freigeistigkeit*) as an organized social movement, founding the German Freethinkers' League (Deutscher Freidenkerbund) in 1881.[83]

In addition to the more philosophically based treaties on materialism that presented human spiritual life as the product of physical life, developments in the biological sciences were blurring the lines between plants and animals, and between animals and humans. With the aid of much improved microscopy, for instance, German biologists were making exciting discoveries about cell division, consolidating the notion of the cell as the basic unit in all organic life, both plant and animal.[84] Most spectacularly, Charles Darwin's *On the Origin of Species by Means of Natural Selection* of 1859, albeit a product of British empiricism more than of German philosophical debates on matter and idea, found a very welcoming audience in Germany.[85] Although Darwin himself resisted comment on the place of human beings in evolutionary theory, others were quick to discern that Darwinism took humans out of their privileged relation with divinity and resituated them squarely in the midst of nature's development. Not only was human activity to be viewed accordingly as a logical extension of animal life; even those features of civilization that seemed to distinguish

80. Ludwig Büchner, *Kraft und Stoff: Empirisch-naturphilosophische Studien* (Leipzig, 1855).

81. Gregory, *Scientific Materialism,* 2.

82. See especially the chapter "Der Gedanke," in Büchner, *Kraft und Stoff,* 146–147.

83. Henning, *Handbuch der freigeistigen Bewegung,* 12; Groschopp, *Dissidenten,* 110–114.

84. Burrow, *Crisis of Reason,* 36. On the importance of cell theory in German Social Darwinism, see Paul Weindling, *Darwinism and Social Darwinism in Imperial Germany: The Contribution of the Cell Biologist Oscar Hertwig, 1844–1922* (Stuttgart, 1991).

85. Paul Weindling notes, "Investigations of the reception of Darwinism have suggested that the theory born in *laissez faire* England found in Germany 'its true spiritual home.'" Weindling, *Darwinism and Social Darwinism,* 15.

human existence from other forms of animal existence—philosophy, religion, ethics, art—might have to be rethought as nothing but especially sophisticated tools in the competition for survival.[86]

Against this background, much of the more secular commentary on the DGEK asked also about the autonomy of ethics, but now in terms of science, materialism, and Darwinism—the three often being conflated in public discussion. The pressing questions on this front were, How is an ethics possible if humans are materially determined? Are human decisions really only reflections of material necessity? Does a truly moral decision necessarily require the ability to renounce material urges? Schmitt, for instance, had assumed that the scientistic logic of the DGEK meant an indebtedness to Darwin and a corresponding understanding of society as a "struggle for existence" (*Kampf ums Daseins*) between individuals.[87] Such a conclusion, he implied, would leave humanity with no possibility for moral decision, as all actions would be subject to this fundamental competition for life. Bousset, on the other hand, making a common connection between materialism, Darwinism, and laissez-faire economics, praised the DGEK on just this point. He objected to the Manchester school of economists because of its advocacy of the "iron law of wages" and the "struggle for existence," and held these maxims to presuppose a material determinism in economic processes that would render futile moral intervention, in the forms of distributive justice or labor regulation, for instance.[88] The efforts by the DGEK to preserve a space for ethics and reform in social life, he claimed, seemed to resist the "morally bankrupt" and determinist logic of economic materialism.[89]

Gizycki responded in the pages of *Ethische Kultur* to the confusion about the DGEK and materialism.[90] Although he did not commit himself or the DGEK to materialism per se, he tried to argue that materialism was not in intrinsic conflict with moral freedom, and he claimed that

---

86. On Darwinism in Germany, see in addition to Weindling's two books, Alfred Kelly, *The Descent of Darwin: The Popularization of Darwinism in Germany, 1860–1914* (Chapel Hill, N.C., 1981).

87. Schmitt, *Warum ist eine religiöse Bewegung Notwendigkeit?* 3–4.

88. Bousset, "Die Gesellschaften für ethische Kultur," 9.

89. Ibid.

90. Georg von Gizycki, "Materialismus und Ethik," *Ethische Kultur* 1, no. 19 (1893): 151–152.

the materialist school had been pushed into a corner by its opponents and consequently forced to say things that it didn't necessarily represent. Distinguishing between "practical" and "philosophical" materialism—where "practical materialism" was supposed to refer simply to the indulgence in physical pleasures and the pursuit of material gain whereas "philosophical materialism" was supposed to connote the "view that the mental life is bound to the material and that a non-embodied spirit does not exist"—he insisted that, contrary to common perception, philosophical materialism in no way leads to practical materialism.[91] Quite the opposite: precisely the material determination of the world enables individuals to view their own moral freedom. With a logic more Kantian than his usual utilitarian stance, he clarified that it is only when one chooses to behave in ways contrary to material desires that one escapes from subservience to material life and can see oneself as morally free. Neither, he added, does the denial of the existence of a God or of an afterlife—claims with which philosophical materialism was commonly associated—preclude moral freedom. "This seems to me just as illogical," he argued, "as if someone were to decide to fill himself up with poison and other deadly things because he believes he cannot nourish himself eternally with healthy nutritional food."[92] The important thing for Gizycki was that one need not necessarily look to a supernatural being or to the beyond for the basis of ethics. Rather, one could find the "good will" in oneself and in the human capacity to make decisions regardless of material circumstances. This reorientation implied a very this-worldly (*diesseits*) ethics that was thus neither in conflict with materialism nor bound to the "practical" materialism of physical pleasure and material gain. In this way, Gizycki felt he had found a rapprochement between moral freedom and materialism.[93]

For some, however, this adherence to a transcendent freedom bespoke precisely the problem of the ethical culture movement—that it remained committed to a philosophical dualism of mind and body, spirit and matter,

91. Ibid., 151.
92. Ibid.
93. Gizycki was the one to spell out the relationship of ethics to materialism, but such sentiments were common among the leadership. Wilhelm Foerster, for instance, noted that "the laws of human essence are much finer than those of mere mechanical works," indicating that something indeed separated human life from mechanical nature. Foerster, *Zur Ethik des Nationalismus*, 17–18.

and was therein more closely bound to conventional religiosity than it recognized. On this point, Haeckel led the charge. Haeckel, who would found the immensely popular Monist League in 1906,[94] commanded a significant if not yet organized following in 1892. In the 1860s, he had established himself as the chief spokesperson for Darwinism in Germany, and his scientific work on biological evolution lent credence to his claims. By the 1890s, Haeckel was busily spreading his monist theories.[95] Drawing philosophically on the pantheism of Baruch Spinoza and scientifically on the evolutionary theories of Darwin, Haeckel created a specifically nineteenth-century variant of monism. Where Spinoza had equated God with nature, Haeckel equated souls with cells.[96] By virtue of the sensate cell, all matter was to be seen as infused with spirituality, and all spirituality to be made up of matter.

Writing from the university town of Jena, where he held a professorship in zoology, Haeckel asked the DGEK to clarify its relationship to established religions, just as Stöcker, Schmitt, and Bousset had done. Where they all viewed the DGEK as venturing too far from religion, however, Haeckel rejected the organization for not going far enough. In his view, as long as the DGEK continued to hold onto the idea of ethics, it could never leave the dualism of established religions behind, "as the two are intimately bound together." For too long, established religions have been "privileged societies" claiming the right "to determine the laws of morality." That connection cannot be broken easily. For Haeckel, the problem with the DGEK rested in its method. The DGEK invested in public debate, assuming that rational discussion among competing philosophical and religious perspectives would ultimately lead to rational, secular conclusions. Insofar as the organization avoided formulating a totalizing *Weltanschauung,* however, Haeckel feared its efforts would be without consequence. In keeping with the "really existing historical conditions," he countered that it was necessary to create a completely new *Weltanschauung,* one that would coincide with the historical and scientific circumstances of the day. Moreover, the

---

94. Henning, *Handbuch der freigeistigen Bewegung,* 45.

95. Weindling, *Health, Race, and German Politics,* 40–41. Niles R. Holt, "Ernst Haeckel's Monistic Religion," *Journal of the History of Ideas* 32, no. 2 (1971): 269.

96. See Baruch Spinoza, *The Ethics and Selected Letters,* ed. and trans. Samuel Shirley (Indianapolis, Ind., 1982); Ernst Haeckel, "Zellseelen und Seelenzellen," *Deutsche Rundschau* 16 (1878): 40–59; cited in Holt, "Haeckel's Monistic Religion," 272.

"building stones" for this new *Weltanschauung* could only be the "clear, rational knowledge of science" set out in a definitively monist fashion.[97]

In this regard, Haeckel's critique mirrored Schmitt's. Both challenged the DGEK's insistence on the autonomy of ethics, as both saw a necessary bond between ethics and established religions. Like Schmitt, Haeckel also held that a socially reinforced *Weltanschauung* was necessary to provide orientation for the lone individual. Yet where Schmitt turned to Christianity, Haeckel held it necessary to provide a new *Weltanschauung* to replace conventional religion. In a related article on the *Weltanschauung* of monism, Haeckel began to clarify what an alternative, secular *Weltanschauung* might look like. Where dualistic philosophies maintain a distinction between spirit or mind and body or matter, monism makes no such distinction. For monism, or *"Einheits-Philosophie"* (unity philosophy), Haeckel clarified, "an immaterial spirit [*Geist*] is just as unthinkable as a 'dead spiritless matter.'" He contested the classification of monism as "materialism," noting that one could just as easily label monism a variety of "spiritualism." In either case, the accuser is still operating in a dualistic system, failing to grasp that monism understands matter and spirit as one and the same. This point was crucial for Haeckel, as he feared that simple materialism emptied the world of spiritual meaning: life appeared fragmented and flat for the individual governed by a materialist *Weltanschauung*. The monist *Weltanschauung,* on the other hand, could be a new religion that would understand materiality as spirituality. Individuals would not look beyond the world for spiritual orientation; they would gain spiritual insights by looking to science for an understanding of the physical world. Only an ethics wedded to this newly articulated *Weltanschauung* would be clearly distinct from Judeo-Christian traditions.[98]

If the intellectual dispute over *Weltanschauung* made it unlikely for Haeckel and the DGEK to work together in the 1890s, Haeckel's effort to combine nationalism with his monist theories made a collaboration impossible.[99] To be sure, Haeckel's nationalist ideas were complex and not

97. Haeckel, "Ethik und Weltanschauung," 310.

98. Ernst Haeckel, "Die Weltanschauung der monistischen Wissenschaft," *Freie Bühne für den Entwickelungskampf der Zeit* 3, nos. 3–4 (1892): 1155–1169.

99. Historians disagree about the relationship of Haeckel's monism to National Socialism. Daniel Gasman has led the effort to link Haeckel and other monists to National Socialism. See especially Daniel Gasman, *The Scientific Origins of National Socialism,* rev. ed.

always supportive of the Prusso-centric German government. Yet as early as the 1860s, as Haeckel was just beginning to formulate his monist ideas, he was linking them to notions of German national superiority. In one of his earliest social-theoretical pieces, Haeckel claimed that the "Indo-Germanic race" had "deviated furthest from the common primary form of ape-like men" and that "the English and Germans" in particular were setting the pace for the advancement of civilization by "laying the foundation for a new period of higher mental development, in the recognition and completion of the theory of descent."[100] Moreover, the development and dissemination of Haeckel's monism was to serve as the evidence for the higher mental development of Germany. But while Haeckel supported German unification, as did most German liberals, he objected to the militarist methods by which it was accomplished.[101] Also like many liberals, he supported Bismarck's campaign against Catholicism known as the *Kulturkampf,* viewing it as a campaign for progress and modernity against residues of superstition.[102] He was less supportive, however, of the antisocialist laws that succeeded the *Kulturkampf,* when the Social Democrats began to emerge as a political force. His opposition did not arise from any sympathy toward Social Democracy but rather from the fact that biology and evolution came under attack and were prohibited from inclusion in public school curricula, as they were seen to lend support to Social Democracy's secular, materialist stance. Haeckel objected that Bismarck's practices not only

---

(New Brunswick, N.J., 2004; first published 1971); and Gasman, *Haeckel's Monism and the Birth of Fascist Ideology* (New York, 1998). For a more subtle argument, see Weikart, *From Darwin to Hitler.* Alfred Kelly introduced a new paradigm when he argued that Haeckel's monism stood for liberalism and scientific progress, and that Nazi appropriation of Haeckel did not reflect the historical circumstances in which his work was legible to contemporaries. Several others have followed roughly in Kelly's path. See Kelly, *Descent of Darwin;* Paul Weindling and Pietro Corsi, "Darwinism in Germany, France, and Italy," in *The Darwinian Heritage,* ed. David Kohn (Princeton, N.J., 1985); and Thomas Glick, *The Comparative Reception of Darwinism* (Chicago, 1988).

    100. Ernst Haeckel, *History of Creation, or the Development of the Earth and Its Inhabitants by the Action of Natural Causes: A Popular Exposition of the Doctrine of Evolution in General, and that of Darwin, Goethe, and Lamarck in Particular,* vol. 2 (New York, 1876), 332; also cited in Gasman, *Scientific Origins,* 41.

    101. Weindling, *Health, Race, and German Politics,* 42.

    102. On liberalism and the *Kulturkampf,* see Michael Gross, *The War against Catholicism: Liberalism and the Anti-Catholic Imagination in Nineteenth-Century Germany* (Ann Arbor, Mich., 2004).

suppressed individual liberties but also seemed to thwart the possibilities of German intellectual grandeur.[103] Only when Bismarck was dismissed did Haeckel fully embrace him and his successful efforts to unify Germany.

Yet Haeckel's attendance at a Bismarck festival in 1892 earned him the scorn and derision of the DGEK founders.[104] If they were anxious about totalizing *Weltanschauungen* in general, they were especially opposed to those that took the form of—or combined with—German nationalism. In this regard, Haeckel's monism was a good example of the ways in which totalizing *Weltanschauungen* tended to coincide with closed or exclusive definitions of community. As early as an inaugural address of 1892, *On the Ethics of Nationalism and of the Jewish Question,* Wilhelm Foerster had raised nationalism as a principal concern for the DGEK. Foerster was interested particularly in a rather vicious inversion that happened to moral sentiment when it became attached to something like nationalism or some other form of strong group identity. He started from the idea that a moral disposition of sympathy for fellow creatures motivates groups to come together and to care for one another. This he viewed as "one of the highest and fortunately most common characteristics of human nature," and as the basis of all forms of cohesive social organization. Moreover, this *"Gemeinschaftsgefühl,"* or sentiment for community, motivates an ethics of self-sacrifice "in which [the individual's] selfishness" disappears and he sacrifices himself for the good of the *Gemeinschaft."* National loyalty might in fact be viewed simply as an "exaggerated elevation" of this sentiment. But here Foerster turned his argument, remarking that precisely the trait that enables a moral sentiment—the willingness to sacrifice oneself for the good of the group—can also turn on itself and become vicious. The strong identification between the individual and the group can cause individuals or groups not only to sacrifice themselves for one another but also to overlook what Foerster called "the naive selfishness of acts of the community as such." Simply put, self-sacrifice for the good of the group may bind an individual so strongly to the group that he fails to recognize the

103. Weindling, *Health, Race, and German Politics,* 43.

104. Haeckel, "Ethik und Weltanschauung," 313. For further evidence of distance between Haeckel and the DGEK, see Wilhelm Foerster's comments in Gizycki, *Mitteilungen,* 21. Here Foerster notes that he is sympathetic with Haeckel on the notion of ethics as independent from religion but that "he is absolutely not in agreement with his *Weltanschauung."*

offenses committed by the group against outsiders. This inversion, Foerster argued, explains "the excesses of patriotism [and] nationalism." With a militarist nationalism in particular, Foerster further argued, the basis for moral sentiment turns in on itself and demands correction.[105]

Felix Adler raised a similar concern when, in response to the first International Ethical Congress in 1896, he reflected on the success that the ethical culture movement had experienced in its first few years in Germany and Austria.[106] According to Adler, Germany had traditionally been an especially spiritual culture, and the difficulties of rapid secularization—at least among intellectuals—had posed particular challenges for Germans. Many individuals were turning back toward religious fervor, a development he found troubling. Even more disturbing for him, however, was the growth of a seemingly secular replacement in the form of a *Pflichtgefühl,* or "sense of duty," that was expressed in nationalist and militarist devotion.[107] By 1896, it was already clear to Adler that a primary task of an International Union of Ethical Societies was to provide alternatives to both fanatical religiosity and nationalist excesses so individuals might again recognize themselves as part of a this-worldly universal humanity, without succumbing to exclusionist conceptions of community.

From Community to Individual

While asking about the relationship of ethics to an overarching *Weltanschauung,* the ethics reform debates addressed primarily how the individual determines the community of moral responsibility. The founders of the DGEK conceived of that community as universal humanity (or, in some cases, as all sentient beings), but the majority of the DGEK's opponents thought of that community in more limited terms, with the particular limitations varying according to intellectual or political position. Implicit in those discussions was another question regarding ethics and autonomy: what exactly constitutes the autonomous moral individual and the individual capable of determining for himself or herself the appropriate community of

105. Foerster, *Zur Ethik des Nationalismus,* 4–7.
106. Adler, "International Ethical Congress," 135.
107. Ibid., 137–138.

moral consideration? This question often remained only implicit, but a face-off between Ferdinand Tönnies and Rudolf Steiner brought it to the fore.

The Austrian-born Steiner was a literary historian who later became founder of the German Anthroposophical Society (1912–1913), an occultist organization celebrating the "wisdom of man."[108] Working in Weimar in the early 1890s on collections of writings from Goethe and Schopenhauer, Steiner was already emerging as a spokesperson for a romantic-individualist strain of German thought that would grow stronger as the century came to a close. While in Weimar, Steiner was invited by Elisabeth Förster-Nietzsche to advise her on the organization of the Nietzsche Archive. Even before this invitation, however, Nietzsche's influence was making its way into Steiner's thought, an influence that guided Steiner's response to the DGEK.[109]

To pose his challenge to the DGEK, Steiner set off the "old Kant" against Nietzsche and "modern thought."[110] In pitting Nietzsche against Kant in this way, Steiner was participating in a growing intellectual fad just as Nietzsche's fame was beginning to blossom into cult status in literary and artistic circles in both Germany and Austria.[111] While Nietzsche himself at times expressed extraordinary admiration for Kant's critical philosophy, it became ever more popular in the course of the 1890s for his disciples to treat Kant with considerably less subtlety.[112] As neo-Kantianism became a

108. Much of the literature on Rudolf Steiner derives directly from the anthroposophical school. For less partisan treatments, see Corinna Treitel, *Science for the Soul: Occultism and the Genesis of the German Modern* (Baltimore, 2004), 97–102; and Robert Sumser, "Rational Occultism in Fin de Siècle Germany: Rudolf Steiner's Modernism," *History of European Ideas* 18, no. 4 (1994): 497–511. On the anthroposophical movement, see Norbert Schwarte, "Anthroposophie," in *Handbuch der deutschen Reformbewegungen, 1880–1933,* ed. Diethart Kerbs and Jürgen Reulecke (Wuppertal, 1998), 595–609.

109. Johannes Hemleben, *Rudolf Steiner: An Illustrated Biography* (London, 2000), 55–57.

110. Rudolf Steiner, "Eine Gesellschaft für ethische Kultur," *Die Zukunft* 1 (1892): 216.

111. On Nietzsche's reception in Germany, see Steven Aschheim, *The Nietzsche Legacy in Germany, 1890–1990* (Berkeley, Calif., 1992); Anton Hain Meisenheim, ed., *100 Jahre philosophische Nietzsche-Rezeption* (Frankfurt am Main, 1991); Geoff Waite, *Nietzsche's Corps/e: Aesthetics, Politics, Prophecy, or the Spectacular Technoculture of Everyday Life* (Durham, N.C., 1996); and R. Hinton Thomas, *Nietzsche in German Politics and Society, 1890–1918* (Manchester, 1983).

112. See, for example, Nietzsche's comments in *Die Geburt der Tragödie,* in *Werke: Kritische Gesamtausgabe,* 25 vols., ed. Giorgio Colli and Mazzino Montinari (Berlin, 1967), sec. 3, vol. 1, 114 (hereafter citations to this collection are given as *Werke,* followed by section

dominant force in German universities in the second half of the century, Kantian philosophy came to represent for some intellectuals outside university culture the staid character of German academics.[113] In contrast, Nietzsche, whose short tenure as a philology professor in Basel precipitated a decade of scathing critique aimed at scholars generally and at German universities in particular, came to be seen as the independent thinker, the philosopher in the street who ran counter to convention.[114]

For Steiner, the contrast between Kant and Nietzsche revolved around the precise constitution of individual moral autonomy. We have already seen how Kantian ethics relied on the premise of individual moral autonomy and freedom from external constraints. For Steiner, however, Kantian ethics—and especially its appeal to universal reason—implied anything but autonomy. Because of its universalist presuppositions, Steiner viewed the Kantian categorical imperative as a homogenizing force that implied that right action could be determined in exactly the same way by very different individuals. It thus did not recognize the fundamental individuality that he took to typify the "modern sensibility," and thereby failed as well to recognize the coercion that society enacts in forcing moral norms onto an individual and making him (or her) identify those moral norms as his or her own.[115] Stressing a highly individualistic reading of Nietzsche, Steiner countered that individuals must always determine moral values in a unique, individualized manner. He thus rewrote Kant's moral maxim to reflect his own understanding of Nietzsche, proposing that one "act always in the way that, according to your unique individuality, only you

number, volume number, and page number). Such expressions were not only a product of his youth. See his comments in *On the Genealogy of Morals,* where Nietzsche praises Kant, together with Plato, La Rochefoucauld, and Spinoza, for his distaste for pity as a moral category. In Friedrich Nietzsche, *Zur Genealogie der Moral,* in *Werke,* sec. 6, vol. 2, 264.

113. On the history of neo-Kantianism, see Thomas E. Willey, *Back to Kant: The Revival of Kantianism in German Social and Historical Thought, 1860–1914* (Detroit, 1978); and Klaus Christian Köhnke, *The Rise of Neo-Kantianism: German Academic Philosophy between Idealism and Positivism,* trans. R. J. Hollingdale (Cambridge, 1991).

114. See especially Ascheim, *Nietzsche Legacy,* 17–51. For an interesting discussion of Nietzsche's relationship to scholars, see Christie McDonald, ed., *The Ear of the Other: Otobiography, Transference, Translation; Texts and Discussion with Jacques Derrida,* trans. Peggy Kamuf (Lincoln, Neb., 1985).

115. Steiner, "Eine Gesellschaft für ethische Kultur," 217.

can act."[116] Nothing short of defining one's own moral framework—an individual "revaluation of values," in Nietzsche's words—would liberate the individual from the constraints of social and traditional norms and consequently qualify as "autonomy" for that modern individual.

Tönnies took it on himself to respond to Steiner's charges in a small publication whose title hid none of his disparagement of Steiner and other disciples of Nietzsche: *"Ethical Culture" and Its Followers: 1) Nietzsche Fools [in the "Present" and in the "Future"]; and 2) Wolves in Fox Furs.* In his response, Tönnies took the strategy of rereading Nietzsche and reframing the question that Steiner had posed. Where Steiner had asked what kind of individual autonomy modernity demanded, Tönnies countered by asking what the historical circumstances were that made individual autonomy an item for discussion in the first place.

According to Tönnies, Nietzsche's real intellectual contribution was his historicization of ethics. Dispelling the notion of ethics as universal, Nietzsche had traced an ethics that might be associated with a Judeo-Christian tradition—kindness, meekness, and justice—back to an origin of cruelty, in which the "weak" tame the "strong" by inflicting on the "strong" bodily pain and punishment. Nietzsche had presented this ethics and its Judeo-Christian heritage as an outdated relic, just waiting to be overthrown in a "revaluation of values." Tönnies heralded Nietzsche for pointing out the enormous burden that the remnants of Judeo-Christian morality placed on a culture that had moved into another, less religious era. Such a burdened society, Tönnies agreed, did not have the ability to "bring forth real, artistic soul." Rather, with rare exceptions, it produced those "mediocre half-geniuses," of which, in Tönnies's view, Steiner was a prime example.[117]

The idea that ethics should be viewed historically corresponded with Tönnies's own stance in his *Gemeinschaft und Gesellschaft.* There he had distinguished between the kinds of moral frameworks that dominate in

---

116. Ibid.
117. Tönnies, *"Ethische Cultur" und ihr Geleite,* 9–11. Because of his opposition to what he considered to be naive Nietzscheanism, Tönnies earned the reputation as a critic of Nietzsche, a reputation he sought hard to contest in letters to Elizabeth Förster-Nietzsche at the Nietzsche Archive. See the collection of letters in the Goethe- und Schiller-Archiv: 72/BW5515, especially the letter of September 1, 1900, where he expressly regrets that his name is included among the enemies of Nietzsche. Also amusing in the same file is a poem Tönnies wrote in honor of the opening of the salon at the Nietzsche Archive, October 15, 1903.

community-based social organizations and the kinds that dominate in society-based social organizations. With the shift from a social organization that privileged group identity and tradition to one that emphasized individual autonomy and rationality, he argued, went a parallel shift from a traditional morality that would be defined by self-sacrifice and group consideration to an ethics of self-assertion, self-interestedness, and future-oriented calculation. If in *Gemeinschaft* a moral code was said to be already in place, the challenge for the individual in *Gesellschaft* was to make individual decisions about moral valuations.[118]

Tönnies thus agreed with Nietzsche that different moral frameworks dominate in different eras. The only problem with Nietzsche's historicization (or "genealogy") of ethics, according to Tönnies, was that it told just half the story.[119] In speaking only of masters and slaves, Nietzsche failed to make visible to the individual in *Gesellschaft* the full range of moral possibilities from which he or she might choose. Nietzsche was right, Tönnies maintained, in pointing to the cruel origins of "slave morality," the morality characterized as "bitter, full of self-pity and self-denial."[120] But Tönnies insisted that there was another, complementary and equally secular, origin for ethics. This he found in the family. Where the master-slave dynamic implied an ethics of contest, the family origin offered an ethics of "help, concern, and duties toward one another."[121]

The idea of a second, complementary origin was crucial to Tönnies's idea of ethics as reform. He acknowledged that Nietzsche was speaking to the dominant mode of morality in *Gesellschaft*. But in trumpeting only "master morality"—the morality of individual competition, of "confidence, bodily strength, size, and beauty"—Nietzsche became nothing but

---

118. Tönnies, *Gemeinschaft und Gesellschaft,* 193–194. The distinction rests on Tönnies's description of two types of will, *Wesenwille* and *Willkür,* both of which are said to be present in all human beings. *Wesenwille* corresponds to nonreflective performance of duty within a given social context whereas *Willkür* corresponds to arbitrary calculation and self-governance or sovereignty. While both are available to all individuals, *Gemeinschaft* nurtures *Wesenwille* in particular, and *Gesellschaft* calls out the *Willkür* in each individual. For the full discussion of the will, see all of book 2, "Wesenwille und Willkür," in *Gemeinschaft und Gesellschaft,* 99–194.

119. Tönnies, *"Ethische Cultur" und ihr Geleite,* 8.

120. Ibid.

121. Ibid.

the "philosopher of capitalism."[122] He was affirming *only* the privileged ethics of *Gesellschaft,* only the aspect of self-interestedness that capitalism demands. After publication of *Gemeinschaft und Gesellschaft,* however, Tönnies had insistently maintained that *Gemeinschaft* and *Gesellschaft* were only sociological models, and that all variants of social order contain dimensions of both *Gemeinschaft* and *Gesellschaft,* even if a particular historical moment emphasized one over the other. In this light he explained that while the logic of *Gesellschaft* does not reward an ethics of social obligation, such an ethics nonetheless remains available as an option for the moral individual.[123] And insofar as the moral individual of *Gesellschaft* is the one who must make individual decisions about morality, he or she is autonomous only if confronted with the full range of available options, or ways to think about morality. In short, for Tönnies, moral autonomy implies not liberation from social influence, as Steiner suggested, but rather open discussion about values as options.[124]

Nietzsche's disciples thus erred fundamentally, in Tönnies's view, when they assumed that individualism stands opposed to all forms of communitarianism, that is, that the individual could be conceived of as an isolated or distinct entity. For Tönnies, conversely, individualism is always only a component of social order. In *Gemeinschaft und Gesellschaft,* he had insisted that the dichotomy between individualism and socialism in particular was unhelpful and ill-informed. Individuals arise only as products of *Gemeinschaft* and as what makes *Gesellschaft* possible, he insisted, while both *Gemeinschaft* and *Gesellschaft* serve as stable forms of social organization. In other words, ideas of the individual and of individualism are fundamentally *social* phenomena and make sense only within specific formations of social order. Insofar as Nietzsche's disciples failed to understand the necessary dynamic between social concord and individualism, they focused solely on what Tönnies considered to be a naive individualism. They thought that the ethics of individualism meant acting solely according to one's own wishes and commands—as if cut off from social order. As a consequence, from Tönnies's perspective, his standoff with Steiner was not one between radi-

122. Ibid., 8, 10.

123. See, for example, Ferdinand Tönnies, "Die sittliche Bestimmung der Frau," *Ethische Kultur* 3, no. 4 (1895): 25–27.

124. Tönnies, *Gemeinschaft und Gesellschaft,* 178.

cal individualism and communitarianism; rather, it was one between naive individualism on the one hand and individual choice within historically specific social constraints on the other. Only the latter, he implied, constituted a viable means through which to consider individual moral autonomy in modern social life.

Ethics as Reform

Tönnies's response to Steiner contained within it the justification for treating ethics as a category of social reform. Like the other founding members of the DGEK, Tönnies stoically accepted that the age of *Gesellschaft* had arrived. But the implications of life in an era of *Gesellschaft* were hardly preordained. One could accept the dominant "morality" of *Gesellschaft,* which Tönnies identified largely as competition and individual self-assertion. Alternatively, however, one could understand the ethics of *Gesellschaft* to be one in which individuals make choices from the wide array of moral possibilities in a given social situation. To encourage the latter option, however, entailed broad public discussion about the most basic categories of social existence, those of ethics, value, and notions of social living. Accordingly, the aim of the DGEK was not to delineate right moral action. Rather, it prompted discussion that would elicit the vast range of choices available to the individual trying to conduct a life. And in doing so, it problematized the social and historical circumstances that make individual moral decisions possible.

The DGEK's focus on ethics and issues of individual moral conscience was anything but a retreat from public and political concern. Rather, the DGEK understood ethics reform as the mechanism through which moral conscience and social change intersected. Moreover, it was in the individual conscience that residues of social tradition and mores existed. Only if these residues become public and available for critical scrutiny could they inform the effort to shape and choose values for a modern world. Such residues did not have to be expunged, but they needed to be made available for public interrogation. At a preparatory meeting for the founding of the DGEK, Adler observed that "our era demands more than ever that we turn inwards. But in order to reach broader circles, our era demands at the same time integration, a firm ground that never fails and that is common

for all those who are serious and striving."[125] Ethics reform sought to provide that firm ground not in a clear definition of community, not in a regulation of individual behavior, not even in a final definition of ethics, but
rather in the ongoing dynamic that revealed the social influences that feed
a moral conscience, and conversely in enabling the individual moral conscience to affect public discourse.

125. Adler, "Rede," 16.

2

THE "NEW ETHIC"

A Particularist Challenge

Oh yes, that suffices for the everyday struggle for existence—but for the
struggle for higher mental goods, for the higher spiritual level—how in that
case does one value humans? "The old tables of morality are broken," but the
new are only half inscribed. And still fully inadequately inscribed.

HELENE STÖCKER

On the forefront of a sexual liberation campaign, Helene Stöcker set
out to define what she called a "New Ethic." The "old ethic," she said, was
"brutal," it was "ascetic, cloistral," and it was "damaging." It conceived
of life and physicality as sinful, individuals as "disobedient sinners," and
the sex drive as "evil in itself." The New Ethic in contrast, would learn
from Nietzsche to resist such "gloomy life renunciation and negation." In
its place the New Ethic would seek to "establish this life, our life, as if
it were valuable."[1] In particular, it would affirm the individual's physical and sexual existence. "Ethics," in Stöcker's terms, would liberate both
men and women from the oppressive reign of what she called *Sittlichkeit,*
or "morality."[2] Hardly alone in these sentiments, Stöcker was praised by

1. Helene Stöcker, "Zur Reform der sexuellen Ethik," *Mutterschutz* 1, no. 1 (1905): 1,
4–6, 8.
2. Ibid., 3. See also Helene Stöcker, "Von neuer Ethik," *Mutterschutz* 2, no. 1 (1906):
5–11; Helene Stöcker, "Das Werden der sexuellen Reform seit hundert Jahren," in *Ehe? Zur
Reform der sexuellen Moral* (Berlin, 1911), 38.

Havelock Ellis, the British sexologist who also sought to create a "new morality" through sexual liberation; in Sweden, Ellen Key pronounced the advent of a new era with love as the basis for a new life, a new ethics, and a new religion.[3]

But why did Stöcker and her fellow sexual liberationists articulate their project in terms of ethics? Did not the language of ethics automatically bespeak a language of regulation? If so, were the liberationists inevitably inviting a new form of regulation into discussions of sexuality? Or were they exploring new ways to talk about ethics and sexuality that could not be fully captured by regulatory frameworks? And were they thus not necessarily evading the problem of regulation, but attacking it at its root and displacing its inner mechanisms?

Stöcker was the individual most closely associated with the New Ethic and sexual liberation in turn-of-the-century Germany. In addition to writing vast numbers of articles, pamphlets, and books on the status of women and sexuality in the modern era, she founded the controversial League for the Protection of Mothers (Bund für Mutterschutz) to lobby for women's reproductive rights and for sexual liberation. Because of this high profile and prolific writing career, her story offers a valuable lens through which to answer these questions, to discern what *work* the language of ethics did for Stöcker and the sexual-liberationist project. Like the early leaders of the German Society for Ethical Culture (DGEK), Stöcker embarked on a project of ethics reform to turn the content of seemingly private considerations into topics of public relevance. As the foremost spokesperson for the New Ethic in Germany, she explained that there are two ways to pursue questions of ethics: to look to the external or public world, and to immerse oneself "in the interiority of the human soul," pulling that interiority to the surface.[4] Pursuing the latter path, and focusing especially on sexual expression, Stöcker used ethics as a means to contest the ways in which the private and intimate were opposed to and cut off from the public and the political.

Although Stöcker approached ethics reform from a radically different angle than the leaders of the DGEK, her project complemented theirs in

---

3. Havelock Ellis, "The Woman Question," *Fortnightly Review* 80 (1906): 123–134; Key, *Über Liebe und Ehe;* Ellen Key, *Das Jahrhundert des Kindes: Studien,* trans. Francis Maro (Berlin, 1902), and *Liebe und Ethik,* trans. Francis Maro (Berlin, 1905).
4. Helene Stöcker, "Einleitung," in *Die Liebe und die Frauen* (Minden, 1906), 5.

surprising ways. Like the spokespersons for the DGEK, Stöcker turned to the newest scientific, historical, and philosophical literature to propagate ethics in explicitly modern, secular—or "this-worldly," in Stöcker's common phrasing—terms.[5] Also, like that of the DGEK, her project was woven with political challenges, asking whether moral subjecthood necessarily coincided with conventional notions of citizenship and national obligation. Where the DGEK lobbed this challenge from the angle of community, however, asking whether the politically defined national community coincided with the community of moral consideration, the New Ethic posed the question from the angle of the moral subject, as Stöcker asked whether the legal model of the citizen-subject coincided with the moral subject. Moreover, where the DGEK relied on the idea of universal humanity as the basis of its critique, the New Ethic appealed explicitly to particularism—to a sexual-liberationist subject of ethics as a different kind of moral subject. Indeed, Stöcker and the New Ethic illustrate especially well how women's noncitizen status could be mobilized by ethics reform, turning as she did to the feminine ethical subject as a model of subjecthood not circumscribed by the law. To see how she drew a strong contrast between the moral subject as envisioned by the New Ethic and the liberal model of the citizen-subject, it is helpful to look first at the set of contexts in which Stöcker proposed her project; second, at how she formulated the New Ethic around an explicitly feminine type of ethical subject; and finally, at how her project might be understood in comparison with several contemporaries, highlighting the political challenge that her contribution to ethics reform sought to make.[6]

5. On the scientific influences on Stöcker and the League for the Protection of Mothers, see Edward Ross Dickinson, "Reflections on Feminism and Monism in the Kaiserreich, 1900–1913," *Central European History* 34, no. 2 (2001): 191–230.

6. A substantial literature exists on Helene Stöcker and the League for the Protection of Mothers. My own interpretation of Stöcker's work is most closely aligned with that of McGuire in "Activism, Intimacy, and the Politics of Selfhood." It is also greatly indebted to Allen, *Feminism and Motherhood,* and Heide Schluppmann, "Die Radikalisierung der Philosophie: Die Nietzsche-Rezeption und die sexualpolitische Publizistik Helene Stöckers," *Feministische Studien* 3 (1984): 10–38. Other examples include Dickinson, "Reflections on Feminism"; Ann Taylor Allen, "Mothers of the New Generation: Adele Schreiber, Helene Stöcker, and the Evolution of a German Idea of Motherhood," *Signs* 10, no. 3 (1985): 418–438; Christl Wickert, *Helene Stöcker, 1869–1943: Frauenrechtlerin, Sexualreformerin und Pazifistin; Eine Biographie* (Bonn, 1991); and Amy Hackett, "Helene Stöcker: Left-Wing

Influences behind the New Ethic

A wide range of well-established trends in Germany and Europe at the turn of the century influenced both Stöcker's New Ethic and the League for the Protection of Mothers. The bourgeois German women's movement was especially prominent both as influence and later as antagonism for Stöcker's project. Conventionally, the German women's movement is dated to the revolutionary year of 1848, when Luise Otto-Peters led an effort to demand gender equality in politics, education, and law. After suffering an abrupt decline in the repressive years that followed, the movement was gaining new steam by 1865 as local groups of the General German Women's Association (Allgemeiner Deutscher Frauenverein) appeared across the German Confederation. Throughout the 1870s and 1880s, the movement concerned itself primarily with women's education and employment opportunities until yet another age of growth in the late 1880s and 1890s. This new phase was marked by the founding in 1894 of the League of German Women's Associations (Bund Deutscher Frauenvereine), an umbrella organization intended to facilitate cooperation and communication among smaller organizations that were themselves devoted to diverse aspects of women's lives.[7] Else Lüders, a contemporary chronicler of the women's movement, identified two dominant concerns that commanded the attention of the movement in the 1890s: the proposal for a new German Civil Code and controversial debates about "morality

Intellectual and Sex Reformer," in *When Biology Became Destiny: Women in Weimar and Nazi Germany,* ed. Renate Bridenthal, Atina Grossman, and Marion Kaplan (New York, 1984), 109–130.

7. On the history of the women's movement in Germany, see Ute Gerhard, *Unerhört: Die Geschichte der Deutschen Frauenbewegung* (Reinbek bei Hamburg, 1990); Ute Frevert, *Women in German History: From Bourgeois Emancipation to Sexual Liberation,* trans. Stuart McKinnon-Evans (Oxford, 1989); Barbara Greven-Aschoff, *Die bürgerliche Frauenbewegung in Deutschland, 1894–1933* (Göttingen, 1981); and Richard Evans, *The Feminist Movement in Germany, 1894–1933* (London, 1976). For accounts of the movement by contemporaries, see Lida Gustava Heymann and Anita Augspurg, *Erlebtes—Erschautes: Deutsche Frauen kämpfen für Freiheit, Recht und Frieden, 1850–1940,* new ed., ed. Margrit Twellmann (Frankfurt am Main, 1992); Else Lüders, *Der "linke Flügel": Ein Blatt aus der Geschichte der Deutschen Frauenbewegung* (Berlin, 1904); Helene Lange and Gertrud Bäumer, *Handbuch der Frauenbewegung* (Berlin, 1901–1902); Lily Braun, *Die Frauenfrage, ihre geschichtliche Entwicklung und wirtschaftliche Seite* (Leipzig, 1901); and Minna Cauer, *Die Frau im 19. Jahrhundert* (Berlin, 1898).

questions" (*Sittlichkeitsfragen*).[8] Although these two concerns energized the movement in the 1890s, they were simultaneously controversial and led to ideological splits between a so-called radical branch and the much larger "moderate" faction. It is helpful to see how the controversies around the Civil Code and the morality questions played out, both to grasp their polarizing effects on the women's movement and to see how Stöcker situated herself and the New Ethic in relationship to them.

Intended to provide a single legal system as a replacement for the multiple codes operating in the individual German states before unification, the draft for the new Civil Code first appeared publicly in 1887. The German Reichstag ultimately approved it in 1896, to go into force by 1900—not, however, before a large group of women organized to protest a wide range of its provisions.[9] The Code was ambivalent toward women. On the one hand, it abolished provisions that had previously prevented women from carrying out financial negotiations: for example, it allowed women to own property and enter into legal contracts in ways formerly prohibited in some German states. On the other hand, the Code was more restrictive regarding marriage and family than many of the local codes that it superseded.[10] Opponents protested the Code's position on family law, especially paragraphs pertaining to marriage regulation and the status of unmarried mothers and their children, and paternalist provisions that allowed only husbands and fathers legally to represent and make decisions regarding women, family, and property. With its stipulations on "parental authority" (*elterliche Gewalt*), the Code recognized joint parental rights in relation to children; yet because of the father's autonomy in the final "right to decision," he retained in practice sole authority over the children. Limitations were also imposed on the right to sue for divorce, which the protesters saw as particularly disadvantageous to women. And

---

8. Lüders, Der "linke Flügel," 23.

9. Ibid., 17–26. For a history of the Civil Code, see Michael John, *Politics and the Law in Late Nineteenth-Century Germany: The Origins of the Civil Code* (Oxford, 1989).

10. Allen, *Feminism and Motherhood,* 137–138. See also Dirk Blasius, *Ehescheidung in Deutschland, 1794–1945: Scheidung und Scheidungsrecht in historischer Perspektive* (Göttingen, 1987), 127–154. For a longer perspective on the Civil Code, see Lynn Abrams, "Companionship and Conflict: The Negotiation of Marriage Relations in the Nineteenth Century," in *Gender Relations in German History: Power, Agency and Experience from the Sixteenth to the Twentieth Century,* ed. Abrams and Elizabeth Harvey (London, 1996), 101–120.

finally, the Code negated any automatic relation between the child of an unmarried mother and the child's biological father, denying the child a right to inheritance from the father. A related measure guaranteed that allegations in regard to the mother's promiscuity could exempt the father from child-care expenses.[11]

With particular reference to the moral undertones that penalized single mothers and their children while protecting biological fathers, critics of the Civil Code charged that it formalized as law a *Doppelmoral,* or double code of morality. The *Doppelmoral,* it was argued, commanded one code of conduct for men and another, more repressive code for women. Marianne Weber, a leading advocate of women's rights and later president of the League of German Women's Associations, argued that the Code reflected the "dynastic-military character of the German state." She maintained that the unlikely and specifically German combination of historical-law and natural-law traditions guiding the Code presented sexual differ-ence *as if* it derived from a natural order. In protest, she countered that "the natural relation of elements such as 'nature' and 'history' is, under closer inspection, always determined by one and the same—the one real—motive: the always recurring consideration for masculine sexual vanity."[12] To women like Weber who had hoped the new Civil Code would bring progressive measures of gender equality, this naturalized legal institu-tion of historically determined gender inequalities proved a momentous

---

11. On how the Civil Code changed the status of women, see Barbara Dölemeyer, "Frau und Familie im Privatrecht des 19. Jahrhunderts," and Beatrix Geisel, "Patriarchal Rechtsnormen 'unterlaufen': Die Rechtsschutzvereine der ersten deutschen Frauenbewe-gung," both in *Frauen in der Geschichte des Rechts,* ed. Ute Gerhard (Munich, 1997), 633–658 and 685–688; Ute Gerhard, *Verhältnisse und Verhinderungen: Frauenarbeit, Familie und Rechte der Frauen im 19. Jahrhundert* (Frankfurt am Main, 1978), esp. 182–188. For contem-porary discussions of the Civil Code as it pertained to women, see Emilie Kempin, *Die Stel-lung der Frau nach den zur Zeit in Deutschland gültigen Gesetzes-bestimmung sowie nach dem Entwurf eines bürgerlichen Gesetzbuches für das deutsche Reich* (Leipzig, 1892); Sera Proelß and Marie Raschke, *Die Frau im neuen bürgerlichen Gesetzbuches: Eine Beleuchtung und Ge-genübersetstellung der Paragraphen des Entwurfs eines bürgerlichen Gesetzbuchs für das deutsche Reich (2. Lesung) nebst Vorschlägen zur Änderung derselben im Interesse der Frauen* (Berlin, 1895); Hermann Jastrow, *Das Recht der Frau nach dem bürgerlichen Gesetzbuch: Dargestellt für Frauen* (Berlin, 1897); G. Planck, *Die rechtliche Stellung der Frau nach dem bürgerlichen Gesetzbuche* (Göttingen, 1899); and Marianne Weber, *Ehefrau und Mutter in der Rechtsent-wicklung: Eine Einführung* (Tübingen, 1907).

12. Weber, *Ehefrau und Mutter,* 412.

disappointment. After the Code passed the Reichstag, the more radical branches of the women's movement began to mobilize forcefully for the vote, having determined that only full political equality would ever lead to legalized gender equality.[13]

Closely related to legal questions were the so-called *Sittlichkeitsfragen* (morality questions) that were commanding the attention of the women's movement in the 1890s. As early as 1876, the General German Women's Association had begun to debate *Sittlichkeitsfragen* when the ideas of Josephine Butler, who was working to abolish state regulation of prostitution in England, migrated to Germany. These ideas became a divisive issue in the German women's movement only in the late 1890s, however, when two opposing approaches to *Sittlichkeitsfragen*—and especially to prostitution— emerged. Both sides lamented prostitution as a sign of moral turpitude, and both followed Butler's "abolitionist" program in opposing the state regulation of prostitution, especially state-run brothels. Yet the first approach, under the heading of *Jugendschutz* (protection of youth), advocated for legal action against all instances of prostitution, whereas the second objected to state involvement in matters of prostitution altogether. This second strand, which eventually crystallized as the German abolitionist movement, also maintained that female prostitutes were far more likely to be arrested for offenses than their male clients. The abolitionists thus saw criminalization of prostitution as discriminatory against women.[14]

An especially tense situation arose with the Lex Heinze affair, in which the opposing factions of the women's movement faced off.[15] First arising

13. Lüders, *Der "linke Flügel,"* 44–45; Heymann and Augspurg, *Erlebtes—Erschautes,* esp. 87–100.

14. Lüders, *Der "linke Flügel,"* 12, 30. On prostitution in Germany, see Sibylla Kraft, *Zucht und Unzucht: Prostitution und Sittenpolizei im München der Jahrhundertwende* (Munich, 1996); Regine Schulte, *Sperrbezirke: Tugendhaftigkeit und Prostitution in der bürgerlichen Welt* (Frankfurt am Main, 1984); Richard J. Evans, *Tales from the German Underworld: Crime and Punishment in the Nineteenth Century* (New Haven, Conn., 1998), 166–212; and Lynn Abrams, "Prostitutes in Imperial Germany, 1870–1918: Working Girls or Social Outcasts?" in *The German Underworld: Deviants and Outcasts in German History,* ed. Richard Evans (New York, 1988), 189–209. A very interesting literary approach is Jill Suzanne Smith, "Reading the Red Light: Literary, Cultural, and Social Discourses on Prostitution in Berlin, 1880–1933" (Ph.D. diss., Indiana University, 2004). A good discussion of Butler in context is Judith Walkowitz, *Prostitution and Victorian Society: Women, Class, and the State* (New York, 1980). See also Jane Jordan, *Josephine Butler: A Biography* (London, 2001).

15. Lüders, *Der "linke Flügel,"* 29–30.

in 1891, after a street hustler murdered a police officer, the Lex Heinze was a bill intended to increase police powers to fight prostitution, pornography, and the "criminal dregs" of urban life.[16] Although the first bill died in committee, it was resuscitated in much more stringent form in 1897. In addition to increased regulation of prostitution and a higher age of consent for girls (up from sixteen to eighteen), the new Lex Heinze contained extremely harsh paragraphs governing "obscenity" in art, theater, and advertising. As the bills progressed, the two sides of the women's movement found themselves in opposition: one faction supported the moral-purity movements (*Sittlichkeitsbewegungen*), especially the Union for the Elevation of Public Morality (Verein zur Hebung der öffentlichen Sittlichkeit) and the General Conference of German Morality Unions (Allgemeine Konferenz der deutschen Sittlichkeitsvereine) as they campaigned for ever more stringent interpretations of "obscenity" and "decency." At the same time, artists, writers, scholars, and performers formed groups known as the Goethe Leagues (Goethebünde) to advocate for free speech and publication rights. Although the Reichstag passed a much less stringent bill in June 1900, the controversy itself had created a high-profile setting for questions of sexuality and public morality.[17]

Stöcker's institutional affiliations consistently fell to the more radical sides of both the women's movement and the *Sittlichkeit* controversies. In 1896, she helped found the Union of Women Students (Verein Studierender Frauen).[18] Then, in 1899, she aided Lida Gustava Heymann and Anita Augspurg in establishing the League of Progressive Women's Organizations (Verband fortschrittlicher Frauenvereine), an umbrella organization for the radical segment of the German women's movement.[19] Formed in the wake of the *Sittlichkeit* controversies, the league addressed morality questions wherever they arose, arguing against state intervention in private life and the *Doppelmoral* in all its manifestations. In addition, the

16. The bill was named for a street hustler who had murdered a Berlin night policeman. See R. J. V. Lenman, "Art, Society, and the Law in Wilhelmine Germany: The Lex Heinze," *Oxford German Studies* 8 (1973): 86–87; Ernst Huber, *Deutsche Verfassungsgeschichte seit 1789*, vol. 4 of 8 (Stuttgart, 1969), 283–385; and Gary Stark, "Pornography, Society, and the Law in Imperial Germany," *Central European History* 14, no. 3 (1981): 200–229.

17. Lenman, "Art, Society, and the Law," 101–102, 109–110.

18. Wickert, *Helene Stöcker*, 28.

19. Ibid., 48.

league reached out to the working-class women's movement, something that distinguished it even more significantly from the bourgeois League of German Women's Associations.[20] In 1902, Stöcker also participated with Heymann and Augspurg in forming the German Union for Women's Suffrage (Deutscher Verein für Frauenstimmrecht), which fought not only for the vote but for women's unlimited entry to the university and to university-related careers.[21] Finally, though her own refusal to condemn prostitution as a moral offense ultimately divided her from the abolitionist movement, Stöcker shared its concerns that economic conditions drove women into prostitution, and she consequently supported the movement's efforts to counter state regulation of prostitution.[22]

Stöcker's intellectual background positioned her well to contribute to both the growing women's movements and the sexual emancipation movements. She was raised in a strict Calvinist family in Elberfeld, where her earliest education consisted largely of religious texts. As a young teenager, however, she rejected the family religion and began her own intellectual quest at the local library.[23] A beneficiary of the work the women's movement had accomplished, Stöcker was among the first generation of women to enter the German universities, first simply as a "guest listener" (*Gasthörerin*) and ultimately as a fully matriculated student when women were finally admitted.[24] In 1896, she began formal study of economics, philosophy, and German literature in Berlin and briefly in Glasgow. To find a suitable dissertation mentor who would accept women as candidates, however, she had to move to Berne, Switzerland. There she studied German romantic thought, which had already caught her interest in Berlin

20. Ibid., 49; Lüders, *Der "linke Flügel,"* 58.
21. On the founding of the Deutscher Verein für Frauen Stimmrecht, see Heymann and Augspurg, *Erlebtes—Erschautes,* 110–113; on Stöcker's participation, see Wickert, *Helene Stöcker,* 49–50.
22. Wickert, *Helene Stöcker,* 50–51.
23. An account of Stöcker's early life can be found at the Swarthmore Peace Collection, Swarthmore, Pa., DG 035, Box 1, Folder 1. See also Hackett, "Helene Stöcker," 110; and Wickert, *Helene Stöcker,* 22.
24. Swarthmore Peace Collection, DG 035, Box 1, Folder 2. See also Wickert, *Helene Stöcker,* 27–29. On women's education, see James Albisetti, *Schooling German Girls and Women: Secondary and Higher Education in the Nineteenth Century* (Princeton, N.J., 1988); and Patricia Mazón, *Gender and the Modern Research University: The Admission of Women to German Higher Education, 1865–1914* (Palo Alto, Calif., 2003).

both through her courses and through an assistantship she held under Wilhelm Dilthey on a research project regarding Friedrich Schleier-macher.[25] In 1901, she finished her dissertation on romantic philosophies of art history[26] and returned to Berlin, where she began lecturing at the Lessing-Hochschule.[27]

If Stöcker's formal education opened up to her the world of German romanticism, her informal intellectual interests brought her in contact with more recent trends in German intellectual culture. Even before leaving her parents' home, she had encountered August Bebel's *Woman and Socialism (Die Frau und der Sozialismus);* and although she never joined the Socialist party—or any political party, for that matter—she had a lifelong sympathy for socialist causes.[28] An equally significant influence was the idea of evolution, which, like socialism, offered Stöcker a critical tool for thinking about social reform and imagining an improved humanity of the future. But the most important lens through which Stöcker came to view the world was the thought of Nietzsche. Before her university days, she had encountered Nietzsche through Ola Hansson's monograph *Nietzsche, His Character and His System (Nietzsche, seine Persönlichkeit und sein System),* and she soon became part of the widespread Nietzsche enthusiasm that swept through much of the German-speaking world.[29] Her own interest in Nietzsche was facilitated by the influence of her short-time love interest, Alexander Tille, who drew considerable fame with the publication of his *From Darwin to Nietzsche (Von Darwin bis Nietzsche)* in 1895.[30] Where Tille fused Nietzsche with Darwin to produce a cold, survivalist logic that would allow the weak to die out, however, Stöcker took Nietzsche in another direction, understanding him primarily as a philosopher of love. In this way Nietzsche's thought became central to her effort to infuse German romantic ideas regarding ethics, sentiment, and gender relations into the radical branch of the women's movement.

25. Wickert, *Helene Stöcker,* 29–30.

26. Helene Stöcker, *Zur Kunstanschauung des XVIII. Jahrhunderts* (Berlin, 1904).

27. Wickert, *Helene Stöcker,* 29.

28. Ibid., 22; Hackett, "Helene Stöcker," 117, 119–122.

29. Wickert, *Helene Stöcker,* 22–23. On feminist appropriations of Nietzsche, see Carol Diethe, *Nietzsche's Women: Beyond the Whip* (Berlin, 1996).

30. Alexander Tille, *Von Darwin bis Nietzsche: Ein Buch Entwicklungsethik* (Leipzig, 1895).

In her appropriation of Nietzsche, Stöcker drew especially on his critique of slave morality. In the logic of slave morality, the self is always measured against the other and ultimately against socially approved norms. In this comparison, the self always comes up short, and the other takes the blame, leading to hostility, rage, and desire to bring down the other. As a social framework, slave morality can take the form of the ascetic principle, which calls on the individual to deny pleasures to the body and the self. For an antidote, Stöcker turned often to Nietzsche's demand "to learn first to love." She was an especially close reader of Nietzsche's philosophical novel, *Thus Spake Zarathustra (Also sprach Zarathustra),* which more than any of his writings emphasized a principle of excessive love, or love as a gift that does not return.[31] Only through such a notion of excessive love does one learn to say yes to the self, to life, and to the other, and therein counter the life-denying tendencies of slave morality.[32]

Formulating the "New Ethic," or the Ethics of "Being Female"

The women's movement(s), the *Sittlichkeit* debates, romanticism, and the Nietzsche explosion thus all worked their independent influences on Stöcker as she was formulating her version of ethics reform in the years around the turn of the century. Yet she inherited none of these factors without changing them to suit her own aims. One of her favorite quotes from Nietzsche was Zarathustra's teaching on true discipleship: "'This is *my* way; where is yours?'—thus I answered those who asked me 'the way.' For *the* way—that does not exist."[33] In response to Nietzsche in particular, she identified the "worker question" and the "woman question" as weak spots

---

31. On Nietzsche and the gift, see especially Hans Alderman, *Nietzsche's Gift* (Athens, Ohio, 1977).

32. Stöcker often refers to this idea of saying yes to life. See, for instance, "Zur Nietzsche-Lektüre," *Der Volkserzieher* 2, no. 45 (1898): 353, collected in Landesarchiv Berlin, B. Rep. 235, Fiche 3593. A longer version of the essay appeared as "Frauengedanken," in *Die Liebe und die Frauen,* 24–29. See also "Unsere Unwertung der Werte," in *Die Liebe und die Frauen,* 7, 14, first published in *Das Magazin für Literatur* 67 (1898): 127–129, 153–155.

33. Stöcker, "Zur Nietzsche-Lektüre," 353. Stöcker appropriately condensed Nietzsche's phrasing here. She writes: "das ist nun mein Weg—wo ist der Eure? Den Weg nämlich—den gibt es nicht!" "Von neuer Ethik," 10. Nietzsche's original reads: "'Das—ist nun *mein* Weg—wo ist der eure?' so antwortete ich denen, welche mich 'nach dem Wege'

that demanded reconsideration.[34] More broadly, she shuffled the entire set of inherited cultural currents to carve out the New Ethic and its reconceptualization of the moral subject. As indebted to the women's movement as to the romantic appeal to love and Nietzsche's critique of slave morality, Stöcker's New Ethic revolved around the formulation of an explicitly feminine subject of ethics.[35] Working through her writings, we can discern the important role that this feminine subject of ethics played: that is, what the articulation of a specifically feminine subject of ethics meant within a critique of moral regulation; how its articulation prompted Stöcker to push for a form of secularization more thorough than the mere removal of "God" and religion from daily life; and how it was wrapped up in her own variant of political critique.

Like Nietzsche before her, Stöcker began her line of thought with a critique of secularization as hitherto incomplete, and with a call to push the process further until it reaches its logical conclusion. Nietzsche had portrayed the idea of "truth"—in its seemingly modern, scientific, and nonreligious sense—as nothing but a substitution for "God." Seekers of this absolute truth, he maintained, were as devoted to an otherworldly pursuit, to pursuit of something outside themselves and outside life, as were seekers of God. They were consequently as prone to asceticism and "life denial" as were their religious counterparts, whom they claimed to be surpassing.[36] Stöcker followed this logic but found the perpetuation of "God" to exist also in gender dynamics. Christian theology, she claimed, had equated masculine with mind and soul, and feminine with matter. It had also consistently privileged masculine soul over feminine matter. So long as cultural norms continue to privilege either the masculine or the spiritual over the feminine

---

fragten. *Den* Weg nämlich—den gibt es nicht!" Friedrich Nietzsche, *Also sprach Zarathustra,* in *Werke,* sec. 6, vol. 1, 241.

34. Helene Stöcker, "Zur Nietzsche-Lektüre," 353.

35. In this sense, she took up the Nietzschean challenge that another writer, Hedwig Dohm, had posed to women. The title alone of Dohm's 1894 novel—*Wie Frauen werden—Werde, die du bist!*—had subtly manipulated Nietzsche's demand that one "become the person that one is." With a small change of pronouns, Dohm converted the masculine neutral to the feminine specific, calling on women to "become the woman that you are." See Dohm, *Wie Frauen werden—Werde, die du bist!* (Breslau, 1894). See also Hedwig Dohm's essay, "Nietzsche und die Frauen," *Die Zukunft* 6, no. 25 (1898): 534–543.

36. Nietzsche gave perhaps the clearest articulation of this phenomenon in the third essay of *Zur Genealogie der Moral,* in *Werke,* sec. 6, vol. 2, 357–430.

or the material, Stöcker concluded, "God" would continue to reign, along with ideas of "the 'absolute truth,' [and] the 'absolute' in general."[37]

Nothing illustrated for Stöcker better this perpetuation of a Christian framework in a seemingly nonreligious world than the historical status of women. A long tradition within Christianity, she maintained, had resisted the idea of woman-as-subject, portraying women rather as "lacking a soul."[38] Without souls, women were precluded from both heavenly transcendence and individual moral decision and action. Women represented mere physical existence and served as temptation to physical sin. Moreover, this portrayal of women mirrored the theological tendency to privilege the spiritual over the physical. Accordingly, the denial of a soul to women provided the foundation for an entire social and religious hierarchy that privileged masculine soul over feminine matter. If, however, the denial of woman-as-subject characterized Christian thought, Stöcker continued, it easily survived secularizing trends. She drew a parallel between the "church fathers" and "men of the new world view," explaining that seemingly secular thought unknowingly perpetuates Christian traditions when it continues to deny to women "the goods of this life," the rights and responsibilities of the modern political, social, and intellectual subject.[39] By excluding women from full participation in political, social, and intellectual life, contemporary gender relations had surreptitiously preserved the religious *form* of the soulless woman. The denial of full political and legal rights evinced this enduring tradition, but it went beyond the legal arena. Indeed, the tendency to view women as naturally self-sacrificing and not as fully desiring subjects perpetuated the tradition in intimate spheres as well.[40]

Accordingly, nothing would be so decisive in delivering the final death knell to the residual investment in "God" and the "absolute," according to Stöcker, than the historical emergence of the woman-as-subject. But what would this woman-as-subject look like who would be so instrumental in bringing about a more comprehensive secularism? Most important, she would not simply replicate man-as-subject. To be sure, according to Stöcker, she would exhibit "something of the old Faustian drive that until

37. Stöcker, "Unsere Umwertung," 15.
38. Ibid., 11.
39. Ibid.
40. Stöcker, "Einleitung," 4.

now the man has believed only he felt"—that is, she would be passionate, and capable of both expressing and achieving her goals and desires. On the other hand, Stöcker insisted, "we want to become much more than men," adding how odd it must be "to want to be 'man' when everything drives at once toward 'being-female.'"[41]

For Stöcker, the masculine model of subjecthood was not neutral. Rather, it contained within itself the very logic that had created gender hierarchies and the complementary hierarchy of mind over matter: the logic that had precluded female subjecthood. How did this work? Stöcker equated the masculine with the analytic, with the proclivity to break down and separate into constituent parts all that it confronts. The analytic divides body from soul, public from private, matter from spirit, rational from sensual. Most damaging in Stöcker's view, the analytic severs ethics from sensuality and love. Thus only the masculine analytic mode could ever have sustained the *Doppelmoral.* Following the logic of the analytic mode, the *Doppelmoral* not only distinguished informally between men's and women's relationship to sexuality, granting men much more flexibility and indulgence in this regard; it also sustained the premise behind the *Doppelmoral* that sensuality itself is sinful, immoral. Operating on the assumption that ethics implies rational denial of physical pleasure, the *Doppelmoral* succeeds at segregating ethics from love and sexuality. If the woman were thus to become subject in the masculine sense, she would write herself out of the game, perpetuating the analytic and with it the *Doppelmoral,* the privileging of spirit over matter and the designation of woman as ill-equipped to form a subject.

Conversely, if "being female" is to have a revolutionary ethical potential—if it is to overcome the ascetic ideal, the *Doppelmoral,* slave morality, and the hidden legacies of God and truth—it must pose an alternative model of woman-as-subject that does not recapitulate the analytic model of man-as-subject. Stöcker thus presented "being female" as a fundamentally "synthetic" mode of being and of apprehending the world via amalgamation and inclusion. Of woman, she explained:

> Yes, we are different from man—and want to remain so eternally! To us everything purely analytical is the greatest offense and a passionate sorrow. To separate the intellect from the life of emotions or drive would seem base

41. Stöcker, "Unsere Umwertung," 11.

to us, contemptuous, immoral. Complete unity, complete desire, feeling, thinking, agreement, harmony—all of these things are what, according to our taste, make us human. To us an analysis without an ensuing synthesis is the enemy, contrariety in itself, that which kills, that which has to be fought eternally. Our will to life, our life itself, is the drive toward synthesis.[42]

In terms of Stöcker's ethics critique, this tendency to synthesis meant above all that woman-as-subject would not distinguish between love, sexuality, and ethics. Rather, the woman-as-subject would weave these categories together. The ethical woman demands "to be a free person, a unique individual, and a loving woman simultaneously."[43] And significantly, she takes pleasure in herself as a sexual being. Stöcker proclaimed of "the modern woman": "She is actually born to love with every fiber of her being, with mind, heart, and sense, with every nerve, because she is in the noble sense…much more sexually desirous than the man."[44] Unlike the moral subject under the *Doppelmoral* who understands sexuality as sinful and as a part of human life to be denied and cut off from the mental, spiritual, and moral dimensions of human existence, Stöcker's woman-as-subject models what it means to be an ethical subject in the new style, in a style not bound to asceticism, to sacrifice, to divisions. Her pursuit of love and sexuality is central to what the female subject *is* and what she *ought to be*.

Most critically and controversially, Stöcker translated the New Ethic and its bearer, the woman-as-subject, into politics to try to reconceive the political subject. She held autonomy to be crucial to political and moral subjecthood. In this regard, she differed little from a liberal tradition that preceded her, and on which she was building, that understood responsible political participation to depend on personal and economic autonomy. But Stöcker viewed moral autonomy primarily as freedom from oppressive

42. Ibid., 16.
43. Ibid., 14.
44. Helene Stöcker, "Die moderne Frau," in *Die Liebe und die Frauen,* 20. See also her comments in "Frauenbewegung und Mutterlichkeit," where she writes: "How men who as doctors and physiologists should have at the very least superficial knowledge of the nervous system of women; how physiologists dare simply to deny to women the senses and the desire for union with a beloved man, that will meanwhile remain a psychological riddle. I must confess that each time when I attempt to comprehend this claim, I am disconcerted and dumbfounded as if one had said that women in general are lacking eyes or hands." Helene Stöcker, "Frauenbewegung und Mutterlichkeit," in *Die Liebe und die Frauen,* 99.

social mores, for one cannot be morally autonomous if one is enslaved to an ascetic ideal or to normative codes of conduct. Consequently, Stöcker's woman-as-subject demonstrates her moral autonomy precisely through the *affirmation* of her desire, not its suppression. Stöcker thus called on the *"Frauenrechtlerin* [advocate for women's rights] in our sense,"[45] the woman who knows that political rights, sexual desires, and moral autonomy must all complement one another. In doing so, she crucially revised what it means to be a subject capable of political participation. Stöcker's woman does not simply enter the political realm from a different angle than does man; she reshapes it. The private is not severed from the public. Instead, autonomy in the private realm is seen as the sine qua non of political and legal rights. Or rather, full political and legal rights would be hopelessly inadequate if not accompanied by freedom to pursue private desires.

The League for the Protection of Mothers

Although Stöcker was a prolific writer and activist, her prominence in Germany and abroad derived primarily from her role as a founding member and long-time president of the League for the Protection of Mothers. For Stöcker, the league served as a tool with which to campaign both theoretically and practically for the woman-as-subject.[46] Founded in 1904, the League for the Protection of Mothers took shape only in 1905, when Stöcker became president of the organization. In January 1905, the league began publishing its weekly periodical, *Mutterschutz: Zeitschrift zur Reform der sexuellen Ethik (Mother Protection: Journal for the Reform of Sexual Ethics)*, later renamed *Die Neue Generation (The New Generation)*.[47]

45. Stöcker, "Unsere Umwertung," 11.
46. For a clear statement of the necessary interconnection between theory and practice, see Stöcker, "Das Werden der sexuellen Reform," 36–37.
47. In 1908, the journal split into *Die Neue Generation* and *Sexual-Probleme*. The former remained under Stöcker's editorial control, and the latter was established by the sexologist Max Marcuse for the more exclusive purpose of scientific and medical-sexual research. For statements from both journals regarding the split, see Helene Stöcker, "Zum Titel- und Verlagswechsel der Zeitschrift," *Die Neue Generation* 4, no. 1 (1908): 39; and Max Marcuse, "'Sexual-Probleme': Ein Wort zur Einführung," *Sexual-Probleme: Der Zeitschrift "Mutterschutz" neue Folge* 4, no. 1 (1908): 1–5.

Stöcker served temporarily as president and then as general secretary of the league, and worked tirelessly as editor of the periodical until its dissolution in 1933. At that time the league was appropriated by the National Socialist regime, which maintained it until 1940. Stöcker herself fled Germany in March 1933, spending the years between 1933 and her death in 1943 in exile, first in Switzerland, then Sweden, Russia, and finally the United States.[48]

At the practical level the league set as its primary goal "the protection of motherhood, married as well as unmarried," but its project extended into a wide variety of areas pertaining to sexuality and reproduction.[49] First and foremost was the need for overall "improvement of the legal situation of unmarried mothers and [their] children."[50] The league saw the legal status of mothers as fundamental to their economic survival; in turn, it held economic self-sufficiency to be crucial for the transformation of custody regulations. Though supportive of all mothers, the league concentrated especially on the plight of single mothers, who numbered about 180,000 in Germany in 1904.[51] Indeed, the idea for the league first came not from Stöcker but from Ruth Bré, who had herself experienced the hardships of being the child of unmarried parents.[52] In the summer of 1904, Bré had embarked on a project to establish a pastoral *Mutterheim* (home for mothers) in Eden near Oranienburg (just outside Berlin). Her grand vision entailed a collection of state-subsidized homes for unmarried mothers at which the women would perform minimal agricultural labor while receiving education and legal advice that would lead to independence. Bré's vision, which included a eugenicist component entailing that only "healthy" women would be allowed to make use of the *Mutterheim,* was ultimately replaced by more urban, less romantic, and less eugenicist plans.[53] By 1908 the league had successfully sponsored homes in Berlin and Frankfurt, and by 1911 several others across Germany were under way. All were devoted to keeping

48. Wickert, *Helene Stöcker,* 133–157.

49. Max Marcuse, "Mitteilungen des Bundes für Mutterschutz," *Mutterschutz* 1, no. 1 (1905): 45.

50. Ibid.

51. Ibid., 46.

52. Allen, *Feminism and Motherhood,* 175.

53. Marcuse, "Mitteilungen," 46; Wickert, *Helene Stöcker,* 60; Evans, *Feminist Movement,* 120–123.

mother and child together.[54] They also aimed expressly to provide an alternative to the existing *Mutterheime* in Germany, the majority of which were run by such organizations as the Protestant Inner Mission (Innere Mission) and were intended to reeducate "fallen women."[55] The league sought to shield unmarried mothers from this moral condemnation and any enforced moral education.[56] In conjunction with the *Mutterheim* projects, the league cooperated with the Social Democrats to petition for state-supported maternity insurance for unmarried and working-class women.[57]

Much indebted to recent advances in contraceptive technologies, the league also made contraception and sexual education the centerpieces of its practical project. Although traditional methods of contraception (for example, coitus interruptus, rhythm method) never went out of favor, their efficacy was greatly outmatched by the modern condoms, diaphragms, cervical caps, and chemical spermicides that were, if still expensive, available to a wide public by 1900 and much more reliable than their traditional counterparts.[58] In 1906, Stöcker and Maria Lischnewska established the Office for Mother Protection (Büro für Mutterschutz), where they distributed advice and information to unmarried mothers and working-class women. Publicly they provided educational lectures on contraception and protested vigorously a Reichstag debate to ban the sale of contraceptives. By the 1920s, these centers had multiplied and were functioning largely to offer advice on matters of sexuality and contraception. Often labeled "neo-Malthusian" (and indeed the league's periodical included the term on its masthead in the years just before the war), the league always supported reproductive rights in the broadest fashion, including abortion. This stand, demonstrated in the organization's work to repeal §218 of the Criminal

54. Wickert, *Helene Stöcker,* 70; Evans, *Feminist Movement,* 125.

55. See, for example, Paula Mueller, "Mutterschutzbestrebungen," in Mueller, *Die "Neue Ethik" und ihre Gefahr* (Berlin, 1908), 10.

56. Evans, *Feminist Movement,* 127–128.

57. Allen, "Mothers of the New Generation," 429. On the history of maternity insurance in Germany, Austria, and Switzerland, see Gerda Neyer, "Die Entwicklung des Mutterschutzes in Deutschland, Österreich und der Schweiz von 1877 bis 1945," in Gerhard, *Frauen in der Geschichte des Rechts,* 744–758.

58. Woycke, *Birth Control in Germany,* 36–43. On contraception among workers, see R. P. Neuman, "Working Class Birth Control in Wilhelmine Germany," *Comparative Studies in Society and History* 20, no. 3 (1978): 408–428.

Code, which forbade abortion, contributed to the exclusion of the league from the umbrella League of German Women's Associations.[59]

Many of the league's auxiliary practical efforts spilled over into other dimensions of sexual emancipation. Members advocated in general against enforced asceticism and the reign of the *Doppelmoral*. They saw prostitution, for instance, not only as a consequence of cruel economic circumstances into which women might fall, but also as a product of the ascetic ideal. Max Marcuse insisted that if the ascetic ideal were dethroned, the need for prostitution would decline.[60] Marriage also came under especially strong critique from Stöcker and the league. In keeping with the New Ethic, Lischnewska claimed that marriage can be fulfilling only as "a union between two equally strong people."[61] And it can be such a free union only so long as neither partner is bound unwillingly to the relationship. Thus both partners must have the right to dissolve the union without significant hindrance. Even more controversially, Stöcker and her colleagues advocated "free love" (*freie Liebe*) as a legitimate form of committed relationship that does not require state or church sanction. Finally, the league lobbied against existing statutes in many German states that required celibacy of female teachers—statutes, Stöcker noted, "under which educated women suffer above all."[62]

Not surprisingly, Stöcker and the league received both adulation and notoriety. Prominent supporters were ready to hand, both in Germany and across Europe. In addition to Stöcker and Bré, the individuals present at the league's first meeting included the German sexologists Max Marcuse and Iwan Bloch and the women's activists Lily Braun, Adele Schreiber,

59. Evans, *Feminist Movement,* 132–136; Wickert, *Helene Stöcker,* 71–72, 74–75.

60. Marcuse, "Mitteilungen," 47. See also Evans, *Feminist Movement,* 43–44.

61. Marcuse, "Mitteilungen," 47.

62. Helene Stöcker, "Die Ziele der Mutterschutzbewegung," in *Die Liebe und die Frauen,* 180. For a consolidated statement on the league's program, at least in its first decade, see Max Rosenthal, "Was heißt: 'Neue Ethik'? Was will der Bund für Mutterschutz?" *Die Neue Generation* 6 (1910): 219–227. On teacher celibacy, see Mechthild Joest and Martina Nieswandt, "Das Lehrerinnen-Zölibat im Deutschen Kaiserreich: Die rechtliche Situation der unverheirateten Lehrerinnen in Preußen und die Stellungnahmen der Frauenbewegung zur Zölibatsklausel," in *Die ungeschriebene Geschichte: Historische Forschung; Dokumentation des 5. Historikerinnentreffens in Wien, 16. bis 19. April 1984,* ed. Beatrix Bechtel (Himberg bei Wien, 1984), 251–258; and James Albisetti, "The Feminization of Teaching in the Nineteenth Century: A Comparative Perspective," *History of Education* 22, no. 3 (1993): 253–263.

and Maria Lischnewska.[63] Alfred Ploetz, founder of the *Archive for Racial and Social Biology (Archiv für Rassen- und Gesellschaftsbiologie)* and the German Society for Racial Hygiene (Deutsche Gesellschaft für Rassenhygiene), also attended the inaugural meeting and supported the league. He criticized it, however, for following a general humanist philanthropic plan rather than endorsing eugenicist selection.[64] The sociologist Werner Sombart lent his support to the organization's periodical and was elected to the league's initial governing board. Sombart's colleagues Friedrich Naumann and Max Weber endorsed the league in absentia, though Weber's wife, Marianne, would soon take serious issue with Stöcker and the New Ethic. International accolades and support were also forthcoming. The social reformer and educational specialist Ellen Key of Sweden lent her support, international prominence, and presence, attending the founding meeting and endorsing the project.[65] Havelock Ellis praised the league from England.[66] Likewise, the British Malthusian Women's League made overtures, citing a shared interest in sexual education and wide availability of contraception, and a shared concern about the economic circumstances that lead women to prostitution.[67] Grete Meisel-Hess, the noted Viennese author, brought attention to the movement when she joined the German branch on her move from Vienna to Berlin in 1908.[68] Sigmund Freud not only supported the Austrian branch of the league when it was founded but also eventually invited Stöcker to Vienna to visit the Vienna Psychoanalytic Society.[69] If less active in the league, cultural magnates such as Alfred Adler, Lou Andreas-Salomé, Wilhelm Stekel, Max Hodann, Auguste

---

63. Marcuse, "Mitteilungen."

64. Allen, *Feminism and Motherhood,* 199.

65. Marcuse, "Mitteilungen," 46–47.

66. Ellis, "Woman Question," 127–128.

67. "Zeitungsschau: Zur Kritik der sexuellen Reformbewegung," *Mutterschutz* 1, no. 3 (1906): 119; "Malthusianische Frauen-Liga: d.h. eine Frauenliga zur Unterdrückung der Armut und Prostitution durch vernünftige Regelung der Geburtenziffer," *Mutterschutz* 1, no. 3 (1906): 125–132.

68. Ellinor Melander, "Toward the Sexual and Economic Emancipation of Women: The Philosophy of Grete Meisel-Hess," *History of European Ideas* 14, no. 5 (1992): 700–704.

69. The Swarthmore Peace Collection, DG 035, Box 1, File 5. See also Ludger M. Hermanns, "Helene Stöckers autobiographisches Fragment zur Psychoanalyse," *Luzifer-Amor* 4, no. 8 (1991): 177–180. Stöcker attended on the evening of March 5, 1913. See *Minutes of the Vienna Psychoanalytic Society,* vol. 4 of 4, ed. Herman Nunberg and Ernst Federn (New York, 1975), 172.

Forel, and Romain Rolland all contributed articles at various times to the league's periodical. Moreover, in 1911, Stöcker led the charge to found an International Union for Mother Protection and Sexual Reform (Internationale Vereinigung für Mutterschutz und Sexualreform).[70] As a result of these local and international accolades, the league created a significant stir, well beyond what its membership numbers—only 3,800 by 1908—might suggest.[71]

Scorn, derision, and alarm, however, were also common contemporary responses to the league. So prevalent were hostilities that, in its first year, *Mutterschutz* ran a regular feature listing opponents' published criticisms. A report in the *Reichsbote (Reich's Messenger)*, for instance, accused the league and the New Ethic of degrading humans and equating them with "livestock" by focusing so much on human physicality.[72] The anonymous author of a report in the *Medizinische Klinik (Medical Clinic)* warned doctors and jurists who might be interested in fighting sexual diseases to keep a distance from the league.[73] An editorial in the *Korrespondenzblattes zur Bekämpfung der öffentlichen Sittenlosigkeit (Correspondence Papers for the Fight against Public Immorality)* called the New Ethic a "hedonist-materialistic master and hetaeren morality" that is the "exact opposite of all true, serious, and healthy ethics."[74] Especially vocal opposition to the league emanated from various branches of the German women's movement, as most moderate leaders sought to distance themselves publicly from Stöcker and her allies. Anna Pappritz, a leading voice against state-regulated prostitution, worked especially hard to make sure the league remained isolated from

70. Wickert, *Helene Stöcker,* 79.

71. Allen argues in *Feminism and Motherhood* that "the League for the Protection of Mothers, although representing a small minority within the German and international feminist movements, thus influenced the development of feminist ideology throughout the Western world during this period" (176). Gudrun Hamelmann suggests that the readership of the journals is particularly hard to estimate. A large number of members likely subscribed to the journals, and they were also widely available at bookstores. See Gudrun Hamelmann, *Helene Stöcker, der "Bund für Mutterschutz" und "Die neue Generation"* (Frankfurt am Main, 1992), 119.

72. "Der Bund für Mutterschutz," *Der Reichsbote* (1905), cited in "Zeitungsschau: Zur Kritik der sexuellen Reformbewegung," in *Mutterschutz* 1, no. 2 (1905): 83. *Mutterschutz*'s section titled "Our Opponents" conveniently directs the historian to a sampling of the most prominent newspaper reports criticizing the organization.

73. Cited in ibid., 82.

74. Cited in Helene Stöcker, "Lex-Heinze Moral," *Mutterschutz* 1, no. 2 (1905): 50.

the mainstream women's movement, insisting that it brought nothing new either theoretically or practically.[75] Even more scathing, Paula Mueller, a prominent leader of the German Evangelical Women's League (*Deutsch-Evangelischer Frauenbund*), designated the New Ethic and the league outright "dangerous." She described the New Ethic as explicitly unethical and accused the league of taking advantage of an inherent public concern about the welfare of children to garner support for its unorthodox projects.[76] Despite its limited membership, the League for the Protection of Mothers clearly succeeded at touching a nerve in activist reform circles.

The Politics of Sexually Differentiated Ethics

Historians have been no more unified in their assessment of Stöcker and the league than were contemporaries. At the center of the controversy has been the relationship of the league to the eugenics movements of the day. General agreement exists that in addition to the controversies around the Civil Code and the *Sittlichkeit* debates, issues of eugenics and population politics that were everywhere on the rise by the late 1890s also played their role in shaping the league. The first significant eugenics movements arose shortly after the 1895 revelation that the German national birth rate, like that of many European countries, was in decline.[77] Furthering the anxiety was the revelation that infant mortality rates were higher in Germany than in other western European countries, a theme that dominated the discussions at the founding of the Munich branch of the League for the Protection of Mothers.[78] While some of the early eugenics movements devoted

75. Cited in "Zeitungsschau: Zur Kritik der sexuellen Reformbewegung," *Mutterschutz* 1, no. 3 (1905): 121–122. For a further effort to distance the abolitionist movement in particular from the Bund für Mutterschutz, see Katharina Scheven, "Selbstbeherrschung oder freie Liebe?" *Der Abolitionist* 4 (1905): 94–96.

76. Mueller, *Die "Neue Ethik" und ihre Gefahr,* 16–21.

77. Woycke, *Birth Control in Germany,* 1; Ansley Coale, "The Decline of Fertility in Europe, 1789–1940," in *Fertility and Family Planning: A World View,* ed. S. J. Behrman, Leslie Gorba Jr., and Ronald Freeman (Ann Arbor, Mich., 1969), 3–19; John Knodel, *The Decline of Fertility in Germany, 1871–1939* (Princeton, N.J., 1974).

78. Marg. Joachimsen-Böhm, "Mitteilung des Bund für Mutterschutz: Gründung der Ortsgruppe München," *Mutterschutz* 1, no. 2 (1905): 89–90. Allen, *Feminism and Motherhood,* 177.

themselves to improving the biological robustness of humanity at large, others had more race- or nation-based agendas.[79] All, however, advocated for influence on the reproductive process in one form or another. In this loose fashion, the eugenics movement crossed easily into the League for the Protection of Mothers. Some historians have seen the league's effort to produce a "healthier" humanity and to link the health of children and the welfare of single mothers to state support as a prelude to a more interventionist racial politics to come.[80] Indeed, the 1911 founding of the International Union for Mother Protection and Sexual Reform carried with it a rather strong connotation of race hygiene, speaking of "selection" (*Auslese*) and "reproduction of the species" (*Gattungsfortpflanzung*).[81] Other historians, however, have pointed to the league's emphasis on individual autonomy in the reproductive process as a sign of its progressive, liberal commitments.[82] Viewing the league within the larger picture of German intellectual culture at the fin de siècle, Ann Taylor Allen, Heide Schluppmann, and others maintain that the language of eugenics was simply the lingua franca, and that Stöcker and the league were at once echoing while remolding that language to suit more progressive aims.[83] Allen adds that the maternalist focus

79. Robert Proctor, *Racial Hygiene: Medicine under the Nazis* (Cambridge, Mass., 1988), 15–17. A large literature on eugenics exists. See, in addition to Proctor, Weindling, *Health, Race, and German Politics;* Sheila Faith Weiss, *Race, Hygiene, and National Efficiency: The Eugenics of Wilhelm Schallmayer* (Berkeley, Calif., 1987); Benoit Massin, "From Virchow to Fischer: Physical Anthropology and 'Modern Race Theories' in Wilhelmine Germany," in *Volksgeist as Method and Ethic,* ed. George Stocking (Madison, Wis., 1996), 79–154; Nancy Stepan, "Biological Degeneration: Races and Proper Places," in *Degeneration: The Dark Side of Progress,* ed. J. Edward Chamberlin and Sander L. Gilman (New York, 1985); Weikart, *From Darwin to Hitler;* and Peter Weingart, "The Rationalization of Sexual Behavior: The Institutionalization of Eugenic Thought in Germany," *Journal of the History of Biology* 20, no. 2 (1987): 159–193.

80. Evans, *Feminist Movement,* 130–139; Marie-Luise Janssen-Jurreit, "Nationalbiologie, Sexualreform und Gebürtenrückgang—Über die Zusammenhänge von Bevölkerungspolitik und Frauenbewegung um die Jahrhundertwende," in *Die Überwindung der Sprachlosigkeit,* ed. Gabriele Dietz (Darmstadt, 1978), 139–175; Rosemarie Schumann, "Helene Stöcker: Verkünderin und Verwirklicherin," in *Alternativen: Schicksale deutscher Bürger,* ed. Olaf Graf (Berlin, 1987), 163–195; Weindling, *Health, Race, and German Politics,* esp. 250–257.

81. Wickert, *Helene Stöcker,* 79.

82. Cornelia Usborne, for instance, in *The Politics of the Body in Weimar Germany: Women's Reproductive Rights and Duties* (Ann Arbor, Mich., 1992), 7–8, points to Stöcker's concern for women's autonomy *and* the league's eugenicist influence.

83. Ann Taylor Allen, "German Radical Feminism and Eugenics, 1900–1908," *German Studies Review* 11, no. 1 (1988): 31–56; Allen, "Mothers of the New Generation," 418–438;

of the league resisted being shunted into the categories of either rights-based individualism or a duty-based, state-oriented communitarianism.[84]

If Allen's argument is relevant more to the practical than the theoretical activities of the league, it nonetheless suggests an approach to Stöcker's more theoretical articulation of the moral subject as something that resisted easy political categorization. Here the question pertains less to the problem of eugenics and more to the mechanisms through which Stöcker's conceptualization of the New Ethic also challenged assumptions about rights, duties, and conceptions of the political subject. By way of contrast, three related contemporary projects, all of which were exploring in some fashion the relationship of ethics to sexuality and politics, serve as useful comparisons. They help to situate Stöcker's project squarely within a milieu in which it made sense to insist that sexuality and moral subjectivity pertained to political status. They also illuminate the vastly different ways in which her contemporaries might arrange the three categories of ethics, sexuality, and politics. At the same time, the comparisons highlight what was unique about how Stöcker configured sexuality and ethics to question conceptions of the rights-bearing, duty-performing citizen.

"Women Have No Existence"

It is helpful to take as a first comparison a most obvious and drastic point of contrast, namely, Otto Weininger's notoriously misogynist and anti-Semitic text *Geschlecht und Charakter (Sex and Character)*. With its self-identification as "antifeminist" (*antifeministisch*) and its stated aim of the "complete devaluation, even negation, of femininity," it may seem an unlikely point of comparison.[85] But Weininger's text, published in Vienna in

---

Allen, *Feminism and Motherhood,* 173–205; Schluppmann, "Die Radikalisierung der Philosophie," 10–38; Hackett, "Helene Stöcker"; Wickert, *Helene Stöcker,* esp. 64–83. The logic is also consistent with Atina Grossmann, *Reforming Sex: The German Movement for Birth Control and Abortion Reform, 1920–1950* (New York, 1995).

84. Allen convincingly argues that the entire women's movement needs to be read in categories other than the standard opposition between individualism and conservatism. See Allen, *Feminism and Motherhood,* 197–202. For a comparable attempt to break out of the "either/or" categories of liberalism vs. eugenics, see Dickinson, "Reflections on Feminism," 206–222.

85. Otto Weininger, *Geschlecht und Charakter: Eine prinzipielle Untersuchung* (Vienna, 1903), vi, ix.

1903 and an instant best seller—issued in twelve editions between 1903 and 1910, and no fewer than twenty-eight by 1947—created a popular stir. Its complexity of thought, though highly idiosyncratic, resonated with wide-ranging discussions about the meaning of gender and sexuality in modern society. Moreover, its aim to investigate the relationship of ethics to femininity makes it a necessary point of comparison that can help to highlight both the cultural and political stakes of Stöcker's project.[86]

From one angle, Weininger exemplified precisely the logic Stöcker sought to contest: that of the "church fathers" and their secular successors, who denied women the "soul" and, with it, moral capacity. To be sure, Weininger distinguished between individual women and femininity as a principle. Treating femininity or "woman" as a principle, however, he claimed not only that it is "wholly sexual," consisting of nothing but matter, but also that "woman must now be denied the possession of a subject."[87] On the premise that "existence" pertains solely to that which transcends the body, he added that "women have no existence and no essence; they *are* not, they are *nothing*."[88] Working with an idiosyncratic reading of Kant, Weininger deduced that woman as mere matter also has no capacity for ethical decision or action.[89] As mere matter, she is solely mortal and has no access to "immortality," which, for Weininger, gives one the intuition of the

86. Misha Kavka, "The 'Alluring Abyss of Nothingness': Misogyny and (Male) Hysteria in Otto Weininger," *New German Critique* 22, no. 66 (1995): 125; John Toews, "Refashioning the Masculine Subject in Early Modernism: Narratives of Self-dissolution and Self-construction in Psychoanalysis and Literature, 1900–1914," *Modernism/Modernity* 4, no. 1 (1997): 34–42. See also Jacques le Rider, *Der Fall Otto Weininger: Wurzeln des Antifeminismus und Antisemitismus* (Vienna, 1985); Nancy Harrowitz and Barbara Hyams, eds., *Jews and Gender: Responses to Otto Weininger* (Philadelphia, 1995); David Luft, *Eros and Inwardness in Vienna: Weininger, Musil, Doderer* (Chicago, 2003); Chandak Sengoopta, *Otto Weininger: Sex, Science, and Self in Imperial Vienna* (Chicago, 2000); and Agatha Schwartz, "Austrian *Fin-de-Siècle* Gender Heteroglossia: The Dialogism of Misogyny, Feminism, and Viriphobia," *German Studies Review* 28, no. 2 (2005): 347–366. The response to Weininger after publication of the book was immense. One spirited reply from within the women's movement was Grete Meisel-Hess, *Weiberhass und Weiberverachtung: Eine Erwiderung auf die in Dr. Otto Weiningers Buche "Geschlecht und Charakter" geäußerten Anschauungen über "Die Frau und ihre Frage,"* 2nd ed. (Vienna, 1904).

87. Weininger, *Geschlecht und Charakter,* 252.

88. Ibid., 388.

89. Weininger's reading of Kant is remarkably idiosyncratic, as were many of the readings of Kant that circulated popularly. Nonetheless, some feminist scholars suggest that the tendency toward distrust of sexuality and women existed in Kant's thought. See, for

noumenal required for moral reflection.[90] As a consequence, woman is not immoral but rather nonmoral; she does not make poor ethical judgments but rather is excluded from the realm of moral judgment altogether.

If Weininger's approach to the category of woman thus stood in polar opposition to Stöcker's view of female subjectivity and sexuality, surprising resonances nonetheless emerged. The unlikely parallels began with Weininger's portrayal of what he called the "female principle." Sharply delineating sexual difference as both biological and "characterological," he said of woman that "her existence is completely filled by [sexual life and reproduction]."[91] Further, she revels in the act of "matchmaking" (*Kuppelei*), beginning with her own sexual union with man but also in the abstract practice of "pairing" in general.[92] Her thoughts are preanalytical, composed of what Weininger called "henids" (*Henide*), or unreflective, unscrutinized instinctual thoughts characterizing a nonreflective "lower grade of consciousness."[93] Although Weininger understood this as a degraded form of thought, it nonetheless bore a certain resemblance in content to the "synthesis" that Stöcker privileged. Like Weininger's preanalytical woman, Stöcker's synthetic woman was supposed to resist the divisive logic of the analytic that Stöcker associated with man. Sexuality in particular was not supposed to be bracketed as an isolated realm of life.

Weininger's thought also resonated with Stöcker's when he discussed political and legal rights. Again, like Stöcker, he held that women should gain political rights *as women,* or only on the understanding "that the most polar opposition imaginable exists between the sexes."[94] Further echoing Stöcker, he envisioned a different definition of rights than would be had in a conventional liberal framework. Women would be endowed with legal rights and political participation not because of their capacity for reason or analysis; rather, rights would have to accrue to women as distinctively sexual beings. Again, the resonance is striking between Weininger's position and Stöcker's suggestion that the right to sexual pleasure is

instance, Robin Schott, *Cognition and Eros: A Critique of the Kantian Paradigm* (Boston, 1988); and Schott, ed., *Feminist Interpretations of Immanuel Kant* (University Park, Pa., 1997).

90. Weininger, *Geschlecht und Charakter,* 385.
91. Ibid., 112.
92. Ibid., 351–353.
93. Ibid., 125.
94. Ibid., 345.

a crucial step in the development of political, legal, and social autonomy. For both Weininger and Stöcker, woman's being—including her political existence—is infused with sexuality. This resonance, however, makes the point of departure between Weininger and Stöcker all the more important. Weininger assumed a completely nonmoral woman; consequently, in the case of woman, political and legal rights were to bear no relationship to moral subjecthood. If the woman accrued rights, she did so as a nonmoral being, and not as a liberal, rational subject of ethics. Stöcker, conversely, portrayed the sexually autonomous subject of ethics as a *supplement* to the conventional model of the liberal, rational subject. In the logic of the New Ethic, it is the woman's ability to pursue, not deny, desire that enables her moral subjecthood and that consequently also enables the autonomy necessary for political subjecthood.

"Moral Destiny of Woman"

As the example of Weininger indicates, Stöcker was not unique in positing ethics as sexually differentiated. Rather, the phenomenon was widespread. In 1894, for instance, *Ethische Kultur* had invited luminaries across Germany, Austria-Hungary, and Switzerland to contribute their thoughts on the "moral destiny of woman." Some participants, such as the Austrian peace activist Bertha von Suttner, refused to consider the idea that women have a different moral disposition than men—understanding disposition itself as a naive concept, and ethics as necessarily universal.[95] The majority, however, entertained happily the notion that women exhibit a different relationship to ethics than men. Many gloried in a distinctively nurturing and edifying feminine ethic, but even here there were differences.[96] Some, such as the Berlin-based neo-Kantian philosopher Friedrich Paulsen, understood gendered ethics to be inherent;[97] others, such as Georgina von Bolberitz of Budapest, insisted on the historical contingency of any differences

---

95. Bertha von Suttner, "Die sittliche Bestimmung der Frau," *Ethische Kultur* 2, no. 12 (1894): 93. See also the contribution from Ottilie Baader in "Die sittliche Bestimmung der Frau: Zweiter Artikel," *Ethische Kultur* 2, no. 19 (1894): 148–149.

96. See, for example, contributions from R. Boughi, Elvira Castner, and A. Dodel, all in "Die sittliche Bestimmung der Frau: Zweiter Artikel."

97. Friedrich Paulsen, in "Die sittliche Bestimmung der Frau: Erster Artikel," *Ethische Kultur* 2, no. 12 (1894): 90.

that cast women as the nurturers of family and men as the guiders of state-craft.[98] One contributor asserted that women enjoy a closer proximity to ethics than do men—"the woman is the categorical imperative"—holding men to more moral behavior than they would otherwise achieve.[99]

Ferdinand Tönnies's contribution stood out in the series not only as the most sustained discussion but also as an express politicization of the question. Tönnies followed the line of Bolberitz, insisting that gender differences could be understood only historically rather than physiologically. Yet he went a step further to argue that the history of social arrangements must be understood as the ongoing realignment of gendered characteristics. Drawing on his recently published *Gemeinschaft und Gesellschaft,* he identified "feminine" qualities as organic, emphasizing memory, tradition, and a relatively closed, local economy. "Masculine" qualities, he claimed conversely, are typified by the market exchange, individualism, and "mechanics." Most cultural epochs, he argued, exhibit one or the other of these sets of traits as dominant, suppressing the alternate set. The "masculine" had the upper hand in modern culture, resulting in a world dominated by capitalism, militarism, and an authoritarian state. But an increase in women's public and political participation would act as a counter to this cultural trinity, as the "moral destiny of woman" stands in direct opposition to the capitalist, militarist, authoritarian dimensions of modern Germany in particular.[100] Women's political participation would thus represent the first, initially destructive (*zerstörend*) step toward the revolutionary overthrow of German society as it was currently constituted.[101] Significantly, for Tönnies, the "moral destiny of woman" was a form of immanent critique insofar as it represented an existing if suppressed dimension of culture. Consequently, no "belief in spirits and gods" was necessary to rejuvenate culture.

98. Georgina von Bolberitz, in "Die sittliche Bestimmung der Frau: Vierter Artikel," *Ethische Kultur* 2, no. 44 (1894): 346–348.

99. Georg von Bunsen, in "Die sittliche Bestimmung der Frau: Erster Artikel," *Ethische Kultur* 2, no. 12 (1894): 90.

100. Ferdinand Tönnies, "Die sittliche Bestimmung der Frau: Sechster Artikel," *Ethische Kultur* 3, no. 4 (1895): 26.

101. Ibid. A variant on this theme would become especially popular among pacifist feminism as well. See, for instance, Anita Augspurg and Lida Gustava Heymann, "Was will 'Die Frau im Staat?'" *Die Frau im Staat: Eine Monatsschrift* 1, no. 1 (1919): 1, which claims that a feminine politics and international cooperation go hand in hand.

Rather, the "moral destiny of woman" represented "the overcoming of culture through culture."[102]

By advocating for women's public and political influence in the name of a specifically feminine ethics, Tönnies was echoing tendencies in the bourgeois women's movement. Building on a long tradition of mobilizing for public influence in the name of a distinctively feminine ethics, more moderate women such as Gertrud Bäumer and Helene Lange were beginning, especially after the turn of the century, to base a campaign for suffrage and direct political participation on the idea of women's nurturing influence, or as "mothers of the community."[103] Others, including many in Stöcker's own circle, argued that women perform a "service" to the nation comparable to men's military service when they accept the risk of childbirth for the production of new, future citizens. Thus both metaphorically and literally, they embody a "maternal" ethic.[104] Few went as far as Tönnies's revolutionary claims, but the premise of a transformative feminine moral subjectivity complemented his logic.

A crucial difference, however, set Stöcker's project apart from this political mobilization of feminine ethics, including Tönnies's more revolutionary variant. The majority of the appeals to gendered ethics as a grounds for political participation remained either metaphorically or literally within the heterosexual, reproductive framework. Accordingly, they tended to assume sexual difference to be complementary, both biologically and culturally. Lange and Bäumer, for instance, understood feminine contributions to society to be "maternal." Tönnies too assumed that the feminine *gemeinschaftlich* and masculine *gesellschaftlich* components exist in all societal formations as necessary and complementary. For him, the "revolutionary" character of women's political participation consisted primarily in bringing to the surface, to public influence, existing feminine elements.

In her New Ethic, however, Stöcker necessarily contested models of gender complementarity. Complementarity in the form of heterosexual relationships, she maintained, relied conventionally on the passivity and

---

102. Tönnies, "Die sittliche Bestimmung der Frau," 26, 27.

103. Allen, *Feminism and Motherhood,* 207.

104. See, for instance, Ellen Key, "Die Frauen und das Wahlrecht," *Sozialistische Monatshefte* 6, pt. 1, no. 7 (1902): 528–531; and Maria von Stach, "Mutterschaft und Bevölkerungsfrage," in *Mutterschaft: Ein Sammelwerk für die Probleme des Weibes als Mutter,* ed. Adele Schreiber (Munich, 1912), 186–200.

self-sacrifice of the woman to the wishes and aims of the man. But for the woman of the New Ethic, the woman "who has found her center in herself," Stöcker countered, "love can no longer mean unconditional sacrifice and submission."[105] And when the woman no longer willingly sacrifices herself and her desires, the complementarity of the active male and passive female no longer holds. Rather, the autonomously desiring woman-as-subject makes life choices even when the path, as Stöcker put it, "does not lead to him"—or, in other words, she goes beyond the heterosexual matrix.[106] To be sure, Stöcker like her contemporaries celebrated the heterosexual couple with child as the most desirable model of human social and sexual relations. But she often repeated that under contemporary historical circumstances, few men exist "from whom we would want children."[107] What did this mean politically? Writing in *Die Neue Generation,* Henriette Fürth remarked that the family—defined as husband, wife, and child—functions as the "foundation and cornerstone of today's state and moral order."[108] When Stöcker questioned the complementarity of the heterosexual couple, threatening the holy trinity of the family by suggesting that the mother and child alone might suffice as a family, she chipped away at the conventional bedrock of a state that had relied on women's self-sacrifice. Her aim was not anarchy. Rather, it was to suggest a political model not reliant on gender complementarity—a political model that accounts for desiring feminine subjects.

Freie Liebe and the Ethics of Marriage

Stöcker tied ethics to sexuality and political participation, working with categories very relevant to her contemporaries but arranging them in ways that pushed at the limits of the bourgeois imagination. Yet Stöcker's project relied equally on a reconsideration of even more basic political and social

105. Helene Stöcker, "Die Liebe der Persönlichkeit," in *Die Liebe und die Frauen,* 153–154. See also Stöcker, "Weibliche Erotik," in *Die Liebe und die Frauen,* 89.

106. Stöcker, "Die Liebe der Persönlichkeit," 157. She added: "Now, however, as we are preparing to go together we notice to our painful astonishment that our way is not the same, that we don't have the same goal." Ibid.

107. Stöcker, "Unsere Umwertung," 12. The allusion is to "Die sieben Siegel," in *Also sprach Zarathustra.* See Nietzsche, *Werke,* sec. 6, vol. 1, 283–287.

108. Henriette Fürth, "Mutterschaft und Ehe," *Mutterschutz* 1, no. 7 (1905): 267.

categories, namely, rights and duties and their relationship to sexual desire and social life, a dimension of her project not at all opaque to contemporaries. In 1909, leaders from the moderate strain of the women's movement published *Frauenbewegung und Sexualethik: Beiträge zur Modernen Ehekritik (The Women's Movement and Sexual Ethics: Contributions to Modern Marriage Criticism),* a collection of essays that addressed the modern problems of ethics, marriage, and sexuality but that were oriented directly against Stöcker and the New Ethic. Unlike the "radical minority," which sought "the solution to the most burning questions in the fundamental restructuring of the moral and legal norms of sexual life," the essays in this book, the foreword maintained, continued to recognize in marriage "the highest moral norms and the only legal norms that provide adequate social responsibility."[109] The justifications for this stance, together with Stöcker's response, reveal what was at stake in the reconsideration of the subject of sexual rights and duties.

Two prominent figures in the moderate women's movement—Marianne Weber and Gertrud Bäumer—articulated the most fundamental opposition to Stöcker's project and her underlying presuppositions about subjectivity and society. Weber and Bäumer would each serve as president of the League of German Women's Associations (Bäumer, 1910–1919; Weber, 1919–1924), and both had recently made substantial intellectual contributions to the movement. In addition to authoring a wealth of articles, Bäumer served as editor of two women's periodicals, *Die Frau (The Woman)* and *Die Hilfe (The Aid),* and had recently coedited with Helene Lange the five-volume *Handbuch der Frauenbewegung (Handbook of the Women's Movement).* Weber, for her part, made her mark with her tome in legal history, *Ehefrau und Mutter in der Rechtsentwicklung (Wife and Mother in the Development of the Law),* a comprehensive study of legal developments from ancient civilizations to the present.[110]

Taking very different tacks in their criticisms of the New Ethic, Weber and Bäumer both identified what they understood as the necessary elements

---

109. "Vorwort," in *Frauenbewegung und Sexualethik: Beiträge zur modernen Ehekritik,* 2nd ed., ed. Gertrud Bäumer et al. (Heilbronn, 1909), vii.

110. Weber, *Ehefrau und Mutter.* Each woman's autobiography sheds interesting light on her life. See Gertrud Bäumer, *Lebensweg durch eine Zeitenwende* (Tübingen, 1933); and Marianne Weber, *Lebenserinnerungen* (Bremen, 1948).

of social existence—elements that, they said, the New Ethic sought to circumvent. Weber contested the New Ethic's approach to nature as an unqualified moral good. She asserted to the contrary that nature itself is neither morally good nor bad, and that only culture produces morality. Moreover, she added, natural urges and cultural laws inevitably conflict, as the exigencies of social existence necessarily limit the individual expression of purely physical desires. Sexuality, she added, bears the complicated fate of resting at the principal intersection between the cultural and natural realms. As biological *Gattungswesen,* or as members of a species, humans are compelled to reproduce; as intellectual beings, however, humans develop individual personalities and can choose the circumstances under which they reproduce (if at all). The conflicts of nature and culture thus play out most deeply at the level of the individual, who is, on the one hand, just one member in a chain of reproduction and, on the other hand, a being who struggles to realize himself or herself as a distinct individual. The conflict can at times be unbearable, especially when laws and regulated moral norms are not in keeping with social practice. Such was the condition in Germany and much of Europe in the early twentieth century, she maintained, as the law had not kept up with economic and social circumstances. Legal reform was thus necessary. Yet no reform of the law, no matter how progressive or suitable to contemporary needs, would ever overcome the *fundamental* conflicts at the heart of social existence and at the heart of the individual's sexual existence.[111]

Bäumer also cautioned that the New Ethic overlooked fundamental conflicts of social life. The history of philosophy, she explained, is filled with vain attempts to balance full expression of individual rights with the demands of social responsibility. Although she admired the German romantics for their efforts to imagine a "New Morality" that would privilege individual pursuit of love and passion, she also found it no surprise that their project could not be sustained and that subsequent efforts in the intervening century such as the Young Germany movement had met similar fates. Ultimately, these movements sought to circumvent the renunciation of desire that is the basic building block of stable social life. In the process, Bäumer surmised, women suffered the consequences. She pointed by

111. Marianne Weber, "Sexual-ethische Prinzipienfrage," in Bäumer et al., *Frauenbewegung und Sexualethik,* 27–29, 37.

contrast to monogamous marriage as a social contract that provides continuity, economic support, and a modicum of individual desire while demanding that both partners sacrifice only a portion of their sexual desires. She acknowledged that economic conditions had changed since the era of the romantics and that women could now support themselves financially and might thus be on a more level playing field with men than before. Nevertheless, she insisted that the law of concessions still held. If women might not be the ones to suffer from the New Ethic, which she saw as just one more instantiation of the effort to circumvent the law of renunciation, the offspring who need the economic infrastructure of a family would bear the brunt of it. Perhaps, she noted ironically, if Stöcker was envisioning a "socialist order" in which children would be raised solely by the state—a comment that spoke as much to the issue of marriage reform as it did to the ongoing divide between the radicals who wanted to cooperate with the working-class women's movement and the moderates who refused to do so—women might be truly free as lovers. She maintained, however, that "insofar as the New Ethic is thought to be realizable in our current circumstances," it can only fail.[112]

Both Weber and Bäumer thus saw Stöcker's project as simultaneously naive and utopian. Where Weber found it merely misguided, Bäumer highlighted its dangerously revolutionary tone. But they both operated under the premise that society and the social subject exist as fundamentally divided, conflicted entities. As a result, both advocated moderate reform while emphasizing that reform had its limits, set by the inherent conflicts of social existence.

Stöcker responded to these criticisms and others by clarifying what she saw as the historical circumscription of her critics. An opportunity arose when, just two years after the publication of *Frauenbewegung und Sexualethik,* a rival collection of articles on marriage and sexual ethics appeared, this one titled *Ehe? Zur Reform der sexuellen Moral (Marriage? On the Reform of Sexual Morality).* Where its rival had sought to understand the limits of sexual and marriage reform, this book promised a much more profound change to come, one that would release sexual relations from

112. Gertrud Bäumer, "Die neue Ethik vor hundert Jahren," in Bäumer et al., *Frauenbewegung und Sexualethik,* 54, 74–77. See also Bäumer's polemic against the New Ethic in "Mutterschutz und Mutterschaftsversicherung," *Die Frau* 16, no. 4 (1909): 193–203.

the "narrow chains of marriage."[113] Stöcker's contribution to the volume is telling in conjunction with the charges made by Bäumer and Weber. To truly realize significant reform, she argued, it was necessary to move beyond their model of conflicted liberalism, first to reconceive how rights and duties pertain to the moral and political subject and then to reconceive the formation of the subject altogether.[114]

Like Bäumer, Stöcker traced the rise of the New Ethic to the German romantics, especially Friedrich Schlegel and Friedrich Schleiermacher. The genealogy, however, was not new for Stöcker. In 1905, after her New Ethic and the League for the Protection of Mothers had endured several months of attacks about their supposed egoism and eudaemonism, she had turned to Schleiermacher to explain how inherently social the New Ethic must be, or rather, to explain what it meant to articulate a socially responsible, individualistic ethics. Schleiermacher had helped her to see how to extend an individual ethics to a social ethics through the mechanism of love for the other. According to Stöcker, the key lay in Schleiermacher's claim that an individual seeking "to cultivate himself as a determinate being must be open to all that he is not." That is, an ethics of self-articulation requires that an individual be able to affirm rather than reject or annihilate the other's existence.[115] Stöcker echoed this premise of Schleiermacher, adding here much as she had done in her earlier publications that one can do this only if one first practices self-definition, that is, self-articulation rather than an understanding of the self only through differentiation from the other. Accordingly, self-articulation *precedes* the potential for responsibility to the other and makes a genuine love for the other possible.

Although Stöcker remained loyal to Nietzsche's legacy, her logic at this point derived considerably more from Schleiermacher—and indirectly Spinoza—than from Nietzsche.[116] She gave little credence to the kind of necessary destruction that the Nietzschean overman exerts in the act of creation, opting more for a model of self-articulation together with care for other existing entities in knowledge that all are temporary

113. "Vorwort," in *Ehe?* 5.
114. Stöcker, "Das Werden der sexuellen Reform."
115. Helene Stöcker, "Neue Ethik in der Kunst," *Mutterschutz* 1, no. 8 (1905): 302.
116. See especially Friedrich Schleiermacher, *Vertraute Briefe über die Lucinde* (Lübeck, 1800).

manifestations of an ever-evolving nature. Stöcker was not a self-professed Spinozist—though she expressed interest when she became familiar with his thought[117]—but she embraced monism as a means to contest the divided subject that underlay the protests of Weber and Bäumer. She thus added in her 1911 piece that the entire project of the New Ethic depends on a reconceptualization of the subject. In opposition to the divided subject, which she associated with the dualism of Kant, the monist subject is not necessarily at war with itself. Rather, its physical and intellectual developments are coincident with each other. Moreover, for Stöcker the monist subject is not a preformed subject that enters into society as a whole, loses something of itself in the process, and exchanges rights for duties and sacrifices along the way. The monist subject instead is a being always in process of becoming; it is not a preestablished whole. In the process of self-articulation, the monist subject defines care for the self and responsibility to the other as complementary acts. Only the long reign of Christianity—and its successors in the form of liberalism and the *Doppelmoral*—force the monist subject into a state of self-division; they demand that the subject experience a conflict between self and other, body and soul. If one operates rather with a monist conception of the subject, the kinds of necessary limits, sacrifices, and divisions in society are not foregone conclusions. But one must move beyond Christianity, beyond the *Doppelmoral,* and beyond the liberal conception of the divided subject to be open to the monist subject in the process of becoming. Only then, according to Stöcker, the logic that Bäumer and Weber articulated—the logic of *either* rights *or* duties, *either* culture *or* nature, and *either* self *or* other—would dissipate.[118]

Beyond the New Ethic

Stöcker's New Ethic posed to her contemporaries challenging questions about the makeup of the rights-bearing, duty-performing subject. While echoing the demands of other women's activists for full legal citizenship,

---

117. Swarthmore Peace Collection, DG 035, Box 1, File 2.

118. For an effort to read the centrality of monism in the League for the Protection of Mothers, and to understand it—quite contrary to my claim here—as typical of nineteenth-century liberalism, see Dickinson, "Reflections on Feminism," esp. 222.

she pushed the challenges further, insisting that participation in politics as a legal, liberal subject would not emancipate women or men from the divided subject that liberalism produced. Her New Ethic, which begins with the self-affirming subject, contested the model of the liberal subject altogether, insofar as the latter is divided between self and other, public and private, mind and body, rights and duties. To be sure, she retained a crucial dimension of the liberal project, namely, a focus on individual autonomy. But she pushed the project to its limit by insisting that sexual desire and its affirmation are necessary components of the politically autonomous agent. Albeit from a very different angle, she thus pointed precisely to the relationship between politics and ethics that the ethical culture movement had done in its own work. If ethics reform did so by trying to excavate the political work of moral claims, and the gap that often exists between conceptions of the political community and the community of moral consideration, Stöcker did so by proposing a reconfiguration of ethics altogether.

Given her expressed criticism of the existing political framework, it should not be surprising that with the advent of World War I, Stöcker turned her thought from sexual liberation and single mothers to pacifism and universal humanity.[119] Back in 1892, she had helped to found the Deutsche Friedensgesellschaft (German Peace Society). An indefatigable critic of the war, she attended the International Women's Congress at The Hague in 1915, and in 1921 she helped to establish the Internationale der Kriegsdienstgegner (International Organization of Opponents of Military Service). In the Weimar era, she served as a leader of the Deutsche Friedensgesellschaft and as vice president of the umbrella organization, the Deutsche Friedenskartell (German Peace Cartel).[120] Just after the war, she explained how the international conflict had made clear to her the inadequacy of focusing solely on the moral life of the individual: "We have experienced how much our individual happiness, our personal enjoyment and satisfaction in love and marriage, in parenting and friendship depends on the circumstances of morality generally, of state relations." Not only had the state torn apart families and love relationships in the course of the

119. Stöcker recounts her turn to pacifism in her autobiographical notes at the Swarthmore Peace Collection, DG 035, Box 1, Folder 6.
120. Wickert, *Helene Stöcker,* 119.

war, but the "psychology of the war" itself, the hatred between groups, must be understood as a consequence of an "old morality" of hatred for the other.[121] Over the next decade, she would develop with ever more intensity the relationship between the New Ethic and a harmonious humanity. She never abandoned her earlier focus on the intimate individual, but she attempted to understand that private individual in relationship to humanity as a whole. In the process, her work came to resemble the early efforts of the German Society for Ethical Culture. Both projects chipped away at the nationally defined citizen and community as the terms through which to think ethics. And both sought to understand and highlight the intimate relationship between individual moral subjectivity and universal humanity.

Clearly, Stöcker's entire project rested on a very pretty, or benign, view of sexuality. According to this view, negative or violent manifestations of sexual drives exist only as a result of societal repression. If oppressive bourgeois ideals are removed, only "healthy" and happy sexual energies will remain. She had also consistently avoided the more violent imagery of Nietzsche's thought. And only much later, while writing her memoirs, did she speculate that Freud's investigations into the inherently perverse and violent components of sexuality might indeed point to the fundamentally irreconcilable tendencies in individual and social life.[122] But long before Freud's own momentous postulation of a death drive that fully integrated violent and sadistic aspects of human desire into the sexual subject, reformers were already intuiting something more complex in sexual drives than anything Stöcker might admit. Marianne Weber's own claim that nature precedes distinctions of good and bad, and is thus not unto itself "moral," was just one hint in this more skeptical direction. The next chapter pursues in more detail a still more skeptical approach to sexuality. It highlights how such a skeptical view might nonetheless align itself with ethics reform even as it worked with and accepted non-negotiable limits to the reformability of the individual subject.

121. Helene Stöcker, "Mutterschutz und Pazifismus!" *Die Neue Generation* 15, no. 2 (1919): 62.

122. Helene Stöcker, "Psychoanalyse 1911/1912," from the Swarthmore Peace Collection, DG 035, Box 1, Folder 5, and reprinted in Hermanns, "Helene Stöckers autobiographisches Fragment," 184.

PART II

The Sexualization of the Moral Subject

3

CONFLICTED SEXUALITIES AND CONFLICTED SECULARISMS

Only insofar as the dull and desultory will is conquered by something
higher is ethical knowledge possible; everything else is just philosophy of
frivolousness, sophistry of drives, free thought of the passions.

FRIEDRICH WILHELM FOERSTER

We saw in the first chapter how secularism as a social movement could
take a variety of forms. Its advocates did not experience secularism as a loss
of religion in private or public life; rather, they experienced it as a project to
be crafted, as a challenge to determine what kind of meaning they wanted
to instill in the world, and hence as a set of choices. For the German Society
for Ethical Culture (DGEK), secularism had meant primarily pluralism
and critical public discussion. Its pluralist agenda, however, met constant
attack as activists of other bents tried to push the project in more decisive
directions: back to religion, forward toward science-as-*Weltanschauung,* or
sideways toward radical individualism. Working from a different angle,
Helene Stöcker was also pushing a project of secularism, understanding
secularism as complete only if it renounced all traces of religion. Further,
she saw sexual regulation and the *Doppelmoral* as products of a religious
heritage, and thus recognized as secular only a project that embraced sexuality and envisioned women as full subjects.

This chapter examines in more detail the variety of effects that sexual liberation—and questions of sexuality more generally—could have on conceptions of secularism as a social project. To do so, it focuses on an institutional conflict within the DGEK that arose when it was confronted with the sexual-liberationist agenda of the League for the Protection of Mothers. From the start, the reform interventions of Ethical Culture and the New Ethic had complemented each other in that both aimed to reshape public rhetoric about ethics. Yet the two projects arose largely independently. With the founding of the league, however, members began to cross over between the two organizations and even to establish the basis for a future institutional affiliation under a broad freethinker (*Freidenker*) umbrella that would eventually take the form of the Weimarer Kartell (Weimar Cartel). The DGEK had to undergo considerable growing pains to accommodate discussions of sexuality, however, as shown in a conflict that broke out in 1904–1905 when the affiliation between the two groups was first suggested.

Challenges to Pluralism in the DGEK

Several factors had combined by 1904–1905 to give the DGEK renewed energy and focus. These events, however, were already testing the pluralist convictions of the early DGEK agenda. First, in 1900, discussions of the Prussian school law resumed, reviving the same controversies that had prompted the founding of the DGEK in 1892. A formal proposal began circulating in 1904, and the law went into effect in 1906. Although in practice the law largely reinforced the status quo, codifying the existing confessionalization of public schools, its very resuscitation placed the relationship of religion, moral education, and citizenship back on the public agenda.[1] In response, the DGEK stepped up its own campaigns for fully secular or at least interconfessional schools. Out of the campaigns arose a branch organization known as the German League for Moral Education (Deutsche Liga für Moralunterricht), which was at times more strident in its explicit hostility to religion than was the DGEK itself.[2]

---

1. Lamberti, *State, Society, and the Elementary School,* 161, 177–209.
2. On the German League for Moral Education's brochures and publications, see, for example, *Konfessionelle oder Weltliche Schule? 3 Ansprachen in der Deutschen Gesellschaft*

In addition, a renewed push within the DGEK to campaign for separation of church and state arose by the end of the nineteenth century in response to actions of the state. In 1897, government officials began consolidating *Sammlungspolitik,* a form of coalition building intended in part to ward off the dangers of the socialist party and in part to consolidate broad support for a large naval buildup [3] The orchestrators of *Sammlungspolitik* sought the cooperation of the Catholic Center Party in government and the reintegration of the Catholic populace into the German nation.[4] The inclusion of the Catholic Center Party overturned a practice of marginalizing Catholics in Prussia and in the united Germany that had begun in the 1860s. It also resurrected a liberal anti-Catholicism that had just as long viewed Catholicism as backward and hence as antithetical to a progressive and secular Germany.[5] Although these developments manifested themselves in the DGEK primarily in terms of calls for a stronger stance against all established confessions, a handful of responses also illustrated the ease with which secularism and anticlericalism could merge. A good example is the comment by Arthur Pfungst, a pedagogy specialist and long-time member of the DGEK. Pfungst contrasted the integration of the Catholic Center Party into the governing coalition with the evolving official state secularism of France, a separation finally embodied in law in 1905, pronouncing Germany to be moving in a reactionary direction as opposed to its rival across the Rhine. He also contrasted developments in Germany to the "Free from Rome" campaign in Austria, a campaign to convert Austrians to Protestantism in preparation for a unification with

---

f. ethische Kultur (Abt. Berlin) 14. Okt. 1904 (Berlin, 1904). The branch founded the periodical *Weltliche Schule,* which ran from 1906 to 1920. Rudolf Penzig gave a firsthand account of the founding of the organization and the periodical in "Was haben wir getan?" *Deutsche Liga für weltliche Schule und Moralunterricht* 1, no. 1 (1906): 1–2.

3. For a skeptical analysis of the role of naval buildup in *Sammlungspolitik,* see Geoff Eley, "*Sammlungspolitik,* Social Imperialism and the Navy Law of 1898," in *From Unification to Nazism: Reinterpreting the German Past* (Boston, 1986), 110–153.

4. Helmut Walser Smith, *German Nationalism and Religious Conflict: Culture, Ideology, Politics, 1870–1914* (Princeton, N.J., 1995), 117–127. On *Sammlungspolitik,* see Hans-Ulrich Wehler, *The German Empire, 1871–1918,* trans. Kim Traynor (Providence, R.I., 1993), 94–99.

5. On official forms of anti-Catholicism and the *Kulturkampf,* see Michael B. Gross, "Kulturkampf and Unification: German Liberalism and the War against the Jesuits," *Central European History* 30, no. 4 (1997): 545–566; and Gross, *War against Catholicism.*

Germany.[6] If the former could symbolize for the DGEK the removal of religion from official state institutions, the latter could only privilege Protestantism over Catholicism.

Finally, in the same years, tensions arose within the DGEK about its relationship both to established confessions and to the growing freethinker movement. The freethinker movement had been developing slowly since midcentury, emerging first as disparate independent organizations, some of which were stridently atheist. By the turn of the century, however, several freethinker leaders began working together to consolidate forces.[7] Committed to tolerance and public discussion, the DGEK had stood initially on the fringes of the freethinker movement. After 1900, however, pressure began to grow from within the DGEK to collaborate.[8] Rudolf Penzig, who had assumed a leadership role in the DGEK and the editorship of *Ethische Kultur,* pushed the DGEK in this direction in order to present a stronger public stance against collaboration between church and state.[9] Not all in the DGEK, however, were happy with the general tendency of the freethinkers. Wilhelm Foerster, for instance, the organization's patriarch, viewed the freethinkers and their commitment to a natural-scientific *Weltanschauung* as a form of "fanaticism" on a par with religious frenzy, and hence in direct contrast to the tolerant rationalism of the DGEK's founding guidelines.[10]

The controversy came to a head at the 1903 annual meeting of the DGEK, where the leadership debated the organization's relationship to established religion. Pfungst and Penzig led the campaign to declare the organization's explicit rejection of all organized religion and won over the sympathies of the majority of attendees. But the long tradition of tolerance and open communication still had a little life left in it, and a full commitment to a freethinking *Weltanschauung* was not adopted, nor was it fully

6. See especially Arthur Pfungst's comments in *Protokoll des siebenten ordentlichen Gesellschaftstages der Deutschen Gesellschaft für ethische Kultur* 7 (1903): 3.

7. Thorough histories of the *freigeistig* movement are Weir, "Fourth Confession"; Groschopp, *Dissidenten;* and Simon-Ritz, *Organisation einer Weltanschauung.*

8. Simon-Ritz, *Organisation einer Weltanschauung,* 106–108.

9. Ibid., 132.

10. Wilhelm Foerster, "Über den Zusammenschluß der freien Geister," in *Lebensfragen und Lebensbilder: socialethischer Betrachtungen* (Berlin, 1902), 185; cited also in Simon-Ritz, *Organisation einer Weltanschauung,* 131–132.

defeated. Under pressure to articulate its own stand, the DGEK leadership navigated the troubled terrain by giving a mixed statement. In "The Position of the Society in Relation to the Religious Communities," the organization announced that it would remain neutral on the "question of world explanation" (*Welterklärungsfrage*) but would push vigorously for complete separation of church and state in all public institutions.[11] If a temporary compromise was reached, however, the uncertainties regarding the DGEK's relationship to established religion hung in the air for several years.

Tensions around secularism and religion in the future of both Germany and the DGEK were thus high when the so-called Foerster-Staudinger controversy of 1904–1905 erupted. Named for its two initial antagonists, Friedrich Wilhelm Foerster and Franz Staudinger, the controversy unfolded in the pages of *Ethische Kultur*. It carried special significance in the DGEK because of the standing of the two antagonists and their relationship to each other. Both Staudinger (1849–1921) and Foerster (1869–1966) had been with the DGEK since its inception in 1892. Both also had backgrounds in philosophy and pedagogy. At the time of the controversy, Staudinger was working as a *Gymnasium* instructor in Darmstadt. Foerster was active as a *Privatdozent* in Zürich, having been excluded from the German education system after 1895–1896, when he had published an article critical of the kaiser and subsequently been convicted of *Majestätsbeleidigung* (defamation of the majesty).[12] Blending the materialism of Marxism with the scientism of neo-Kantianism, Staudinger had published numerous books on ethics, politics, and *Volkspädagogik* (popular pedagogy).[13] More hostile to Marxism, Foerster had concentrated directly on Kantian ethics before turning explicitly to questions of moral pedagogy.[14] The two had occupied opposing sides in recent developments in the DGEK. At the 1903 meeting, Foerster

---

11. *Protokoll*, 7:9.

12. The article was "Der Kaiser und die Sozialdemokratie," *Ethische Kultur* 3, no. 37 (1895): 289–290. For Foerster's own reflections on the events, see his *Erlebte Weltgeschichte, 1869–1953: Memoiren* (Nürnberg, 1953), 114–119.

13. See, for example, Franz Staudinger, *Die zehn Gebote im Lichte moderner Ethik* (Darmstadt, 1902); *Ethik und Politik* (Berlin, 1899); *Beiträge zur Volkspädagogik* (Bern, 1897); and *Die Gesetze der Freiheit* (Darmstadt, 1887).

14. As an example of Foerster's early Kantian work, see *Der Entwicklungsgang der Kantischen Ethik bis zur Kritik der reinen Vernunft* (Berlin, 1893); more indicative of his later pedagogical work is *Jugendlehre: ein Buch für Eltern, Lehrer und Geistliche* (Berlin, 1904).

had been Pfungst's primary object of attack, not only because Foerster had written and subsequently defended the initial bylaws of the DGEK, but also because he had begun a personal conversion process away from pluralist secularism and toward a direct reintegration of Christianity into his work on ethics. Staudinger had been sympathetic to the arguments of Pfungst and Penzig but explicitly sought to find an accommodation with Foerster.[15] By 1905, however, he renounced his attitude of compromise.

The controversy between Foerster and Staudinger, which played out in a series of short articles in *Ethische Kultur,* centered initially on the role of religion and reason in modern ethics. In his contributions, Foerster argued for the revival of intuition and "inner experience" in the DGEK. Reason alone, he warned, leads the individual into a dangerous overconfidence in his or her own autonomy in questions of moral significance. To ward off this danger, the individual needs the influence of community and tradition in the formation of his or her moral self—a fact, Foerster lamented, modern individualism fails to acknowledge. Foerster thus advocated a specific form of intuition as an ethical guide, a form that can originate only in social tradition, or in what he referred to repeatedly as the "consensus of the wise." Through this intuition, the individual perceives from the depths of his or her own self the moral norms of tradition, an internalized form of community monitor. In this guise, intuition connects the individual to a community and a history in a way that reason alone—in its modern, individualist form—cannot.[16]

Staudinger, conversely, responded by defending reason as the singular basis of ethics. He acknowledged the powerful effects that strong emotions can have on the individual. He also recognized how such emotions can motivate the individual to moral action by providing a sense of belonging to something much larger than the self. But he warned that powerful emotions can overtake the individual's sense of judgment, inducing confusion in moral matters. Staudinger offered as an example his own memory of national pride that he had felt in the wake of the Franco-Prussian War.

15. *Protokoll,* 7:7.

16. Foerster outlined the major theses of his argument in "Die Grenzen des bloßen Verstandes in Fragen der Lebens- und Menschenkenntnis," *Ethische Kultur* 13, no. 1 (1905): 3–4. He followed up with comments in "Sprechsaal," *Ethische Kultur* 13, no. 3 (1905): 22–23; "Sprechsaal," *Ethische Kultur* 13, no. 6 (1905): 47; and "Erklärung," *Ethische Kultur* 13, no. 12 (1905): 93–94.

Carried away by the "intoxication" (*Rausch*) of victory, he had temporarily forgotten his own moral sense that killing is wrong under any circumstances, including war. The example was not innocent but rather was sent as a direct message to Foerster: an ethics derived from emotion or "inner experience" may not have the tools to distinguish between desirable and nondesirable forms of emotion such as religious intuition and nationalist frenzy. Reason, Staudinger countered, offers a much more solid, stable guide for moral decisions, as it is not vulnerable to the winds of change. Moreover, when cultures undergo profound transformation—as he considered Germany to be doing—the stability of moral guidelines proves especially crucial. When appealing to reason as the absolute guide, he acknowledged, one does not have to deny the work of emotion altogether. But those emotions must be guided and tamed by reason as the final arbiter. Only in this way can one be confident that one won't fall prey to either nationalist intoxication or religious excess.[17]

After multiple volleys between Staudinger and Foerster, Bruno Meyer stepped into the fray to call for Foerster's resignation from the DGEK. Meyer, an ally of Staudinger and a fellow founding member of the DGEK, claimed that Foerster's position was inconsistent with the DGEK because it departed from the organization's humanist basis. Though the DGEK fostered debate about the meaning of ethics, he noted, there must be limits. The acceptable range would include only an ethics "that knows nothing further than the human with all that belongs to [the human] as verifiably and recognizably human." To clarify his point, he distinguished between religion and *Wissenschaft* as the foundation for an ethics. He recognized that "an ethics founded upon religious assumptions can also be a *Wissenschaft*," in the sense that it can be an organized field of knowledge. Accordingly, both *Wissenschaft* and religion can provide normative guidelines for moral life. But *Wissenschaft*, he argued, has a human foundation whereas religion relies on something beyond human reason. Any ethics that takes its cue from a transcendent principle within a religious framework is thus contradicting the humanist premise of the DGEK. To preserve this premise,

---

17. Staudinger elaborated his argument in "Das Gemüt und die Wahrheit," *Ethische Kultur* 12, no. 22 (1904): 171–172; he followed up with comments in "Sprechsaal: Die Grenzen des Verstandes in Fragen der Lebens- und Menschenkenntnis," *Ethische Kultur* 13, no. 2 (1905): 15, and "Sprechsaal: Wer setzt die Autorität fest?" *Ethische Kultur* 13, no. 4 (1905): 30–31.

Meyer challenged Foerster either to acknowledge a purely human ethics or to recognize that he no longer belonged in the DGEK.[18]

Foerster made one last protest, admitting that he had indeed recently turned to religion but calling as well for the DGEK to return to its pluralist roots.[19] And with this standoff the stakes were clear: participants were not really talking about the intellectual question of reason versus emotion in ethics—a topic that still tended to be tolerated within the ethics debates. Instead, they were using the discussion of reason versus emotion to speak about the larger choice confronting the DGEK: whether it was going to adhere to its original understanding of secularism as pluralism or opt for a more explicit stance against all manifestations of religion. What drove the DGEK to this point of polarization? When we turn to the role that sexuality played in the debates, we can see that Meyer's emphasis on the "human" points to the answer, that is, that the two sides had come to be working not just with different interpretations of ethics and its origins but with radically different ideas of the human as moral potential. And it was, at least for Foerster, the rise of sexuality as central to ethics that caused him to rethink his understanding of the formation of the moral subject in ways that made his very interest in ethics reform stand in opposition to those of Staudinger, Meyer, and the evolving radical leadership of the DGEK. To be sure, the DGEK had already been undergoing radicalization in recent years.[20] But the entrance of questions of sexuality and sexual liberation into the debates brought out the irreconcilability of the two sides and their radically different motivations for ethics reform.

The Consolidation of the Individualist, Sexual-Liberationist, Antireligious Agenda

Issues of both gender and sexuality had of course arisen in the DGEK long before this interchange between Staudinger and Foerster. In 1896, when

18. Bruno Meyer, "Der Aufstand des Gefühls gegen die Vernunft," *Ethische Kultur* 13, no. 12 (1905): 90–93.

19. Foerster, "Erklärung," 93–94.

20. Treating the DGEK at an institutional level, historians such as Groschopp and Simon-Ritz have explained the polarization in the DGEK in terms of the change in leadership. I do not take issue with their claims, but I seek to understand as well the theoretical problems that coincided with institutional developments.

the International Ethical Union met in Zurich, it established as a guideline an endorsement of monogamous marriage, though it was left to each local branch to determine if and how this guideline might be supported or facilitated.[21] Plenty of early participants in the DGEK were happy to follow this line and to take moderate to conservative stances on issues of sexuality in their own domain. Like many in the DGEK, Friedrich Jodl, for instance, was a well-known supporter of women's political and legal rights; yet as an official referee of Otto Weininger's *Geschlecht und Charakter,* which he publicly praised, he also earned a reputation for opposition to sexual liberation.[22] Even more high-profile was the campaign he led against the paintings of Gustav Klimt that were to adorn the main building of the university in Vienna. Klimt's Schopenhauerian paintings depicted a world of flux, suffering, and primordial sexuality. If Jodl opposed the paintings largely for their celebration of the irrational, his campaign against Klimt situated him also in a more conservative crowd that objected to the artist's brute depiction of nude female sexuality.[23] Yet Jodl had already been forced to resign from the DGEK on acceptance of a professorship at Vienna, and his slightly more conventional ways were not necessarily indicative of the direction of the organization.

Perhaps more prescient was the position taken by Wilhelm Foerster, father of Friedrich Wilhelm Foerster, when matters of reproduction, contraception, and sexual regulation arose in *Ethische Kultur* in 1896. Until this point, no one had taken a strong stance on matters of sexuality in the DGEK or in *Ethische Kultur.* Soon after news of the decline in the German birth rates, however, Julius Platter from Zürich had submitted an article expressing his concern about the future of the German population. On the assumption that individuals would be more inclined to reproduce if married, he advocated a national law (for Germany) that would forbid sexual relations outside marriage. By creating the circumstances in which reproduction would be welcome, he claimed, the birth rate would supposedly rise.[24] In response, Wilhelm Foerster denied that regulation of sexual relations could in any way benefit either individual ethics or social

---

21. Adler, "International Ethical Congress," 146. For a longer perspective on the meeting at Zurich, see Börner, *Die ethische Bewegung,* esp. 12.

22. On Jodl's role in Weininger's defense, see Gimpl, *Vernetzungen,* 101–219.

23. See Schorske, *Fin-de-Siècle Vienna,* 208–273. See also Gimpl, *Vernetzungen,* 172–180.

24. J. Platter, "Ein ethisches Problem," *Ethische Kultur* 4, no. 17 (1896): 129–132.

welfare. Rather, he took the position—similar to that argued by the young Stöcker—that women needed to be emancipated "from the sexual slavery of marriage," and that such emancipation would also lead to the emancipation of men from their self-imposed slavery.[25] While he expressed concern about the decline in the birth rate, he held firm that regulation of individual sexual choices would not be an acceptable response.

Wilhelm Foerster's position had no official or institutional weight behind it, yet it foreshadowed the stance of the DGEK in future years. By 1904–1905, individuals such as Meyer, who helped to found both the DGEK and the League for the Protection of Mothers, were building connections between the two organizations.[26] Initially based on the crossover of a few individuals, these connections were formalized with the establishment of the Weimarer Kartell, under formal discussion in 1907 and founded officially in 1909.[27] If Wilhelm Foerster's argument anticipated the future of the DGEK and its openness to issues of sexual liberation, it nevertheless gave no indication of the substantial work and compromise that would have to be made to consolidate such an orientation. Nor did it hint at the growing polarization of the secularist project, with which questions of sexuality would become intertwined.

To see the substantial work and compromise that the move to accommodate sexual liberation necessitated, it is useful to look at the seemingly contradictory ways in which Staudinger and Meyer approached the question. Indeed, nothing would suggest that Staudinger, who had only the previous year published a playful book of aphorisms critical of Nietzschean "master morality," and Meyer, who was greatly informed by Nietzsche, would find common ground.[28] Taking up the question within the context of his standoff with Foerster, Staudinger stuck to his rationalist line. Just as he argued about emotions generally, he insisted that matters of sexuality "are to be handled like any other," and can thus be addressed and contained solely within the realm of reason, or as a physical phenomenon that reason

---

25. Wilhelm Foerster, "Sexual-Ethik und Frauen-Befreiung," *Ethische Kultur* 4, no. 17 (1896): 132–133.

26. On Meyer's participation in the founding of the League for the Protection of Mothers, see "Gründung des Bundes für Mutterschutz," *Mutterschutz* 1, no. 1 (1905): 45–48.

27. Max Henning, *Handbuch der freigeistigen Bewegung,* 20–23.

28. Franz Staudinger, *Sprüche der Freiheit: Wider Nietzsche's und anderer Herrenmoral* (Darmstadt, 1904).

could and should trump.[29] For Staudinger, religion thus had no place in the regulation of sexuality, as reason alone should be the final arbiter.[30] In a separate context in which he was evaluating the Ten Commandments "in light of modern ethics," he had made a slightly different argument, noting that no modern moral ground can justify the commandment to abstain from sexual relations outside marriage. Rather, the commandment's relevance derived solely from the practical reason that modern economic conditions make individuals in a family reliant on one another.[31]

Writing not in *Ethische Kultur* but rather in *Mutterschutz,* Meyer conversely held fast to a sexual-liberationist monism not very different from Stöcker's. Echoing Stöcker, he saw sexual regulation as the primary constraint on individual moral autonomy, and hence liberation from this form of "priestly" control as the only means to authentic moral autonomy. He also agreed with Stöcker (and Nietzsche) that the mind-body dualism was a mechanism of priestly control that required the individual to regulate his or her own desires. More biologistic than Stöcker, he argued that the priests had come to focus on sexuality because it was the one physical drive that the individual could renounce without physical demise (unlike eating or sleeping). But such abstention, he maintained, works against nature, as nature requires the individual to reproduce. When priestly religion insisted that individuals abstain from sexual enjoyment, individuals were cut off from biologistic demands. In other words, religion introduced the mind-body dualism that sexual liberation worked to undo.[32]

Staudinger and Meyer were thus working with radically different understandings of the makeup of the moral subject: variants of dualist and monist subjects, respectively. For the Nietzsche-influenced Meyer, Staudinger's reliance on reason would seem to resurrect the mind-body dualism associated with slave morality; for Staudinger, Meyer's appeal to the biological drives to which the individual must yield spoke potentially to the irrational influences on the individual's moral subjecthood. This was no small difference, if we remember how central the critique

29. Franz Staudinger, "Sprechsaal: Wer setzt die Autorität fest?" *Ethische Kultur* 13, no. 4 (1905): 30.

30. Ibid.

31. Staudinger, *Die zehn Gebote,* 8–9.

32. Bruno Meyer, "Zur Psychologie der Geschlechtsmoral," *Mutterschutz* 1, no. 1 (1905): 12–26.

of asceticism was to Stöcker's liberationist project. Yet Staudinger and Meyer agreed on one fundamental principle: the importance of *individual* autonomy. Moreover, they agreed that only historically contingent factors interfere with individual autonomy, that is, religion and social mores are *historical* phenomena that colonize individual behavior and conscience. They thus agreed that ethics reform faced the primary task of liberating the historically weighted individual—however defined—from these social constraints.

This compromise between Staudinger and Meyer on the individualist rational subject helps to clarify an oddity of the debate between Staudinger and Foerster: both had made their claims in the name of Kantian ethics and yet were far apart in their conclusions about the direction of the DGEK. For Staudinger, Kant remained the preeminent philosopher of ethics, and rationality provided the only viable ground on which the individual might make moral decisions when confronting physical pressures and desires. For Foerster, on the other hand, Kant represented first and foremost the philosophy of intuition. According to Foerster, Kant had explored the "limits of pure reason in relation to that which lies beyond the external experience." He did not, however, follow Kant's own next logical step, which was to ground ethics in the realm of pure practical reason. Rather, for Foerster, the next logical step was to recognize "there is also something in the inner life of people that lies beyond external experience" and that is "at least as important for the determination of ethical norms as anything that reason can disclose to us."[33] In a move surprisingly resonant with a religious romanticism, Kant—the beacon of the German Enlightenment—became for Foerster the philosopher of internal perception, of an unnameable, unidentifiable, but intuitively perceptible inner voice of conscience.

Foerster and Staudinger were thus both operating with "Kantian" subjects in opposition to the Stöcker-Meyer appeal to a Nietzschean subject-in-process. Much more significant for both Foerster and Staudinger than their point of agreement, however, was their point of departure. While Staudinger found a knowable reason to be that which transcends the sensuous, embodied subject, and that which provides the individual the rational

33. Foerster, "Die Grenzen des bloßen Verstandes," 4.

capacity to resist physical desires and social pressures, Foerster's transcendent brought a whiff of the mysterious, that which is inexplicable to reason.

Beyond Reason: The Christian, Communal Ethics of Sexual Regulation

In turning to aspects of the self that exceed the isolated, rational individual, Foerster was in remarkably good company. Across Central Europe, skepticism about the rational autonomous agent was flourishing. Psychoanalysis, which only belatedly came to be the most well known instance of this turn, began with the explorations of Sigmund Freud and Josef Breuer into hysteria and talk therapy, in which they found that repressed memories of early childhood trauma were causing physical ailments in their patients. These studies, together with Freud's massive *Interpretation of Dreams* (1900), initially were read primarily by the medical profession. Freud's very accessible *Psychopathology of Everyday Life,* however, which appeared for a popular audience in 1904 and which depicted how little conscious control the everyday individual—the healthy and the unhealthy alike—has over his or her thoughts and actions, reached a far wider audience.[34] But Freud was certainly not alone in his efforts to map the unconscious and irrational aspects of the human mind. Interest in occult phenomena, for instance, was on the rise in the same period among individuals who looked to parapsychology to tap into dimensions of the self normally hidden under the constraints of bourgeois individualism.[35] In the realm of law, the courts were finding a rise in cases of "diminished legal responsibility" (*geistige Minderwertigkeit*), in which perpetrators of

---

34. Sigmund Freud and Joseph Breuer, *Studien über Hysterie,* in *Gesammelte Werke, Chronologisch Geordnet,* 18 vols., ed. Anna Freud, Edward Bibring, Willi Hoffer, Ernst Kris, and Otto Isakower (London, 1940–1952), 1, 75–312; hereinafter abbreviated *GW;* Sigmund Freud, *Die Traumdeutung, GW* 2–3; Sigmund Freud, *Zur Psychopathologie des Alltagslebens, GW* 4. *Zur Psychopathologie* first appeared in the *Monatsschrift für Psychiatry und Neurologie* 10, nos. 1–2, in 1901, and then as a book available for the public in 1904. On the early years of psychoanalysis, see Peter Gay, *Freud: A Life for Our Time* (New York, 1988), 103–149.

35. Treitel, *Science for the Soul.* See also Harrington, *Re-enchanted Science.*

crimes could not necessarily be held responsible for their actions.[36] And in literature and art—from Hedwig Dohm to Arthur Schnitzler, Paul Klee, and Wassily Kandinsky—artists and writers of all kinds were exploring the liberation of the self from bounded individualism and the constraints of rationality.

Such challenges to the rational and bounded self turned up in the DGEK in 1900 when the Swiss psychiatrist and sexologist Auguste Forel addressed the Swiss branch of Ethical Culture. Speaking to the audience about the "accountability [*Zurechnungsfähigkeit*] of the normal person," Forel explained that the greater part of an individual's actions are determined by unconscious factors, and that it is thus difficult for science to draw clear lines between the mentally healthy and the mentally ill.[37] "The illusion that we have freedom of the will," he added, "derives only from our ignorance regarding the motives for our actions."[38]

Foerster's own turn to the irrational dimensions of the self emphasized the effects of sexuality on moral potential, critiquing modern individualism in the name of a very modern approach to Christianity. In his debate with Staudinger in *Ethische Kultur,* Foerster had only begun to hint at the relationship of this "intuition" to sexuality by making the sexual-liberationist project his primary example of the limits of individualist reason. He had pointed to the sexual-liberationist projects of women activists such as Ruth Bré of Germany and Ellen Key of Sweden, who, along with Helene Stöcker, were leading the charge for the "new ethic" of sexual liberation. The problem, Foerster insisted, was not their focus on sexuality per se but the particular form that "modern" sexuality—in the guise of the New Ethic—took. In the sexual-liberationist paradigm, according to Foerster, sexuality serves only the immediate and rational interests of the individual. The paradigm consequently fails to understand how sexuality affects the deepest interiority of the moral subject, that is, it fails to acknowledge "the limits of mere reason."[39] As a consequence, it works only

36. Richard Wetzell, *Inventing the Criminal: A History of German Criminology, 1880–1945* (Chapel Hill, N.C., 2000), 79–83.

37. August Forel, *Ueber die Zurechnungsfähigkeit des normalen Menschen: Ein Vortrag gehalten in der Schweizerischen Gesellschaft für ethische Kultur in Zürich,* 4th ed. (Munich, 1902), 6.

38. Ibid., 7.

39. Foerster, "Die Grenzen des bloßen Verstandes," 3.

to foster individualism and to strengthen the outer shell of the individual. In the process, it cuts the individual off from, makes him or her deaf to, "intuition." Insofar as social relations result from sexual liberation, they are rationalized social relations, not social relations that connect the deepest interiority of one individual to another.[40]

In *Ethische Kultur,* Foerster had criticized sexual liberation only as the utmost example of modern individualism and its naive reliance on the rational self. Soon thereafter, however, he proceeded to outline the more intimate and necessary relationship of sexuality to moral autonomy. No longer contributing to *Ethische Kultur,* Foerster looked elsewhere to pursue the connection. He turned first to the German Society for Fighting Sexual Diseases (Deutsche Gesellschaft zur Bekämpfung der Geschlechtskrankheiten), a moral purity movement that emphasized abstention outside monogamous heterosexual marriage, and then to *Die Frau (The Woman),* a periodical of the mainstream German women's movement. The choice of these two sites presaged the full antiliberationist stance he would formulate by 1907 in his book-length polemic *Sexualethik und Sexualpädogogik: Eine Auseinandersetzung mit den Modernen (Sexual Ethics and Sexual Pedagogy: A Confrontation with the Moderns).*[41] In this popular book—it saw six editions in German and was reprinted as late as 1952—Foerster not only drew the *necessary* connection of sexual regulation to Christianity; he also came to view sexuality and sexual regulation as the foundation of the moral subject.

Foerster began his polemic in *Sexualethik* by echoing the common sentiment that profound social transformations were under way. He compared his era to that of "Socrates—a time in which all traditional moral orders have been dissolved and individual drives and passions are to be seen as forfeiting all earnest discipline in the name of freedom and of a strong life."[42] To provide stability in such times, he advocated a return to "character," by which he meant a moral self that could master the physical drives.

40. Ibid., 3–4.

41. Friedrich Wilhelm Foerster, *Sexualethik und Sexualpädagogik: Eine Auseinandersetzung mit den Modernen* (Kempten, 1907). The book was an extension of a lecture given to the Deutsche Gesellschaft zur Bekämpfung der Geschlechtskrankheiten. See also Friedrich Wilhelm Foerster, "Bemerkungen zu Ellen Keys 'Lebensglauben,'" *Die Frau* 14, no. 2 (1906): 65–73.

42. Foerster, *Sexualethik,* 19.

To clarify, he distinguished between "mastery by nature" and "mastery by the self," in which the self refers exclusively to the mental command of a person. Using these terms, he identified sexuality as the quintessential example of a phenomenon that falls immediately under "mastery by nature" but that can be converted to "mastery by the self." When an individual learns to master and negate sexual drives, he or she converts sexuality from a phenomenon that seems to come from outside the self, that is, from nature, into one that actually contributes to the formation of "character," or the self. In other words, according to Foerster, the act of learning to deny something as powerful as the sexual drives helps to bring the self into being, the self that will subsequently be equipped to make moral decisions in other realms of life. Recognizing that sexual drives cannot be eliminated altogether, Foerster celebrated the institution of marital monogamy. Because marital monogamy is situated within a range of religious, legal, economic, and familial institutions, it works as a form of sexual practice that emphasizes the individual as more than a sexual being. It is the one form of sexual practice, he explains, that works "to protect the unity of the human personality [*Persönlichkeit*] also in our sexual activities."[43]

To consolidate this self capable of moral decision, Foerster maintained, the individual needs two related aids. First, an education can help him or her to establish a clear and solid hierarchy between physical and spiritual concerns. Such education would not "despise or strangle nature" but rather would educate nature—and the natural drives—"to complete obedience under mind."[44] Second, a clear sense of moral community and a well-grounded cultural tradition can reinforce the individual's education. Natural drives are forceful, and the individual would be powerless against them if left to himself or herself. Fortunately, as an already established cultural tradition, Christianity was uniquely prepared to fill this role. Not only did Christianity privilege spirit over matter, but it came equipped with social reinforcements that could guide the individual in the grueling quest for character—institutions such as history, mottoes, cultural heroes, and even a legal tradition. To recall the terms he had used in the dispute with Staudinger, Christianity would serve as the "consensus of the wise," coming to the aid of the individual as he or she confronts physical temptations,

43. Ibid., 23.
44. Ibid., 47.

simultaneously integrating itself into the moral self that emerges. The individual would experience "intuition" as something that originates from the innermost depths of the self and at the same time as a voice that seems to come from beyond the self. To perform this dual task is the privileged and "liberating" dimension of Christianity.

In Foerster's view, the sexual liberationists were thus mistaken on two fronts. First and foremost, they failed to recognize how important mastery of natural drives is in the formation of the moral self: only the mastery of natural drives—and especially of sexual drives—allows the individual to form the sense of moral self that will enable him or her to make moral decisions in other realms of life. Instead, by celebrating indulgence in one's own sexuality, the liberationists started themselves and their followers down a doomed path that would enslave them forever to natural drives. Second, in denouncing the Christian moral tradition, the liberationists refused the lone individual the kind of institutional support that would ease his or her burden in the battle against natural drives. For such an individual, real moral autonomy would be nearly impossible to achieve.

Why, in Foerster's view, were the liberationists so naive? First, he argued, they greatly underestimated the force of natural sexual drives and "the dark abysses of human nature." Consequently, they underestimated the challenge the individual confronts when making decisions about his or her sexual activities.[45] Second, they failed to recognize these "dark abysses" because they inadequately grasped the moment of history in which they were living. Although Foerster viewed the moment as one of profound transformation, he also perceived the enduring influence that "tradition" still exerted on individuals. Adults living in 1907 had long ago internalized the "consensus of the wise," whether they liked it or not. As a result, "the instincts are still quieted and domesticated by the aftereffects of a powerful religious and ethical tradition." If, however, the liberationists succeeded in their individualist and antitraditionalist agenda, cultural transformation would ultimately succeed. Individuals from later generations would then grow up without the benefits of moral education and would no longer be able to develop moral autonomy, allowing the "dark abysses" of human nature to run wild.[46]

45. Ibid., 38.
46. Ibid., 46.

Amid this tradition-or-else logic of Foerster's argument is a noteworthy organization of the religion-sexuality-ethics triad. Foerster did not identify secularization as the most pressing threat to individual morality. Never, for instance, did he suggest that culture was in crisis due to a drop in church attendance, or to an atrophy in religious belief, or even to any separation of church and state. Rather, according to Foerster, culture was in crisis because of the transformations in sexual norms. Consequently, in his analysis, sexuality came to be the most fundamental term to which both religion and ethics were subordinated. While sexual drives emerged from his discussion as transhistorical phenomena, both ethics and religion emerged as contingent. Sexual drives were in fact the very reason why both ethics and religion must develop: sexual drives need regulation, and the individual requires assistance in that regulation.

In short, for Foerster, Christianity is not the reason for sexual self-mastery; it does not compel the individual to abstain from illicit sexual behavior. Rather, Christianity is merely a tool in the process of individual moral development. In other words, it was not coincidental that Christian-based schools of ethics were prone to regulate sexual behavior; such schools of ethics existed *in order to* regulate sexual behavior. Later Foerster would come to identify his faith as "applied religion" that "does not begin with theology, but rather with the reality of life [*Lebenswirklichkeit*]."[47] That is, religion serves a social *purpose*. In this fashion he was almost paralleling Émile Durkheim's understanding of religion and God as "social facts," or as phenomena that have their reality in their effects on social life.[48]

To be sure, Foerster's religiosity cannot be taken as typical of the period. Indeed, raised in a freethinker milieu and coming to Christianity only late in life, he was quite an exception not only in the reform milieu but also in Central European culture more generally. When he did turn to religion, it was out of an interest in the role of "mystery" in life, more so than for reasons of belief, and he was extremely open in his religious pursuits. He read Catholic texts as happily as Protestant ones, and admired the moral possibilities enabled by East Asian religions.[49] Yet precisely because of his

---

47. Foerster, *Erlebte Weltgeschichte,* 35.

48. See especially Émile Durkheim, *Elementary Forms of Religious Life,* trans. Karen E. Fields (New York, 1995).

49. Foerster, *Erlebte Weltgeschichte,* 155–164.

exceptional biographical path to religion, Foerster illustrates the mobility and functional possibilities of modern religious identities. He fully recognized religion as a choice and put particular emphasis on its social function.

In many ways his contributions to the sexualized ethics debates after his religious turn look no different than those of Paula Mueller, for instance, the leader of the German Evangelical Women's Movement (Deutsch-Evangelischer Frauenbund), or even the comments of Adolf Stöcker. They all spoke to the valuable role Christianity can play in defining moral behavior and binding the individual to the social. Yet where Stöcker and Mueller tended to assume a deep and unchanging Christianity—Stöcker speaking of the "centuries-long" role of Christian women, and Mueller of the "eternally valid moral commandments"—Foerster was aware of the invention and mobilization of a Christian tradition as a modern social tool.[50]

Reform and the Sexualized Moral Subject

In this chapter I have demonstrated what might seem commonsensical: those arguing against religion tended to support sexual liberation; those arguing from a religious position tended to endorse only heterosexual monogamy. Yet these positions were not inevitable. The endorsement of monogamy by the International Union of Ethical Societies is itself evidence to the contrary. Moreover, the conflict within the DGEK reveals the intellectual work and compromise that went into forging the polarized stances toward ethics and sexuality. In addition, we see at least as many parallels as differences in the two stances. The very work of establishing opposing arguments circled around the shared assumption of a sexualized moral subject. For Foerster, individuals must be able to master sexual drives in order to develop the moral capacity for self-renunciation; for Meyer and the liberationist camp, only sexual liberation would allow individuals to realize the kind of autonomy necessary for independent moral decision.

50. Adolf Stöcker, "Die Aufgaben der Frau in der Gegenwart," *Evangelische Frauenzeitung* 5, no. 5 (1905): 39–40; Paula Mueller, "Der Bund für Mutterschutz und die 'neue Ethik,'" *Evangelische Frauenzeitung* 6, no. 1 (1905): 3–5.

Yet significantly, they both saw sexuality as the site at which ethics reform must operate.

Furthermore, both agreed that a primary purpose of religion is to regulate sexuality. They differed solely on whether they endorsed or opposed such regulation. Exceptions existed, of course, as in the case of Staudinger, who clung steadfastly to reason as the foundation of ethics. But as we have seen, even Staudinger's arguments could, because of their strident antireligious character, be co-opted by Meyer in the service of a sexual-liberationist ethics. Yet if the example of the DGEK suggests that a consensus around a sexualized moral subject was growing, it also illustrates how little consensus existed about the meaning or implication of the sexualized moral subject. It could work for religious as well as antireligious purposes; it could coincide with a fundamentally historicist perspective as easily as with a primitive-universalist conception of the subject.

Still further, the different approaches to the sexualized moral subject did not necessarily determine attitudes toward reform as a project. Rather, the different approaches simply shaped what kinds of tools reformers were likely to use. Thus, for Meyer and Staudinger, reform relied on two things: the autonomous individual and the elimination of religion from public life. They could turn either to biology or to reason as their grounds for this type of reform. For Foerster, conversely, reform relied primarily on the promotion of ethics as a mechanism of tying the individual to the social, and he thus turned to a functionalist Christianity as a tool.

In this view, Foerster differed very little from his pluralist-turned-antireligious counterparts. Despite their differences, they all remained fundamentally committed to the idea of reforming society through ethics. Their standoff simply highlighted the shift in emphasis on the mechanics of ethics reform. For Foerster, ethics remained the central focus of reform, and religion an important tool; for Meyer and Staudinger, antireligion became the mechanism through which ethics could be reformed. Nothing about Foerster's turn to religion thus implied any retreat from progressive reform projects altogether. Indeed, his ongoing commitment to reform explains how he, much like Helene Stöcker, could find himself embracing the pacifist movement in the wake of World War I. After holding several university positions in Switzerland and Austria, he had finally received a chair in Germany in 1914, only to have to abandon it in 1918 when his publications against German war politics brought the attention of the police.[51] The war may have dampened Foerster's and Stöcker's enthusiasm and caused them to take up more global concerns, but they both continued to hold out the possibility that, through ethics, a better humanity could be nurtured.

If the activists of this chapter saw no limits to reform, however, some of their contemporaries were beginning to express doubt. In the next chapter, we examine the more global context in which the ethics reform movements unfolded. There we see how the sexualization of ethics in a global perspective could still symbolize for some the means for radical reform of society, while inducing others to question the limits and even desirability of changing the world through attention to the sexuality and conscience of the individual.

51. Foerster, *Erlebete Weltgeschichte,* 197.

4

GLOBAL INFLUENCES, LOCAL RESPONSES

There were evidences of increasing moral sensitiveness in the world, but
moral sensitiveness was sometimes the epiphenomenon, the back-wash
effect, of movements in an unmoral direction. Macbeth's conscience was
preternaturally alert when he was about to commit murder. Some pessimists
interpret the sensitiveness of the modern conscience as the result of the
aggressiveness of civilisation towards primitive races and peoples.

FELIX ADLER, *at the Universal Races Congress*

Thus far we have observed the ethics debates primarily in their Central European context. Yet they played out in an era when changes in transportation and communication were fundamentally altering the way individuals perceived humanity and the globe. Railways and steamships enabled previously unimaginable transcontinental and transoceanic travel and commerce, while the invention of the radio revolutionized the transmission of information. Indeed, these technologies had made possible the international organization of ethics groups that we have already seen, just as it gave birth more broadly to the phenomenon of nongovernmental internationalist activism in the last years of the nineteenth century. Significantly, these were the same technologies that also facilitated the dramatic increase in European colonization that would shortly make World War I a truly global war.

This chapter explores the effects of global dynamics on ethics reform. It examines in particular how globally informed categories such as cultural difference, universal humanity, and race could influence reformers' understanding of "moral conscience." Three examples demonstrate how diversely the global condition could influence ethics discussions: the work of Prague philosopher Christian von Ehrenfels, who transformed a philosophy of value theory into a racially informed Darwinist model of sexual reform; Freud's first foray into the field of ethics, a response to Ehrenfels; and the Universal Races Congress, an international ethics reform effort to think critically about race in the global context of imperialism.

At first glance, these moments seem remarkably diverse, yet they are all direct products of or responses to ethics reform. Moreover, they all illustrate how questions of sexuality had become central for ethics reform— not only in terms of individual moral formation, as we saw in the last two chapters, but also in conceptions of cultural formation, cultural difference, and universal humanity. They thus reveal the diverse ways in which the global context informed contemporaries' understanding of the relationship between sexuality and moral conscience.

Ehrenfels: On Cultural and "Constitutional" Development

As a professor of philosophy in Prague from 1896 until his death in 1932, Ehrenfels was already an established name in academic philosophy when he began writing in the field of sexual ethics.[1] He studied with Franz Brentano, corresponded with Freud, and included among his Prague acquaintances writers such as Max Brod, Felix Weltsch, and, in passing, Franz Kafka.[2] As a student of Brentano, who had made his own career in studies of inner perception, Ehrenfels developed an interest in questions of perception and devoted much of his early work to psychological study. With an essay in 1890 titled "On 'Gestalt Qualities,'" he helped to shift the paradigm of Central European psychology from a view that emphasized the discrete entities of mental experience to one that emphasized the unity of mental experience. In addition to this contribution to gestalt theory,[3]

1. On Ehrenfels's life, see R. Fabian, "Leben und Wirken von Christian v. Ehrenfels: Ein Beitrag zur intellektuellen Biographie," in *Christian von Ehrenfels: Leben und Werk,* ed. Fabian (Amsterdam, 1986), 1–64.

2. Barry Smith, *Austrian Philosophy: The Legacy of Franz Brentano* (Chicago, 1994), 243.

3. On Ehrenfels and gestalt theory, see Barry Smith, "Gestalt Theory: An Essay in Philosophy," in *Foundations of Gestalt Theory,* ed. Smith (Munich, 1988), esp. 11–16; Smith,

Ehrenfels wrote on metaphysics, economics, the philosophy of mathematics, and epistemology. Especially relevant to his subsequent interest in ethics reform were his writings in the late 1890s on "value theory" (*Werttheorie*), which I discuss below and which proved an important influence on the Anglo-American development of emotivism as an ethical theory.[4]

Shortly after the turn of the century, Ehrenfels turned his energies to more popularly oriented work in the realms of sexual ethics, eugenics, and racial ideology, and in this capacity participated in the discussions on ethics reform. He contributed a flurry of articles on sexuality and racial hygiene to Alfred Ploetz's *Archiv für Rassen- und Gesellschaftsbiologie (Archive for Racial and Social Biology)*, to Ludwig Woltmann's *Politisch-Anthropologische Revue (Political Anthropological Review)*, and to Max Marcuse's *Sexual-Probleme*, the offshoot rival of Helene Stöcker's *Mutterschutz*. He corresponded with Ellen Key about sexual ethics, and he followed closely the developments of the League for the Protection of Mothers.[5] Yet Ehrenfels had somewhat different motives than these other participants in ethics reform. He was not concerned with either "universal humanity" or the sexual emancipation of women. Motivating his polemic rather was his conviction that the "white race" was on the biological decline and threatened by the "yellow danger" (*gelbe Gefahr*).[6] Accordingly, he sought to ground a biologistic ethics that would reverse the trends that worried him most.

Ehrenfels's academic writings from the 1890s are often treated by scholars separately from his reform-oriented work from the first decade of the twentieth century. Yet his work on value theory formed the intellectual background for his subsequent racialized approach to sexuality. The two phases were tied together by a model of evolutionary ethics based loosely on Darwin.

Austrian Philosophy, 243–280; and Mitchell Ash, *Gestalt Psychology in German Culture, 1890–1967: Holism and the Quest for Objectivity* (Cambridge, 1995), 84–93.

4. Stephen A. Satris, "The Theory of Value and the Rise of Ethical Emotivism," *Journal of the History of Ideas* 43, no. 1 (1982): 109–128.

5. See "Brev till Ellen Key," L 41:63:3, pp. 45–54, in the Ellen Key Nachlass at the Kungliga Biblioteket, National Library of Sweden. See also letters from Max Marcuse to Ehrenfels in the Ehrenfels Nachlass; copies are held at the Forschungsstelle und Dokumentationszentrum für Österreichische Philosophie in Graz.

6. The phobia infuses all of Ehrenfels's writings throughout the decade. One concentrated treatment is his "Die gelbe Gefahr," *Sexual-Probleme* 4 (1908): 185–205.

Ehrenfels had begun writing about ethics in the 1890s while working in what has come to be known as the "second school" of Austrian value theory, a school that extended the study of values beyond economics to include moral and cultural phenomena.[7] Ehrenfels's approach to the field was to say that values—both economic and moral—exist as a result of desire for an object, wherein an object is understood in the broadest possible sense to include such things as processes, emotions, and abstractions. As Ehrenfels put it, "we do not desire things because we grasp in them some mystical, incomprehensible essence 'value'; rather, we ascribe 'value' to things because we desire them."[8] Because values do not inhere in objects, they are subject to change over time. As individual and social conditions evolve, so too will the values that individuals and societies desire. Values, including moral values, consequently compete in what Ehrenfels labeled a "struggle for existence."[9]

By applying value theory to ethics, Ehrenfels depicted a universe of moral values in evolutionary conflict with one another. He broke ethics down into two primary categories, the categorical and the dispositional. Categorical morality referred to categorically proscribed acts such as killing or lying that are, if not absolutely universal, fairly stable across time and cultures. Against the slow-moving categorical morality, he juxtaposed "dispositional morality," which emphasizes the disposition of the moral agent—for example, the disposition to generosity or kindness or to cruelty and miserliness. Howard Eaton offers the example of Robin Hood, whose act of stealing from the rich to give to the poor is *categorically* wrong in most societies, but in a context that privileges economic equality, the disposition behind the act might be socially valued nonetheless.[10] Next

---

7. The "first" school of value theory centered on Carl Menger, one of Ehrenfels's teachers. See Carl Menger, *Grundsätze der Volkswirkschaftslehre* (1871), as reprinted in his *Collected Works,* ed. F. A. von Hayek (London, 1933).

8. Ehrenfels, "Werttheorie," in *Christian von Ehrenfels, Philosophische Schriften,* vol. 1, ed. Reinhard Fabian (Munich, 1982), 219; also cited in Smith, *Austrian Philosophy,* 283.

9. On Ehrenfels and value theory, see Smith, *Austrian Philosophy,* 281–297; Howard O. Eaton, *The Austrian Philosophy of Values* (Norman, Okla., 1930); and Reinhard Fabian and P. M. Simons, "The Second Austrian School of Value Theory," in *Austrian Economics: Historical and Philosophical Background,* ed. Wolfgang Grassl and Barry Smith (London, 1986), 37–101. On Ehrenfels's relationship to the first school of value theorists, see Wolfgang Grassl, "Introduction: Christian von Ehrenfels als Werttheoriker," in Fabian, *Ehrenfels, Philosophische Schriften,* esp. 1:3–12.

10. Eaton, *Austrian Philosophy of Values,* 272.

to these two fundamental dimensions exist the concrete manifestations of social custom (*Sitte*) and law (*Recht*). Because of the historical evolution of value, dispositional morality often comes into conflict either with categorical morality or with custom and law. Ethics, in Ehrenfels's Darwinian framework, is the product of both the struggle or competition for value that ensues as well as its temporary resolution. In a contribution to Adler's *International Journal of Ethics,* Ehrenfels remarked that he considered his chief contribution to the philosophy of ethics to be his analysis of how the individual and social value of moral categories changes with time due to this discord between its different elements.[11]

When Ehrenfels returned to the theory of ethics in 1907, the Darwinian metaphors of his earlier work became more literal. At this point he had already published a spate of articles advertising his racialized reform project. Two books on ethics of 1907, *Grundbegriffe der Ethik (Fundamental Concepts of Ethics)* and *Sexualethik (Sexual Ethics),* provided the theoretical framework for his ongoing campaign. Both appeared in the same series, *Grenzfragen des Nerven- und Seelenlebens (Limit Questions of the Nervous and Mental Life),* and were intended for an educated but not philosophically specialized audience. The *Grundbegriffe* is a clear, systematic introduction to Ehrenfels's updated theory of ethics which builds on and expands his earlier thought on the topic. It was intended, he stated explicitly, as a theoretical prequel to the more reform-oriented *Sexualethik.*[12]

In the *Grundbegriffe,* Ehrenfels built on his early model of ethics as a dynamic process of conflict. He retained his distinctions among ethics, morality (both dispositional and categorical), law, and custom. To this list, however, he now added a new element, the "constitutional," which demands that individuals and societies strive for physical self-preservation. Human communities, Ehrenfels explained, develop both constitutionally and culturally. But the constitutional tends to develop far more slowly than the cultural, and the discrepancy raises a problem for ethics. Ethics now had to be understood not only as the reconciliation of dispositional morality

11. Christian von Ehrenfels, "The Ethical Theory of Value," *International Journal of Ethics* 6, no. 3 (1896): 371–384.

12. Christian von Ehrenfels, *Sexualethik* (Wiesbaden, 1907), 7. The series was published by the J. F. Bergmann Company in Wiesbaden and included contributions from such prominent writers as Sigmund Freud, Werner Sombart, Paul Möbius, and August Eulenburg.

with law and customs, but also as the effort to assess whether mores are inhibiting the physical flourishing of a society. "Not all commands and prohibitions," he insisted, are "biologically valuable for all times, all circumstances, all human communities."[13]

Ehrenfels stayed philosophically neutral in the *Grundbegriffe*, lamenting only the excessive individuation of modern society. Yet embedded in his critique was a further dimension of his ethical theory: the conscience. Conscience, he insisted, was a fairly recent development in the evolution of ethics, as it could have arisen only in a highly individualized society that places enormous emphasis on individual autonomy. Moreover, its reign further reinforces the prevalent subjective sense of individuation, as each individual perceives the superiority of the call of conscience over and above the "relativity of social morality." Before the conscience, Ehrenfels explained, "all human voices are silenced."[14] Yet this circular reinforcement of individuation misses a crucial point about the conscience that Ehrenfels wanted to explain: it is not individual. Rather, he insisted, conscience is not only social but also tied to primordial human existence. And as a conduit to primordial human existence, it is in position to guide the individual toward an awareness of constitutional morality—to an insight into the biological well-being of society.

Interestingly, Ehrenfels's mode of conscience differed little in form from Friedrich Wilhelm Foerster's, discussed in the previous chapter. Both Ehrenfels and Foerster understood conscience to be the voice of a larger human circle that guides the lone individual. Yet the *content* of Ehrenfels's conscience differed fundamentally from that of Foerster, in that Foerster's still spoke in principle to ideal human sociality that transcends physicality whereas Ehrenfels understood the voice of biology to be making demands on the individual. Ehrenfels had simply taken those biological drives and turned them into an ideal form by way of conscience. For his part, however, Foerster questioned Ehrenfels's model, asking whether human morality demanded something more idealistic than the mere achievement of biological ends.[15]

13. Christian von Ehrenfels, *Grundbegriffe der Ethik* (Wiesbaden, 1907), 17.
14. Ibid., 27–28.
15. Friedrich Wilhelm Foerster, *Sexualethik und Sexualpädagogik: Eine neue Begründung alter Wahrheiten,* 4th ed. (Kempten, 1913), 81–82.

Building on the ethical theory laid out in the *Grundbegriffe,* Ehrenfels devoted the entirety of his *Sexualethik* to the legitimation of his racialist approach to sexual and ethical reform. He explained the urgency of reform in response to two supposed dangers confronting Europe: one internal and one external. First, like many of his contemporaries concerned with "degeneration," he maintained that Europe's efforts to advance culturally had come at the cost of biological and moral "virility." If Europe continued along this path, he claimed, it would soon be too physically weak to sustain itself: it would mean "the death of the *Volk* of occidental culture, thus of the white race."[16] Reform of sexual ethics should thus set the reversal of this devirilizing trend as its primary goal.

Second, according to Ehrenfels, Europe faced an external threat in the form of the "yellow danger" (*gelbe Gefahr*).[17] In his view, European and East Asian societies stood in marked contrast. Where Europe suffered under unequal development in the cultural and biological realms, East Asian societies had managed to cultivate a productive balance between the two. This balance was evidenced in a rigidly organized but virile sexual morality that allowed Asian societies to grow in number and in cultural and technological sophistication such that they could not only survive but expand. At the outset of the decade, Ehrenfels had been impressed primarily with China and its population of 400 million—a number that seemed to captivate him, as he repeated it often—and saw it as a model for the improvement of the biological lot of humanity altogether.[18] After Japan's military defeat of Russia in 1905, however, he came to see the struggle for survival as a global affair between races, and began to emphasize the possibility that Japan or China might conquer Europe either militarily or economically.[19] Accordingly, in his writings about ethics, he came to focus

16. Ehrenfels, *Sexualethik,* 75.

17. Ibid., 88.

18. Christian von Ehrenfels, "Monogamische Entwicklungsaussichten," *Politisch-Anthropologische Revue* 2 (1903): 714.

19. Christian von Ehrenfels, "Die konstitutive Verderblichkeit der Monogamie und die Unentbehrlichkeit einer Sexualreform," *Archiv für Rassen- und Gesellschafts-Biologie* 4 (1907), 615–617; *Sexualethik,* 86. On the evolution of Ehrenfels's anxiety about an Asian colonization of Europe, see Edward Ross Dickinson, "Sex, Masculinity, and the 'Yellow Peril'": Christian von Ehrenfels' Program for a Revision of the European Social Order," *German Studies Review* 25, no. 2 (2002): 255–284.

not on "sexual reform for the whole of humanity, but rather only for the Christian, white race, the bearers of occidental culture."[20]

As a response to these two imminent "threats," Ehrenfels called for a complete reconsideration of sexual ethics in Europe as a means to revitalize its "virility factor" (*virile Faktor*).[21] Drawing on the language of the *Grundbegriffe,* he argued for the reconciliation of constitutional morality with both custom and dispositional morality. More concretely, he asserted that contemporary sexual mores that demand abstention from sexual relations outside marriage do not support the biological well-being of the individual and the whole. Ehrenfels thus aimed his campaign of sexual ethics reform primarily against the institution of monogamous marriage and the *Doppelmoral* that many in the women's movement also targeted.[22]

Yet Ehrenfels's critique of the *Doppelmoral* differed markedly from those of other reformers, which tended to take one of two forms. Most prevalent among his contemporaries was a quest to restore sexual activity solely to the realm of monogamous heterosexual marriage, a position well represented by Friedrich Wilhelm Foerster but also by most of the mainstream women's movement and its evangelical branch. Ehrenfels, however, held that all forms of sexual restraint were inherently "feminine" in nature. Consequently, in his view, the first and most prevalent criticism of the *Doppelmoral* demonstrated nothing but the fact that this "feminine trait" had infused popular mores.[23] Less common but perhaps as prominent because of its notoriety was the call for gender equality in the pursuit of "free love," epitomized by Helene Stöcker, Ellen Key, Bruno Meyer, and others. Ehrenfels, however, was equally alarmed by this second criticism of the *Doppelmoral,* labeling it the " 'Jacobinism' of the sexual revolution"[24] because of its seeming devotion to absolute equality in sexual liberties. For Ehrenfels, any effective critique of the *Doppelmoral* must take into account the fundamental biological difference between the sexes and the consequent difference in constitutional morality. Women, he argued, are biologically predispositioned for a sense of modesty and chastity, as indicated

20. Ehrenfels, "Die konstitutive Verderblichkeit," 615.
21. Ehrenfels, *Sexualethik,* 10.
22. Ibid., 23.
23. Ibid., 18.
24. Ibid., 26.

by the fact that the genitals are hidden from view.[25] Men, however, exhibit "no sexual virtues," at least not in the popular understanding of the term that conflates chastity with virtue.[26] Men's external sexual organs, in contrast to women's hidden ones, indicate their lack of natural modesty. In place of modesty, they are compelled by their constitutional morality to demonstrate their virility and to compete for women and for the right to reproduce.

Because of the physiological differences between men and women, Ehrenfels maintained that there *should* be dual, sexually differentiated codes of morality. The challenge was only to find the right ones. Since the *Doppelmoral,* as conventionally understood, actually conformed to women's natural disposition toward modesty and chastity, whereas men have truly suffered under it, Ehrenfels proposed a terminological change, criticizing not the *Doppelmoral* but rather the *"doppelte Männermoral"* (doubled male morality), or the double bind in which men find themselves under current social mores.[27] On the one hand, social mores demand monogamy from the individual male, even if they tacitly allow him indulgence in extramarital sexual relations. On the other hand, constitutional morality demands that the man seek sexual exploit. In keeping with his assessment that the task of ethics is to compel constitutional considerations to contest social mores that are out of step with historical and biological circumstances, Ehrenfels called for "male emancipation" (*Männeremanzipation*) in the name of ethics reform.[28]

As a corrective, Ehrenfels advocated the practice of *polygynie* in Germany and Europe.[29] In this system, the men would compete with one another to reproduce with the women, the only constraint being that a man can only take as many "wives" and children as he could financially support.

---

25. Ibid., 16.

26. Ibid., 14.

27. Ehrenfels, *Sexualethik,* 69. See also Christian von Ehrenfels, "'Doppelte' und differenzierte Moral," *Sexual-Probleme* 4 (1908): 66–82.

28. Ehrenfels, *Sexualethik,* 77–83.

29. "The expressions 'polygynous' and 'polygyny' are used here instead of the more common 'polygamous' or 'polygamy' because the latter are ambiguous and can also potentially refer to that which is in strict opposition to the naturally healthy, namely, polyandrous relations, [or] to the simultaneous sexual intercourse of one woman (or young woman) with multiple men (or young men)." Ehrenfels, *Sexualethik,* 11.

Women would live together communally and retain full custody of their children; men would pay a monthly allowance to support the mother and child. Less healthy men, those unable to win or afford a wife and children, would pursue sexual experiences with *Hetären,* or courtesans—women who cannot or choose not to reproduce. As a result, the healthiest and wealthiest men would reproduce bountifully, and the overall biological stock in Europe would improve. This system, Ehrenfels maintained, best matched the biological proclivities of men and women while improving the health of the "white race" altogether.

Edward Ross Dickinson has made the convincing case that despite the seemingly eccentric quality of Ehrenfels's racialized defense of a virile masculinity and a chaste femininity, his overall approach to modernity was not at all unique at the fin de siècle.[30] The interweaving of race, gender, and sexuality—or, rather, their inseparability—was indeed ubiquitous at the time Ehrenfels was writing. In this regard, Ehrenfels stands out only in that his own anxiety about race adopted neither of the more popular variants: racialized anti-Semitism or anxiety about "tropicalization" through contact with colonized subjects. His particular fear of the "yellow danger" also put him in solid—and international—company. In fact, he looked to the U.S. effort to stop the immigration of Chinese workers as an important if ultimately insufficient first step in warding off a population takeover. And it was Arthur de Gobineau, the French racial theorist, who had first provided a racialized argument about the industriousness of Chinese workers.[31] In Germany, the rhetoric of yellow peril really took hold in the last decade of the century. Social Darwinists and Social Democrats alike spoke out against the dangers of Chinese labor.[32] Kaiser Wilhelm II added a political-religious dimension to the sentiment in 1895 when he commissioned and then circulated to his friends—both domestic and international—a drawing depicting France, Germany, Russia, England, and Italy standing on a rock, being protected by the archangel Gabriel from a Chinese dragon bearing a Buddha, with a caption reading: "Nations of

30. Dickinson, "Sex, Masculinity," esp. 264–265.
31. Gregory Blue, "China and Western Social Thought in the Modern Period," in *China and Historical Capitalism: Genealogies of Sinological Knowledge,* ed. Timothy Brook and Gregory Blue (Cambridge, 1999), 79.
32. Heinz Gollwitzer, *Die gelbe Gefahr: Geschichte eines Schlagworts* (Göttingen, 1962), 168–173.

Europe: Join in the defense of your faith and your home."[33] Ehrenfels simply augmented the yellow-peril rhetoric by tying it directly to domestic matters of sexual reproduction.

Equally symptomatic of the era, however, was Ehrenfels's understanding of ethics as the language with which to ground and justify reform. Writing explicitly in dialogue with Stöcker and her circle, Ehrenfels too understood his own call for reform to pertain directly to the private lives and consciences of individuals. If with a radically different politics, he likewise understood the need to engage the conscience and desire of the individual to effect social reform. And yet he saw that conscience not just as a social product (in the manner of Foerster) but as a social-biological link to the race. Understanding the desires of the liberal individual as the only mechanism for social reform, and thereby granting enormous importance to the seemingly autonomous individual even while contesting the autonomy and individuation of that individual (both male and female), he too thus worked with and revised the logic of liberal individualism in ways not atypical of ethics reform at large. Of course, his ultimate vision was a much more regulatory model than Stöcker or the DGEK would ever consider, justified by the socially informed "conscience" that morally compels the individual to work for the good of the race. Moreover, if Ehrenfels's vision did not privilege the state, treating it more as a tool of ethics reform than its engine, his vision at least partially anticipated the racialized regulatory regimes of the future, including their need to tap the desires and private lives of individuals for their effective survival. In this regard, his vision points to the unstated and usually unintended potential consequences of the progressive ethics reform era, or at least to its hidden underbelly. If ethics reform sought generally to emancipate the individual conscience for purposes of critique, it remained open as to how specific reformers would consequently understand both "emancipation" and "critique."

Furthermore, the case of Ehrenfels indicates the ways in which a global awareness pervaded the context of ethics reform. Within ethics reform, Ehrenfels stood out for his rhetoric about a "yellow danger." But underlying his concern was a common awareness of the possibilities of global migration and of a growing if diverse effort to reconceptualize global humanity

33. Cited in R. A. Thompson, *The Yellow Peril, 1890–1924* (New York, 1978), 1–2.

and the place of the individual within it. We have already seen examples of such efforts: the DGEK always concerned itself with the idea of "universal humanity," and Stöcker and Foerster both turned their energies to universal peace and international cooperation in the wake of World War I, also in the name of "universal humanity." Ehrenfels's own intervention in this regard simply reveals that global awareness did not necessarily point in a cosmopolitan direction. In the next section, we see how a global awareness also informed Freud's reflections on the evolution of the individual conscience and its relationship to ethics and ethics reform. Freud turned away from Ehrenfels's biologism but nevertheless echoed Ehrenfels's concern about conflicting moral commands and their effects on the health of the individual moral agent.

Freud and the "Universal" Conflict of Ethics

Freud is not usually treated as a reformer or activist, in large part because he carefully defended psychoanalysis as a science so it would not be criticized for any particular political stance. Throughout the first decade of the twentieth century, however, relations between psychoanalysis and reform were on the rise, if always loose and ambivalent. Stöcker and others articulating the New Ethic found in Freud an inspiring scientist fighting the neuroses induced by sexual repression. Working from quite a different perspective—and providing us a glimpse into how fluid the party lines were in the culture of ethics reform—Foerster also saw in Freud at least at times a fellow traveler. In particular, Foerster admired the insights that the new field of psychotherapy offered the individual in pursuit of "character" that can master physical drives.[34]

Freud himself also gave occasional approving nods in the direction of ethics reform. He endorsed the founding of a Viennese chapter of the League for the Protection of Mothers, and in 1913 he hosted Stöcker at a meeting of the Vienna Psychoanalytic Society.[35] Perhaps more telling, Freud's first real reflection on issues of ethics, an article titled " 'Civilized'

34. Foerster, *Sexualethik und Sexualpädagogik,* 1907, 20, 40–41.

35. Hermanns, "Stöckers autobiographisches Fragment"; Nunberg and Federn, *Minutes of the Vienna Psychoanalytic Society,* 4:172. See also Stöcker's entry on psychoanalysis in

Sexual Morality and Modern Nervousness," appeared in the context of reform, notably in Marcuse's *Sexual-Probleme*. Although Marcuse's periodical was founded as part of his split with Stöcker's New Ethic, it was still very much in dialogue with ethics reform and its sexual turn. Indeed, the correspondence between Marcuse and Ehrenfels regarding the "doppelte Männermoral" indicates less a lack of interest in ethics on the part of Marcuse than an antipathy to the particular form of Stöcker's New Ethic, as Marcuse strongly encouraged Ehrenfels to embolden his claims about ethics and to publish them in *Sexual-Probleme*.[36] Freud's own intervention in ethics reform took Ehrenfels's *Sexualethik* as its point of departure, referring to it as a "meaningful line of thought" worthy of serious consideration.[37] Nor did Freud limit his interest in Ehrenfels to this isolated instance, for he also invited Ehrenfels to give a lecture at the Vienna Psychoanalytic Society.[38]

To be sure, Freud took a very different line of argument from Ehrenfels, with no interest in the Prague philosopher's fear of a "yellow danger" and only a seemingly ironic concern about European virility. So what was it in Ehrenfels in particular that interested Freud, such that he explicitly identified Ehrenfels as his interlocutor? And how did Freud's interest in Ehrenfels—even as a point of departure—situate his reflections on ethics within the reform context? In the next section, we see how Freud built on Ehrenfels's elaboration of ethics as a site of conflict. Moreover, like Ehrenfels, Freud would come to view sexuality as the privileged interface between competing moral claims, or as the site at which the conflict in ethics occurs. Unlike Ehrenfels, however, Freud came to understand ethics as constitutively conflicted, that is, he came to see an inherent dilemma in the construction of a moral subject.[39]

---

her unpublished autobiographical sketch at the Swarthmore Peace Collection, DG 035, Box 1, Folder 5.

36. See the letter from Marcuse to Ehrenfels dated November 22, 1907, at the Forschungsstelle und Dokumentationszentrum für Österreichische Philosophie, Graz.

37. Sigmund Freud, "Die 'kulturelle' Sexualmoral und die moderne Nervosität" (1908), in *GW* 7, 143; first published in *Sexual-Probleme* 4 (1908): 107–129.

38. Nunberg and Federn, *Minutes of the Vienna Psychoanalytic Society,* 2:82, 93–100. See also 1:43 for Freud's early reference to Ehrenfels's work.

39. For representative analyses of Freud, psychoanalysis, and ethics, see Kenneth Reinhard, Eric Santner, and Slavoj Žižek, *The Neighbor: Three Inquiries in Political Theology* (Chicago, 2006); Ernest Wallwork, *Psychoanalysis and Ethics* (New Haven, Conn., 1991); Philip

Civilized Sexual Morality

In "'Civilized' Sexual Morality," Freud repeated his long-standing claim that sexuality did not belong primarily to the realm of biology. Indeed, according to Freud, it takes considerable cultural work to train an individual's sexual desires and pleasures to focus on the genital and reproductive, and Freud made the effects of this cultural work on the individual the topic of his intervention in ethics reform. In his appropriation of Ehrenfels, he thus dropped altogether the reference to constitutional morality that was so central to Ehrenfels's concerns. But Freud did pick up on the *form* of Ehrenfels's investigation. That is, like Ehrenfels, he began to understand ethics as a necessary site of conflict for the sexual subject. Where Ehrenfels saw this as a conflict between constitutional and cultural morality, Freud came to articulate it as a conflict *within* the logic of cultural morality—within the logic of training the sexual drives.

Freud's primary focus at this point was not on morality per se but rather on the neuroses that sexual morality produces when a society recognizes as legitimate only reproductive sexual activity within heterosexual, monogamous relationships. In this regard, he found civilized sexual morality to affect women with special ferocity. Women were largely trained to avoid sexual enjoyment outside marriage but were expected to find pleasure in sex within marriage. Years of training the psyche away from pleasure, however, made "legitimate" enjoyment virtually impossible, and the conflict routinely produced varying degrees of neurosis.

Yet when he turned to men, Freud talked as much about a moral double bind as he did of neurosis. Tellingly, Freud repeated Ehrenfels's term, the "doppelte Moral," rather than the more common *Doppelmoral* that sexual liberationists and women's-rights activists such as Stöcker deployed. Like Ehrenfels, however, Freud was interested not in the two codes of morality that pertained to men and women respectively, but rather in the two codes of morality that put irreconcilable demands on the modern man, who is at once expected to pursue sexual pleasures and simultaneously to hide his pursuit of those pleasures. This twofold relationship to sexual pleasures

---

Rieff, *Freud: The Mind of the Moralist* (Garden City, N.Y., 1961); Jacques Lacan, *The Ethics of Psychoanalysis, 1959–1960: The Seminar of Jacques Lacan, Book 7,* trans. Dennis Porter (New York, 1992); and Erich Fromm, *Psychoanalyse und Ethik* (Frankfurt am Main, 1978).

compels the man to dishonesty, which is also incompatible with the moral codes he has largely accepted. Women are shielded from this moral conflict only because they are said to have a lesser sexual drive; somehow the drive itself does not place as much of a moral demand on them as it does for men. Citing Ehrenfels, Freud noted that "a society that lets in this doubled morality cannot carry 'love of truth, honesty and humanity' beyond a definite, narrowly limited measure, and must lead its members to the concealment of the truth, to rosy glasses, to self-deception, and to deception of others."[40] Where Ehrenfels feared that this conflict reduced the virility of the European population, Freud worried that it raised the level and frequency of neurosis—a development, he noted, which itself might have as a by-product an effect on rates of reproduction.[41]

Totem and Taboo

Interested primarily in the cause of neurosis in " 'Civilized' Sexual Morality," Freud had simply identified a sweeping conflict that the male moral subject experiences. He made no attempt to identify its origin, however, or to understand why it makes such a strong impression on the individual as potentially to induce neurosis. Like Ehrenfels, he was grappling with the idea that sexual drives make a moral demand on the subject. And although he was concerned less with the strictly biological drive to reproduce that interested Ehrenfels, and more with a moral demand to pursue pleasure, he nonetheless echoed Ehrenfels when he identified sexuality as the site at which these conflicting moral demands play out, and hence as the site that ethics reform must target if it hoped to be successful.

Yet Freud was not satisfied with the cursory treatment he gave to ethics in his 1908 article, and he continued to dwell on the problem. In 1912–1913, he returned to the theme in a set of four essays that eventually became *Totem and Taboo*. In this effort, he retreated from the activist realm of ethics reform to the more scientific domain of psychoanalysis, withholding comment entirely on the prospects of reform. Yet his reflections, published

---

40. Freud, "Die 'kulturelle' Sexualmoral," 144.
41. Ibid., 167. Freud returned often to this problem of a double code of morality and the neurosis it induces in the individual subject. See, for instance, Sigmund Freud, "Einleitung zu *Zur Psychoanalyse der Kriegsneurosen*," in *GW* 12, 321–324; and "Über die Psychogenese eines Falles von weiblicher Homosexualität," in *GW* 12, 271–302.

first in *Imago*, a recently founded journal intended for the exploration of the cultural relevance of psychoanalysis, posed indirectly a significant challenge to ethics reform as a whole. Here Freud sought to identify the cultural origin of ethics and of its conflictual character. In doing so, he returned to his own conception of ethics as conflicted, now providing anthropological support to claim that ethics is *constitutively* conflicted, universally—regardless of definition—and hence positively resistant to use as a category for social reform.

In *Totem and Taboo*, Freud approached the topic of ethics through a psychoanalytic explanation of totemism, a phenomenon commonly described by contemporaries as the earliest, most "primitive," and most originary formation of religion and cultural morality. In his interest in totemism, Freud had a flourishing literature on which to draw. His own account of totemism engaged the anthropological studies of J. G. Frazer, W. Robertson Smith, and Franz Boas; the sociological studies of Émile Durkheim; and the evolutionary theories of Charles Darwin, to name just the most prominent sources. Most urgently, however, Freud understood *Totem and Taboo* chiefly as a psychoanalytic corrective to recent publications from Carl Gustav Jung and Wilhelm Wundt, both of whom were actively exploring the relationship of individual psychology to custom, myth, and religion. Wundt was especially well known in the field, immersed as he was in a ten-volume study of "folk psychology" (*Völkerpsychologie*). By the 1870s and 1880s, Wundt had established himself as a founder of experimental psychology, often referred to as "physiological psychology." Although his emphasis on the empirical observation of consciousness and sense perception situated him quite far afield from Freud's interest in the unconscious, the two men shared a general concern for the interaction of the mind and the body. Especially significant in terms of ethics reform, Wundt had also published in 1886 a well-regarded, psychologically and empirically informed study of ethics that provided for many reformers a model of what a modern "scientific" ethics might look like. When he turned to folk psychology after the turn of the century, he brought together these two strains of his work, seeking to understand the empirical history of custom and morality and its interaction with individual psychology.[42]

42. For Wundt on experimental psychology, see especially *Grundzüge der physiologischen Psychology,* 2 vols. (Leipzig, 1873–1874); on ethics, see *Ethik: Eine Untersuchung der Tatsachen und Gesetze des sittlichen Lebens* (Stuttgart, 1886); on "folk psychology," see

In contrast to Wundt, Jung was deeply engaged in the psychoanalytic method. Freud's critique of Jung thus pointed not to the tension between experimental psychology and psychoanalysis but rather to the tension over the future direction of psychoanalytic inquiry itself. Freud had once looked to Jung as one who might help to publicize psychoanalysis and prevent it from being ghettoized as a "Jewish science." By 1911–1912, however, the once promising partnership was severely frayed, in large part because of competing understandings of libido theory and the extension of psychoanalysis to cultural interpretation.[43] For Freud, the chief psychoanalytic intervention had been the discovery of a fundamentally sexual libido, whereas Jung was looking for other contributions to the makeup of the libido, such as deep cultural roots, archetypes, and a collective unconscious. Freud thus quickly dismissed Jung's breakthrough "Wandlungen und Symbole der Libido" ("Transformations and Symbols of the Libido") of 1912 as falsely trying to understand "social psychology" as a means to explain individual psychology.[44] What disturbed Freud, whose inclination toward liberal individualism never failed him, was the idea that social customs, social life at large, social existence could *intrinsically* make demands on the individual psyche. Rather, in *Totem and Taboo,* Freud would insist that social existence and the demands that it makes on the individual must be explained through reference to the organization of *individual* desires.[45]

In response to Wundt, Jung, and his own earlier reflections in "'Civilized' Sexual Morality," Freud thus set out in *Totem and Taboo* to provide a psychoanalytically informed theory of human religion and ethics. In this account, he sought to explain what motivates the individual to give over some of his or her autonomy to a group or to a deity. In doing so,

---

Völkerpsychologie: Eine Untersuchung der Entwicklungsgesetze von Sprache, Mythus und Sitte, 10 vols. (Leipzig, 1911–1920); also see Wundt, *Elemente der Völkerpsychologie: Grundlinien einer psychologischen Entwicklungsgeschichte der Menschheit* (Leipzig, 1912). On Wundt and *Völkerpsychologie,* see Woodruff D. Smith, *Politics and the Sciences of Culture in Germany, 1840–1920* (New York, 1991), 120–128.

43. See Gay, *Freud,* 197–243.

44. Sigmund Freud, *Totem und Tabu,* in *GW* 9, 3.

45. Another early effort within psychoanalysis to theorize ethics was Carl Furtmüller, *Psychoanalyse und Ethik: Eine Untersuchung* (Munich, 1912). Significantly, Furtmüller, who also sought to find a *social* instinct as a means to think about ethics, had to publish his reflections in the *Schriften des Vereins für freie psychoanalytische Forschung,* the journal of a group that had been forced to split off from the Vienna Psychoanalytic Society.

he translated the Oedipus narrative into the origin of culture. He took as his starting point his observation that "modern neurotics" and totemism have much in common: both were compulsively bound to rules and absolute taboos that couldn't be explained consciously or rationally but that nonetheless compelled unwavering obedience. To explain the origin of totemism, Freud hypothesized the existence of a primal horde whose father had monopolized for himself all sexual rights to women of the group. The sons, a band of brothers, had supposedly tired of the situation, joined forces, and killed and devoured the father. Afterward, however, ambivalence reigned. The brothers, who had loved the father even as they envied him, felt remorse for their act, yet they would kill him again if he returned to monopolize the women. Likewise, they would kill a brother if one emerged as dominant. To prevent fratricide, the brothers thus internalized the monopoly the father once held and placed on themselves a ban against all sexual relations between the brothers and the women of the clan. This, according to Freud, represented the first moment of self-imposed sexual regulation within a human group. And it was, he added, "the beginning of so many things—of social organization, of moral restrictions, and of religion."[46]

Over time, as the brothers retroactively honored the father due to guilt and remorse, he retreated in memory, becoming a deity. This father-turned-deity, however, had to change forms, as memory of the father's literal figure inspired an intolerable ambivalence.[47] Drawing on W. Robertson Smith's emphasis on sacrifice, Freud decided that the father's memory had once been replaced with that of a substitute token animal, which then became the clan's totem guardian. The resulting system of taboos organized around the clan's totem would function to repress the primal memory and to obscure the system's own origin and motivation. Only the absolute necessity to honor the deified totem and to adhere rigorously to the code of sexual regulation remained. Qualifying the speculative dimension of the argument, Freud noted in his conclusion that the factual occurrence of the deed is not necessarily the prerequisite for the validity of his claims: "Accordingly the mere hostile *impulse* against the father, the mere existence of a wishful *fantasy* of killing and devouring him, would have been

46. Freud, *Totem und Tabu*, 172.
47. Ibid., 175.

enough to produce the moral reaction that created totemism and taboo."[48] Even if the primal patricide never actually occurred, Freud suggested, the mechanism of ethics—of which totemism and its taboos were just the earliest example—would always be marked by murderous ambivalence, an unstable mix of desire, hostility, and remorse that the moral subject must deny at all turns.

The broad implications of the primal patricide for considerations of ethics were central to Freud's aims in *Totem and Taboo,* especially, he added, as they "can throw a light on the dark origin of our own 'categorical imperative.'"[49] According to Freud, the two mechanisms had much in common, deriving from their strict formalism. "Taboo prohibitions," Freud insisted, "have no grounds and are of unknown origin."[50] They are consequently beyond the reach of critical contemplation. Accordingly, he added, "external threat of punishment is superfluous" for their observance, "for there is an internal certainty (conscience) that any violation will lead to intolerable disaster."[51] Likewise, Kant's concept of the categorical imperative must have no ground, content, or external guarantee. There can be no preexisting "good" to which the moral law or the moral agent would be subservient, a pure formalism that, in the Kantian framework, aims to preserve the rational autonomy of the moral agent.[52] In his comparison of the categorical imperative to the mechanisms of the taboo, however, Freud was suggesting a psychoanalytically more complex explanation. As we have seen, totemism and its corollary taboos were a means to forget the original patricide, along with the sexual desire and ambivalence that endure in unconscious fashion. The corollary suggestion regarding the categorical imperative would then be that its very presupposition of formality forgets, or serves to obscure, ambivalent desires. These are not the elements of self-interest that the categorical imperative demands the moral agent bracket when making a moral decision; rather, these are the unconscious desires and ambivalences that accompany *compliance with* the categorical

48. Ibid., 192.
49. Ibid., 32.
50. Ibid., 19.
51. Ibid., 36–37.
52. In Kant's writings there are many variations in terms of his presentation of the categorical imperative. My comments here relate to Immanuel Kant, *Critique of Practical Reason,* trans. and ed. Mary Gregor (New York, 1997).

imperative. In short, then, according to Freud, the moral decision is never disinterested but is, rather, always *motivated:* it always serves the ambivalent interests of sexual desire and aggression.

For Freud, *Totem and Taboo* universalized the dilemma he had identified in "'Civilized' Sexual Morality": if the modern individual was more likely to succumb to neurosis than an individual in another regulatory regime, the ambivalence and double bind at the heart of ethics now had to be recognized as universal. It is moreover not insignificant in this context that Freud chose the Kantian categorical imperative to compare with totemic taboos. The majority of moral frameworks available to Freud—the ones we saw in chapter 1—left open some room for cultural specificity: the general moral command to love the neighbor left open the question of which neighbor; the utilitarian pursuit of "the greatest good for the greatest number" left open the questions not only of what constitutes the "good" but also of what exactly constitutes the "greatest number" (for example, a small community, humanity at large, all sentient beings, and so forth); and an ethics of pity begged the question of what constitutes suffering. Yet the formality of the categorical imperative was supposed to be the epitome of rationality and hence to be universally applicable. No cultural content could ever taint the categorical imperative because it was said to have no content. By comparing totemic taboos to the categorical imperative, Freud thus found the seemingly most universal application of his critique of ethics.

One last step remained in Freud's early reflections on ethics. He observed in an essay of 1914, "An Introduction to Narcissism," that a moral code is compelling for an individual only if "he takes it as his own measure and submits himself to its demands."[53] Freud thus needed to reflect on the formation of the moral individual to assess what motivates him or her to form a moral conscience and to accept specific moral demands as personally meaningful. In the essay on narcissism, he set out to understand the early formation of the desiring subject, a process he would equate with the early history of the moral subject.[54] According to this narrative, the infant begins as an undifferentiated, pleasure-seeking entity in which instincts

53. Sigmund Freud, "Zur Einführung des Narzißmus," in *GW* 12, 160.
54. "It is a necessary assumption that a unity such as an I [ego] is not to be found in the individual at the outset; the I must be developed." Freud, "Zur Einführung des Narzißmus," in *GW* 12, 142.

of self-preservation (ego instincts) and sexual instincts are indissociable. Over time, the child begins to differentiate these drives when it learns to renounce some pleasures in favor of others. Drawing again on the Oedipal story, Freud found the fear of castration to be the starkest instance in which the child renounces sexual desires in favor of self-preservation.[55] Yet something new happens now: in this process the child has not only internalized the critical parental voice; the child has done so by establishing a new component of the psyche, what Freud now began to call the "ego ideal" (*Ich-Ideal*). The sexual desires that were once aimed at an external object (for example, the mother) are now invested in this internalized ego ideal. In this manner, social morality as represented by the internalized parental censor or ego ideal becomes meaningful for the child, the object of libidinal attraction that the child strives to please.[56]

The story of the formation of the moral subject in "An Introduction to Narcissism," however, left ethics in as precarious a position as had the primal patricide of *Totem and Taboo,* if not more so. In *Totem and Taboo,* ethics masked an ambivalent hostility and desire. In his study of narcissism, Freud found a mechanism through which the ambivalent hostility grows: as the subject strives to please the ego ideal, it diverts ever more sexual energy away from external objects and toward the ego ideal. In doing so, it feeds the ego ideal, making it both stronger and more demanding. As a consequence, the ego ideal continues to set the bar ever higher for the moral subject, who in turn can never reach the ideal. Just a few years later, when Freud finally completed his structural theory of the mind in his *The Ego and the Id,* the ego ideal, which had both a loving and demanding component, became the voracious or cruel superego (*Über-ich*), making impossible demands against which the moral subject feels inevitably inferior and bringing out potential aggression and resentment on the part of the self it regulates. The desire, ambivalence, and hostility that Freud found at the origin of culture now manifested itself at the origin of the moral subject *tout court.*[57]

With *Totem and Taboo* and "An Introduction to Narcissism," Freud had thus provided both a cultural and an individual narrative to explain the

---

55. Ibid., 159–160.
56. Ibid., 161–163.
57. Sigmund Freud, "Das Ich und das Es," in *GW* 13, 237–289.

phenomenon that many ethics reformers had come to accept: that sexuality lies at the heart of ethics. But he did so in ways that challenged the assumptions of almost all the sexual-ethical reform efforts. Like both Friedrich Wilhelm Foerster and Ehrenfels, Freud was looking for the *origins* of individual moral conscience. For Foerster, who understood the rise of this moral conscience in ways not wholly dissimilar to Freud, the individual simultaneously learns to resist particular physical desires while internalizing the voice of social tradition. Yet a crucial point marks the difference between Freud and Foerster on this matter. Foerster understood morality as the product of the renunciation of sexual desire; the individual takes on a moral character through renunciation of sexual drives. Freud, conversely, understood morality as the *redirection* of sexual desire, or rather as an alternative and highly ambivalent expression of that sexual desire. The difference was decisive for their attitudes to reform. Although the moral individual in Foerster's view suffers from an internal conflict around his or her moral subjectivity, ethics reform remains possible because the rightly constructed moral voice of society, or moral tradition, can actually *help* that individual and minimize the internal conflict. Or rather, the moral voice of tradition helps ease the conflict between the physical and mental that otherwise plagues the lone individual. Foerster thus criticized Freud for remaining too focused on the production of healthy individuals, at the expense of hundreds of years of moral education that could be helpful to those individuals.[58] Something similar could be said about Ehrenfels, although he was working from a very different perspective. The goal of ethics reform in Ehrenfels's framework was also to reduce the conflict between unconscious biological demands—which may take the form of an internal moral conscience—and social mores. For both Foerster and Ehrenfels, reform implied the minimization or elimination of a conflict between the physical and the mental. For Freud, conversely, ethics reform as the reduction of conflict remained impossible, as the conflict lay *in ethics itself*, in the very way in which the physical and the mental, the social and the individual get articulated *as moral relations*. According to this perspective, one cannot remain within the language of ethics and eliminate the conflict at the same time, as ethics is the conflict itself.

58. Foerster, *Sexualethik und Sexualpädagogik*, 4th ed., 1913, 139–140.

Stöcker's liberationist argument that painted sexual desire in opposition to moral regulation fared no better in light of Freud's challenge. Despite his own bourgeois inclinations, Freud sympathized with her overall critique of excessive sexual regulation and repression, though he was concerned less with the *ressentiment* and more with the nervous illnesses that such repression induces. Yet if Freud had worried that certain regimes of sexual morality are unhealthy, his overall approach to ethics no longer enabled liberation as a mode of ethics reform. Stöcker had understood sexual liberation as a means for the autonomous subject to realize his or her own ethical potential. Freud, however, found sexual desire and moral regulation to be complementary components of the autonomous subject. For the individual to learn self-preservation and to distinguish the self from the other, according to Freud, he or she must internalize normative sexual regulation. That is, social morality must be incorporated as part of the self, and hence as something from which the autonomous subject cannot be liberated.

To an extent Freud's challenge most closely resembled the liberal-individualist critique that Marianne Weber and Gertrud Bäumer had mounted against Stöcker's New Ethic. In that critique they had asserted as universal the conflict between individual desires and social welfare. Yet for Freud, the very distinction between individual and social evolves as a *moral* distinction rather than as an ontological one. Where Weber and Bäumer both took for granted the clear existence of the individual in opposition to the social, Freud was interested in the process by which the individual subject as both self-reflective and moral emerges as distinct from the social. And he found that process to occur in the very formation of the individual psyche at the moment when the individual evolves to be a distinct moral subject. Weber and Bäumer had understood ethics thus as a universal conflict between conscious pursuit of self-interest and willingness toward self-sacrifice; Freud found the conflict equally universal, but one that plays out at least partially unconsciously in the torture chamber of the moral subject's psyche. Despite these significant differences, however, Freud's overall challenge to ethics reform resembled those of Bäumer and Weber, in that it highlighted a set of conflicts that could not be resolved—not through retreat to religious tradition, investment in biological drives, or emancipation of sexual desires.

But just how "universal" were these claims? Freud has sustained considerable criticism from subsequent theorists for his assumptions about universal cultural patterns (the nuclear family, the Oedipus myth) and for his relative lack of interest in the specificities of non-European cultures.[59] On this front, his comparison of "primitive" cultures to "modern neurotics" does not help his case.[60] Seen against the racialist arguments of Ehrenfels, however, Freud's rhetoric of universalism takes on other, more local implications. Ehrenfels's primary fear was that Europe would be overrun economically and reproductively. Global interconnection and awareness of a universal humanity made that fear for him a pressing danger that ethics reform was supposed to resist. Freud's response to global awareness was not only to remove the biological from the equation but also to denote cultural difference as, at bottom, insignificant as a question of ethics. In this light, his universalism worked as much to cast doubt on the grand schemes of reform that Ehrenfels and others envisioned as it did to counter Ehrenfels's particular form of racialist logic and fear of non-European cultures.[61]

Yet a universalist logic did not necessarily imply an antiracist logic, nor did it necessarily counter cultural supremacy. Freud's own use of the rhetoric of "primitive" and "civilized" was in fact symptomatic of the era and one variant of its universalist tendencies—a tendency that saw "universal humanity" as made up of distinct cultures situated at different levels of civilizational progress. Accordingly, reformers often looked to so-called primitive societies for insights into their own cultural past. Significantly, this variant of universalism could just as easily celebrate the fundamental equality and freedom of humanity as it could justify colonialism and the "civilizing mission" as a means to help "backward" people realize their "universal" potential. In the next section, we return to the ethical culture movement and its participation in a global meeting of scientists and

59. A recent critique is Ranjana Khanna, *Dark Continents: Psychoanalysis and Colonialism* (Durham, N.C., 2003). See also Jean-Paul Sartre, *Black Orpheus,* trans. S. W. Allen (Paris, 1963); Wulf Sachs, *Black Hamlet* (Baltimore, 1996); Frantz Fanon, *Black Skin, White Masks,* trans. Charles Lam Markmann (New York, 1967); Octave Mannoni, *Prospero and Caliban: The Psychology of Colonisation,* trans. Pamela Powesland (New York, 1964); and Jacques Derrida, "Geopsychoanalysis," in *The Psychoanalysis of Race,* ed. Christopher Lane (New York, 1998).

60. On Freud and primitivism, see especially Ashis Nandy, *The Savage Freud, and Other Essays on Possible and Retrievable Selves* (Princeton, N.J., 1995).

61. On Freud and race, see in addition to the sources mentioned in note 59 Sander Gilman, *Freud, Race, and Gender* (Princeton, N.J., 1993); and Lane, *Psychoanalysis of Race.*

activists who were grappling with precisely this ambiguity of universalism and its implications for moral conscience and reform.

Ferdinand Tönnies at the Universal Races Congress

At a 1906 meeting of the International Union of Ethical Societies in Eisenach, Felix Adler proposed an international conference to deal with questions of race and ethics.[62] Through the joint efforts of the International Union of Ethical Societies and the Interparliamentary Union, this conference came to fruition in the form of the Universal Races Congress (URC), a three-day event held in London in July 1911. Although the URC was dominated by Europeans, and especially by local London attendees, it could nonetheless boast a list of participants that was truly global. With roughly 2,200 participants, the conference attracted individuals from six continents and more than fifty countries.[63]

The purpose of the URC was, in the words of its logistical coordinator, Gustav Spiller, "to discuss, in the light of science and the modern conscience, the general relations subsisting between the peoples of the West and those of the East, between so-called white and so-called coloured peoples, with a view to encouraging between them a fuller understanding, the most friendly feelings, and a heartier co-operation."[64] Organizers maintained that sentiments of "race supremacy" were a primary cause of international conflict, and they thus charged the URC with the task of contesting the premises underlying such sentiments. Moreover, as Spiller's statement suggests, science was supposed to enable the explicitly moral ambitions.

But despite the commitments to human equality, and despite the genuinely antinationalist and anti-imperialist commitments of many orga-

---

62. Börner, *Die ethische Bewegung,* 12.

63. A sampling of the international participation can be seen in a short list of the most luminary contributors: Franz Boas (Germany, United States), W. E. B. DuBois (United States), Mohandas Gandhi (India), General Légitime (Haiti), Ferdinand Tönnies (Germany), Mojola Agbebi (Nigeria); Brajendranath Seal (India), Wu Ting-Fang (China), Tongo Takebe and Teruaki Kobayashi (Japan), and J. Tengo Jabavu (South Africa).

64. "Circulars Issued by the Executive Council," in *Papers on Inter-racial Problems Communicated to the First Universal Races Congress Held at the University of London July 26–29, 1911,* ed. Gustav Spiller (London, 1911), xiii.

nizers and attendees, it is difficult to describe the event wholly as "antinationalist" or "anti-imperialist." The congratulatory notes that leaders of imperial powers sent to the congress alone are enough indication to the contrary, as are the national and imperial sponsorships of many attendees.[65] The location of the event in London clearly situated it also at the heart of the imperial world. Furthermore, although all participants were encouraged to speak in their native language (or in Esperanto), the two official languages of the URC, French and English, indicate how dependent the congress was on the reach of colonial practices.

Such tensions were not lost on the participants. Bound like Freud to a rhetoric of "civilized" and "primitive," "backward," or "uncivilized," they struggled especially with imperialism and issues of cultural difference. Some called for the immediate cessation of imperialism, but the official resolutions adopted the "civilizing" logic of "preparing" the colonized nations for self-government.[66] Observing the conflict, one participant noted even before the URC convened that "it really amounts to confessing that all peoples who have not hitherto governed themselves are relatively undeveloped; that, in short, self-government is the pre-requisite of any high level of social organisation and general capacity."[67] Moreover, participants labored mightily to affirm the basic equality of "universal humanity" while respecting distinct cultural traditions.[68] Yet although the refrain of preserving important and unique cultural traditions resonated throughout the three days, it was largely lost when participants considered what constitutes "preparedness" for self-government, as calls for "universal education" and "universal morality" took over.[69]

A further controversy plagued the URC, especially in terms of its organizing theme of race. As noted, organizers assumed that a global

65. *Record of the Proceedings of the First Universal Races Congress, Held at the University of London, July 26–29, 1911* (London, 1911), 48, 58. For sponsorships, see 15–20.

66. Ibid., 10.

67. John M. Robertson, "The Rationale of Autonomy," in Spiller, *Papers on Inter-racial Problems,* 40–41.

68. On the event as a model of the "new cosmopolitanism," see Robert John Holton, "Cosmopolitanism or Cosmopolitanisms? The Universal Races Congress of 1911," *Global Networks* 2, no. 2 (2002): 155, which paraphrases an argument from Bruce Robbins, "Actually Existing Cosmopolitanism," in *Cosmopolitics: Thinking and Feeling beyond the Nation,* ed. Pheng Cheah and Bruce Robbins (Minneapolis, 1998).

69. *Record of the Proceedings,* 8.

convention on science would shed light on issues of race and would correspond to the moral aims of the congress both to work toward harmony among humankind and to eliminate conceptions of race superiority. Yet this assumption was harder to support when the actual discussions of race got under way, a fact quickly acknowledged by Ferdinand Tönnies, who represented the DGEK and the German Sociological Society (Deutsche soziologische Gesellschaft) at the URC, and who was also a member of the Honorary Planning Committee and chief popularizer of the event in Germany.[70] The discussions of race played out in unpredictable ways, and discussions of miscegenation in particular prompted Tönnies to reconsider the relationship of science to moral conscience in a global framework.[71]

The organizers' assumption that science and ethics would complement one another was already present in the invitational circular they sent out in advance of the congress. In it, organizers had asked participants to consider a specific set of questions, several of which reflected the anthropological language of race prevalent at the turn of the century and that asked accordingly for "descriptive" or "scientific" responses:

> (a) To what extent is it legitimate to argue from differences in physical characteristics to differences in mental characteristics? (b) Do you consider that the physical and mental characteristics observable in a particular race are (1) permanent, (2) modifiable only through ages of environmental pressure, or (3) do you consider that marked changes in popular education, in public sentiment, and in environment generally, may, apart from intermarriage, materially transform physical and especially mental characteristics in a generation or two?

70. See the letters of May 17, 1909; December 1 of unnamed year (presumably 1909 or 1910); and May 22, 1911; from Gustav Spiller to Tönnies, in the Ferdinand Tönnies Nachlass at the Schleswig-Holsteinsche Landesbibliothek, Collection CB 54, File 65:03.

71. I examine the broader discussions at the URC in "Internationalist Activism at the Height of Nationalism: The Universal Races Congress of 1911," in *Global History: Interactions between the Universal and the Local,* ed. A. G. Hopkins (New York, 2006), 131–159. For recent literature on the URC, see Holton, "Cosmopolitanism or Cosmopolitanisms?"; Susan D. Pennybacker, "The Universal Races Congress, London Political Culture, and Imperial Dissent, 1900–1939," *Radical History Review* 92 (2005): 103–117; Mansour Bonakdarian, "Negotiating Universal Values and Cultural and National Parameters at the First Universal Races Congress," *Radical History Review* 92 (2005): 118–132; and Gabriele Schirbel, *Strukturen des Internationalismus: First Universal Races Congress, London 1911,* 2 vols. (Münster, 1991).

In keeping with the political motivations of the organizers, however, the circular also asked, "How would you combat the irreconcilable contentions prevalent among all the more important races of mankind that *their* customs, *their* civilisation, and *their* race are superior to those of other races?"[72] In other words, how can one think in a politically and morally critical fashion about race? In short, the descriptive and normative questions were not to be separated. In this light, Adler celebrated after the fact the scientific consolidation of the monogenesis thesis of race, or the idea of a single origin of humanity, as the great achievement of the congress.[73] Although Adler was correct that the participants at the congress had indeed been unanimous on the monogenesis/polygenesis issue, he assumed also a consensus about the moral implications of monogenesis, and in this he overstated the case. Indeed, participants were far from unanimous on the moral implications of their consensus—and here the troubled relationship of ethics to science began.

The questions about race were directed at and primarily discussed by the anthropologists in attendance, and the answers fell roughly into two categories. First was the position of Felix von Luschan, the Berlin anthropologist whose attendance at the URC was sponsored by the Berlin Society for Anthropology, Ethnology, and Prehistory (Berliner Gesellschaft für Anthropologie, Ethnologie und Urgeschichte) and whose contribution to a volume of precirculated papers earned him notoriety at the congress.[74] In his essay, "Anthropological View of Race," Luschan outlined the advances his discipline had made in its conception of human history. Not only had anthropology long ago abandoned the polygenesis thesis, he explained, but it had also abandoned the practice of dividing "races"—a term he expressly contested at the URC itself—into "active" and "passive," or "day" and "night," or even "civilized" and "savage." To be sure, local groups had evolved

72. Gustav Spiller, "Questionnaire," in *Papers on Inter-racial Problems,* xiv–xv.

73. Felix Adler, "Report of the First Universal Races Congress, Held at London July 26–29 1911," in *Report of the Commissioner of Education for the Year Ended June 30, 1911,* vol. 1 (Washington, D.C., 1912), 611. Paul Rich also celebrates the popular consolidation of the monogenesis thesis as the great achievement of the URC, in "'The Baptism of a New Order': The 1911 Universal Races Congress and the Liberal Ideology of Race," *Ethnic and Racial Studies* 7, no. 4 (1984): 536. See also Rich, *Race and Empire in British Politics* (Cambridge, 1990), esp. 44–49.

74. *Record of the Proceedings,* 16.

over time to develop distinct physical characteristics, he maintained. These developments, however, had always been contingent and unstable products of human "migration and colonization." To the extent that there is a "natural" organization of human groups, Luschan suggested, it is a fluid one of constant intermixture and transformation.[75] Scientifically speaking, "humanity" exists at bottom solely as a singular and "universal" race.

Yet Luschan nonetheless concluded that those contingent "groups" that exist in the modern era should be preserved at all costs. His moral justification for this surprising turn in his argument was that "the brotherhood of man is a good thing, but the struggle for life is a far better one." War and struggle are not only necessary components of human existence but invaluable components: "Nations will come and go, but racial and national antagonism will remain; and this is well, for mankind would become like a herd of sheep, if we were to lose our national ambition and cease to look with pride and delight, not only on our industries and science, but also on our splendid soldiers and our glorious ironclads." Luschan reinforced his call to arms with a strong stance against a "mixture of Europeans with the greater part of foreign races." Appealing to his scientist's credentials, he added that "it may be permitted to anthropology to wish a separate evolution of the 'so-called white and the so-called coloured peoples.'"[76]

Oddly enough, Luschan's position had the strange quality of satisfying the URC's two-pronged agenda: simultaneously to affirm universal humanity and to respect cultural difference. He thus found his share of supporters at the URC, even if few echoed his celebration of war. Rather, Luschan's supporters tended to endorse his argument explicitly in terms of antimiscegenation. Ignaz Zollschan of Austria, a representative of the

75. Felix von Luschan, "Anthropological View of Race," in Spiller, *Papers on Inter-racial Problems,* 13–24, esp. 18, 21.

76. Ibid., 23. For Luschan's thoughts after the URC, see Felix von Luschan, "Der Rassen-Kongreß in London 1911," *Koloniale Rundschau* 3 (1911): 597–623; and "Rassen-Anthropologie," *Die Umschau: Übersicht über die Fortschritte und Bewegungen auf dem Gesamtgebiet der Wissenschaft und Technik* 36, no. 2 (1911): 733–737. Regarding this kind of regular inconsistency in Luschan's thought, John David Smith makes a strong argument that Luschan was almost always working to disprove racialist premises and that it was W. E. B. DuBois—whose acquaintance Luschan presumably first made at the URC—who first identified the contradiction between many of Luschan's progressive and racialist tendencies. See Smith, "W. E. B. DuBois, Felix von Luschan, and Racial Reform at the *Fin de Siècle,*" *Amerikastudien* 47, no. 1 (2002): 23–38.

World Zionist Organization, for instance, extolled the distinctiveness of all "races" and argued that it was important to preserve their distinctiveness by "discouraging race-fusion."[77]

The majority of participants, however, found Luschan's argument distasteful. And like his supporters, his critics too tended to focus on miscegenation as the crux of the argument. Most common was the move simply to invert Luschan's argument and advocate for miscegenation, or "race-fusion." In these inversions, Luschan's antagonists did not contest his scientific claims; rather, they simply derived alternative moral conclusions. They thus endorsed his premise of a migrating humanity, but they argued that mixing rather than preserving races was beneficial to the physical and cultural welfare of the human population, and something thus to be positively, morally cultivated. Earl Finch of the United States, for instance, cited a range of studies that suggested, contrary to preconceptions, that miscegenation might improve either the physical or mental capacity of offspring.[78] Sir Sydney Olivier of Jamaica supported Finch's argument, noting that "as soon as you got a mixture of races, black or white, you got a better and more flexible vehicle for human genius."[79] Interestingly, however, these arguments tended to mirror Luschan's, in that they saw biological phenomena as the mechanisms through which humanity would be "improved." Like Luschan, moreover, these pro-miscegenists operated on the assumption that moral implications could be read in a straightforward fashion from biological data. They thus shared with Luschan the scientific thesis of a universal and migrating humanity—though Luschan's critics at times unintentionally rehabilitated the stable "races" that Luschan's description negated. The premise of universal humanity as a race was consequently not a point of contention; rather, moral decision seemed to break off from scientific observation precisely at the point of sexual reproduction.

A dilemma consequently emerged for the ethicists at the meeting: the very science that organizers had invested with moral authority seemed to enable completely conflicting moral responses. The tactic of Wilhelm Foerster, who represented the International Union of Ethical Societies, illustrates one available option. Taking no stance whatsoever on the question of

77. *Record of the Proceedings,* 28.
78. Ibid., 31–32.
79. Ibid., 32–33.

miscegenation, Foerster insisted that the URC focus primarily on its moral mission and that it sever morality from science altogether. He thus praised the scientific value of Luschan's work but lamented the moral dimension of Luschan's affirmation of war.[80] Ironically, Foerster's logic duplicated that expressed by Ploetz in his *Archiv für Rassen- und Gesellschafts-Biologie.* Announcing the URC to his readers, Ploetz described it as naive from the outset in that it assumed ethics and science could inform one another.[81] Ploetz in fact lamented the lost opportunity of the congress, which he thought could have had important scientific value if it were not weighted down by its moral aims. Although working from opposing angles, Foerster and Ploetz mirrored one another in their willingness to keep science and ethics in separate realms.

Tönnies, however, took a position more similar to that of Brajendranath Seal, a professor of Cooch Behar's College in India. A leading enthusiast of the event, Seal had nonetheless mocked the miscegenation controversy, noting that he "did not know whether he was a miscegene because he did not possess the genealogical records of his family from Adam downwards. Those more happily situated in that respect might pride themselves on purity of race."[82] Yet Seal's Hegelianism, which led him to speak often of the *Zeitgeist* and the inevitable progress in the world, also led him to insist that "there was no conflict between the teachings of science and the demands of the modern conscience."[83] Ethics and science, for Seal, must go hand in hand, because that is how history rationally proceeds. If they do not seem to fit perfectly, history must further evolve. Either science or ethics was imperfect until it complemented the other. Albeit less informed by Hegelian logic, Tönnies too insisted that ethics and science must coincide. His observation of the miscegenation controversies, however, prompted him to assess how ethics and science could be retheorized in a global framework and thus brought back into alignment.

Before the congress, Tönnies had submitted for the precirculated collection an article titled "Science and Art, Literature and the Press." In this

---

80. Ibid., 25.
81. Alfred Ploetz, "First Universal Races Congress," *Archiv für Rassen- und Gesellschafts-Biologie* 8, no. 3 (1911): 412–413.
82. *Record of the Proceedings,* 34.
83. Ibid., 66.

short essay, he reminisced about the great "cosmopolitan thinkers" of the eighteenth century who understood that "any scientific question, wheresoever it may be discussed, appeals to all cultivated nations."[84] This position was not considerably different from the one he had taken in the 1890s when he supported the founding of the DGEK. There, as we saw in chapter 1, he articulated a modern, secular, universalist ethics on the singular basis of science.

After hearing the anthropological discussions, however, Tönnies began to qualify his celebration of science, reminding himself and others that "the Congress had a scientific as well as a moral and practical character."[85] While scientific observation was crucial to the kind of work the URC sought to do, it could not be taken alone. Likewise, the moral project of the URC would end in egregious error if it failed to listen to and account for scientific evidence. But somehow, the relationship of ethics to science needed to be better theorized. Tönnies thus took the opportunity, in his busy reporting after the URC, to further reflect on the often uncomfortable relationship between science and moral valuation that had arisen. Writing almost one year later, he again celebrated the event's basic intentions: "It was a grand idea to observe these matters 'in the light of science and the modern conscience.' "[86] But he wondered now if the organizers had been expecting too much in this regard. In matters of global relations, "science and conscience should be consulted," he concurred, but unfortunately science is not unanimous on issues of race and its meanings for human interaction. To be sure, he held to the idea that *only* science was in the position to provide a common language for all of humanity: "The fact is that scientific thought and consciousness of humans of all nations and races is binding and uniting, that the mission of science is directed toward universal humanity." This he contrasted to "morals, institutions, religions and related opinions" that do not necessarily enable communication across cultural difference. But unlike the optimistic organizers of the URC, he had to conclude that science does not *guarantee* such global communication. Science cannot "in general

---

84. Ferdinand Tönnies, "Science and Art, Literature and the Press," in Spiller, *Papers on Inter-racial Problems,* 233.

85. *Record of the Proceedings,* 33.

86. Ferdinand Tönnies, "Nachreden des Rassenkongresses," *Ethische Kultur* 20, no. 12 (1912): 89.

repudiate what is expressed in sentiment and will," he lamented, nor "can it prove that it is good and just to encounter all humans as human." Indeed, he came to believe after the URC that science has a tendency to *avoid* moral considerations: "Scientific thought wants to provide moral considerations. And the race question was said to be discussed in a scientific manner at the Congress. [But] this required that ethical feelings were suppressed. And in that lay the fundamentally contradictory character of the gathering."[87]

For Tönnies, the challenge was thus to sort out how science and ethics might operate together, that is, how one must delimit science such that its moral potential is realized rather than avoided. He had thus been unable to join Foerster, his fellow representative of the DGEK, when Foerster simply rejected the moral claims asserted by Luschan. To do so would be to allow morality and science to continue to operate in two radically separate registers, such that the one could not influence the other. Tönnies's own response was first to differentiate between different kinds of sciences, in particular between anthropology and sociology. So long as anthropology concentrated on physical human characteristics, it was vulnerable to the mistake "of assuming that physical and mental, intellectual and moral characters always coincided."[88]

Second, like Freud, Tönnies insisted that moral considerations must play out *solely* within the realm of the cultural: only sociology was equipped to discuss the kinds of cultural interactions that were the object of the congress. In his precirculated paper, Tönnies had stated sociology's object of concern to be "social life as a problem," or "the problem of moral life, which, to a large extent, means the peaceful life of a people."[89] Concerned only with the social life of a people, and concerned simultaneously with what makes *peaceful* life possible, sociology need never get itself caught up in the biological morass that threatened to undermine the moral ambitions of the congress. And yet, for Tönnies, sociology retained all the characteristics of a science—a science compatible with morality because it takes culturally specific morality as its object of study. At the URC itself, he hesitantly began to entertain the notion of "comparative sociology," in which the *methods* of talking about cultural moralities would be universal

87. Ibid., 89–90.
88. *Record of the Proceedings,* 34.
89. Tönnies, "Science and Art," 239.

while the *object* of study—distinct cultures—would acknowledge and affirm cultural difference. Like Luschan, Tönnies thus found a way to talk about universalism and cultural difference together; unlike Luschan, however, he could do so only by excluding altogether questions of biological reproduction.

The Limits of Reform

It is noteworthy that all three cases explored above found sexuality to be the troubled site at which, in a moral framework, ethics and moral conscience must be reconsidered. Each perspective brought together, in its own way, considerations of the most global and the most local. In previous chapters, we have seen how considerations of sexuality and ethics could be meaningful for notions of citizenship, or for an understanding of how the individual relates to a social and political community. In this more global context, the same holds true, though here the widely diverse possibilities come to the fore: the three cases suggest that the intersection of the global and the sexual were part of a broad effort to reconceptualize the individual's relationship to social groups, but that the same intersection at the point of moral conscience carried no singular or necessary implication. For Ehrenfels (and for Luschan), for instance, the sexual played a crucial role in the Darwinian struggle for survival in an era of global commerce and migration. For Freud, the sexual implied the shared fate—and shared moral and cultural dilemma—of global communities. For Tönnies, who was most explicitly engaged in the URC's project of contemplating a community of global citizens, the sexual meant trying to think about the aspects of human existence that transcend cultural difference. Significantly, the rise of questions of sexuality and especially of biological reproduction at the URC also highlighted for Tönnies the need to problematize the relationship of ethics to science.

How, then, did these diverse global perspectives relate to reform? Of the three, Ehrenfels articulated the most dramatic and comprehensive vision of reform. When confronted with combative visions of racialized ethics, however, both Freud and Tönnies sought possibilities of the universal in humanity; at the same time, they both began to put a brake on reform. Observations by recent theorists of race and racism might help shed some light on this development. Ann Stoler, for instance, has suggested that we understand "race, racism, and its representations" not as departures from progressive, liberal ideals but rather as "structured entailments of post-enlightenment universals, as formative features of modernity, as deeply embedded in bourgeois liberalism." In short, racial thinking is part and parcel of a progressive modernity; it "harnesses itself to varied progressive projects and shapes the social taxonomies."[90] In these terms, Ehrenfels must be seen as the most "progressive" of the three examples examined here. He was most invested in the emancipatory possibilities of both social technologies and scientific knowledge. It is significant that Ehrenfels himself did not frame his racialized campaign explicitly in terms of colonialism, empire, and the common anxieties about miscegenation—the sites where Stoler and other race theorists have suggested "modernity" in its industrialized, socially engineered, and racially denoted form evolved. Rather, Ehrenfels illustrates how flexible and productive fantasies of race could be even when they were not tied directly to colonial projects.[91]

This view of race as a "progressive" logic provides a way to interpret as well the brakes that Freud and Tönnies put on reform. Both seemed to be splitting their indebtedness to an Enlightenment legacy. Tönnies would not renounce science as the basis for modern ethics, but he called for critical attention to the limits of science and to the proper *objects* of scientific knowledge. Freud, conversely, never renounced his liberal individualism and his search for a complementary ethics within psychoanalysis. Yet he simultaneously contested models of the liberal individual and of mechanistic configurations of the moral law.

In a similar vein, the interventions by Freud and Tönnies speak also to a more "local" issue of reform culture identified by the German historian Detlev Peukert. Like Stoler and her identification of racialist logic with modernity and progress, Peukert found in the reform culture of the fin de siècle a more ominous dimension of progress and the seeds of the "Final

90. Ann Laura Stoler, *Race and the Education of Desire: Foucault's History of Sexuality and the Colonial Order of Things* (Durham, N.C., 1995), 9. For a complementary argument, see Anne McClintock, *Imperial Leather: Race, Gender, and Sexuality in the Colonial Contest* (New York, 1995).

91. The classic statement on the role of fantasy in German formations of race and empire is Susanne Zantop, *Colonial Fantasies: Conquest, Family, and Nation in Precolonial Germany, 1770–1870* (Durham, N.C., 1997).

Solution." According to Peukert, the nascent human sciences and affiliated reform movements mobilized their Enlightenment idealism to seek ways to improve life for all. These movements, however, were prone to rationalization and professionalization over time, such that their mechanisms of reform could survive even when the aims changed. With regime change in 1933, and a corresponding redistribution of support within the sciences, efforts at social perfection easily shifted focus without shifting methods, from life to "life unworthy of life."[92] Peukert's narrative focuses on the survival of a mechanistic reason that colonizes what members of the Frankfurt School liked to call "critical reason."[93] Yet the examples of Freud and Tönnies give us pause to consider the narrative anew. To be sure, neither Freud nor Tönnies seemed to be reading the future or intuiting the murderous potential of reform. But both seemed to be sensing the mechanistic and social-regulatory possibilities implicit in reform. In their efforts to check those possibilities, their examples suggest the existence of a critical awareness within the reform culture regarding the regulatory potentials of modernity—in both its racialist and its mechanistic variants.

92. Peukert's most concise and extreme formulation of the narrative came in his short essay, "The Genesis of the 'Final Solution' from the Spirit of Science," in *Re-evaluating the Third Reich,* ed. Thomas Childers and Jane Caplan (New York, 1993). More elaborated and subtle versions are in *Grenzen der Sozialdisziplinierung: Aufstieg und Krise der Jugendfürsorge von 1878 bis 1932* (Cologne, 1986). For responses to Peukert's work, see the collection edited by Frank Bajohr, Werner Johe, and Uwe Lohalm, *Zivilisation und Barbarei: Die widersprüchlichen Potentiale der Moderne* (Hamburg, 1991), especially Bajohr, "Detlev Peukerts Beiträge zur Sozialgeschichte der Moderne," 7–16, and Geoff Eley, "Die deutsche Geschichte und die Widersprüche der Moderne: Das Beispiel des Kaiserreiches," 17–65.

93. See, for example, the introduction to Theodor Adorno and Max Horkheimer, *Dialektik der Aufklärung: Philosophische Fragmente* (Amsterdam, 1947); or Jürgen Habermas, "Technology and Science as 'Ideology,'" in *Toward a Rational Society: Student Protest, Science, and Politics,* trans. Jeremy J. Shapiro (Boston, 1968), 81–127.

5

MORAL LAWS AND IMPOSSIBLE LAWS

The "Female Homosexual" and the Criminal Code

The grounds that justify the punishment of unnatural fornication
between men lead logically to the punishment of unnatural fornication
between women as well, even if the latter is neither
so common nor so public as the former.

Proposal for a German Criminal Code, 1909

"Female homosexuality, which is certainly not less common than male homosexuality, although much less obvious, has not only been overlooked by the law, but has also been neglected by psychoanalytic research." Thus opened Freud's 1920 study, "On the Psychogenesis of a Case of Female Homosexuality."[1] The reference to the law makes it a rather peculiar opening for his first sustained treatment of female homosexuality, as the article never returned to the legal theme. The opening sentence takes on an even more peculiar character when one realizes that it is factually incorrect.

Significant portions of this chapter were first published as "In the Name of the Law: The 'Female Homosexual' and the Criminal Code in Fin de Siècle Germany," by Tracie Matysik, from *Journal of the History of Sexuality* 13, no. 1, pp. 26–48. Copyright © 2004 by the University of Texas Press. All rights reserved.

1. Sigmund Freud, "Über die Psychogenese eines Falles von weiblicher Homosexualität," in *GW* 12, 271.

Female homosexuality had been criminalized in Austria since 1532.[2] Moreover, although female homosexuality was not punished in Germany at the time, it had not gone unnoticed by the law there either. To the contrary, the 1909 publication of the government-commissioned *Proposal for a German Criminal Code* rewrote the existing Criminal Code's §175, which already designated male homosexuality as criminal, as §250, extending the criminal designation to female homosexuality. Where §175 had criminalized *"widernatürliche Unzucht"* (unnatural fornication) between men and between humans and animals, the proposed §250 would punish *"widernatürliche Unzucht"* between women as well.[3] In addition, §250 increased the severity of punishment over §175: whereas hitherto male homosexuality could result in prison and loss of civil rights, the new paragraph retained those stipulations while adding that a sentence of no less than six months and up to five years of jail would be mandatory.[4]

The point is not to dwell on Freud's factual oversight. Rather, it is to ask whether, despite the explicit factual incorrectness, there wasn't something more accurate in Freud's claim that the law had overlooked female homosexuality. In the case of psychoanalysis, female homosexuality had long made its presence felt. Yet it was routinely marginalized, as it did not correspond to psychoanalytic laws of desire.[5] The discussion

2. Claudia Schoppmann, *Verbotene Verhältnisse: Frauenliebe, 1938–1945* (Berlin, 1999), 126. See also Hanna Hacker, *Frauen und Freundinnen: Studien zur "weiblichen Homosexualität" am Beispiel Österreich, 1870–1938* (Weinheim, 1987).

3. As becomes clearer below, the debates focused largely on legal terminology. Two terms in particular were contested by opponents of §250: *widernatürliche Unzucht,* which could be translated roughly as "unnatural fornication"; and *Beischlafähnliche Handlungen,* meaning something like "deeds similar to intercourse." Such sexual euphemisms functioning as legal terminology were perhaps particularly prone to multiple interpretations. In order to highlight the disagreement around these central terms and to minimize my own interpretive distortion, I leave them in the original.

4. *Vorentwurf zu einem Deutschen Strafgesetzbuch* (Berlin, 1909), 691; *Strafgesetzbuch für das Deutsche Reich,* 22nd ed. (Berlin, 1907), 159–160. Austria also published a penal code in 1909 that punished female homosexuality with imprisonment (*Vorentwurf zu einem Österreichischen Strafgesetzbuch* [Berlin, 1909]). But because this simply continued an existing practice, it did not elicit the same public outcry as in Germany.

5. See especially the scant treatment in "Drei Abhandlungen zur Sexualtheorie," 1905, in *GW* 5, 27–145, in which Freud treats male homosexuality in relative depth, only to avoid the topic of female homosexuality on its own by suggesting that the analysis of male homosexuality applies. See also "Bruchstück einer Hysterie-Analyse," also 1905, in *GW* 5, 161–286, in which mention of Dora's possible homosexual inclinations is relegated to a footnote. Teresa

surrounding §250 in Germany suggests that a parallel logic pertained in the legal arena.

Commissioned by the government, the 1909 *Proposal* was intended to be publicly debated and, after revision, adopted to replace the Prussian-dominated Criminal Code of 1871. It appeared in a context of broad efforts at legal reform that were spreading across Europe.[6] Although never adopted—in large part because of the interruption of the war—the *Proposal* nevertheless elicited considerable controversy, drawing on a public that had already been mobilized in the wake of the German Civil Code in preceding decades. Throughout the nineteenth century, liberal factions had advocated for legal codification as a vehicle of state and social modernization. The Civil Code was characterized by contemporaries, however, as a mixed bag of progressive and reactive tendencies, at once extending equally to the entire Reich, if not applying equally to all individuals within the Reich.[7] Contemporaries consequently learned to view codification as a somewhat ambiguous project. To be sure, the *Proposal* and its §250 elicited less commentary and mobilization than did its Civil Code predecessor. Yet those contemporaries with an interest in the matter one way or another had learned much from the Civil Code controversy and were well prepared to discern the ambiguities and questionable appeals to equality that appeared in the new *Proposal* and its §250. While some heralded the *Proposal* as introducing a new level of equality, especially insofar as punishment pertained to men and women, others lamented that it tended toward

---

de Lauretis argues that Freud's model of desire was incompatible with his model of female homosexuality, and that the disjuncture prohibited the recognition of the lesbian as subject. De Lauretis, *The Practice of Love: Lesbian Sexuality and Perverse Desire* (Bloomington, Ind., 1994), 29–78. Diana Fuss has discussed in figurative terms Freud's reference to the law in the "Psychogenesis" case. Arguing that Freud associates homosexuality with identification rather than with desire, she traces how in his argument the homosexual woman "falls"—according to Newtonian laws of physics—from desire to identification. See Fuss, *Identification Papers* (New York, 1995), 57–82.

6. Proposals for new criminal codes appeared at roughly the same time for Germany, Austria, Switzerland, Serbia, Sweden, and Japan. A recent history of legal culture and its reform in the German Kaiserreich is Benjamin Hett, *Death in the Tiergarten: Murder and Criminal Justice in the Kaiser's Berlin* (Cambridge, Mass., 2004). On reforms in criminology that fed into legal reform, see Wetzell, *Inventing the Criminal*.

7. Michael Stolleis, *Konstitution und Intervention: Studien zur Geschichte des öffentlichen Rechts im 19. Jahrhundert* (Frankfurt am Main, 2001), 195–196. On the politics of the Code, see John, *Politics and the Law*.

more severe punishment, particularly in the realm of moral offenses, and only increased the state's intervention in the private lives of citizens.

The controversy around §250 proved to be a site at which the ambiguities of legal (and cultural) struggles with modernity condensed, and it is especially illuminating in the broad picture of the ongoing public ethics discussions. Central to the debate around §250 was the question of what exactly produced the criminal character who could be prosecuted for female-female sexual acts, and what physiological, social, and moral factors might combine to bring this character about. It presupposed from the outset a sexualized moral subject, though a subject who could be criminalized for a sexuality deemed immoral. But this subject, the "female homosexual," was a new category in the landscape, one previously defined neither by the law nor by ethics discussions. The debates that followed the publication of the proposal reveal the diverse language and approaches contemporaries could use to talk about the relationship of state-enforced legal codes to the moral law, as well as the ways critics could mobilize the moral law against state-enforced law. The debates also illustrate the multiple interpretations and uses contemporaries could find for the sexualized subject. Indeed, the debates not only demonstrate how difficult it was to regulate the "female homosexual" as a category; they indicate as well how the unregulatability of this new criminal subject could have spillover effects, bringing out the instability that lay latent in otherwise seemingly stable sexualized moral identities such as the homosexual man and the heterosexual woman.

The positions taken in the §250 controversy fell into roughly three categories: (1) advocacy for the paragraph, coming primarily from the authors of the *Proposal* itself; (2) critique of the paragraph from a legal-medical standpoint; and (3) critique of the paragraph from a feminist standpoint. (I have found no instances of self-identified female homosexuals participating in the discussion.) Before we turn to these positions in detail, however, it is helpful first to view a few background events and circumstances that informed the various arguments for and against criminalization.

Background: §175

The *Proposal*'s §250 came as a severe setback to the homosexual emancipation movement, which had historically crystallized around protest of

§175.[8] As an organized movement, homosexual emancipation first gathered steam in 1897, when the Berlin medical doctor Magnus Hirschfeld joined forces with the Leipzig publisher Max Spohr and the ministerial official Erich Oberg to form the Scientific Humanitarian Committee (Wissenschaftlich-humanitäre Komitee). Together they brought to the public a sudden wave of publications on homosexuality (23 by 1899) and founded Hirschfeld's *Jahrbuch für sexuelle Zwischenstufen (Yearbook for Sexually Intermediate Types)*. The movement against §175 seemed to be making steady progress, which leaders of the movement attributed to the successful circulation of scientific studies about homosexuality.[9] The success came to an abrupt halt, however, when in 1906 a series of public scandals erupted, involving the supposed homosexuality of many of Kaiser Wilhelm II's closest friends and advisers. A stream of libel suits, perjury charges, and criminal trials that involved the kaiser's advisers, the chancellor, military officers, and civilians left the kaiser and his regime of "personal rule" fundamentally weakened.[10] As a result, one participant observed, "no one would dare anymore to speak in public about the lifting or even softening of §175."[11]

Without a §175 to contest, there existed less pressing motivation for an organized female homosexual movement at the turn of the century.[12] To the extent that such a movement existed, it had been intertwined closely with the women's movement more generally, which was itself, as we have

8. Examples of the historiography on homosexuality and the homosexual emancipation movement in Germany include James Steakley, *The Homosexual Emancipation Movement in Germany* (New York, 1975); Gisela Bleibtreu-Ehrenberg, *Tabu Homosexualität: Die Geschichte eines Vorurteils* (Frankfurt am Main, 1978); Hans-Georg Stümke, *Homosexuelle in Deutschland: Eine politische Geschichte* (Munich, 1989); Freunde eines schwules Museum in Berlin e.V., ed., *Die Geschichte des §175: Strafrecht gegen Homosexuelle* (Berlin, 1990).

9. August Eulenburg, "Homosexualität und neuer Strafgesetzentwurf," *Deutsche Montags-Zeitung,* December 19, 1910.

10. On the political repercussions of the scandal, see Isabel V. Hull, *The Entourage of Kaiser Wilhelm II, 1888–1918* (New York, 1982), 145.

11. Eulenburg, "Homosexualität," 1.

12. Studies devoted explicitly to female homosexuality include Lillian Faderman and Brigitte Eriksson, eds., *Lesbians in Germany, 1890's–1920's* (Tallahassee, Fla., 1990); Claudia Schoppmann, *Der Skorpion: Frauenliebe in der Weimarer Republik* (Hamburg, 1985); Marti M. Lybeck, "Gender, Sexuality, and Belonging: Female Homosexuality in Germany, 1890–1933" (Ph.D. diss., University of Michigan, 2007). A useful historiographical survey is Bernd-Ulrich Hergemöller, *Einführung in die Historiographie der Homosexualitäten* (Tübingen, 1999).

seen, internally divided in 1909 over such issues as equality and suffrage, as well as so-called radical sexual politics. As Lillian Faderman and Brigitte Eriksson note, the areas of education reform, expanded female work opportunities, and female suffrage "were of concern to many German women in general," but "to lesbians they were vital." For the latter, "they were the *sine qua non* of their ability to live as lesbians without submitting to heterosexual marriage for the sake of maintaining middle class lifestyles."[13] Despite shared concerns, however, relations between heterosexual and homosexual women within the women's movement were not always easy. Anna Rueling, for instance, had openly criticized the women's movement in 1904 for its failure to advocate for homosexual women's rights, despite the contributions by homosexual women to the movement. The "injustice," Rueling had argued, derived in part from the refusal to acknowledge that many within the women's movement were homosexual, and in part from fear of scorn from "the still blind and ignorant masses" if the news were to get out.[14]

Proposal for the Law: §250

Controversies surrounding the homosexual emancipation movement, the matter of state interest in private sexual lives, and the question of women's legal equality were thus all in play before the *Proposal* appeared, and they all surfaced in the official justification for the proposed §250. In reference to male homosexuality, the authors defended the paragraph first and foremost in the name of state interest: "*Widernatürliche Unzucht,* especially between men, is a danger for the state, as it effectively and most severely damages men in their character and in their civil existence, shatters healthy family life, and corrupts male youth." It also derives from "questionable drives" that "often have the most severe consequences, such as

13. Faderman and Eriksson, *Lesbians in Germany,* xii–xiii.

14. Anna Rueling, "What Interest Does the Women's Movement Have in the Homosexual Question?" in Faderman and Eriksson, *Lesbians in Germany,* 91–92. On Rueling's address, see Biddy Martin, *Femininity Played Straight: The Significance of Being Lesbian* (New York, 1996), 49–54. Martin demonstrates how Rueling depends on a notion of lesbian "extraordinariness" in relation to heterosexual women. This contested similarity or dissimilarity, I argue, is very much at stake in the feminist response to the *Proposal.*

death, crime, and the ruin of entire families." To ward off these threats, the authors concluded, "it is in the urgent interest of the state to confront rigorously this diffusive type of *Unzucht,* and also, through maintenance of the criminal injunction, to resist efforts to establish [homosexuality] as a mere physical and psychological anomaly."[15]

With this last reference, the authors transitioned from the matter of state interest to a direct statement against the homosexual emancipation movement, adding: "The *Proposal* rejects as unproven and in contradiction with the experiences of practical life the currently common view that same-sex *Unzucht* has to do with an irresistible pathological natural drive, [a view] that would eliminate or significantly reduce criminal responsibility." To further their argument, the authors spoke of the "moral deterioration" behind claims about innate sexual disposition. They compared the homosexual individual to "many normally sexually dispositioned people" who "suffer from an abnormally high sexual drive," and noted that the latter is a condition that "a judge could not and does not take into consideration" in legal matters. Bolstered by the comparison, the authors concluded that "a concession to that view [that homosexuality is natural] would thus be equally unjustified as it could lead to a critical reversal of the moral perspective." That is, legal recognition of sexual orientation as natural would undermine a popular moral judgment against homosexuality.[16]

The justification for extending the paragraph to women was brief, largely restating the case against men: "The grounds that are standard for the punishment of *widernatürliche Unzucht* between men leads logically also to the punishment of *Unzucht* between women, even if this is not so common or does not appear so often in public. The danger for the life of the family and the youth is the same." Nevertheless, in a backhanded response to advocates for women's equal rights before the law, the authors maintained that the revised wording that would criminalize *widernatür-liche Unzucht* between "persons of the same sex," and not simply between men, "removes the previous inequality."[17] In other words, if women wanted equal rights under the law—which they did not have—they would have to be subject to equal punishments as well.

15. *Vorentwurf zu einem Deutschen Strafgesetzbuch,* 689–690.
16. Ibid., 690.
17. Ibid., 691.

In short, the authors set out in the *Proposal* the terms of the controversy around §250: (1) the relationship between law, state interest, and public and private morality—notably leaving the constitution of "morality" undefined; (2) the scientific understanding of sexuality and the relationship of science to both law and morality; and (3) the notion of gender equality before the law. One further source of contention arose out of the *Proposal,* and that was precisely the one of *naming* the object of concern. Regarding legal definitions, the authors explained that *"widernatürliche Unzucht"* would remain defined as it had been under §175: as *"beischlafähnliche Handlungen"* (actions similar to intercourse).[18] Perhaps more than any other part of the *Proposal,* this definitional clarification, which appeared almost as an afterthought, presented protesters with their strongest grounds for challenging §250.

Legal-Medical Protest

Much of the initial response from the protesting sexologists and jurists took the issue of legal definition as its starting point. As Hermann Rohleder, a medical doctor from Leipzig, pointed out in "Paragraph 250, the Replacement of Paragraph 175 in its Potential Consequences for the Female Sex," the terms *widernatürliche Unzucht* and *beischlafähnliche Handlungen* had long histories of legal uncertainty. In 1880, when the term was under legal scrutiny, it was suggested that *widernatürliche Unzucht* refer solely to "the introduction of the penis into a natural or artificially constructed bodily hole," but the supreme court had ruled against such a limited definition. Subsequent discussions had considered "friction," a generalized "introduction of a body part into the body of another," or "the least short touch of the lower bodies against one another." All these, Rohleder claimed, had only diluted the term's legal precision. He thus demanded "a more exact definition of the details of *widernatürliche Unzucht* from the purely medical standpoint."[19]

---

18. Ibid., 692.

19. Hermann Rohleder, "Paragraph 250, der Ersatz des Paragraph 175, in seinen eventuellen Folgen für das weibliche Geschlecht," *Reichs-Medizinal-Anzeiger* 36, no. 3 (1911): 67–68.

If terminology proved to be a legal complication in the case of male homosexuality, it was even more complicated in reference to female homosexuality. Unlike many of his fellow protesters of the paragraph who simply held the notion of female-female *beischlafähnliche Handlungen* as altogether inconceivable, Rohleder did not rule out the possibility. Rather, he delineated what he took to be the four possible "types" of female-female sexual acts (1) "mutual masturbation," or "mutual rubbing with the fingers...(possibly inserted into the vagina)"; (2) "lambendo genitalia," or cunnilingus including the "introduction of the tongue into the genitals"; (3) "tribadism," defined as the "mutual rubbing" of the genitals; and (4) "female cunnilingus," consisting of the excitation of the clitoris. Acknowledging that each of these acts bears similarities to *beischlafähnliche Handlungen,* he nevertheless insisted that "despite their perverse character," none qualified technically if *beischlafähnliche Handlungen* were to be understood as penetrative intercourse. Drawing his conclusions from what he took to be the basic facts of female physiology, that is, "the lack of an active reproductive organ akin to that of the male sex," he argued that in the female case it is impossible to determine "where *beischlafähnliche Handlungen* ... should begin, what belongs to [the concept], and what not."[20] In short, the female-female sexual acts did not conform to existing and legitimate legal categories—including those of the *Proposal*—and thus would necessarily remain impervious to legal discourse.

Rohleder then took the opportunity of §250 to argue logically against antihomosexuality legislation altogether. Before the publication of the *Proposal,* he had maintained that on grounds of legal equality, §175 would be legitimate only if it were extended to women. According to his analysis of the legal language of the paragraph, however, the female homosexual could never qualify as a criminal for a concrete act in the manner of the male homosexual. That is, although something called the "male homosexual" could be tied to a specific illegal sexual act known as *beischlafähnliche Handlungen,* and thereby could be declared a criminal subject, no such direct linkage could be made between a female homosexual and a concrete act. The female homosexual as subject responsible for performing the acts that would be said to define her could not be concretely identified. Since

20. Ibid., 69.

the paragraph thus could not effectively punish the female homosexual, Rohleder maintained, it would have to renounce its claims to punish the male homosexual as well, at least if it were intended to apply equally to male and female homosexuals. Logically, the paragraph would have to fall by the wayside.

Rohleder's argument slyly inverted the equalizing claims of the *Proposal* to argue against the paragraph altogether. Yet, though such an argument was put forth for progressive purposes—that is, to counter a law that many held to be a relic of medieval prejudices—one cannot overlook the fact that the logic of the argument relied on the banishment of the female homosexual as subject, on her terminological effervescence. Male homosexuality could be tied to concrete agents performing identifiable acts within the language of the law. Female homosexuality, on the other hand, could not be broken down into agent and act, and thereby defied legal discourse. Rohleder's argument for the legal emancipation of male homosexuality thus rested on this technical obfuscation of the homosexual woman as agent of her deeds.

To an extent this component of the discussion resonated with a long history of legal incomprehension in the face of female homosexuality. For example, the 1721 case of Catharina Margarethe Linck, thought to be the last woman executed in Germany for homosexuality, demonstrated a juridical struggle to discern if a woman could be capable of a sexual crime according to the letter of the law. Jurists involved in that case sought to deduce from biblical writings what exactly constituted female-female sex and whether or not it was unholy. That is, they aimed to interpret the "divine" ruling.[21] On this score, however—on the grounds from which law derives its legitimacy—the discussion around §250 departed from its historical predecessors, reflecting rather the uniqueness of the fin-de-siècle legal climate.

Historians have often suggested that nineteenth-century legal codes witnessed a reversal of Enlightenment legal philosophy, reinserting "morality"

21. For a complete history of the Linck case, see "A Lesbian Execution in Germany, 1721: The Trial Records," trans. Brigitte Eriksson, in *Historical Perspectives on Homosexuality,* ed. Salvatore J. Licata and Robert P. Petersen (New York, 1981), 27–40. In "The Myth of Lesbian Impunity: Capital Laws from 1270 to 1791," pp. 11–25 in the same volume, Louis Crompton situates the case in long-term historical perspective, arguing that contrary to common claims, female homosexuality was indeed punishable and punished in the Middle Ages.

concerns that had been purged by their Enlightenment predecessors.[22] As the *Proposal* did little but strengthen laws "against morality" (*wider Sittlichkeit*), it conformed at least somewhat to that pattern. Yet the discussions around §250 would suggest anything but an antimodern public approach to legal culture. Especially common among both medical and juridical critics of the *Proposal,* in fact, was the direct appeal to science as the basis of law. As the jurist Joseph Kohler exclaimed: "Science is not something simply to invoke in order to write volumes on the present condition of criminal law. It belongs above all to the legislative realm!"[23] Likewise, Rohleder's demand for precise legal-scientific definitions reflected the prevalent attempts among critics of the *Proposal* to understand both sexuality and the law scientifically. This commitment held that specific, identifiable acts were to be punished, not the soul or the general disposition of their bearer. The appeal to science did not necessarily pit Enlightenment rationality against moral appeals. In play rather was a struggle over the very definition of morality itself, as the legal and medical opponents of §250 offered their own notion of morality as a fusion with science.

Hirschfeld, for instance, appealed to a scientifically informed approach to morality in his opposition to §250. Deducing that the primary motivation for §250 had been social "feelings of antipathy" against homosexuality, Hirschfeld questioned the reliability of the "sensibility of the people" as the ground on which to construct a legal or moral order: "The science of morality demonstrates not only that the subjective perspective of the public derives from often errant assumptions, but also that it is very unstable." Countering reliance on traditions of public sentiment, he suggested that "ethics and law are indebted for their existence and necessity to the inadequacy of this perspective." That is, ethics and law are to be rational correctives to the historical vicissitudes of public opinion. His argument for the objective purity of the law derived in part from what he took to be the law's own power of influence: "In reference to the sentiment of the

22. David Blackbourn, "The Discreet Charm of the Bourgeoisie: Reappraising German History in the Nineteenth Century," in Blackbourn and Geoff Eley, *The Peculiarities of German History: Bourgeois Society and Politics in Nineteenth-Century Germany* (Oxford, 1984); Isabel V. Hull, *Sexuality, State, and Civil Society in Germany, 1700–1815* (Ithaca, N.Y., 1996), esp. 333–370.

23. Josef Kohler, "Der deutsche und der österreichische Vorentwurf eines Strafgesetzbuchs," *Archiv für Strafrecht und Strafprozess* 56 (1909): 285.

people, it is necessary further to recognize the high degree to which it is influenced by the punishment regulations themselves and by the measures of the state-sponsored legal profession."[24] In other words, the existence of particular laws may themselves produce certain "moral" prejudices. It was consequently incumbent on lawmakers to purge antiquated prejudices from the law rather than to understand law simply as a mirror of autono mously existing moral sentiments. Hirschfeld thus tried to argue on the one hand that the law is productive of social morality and, on the other, that the law should extract itself from the arbitrary character of public sentiment and its historically contingent mores. This "progressive" alternative favored an "objective" legal code informed by the dictates of science.

Heinrich Winzer went into more detail on this score. On the one hand, he called for a scientifically enlightened legal code, aligned with the principles of the legal state and free from the "ghosts" of the past. Law should not, however, limit itself to this merely negative definition of eliminating ghosts. Rather, he maintained, it should play a more productive and edifying role. Taking Hegel as his guide, he held that the conditions of legitimate law would thus be "first, that the laws are necessary, sufficient, and *justified;* and second [that they provide] for the citizens a moral certainty, education, and insight." On its own, Winzer maintained, "the majority can be backward and in certain points inferior, even immoral." It is the task of the state as a rational entity to facilitate public development to "moral maturity": "It is not because the 'state' represents the public that its regime should be honored....History knows a *progress* of moral attitudes. But rather, the citizen bows obediently to its coercion insofar as the state represents the reasonable and meaningful, the superior and the moral, and that which represents well-being in the most noble sense."[25] In short, an enlightened, scientifically informed law should bring about an equally enlightened, scientifically informed popular morality.

Following a parallel line of thought, Kohler also demanded that the law have an edifying effect. He developed his stance, however, explicitly in opposition to what he called "the false individualism of Kant." Kohler

---

24. Magnus Hirschfeld, "Kritik des §250 und seiner Motive im Vorentwurf zu einem Deutschen Strafgesetzbuch," *Archiv für Kriminal-Anthropologie und Kriminalistik* 38 (1910): 94.

25. F. Heinrich Winzer, *Der neue §175 RStGB! §250 des "Vorentwurfs zu einem Deutschen Strafgesetzbuch": Kritik und Vorschläge* (Leipzig, 1910), 3–5.

objected to Kant's treatment of the problem of free will, insisting that it is misleading to consider "the question of free will as a metaphysical question; it is [rather] a purely psychological, even a psychological-empirical question." Arguing that Kant was misguided when he located free will in the "beyond," Kohler called rather on a "material" free will:

> And when one maintains that free determination of the will stands in contradiction with causality, so those determinists who believe themselves to be moving completely within the terrestrial demonstrate that they get caught forever in the metaphysical wake; for the claim that causality is structured so as to make free determination of the will impossible is not a product of observation and of science based on observation, but rather a product of the mechanical world view. The mechanical world view is also metaphysical because it denies everything non-mechanical, a denial which can only be justified on the basis of a metaphysical standpoint.

Kohler then equated the materiality of free will with an explicitly embodied will—in contrast to the *Proposal,* which, he maintained, conceived of free will "in the popular sense, and that is in the sense of indeterminism." He explained that "the whole *Volksanschauung* [outlook of the people] founds criminal law on the idea that the individual could also have done otherwise, and regards the individual being as an autocrat in the realm of determination of the will, that is as an autocrat which is dependent neither on the internal nor the external, and is coerced neither by the internal nor by the external."[26]

Kohler's and Winzer's arguments coincided conveniently with Hirschfeld's scientific interpretation of "sexually intermediate types," often referred to as the "third sex."[27] According to Hirschfeld's theory, homosexual men and women were usually found to have bodily characteristics of the opposite sex. These features could range from genital developments to hair growth, voice, build, and comportment "typical" of the other sex. This theory of sexual crossing both assumed and argued that sexual orientation derived from bodily composition. Sexual orientation accordingly took on a

---

26. Kohler, "Der deutsche und der österreichische Vorentwurf," 297.

27. James Jones, *"We of the Third Sex": Literary Representations of Homosexuality in Wilhelmine Germany* (New York, 1990), 43–91.

"natural" status, derived from bodily "law," a fin-de-siècle variation on the idea of "natural law." Applying Hirschfeld's theory, Rohleder asserted that *widernatürliche Unzucht* was an impossible concept when applied to homosexuality: "These homosexual acts are 'contrary to nature,' however, only from the standpoint that they do not serve in the production of descendants or in the preservation of the species. But this standpoint is one-sided insofar as nature also produced homosexuality, and for the pure *Urning* [homosexual] normal intercourse is contrary to nature, while same-sex is natural."[28] Punishment would consequently be a violation of the "natural law" of the body, or of the "moral" order governing the "universe" of the individual body. From this perspective, sexual orientation would be part of the materially determined context (the material free will) in which the subject acts. One is of course to be held accountable for one's actions, but only for those which the agent could control or change, that is, only for those which could be otherwise. If sexual orientation were innate, following one's inclinations could not be a punishable offense.

Yet there was a slight discrepancy between this argument for innateness and identity, which would appear so effective in combating §175, and the argument described above that specifically addressed female homosexuality. Exemplified by Rohleder's explication, the argument against punishing female homosexuality depended on a distinction between the act and its perpetrator. The female homosexual, Rohleder had claimed, could not be punished because no single act could be designated criminal. Modern law should not punish the "soul" or the disposition of a person, but only the specific acts they commit. Conversely, the innateness argument led its spokespersons away from a consideration of acts and toward the "entire mental life" of a person, in which acts make sense only if they are seen within the material free will and moral disposition of the total sexual person. In short, protesters had talked themselves into separate corners: some were holding that it was the sexual "essence" of a person that either should or should not be considered under criminal law, even as others wanted to assert a distinction between individuals and their acts.

28. Rohleder, "Paragraph 250," 68. See also Kurt Hiller, "Homosexualismus und Deutscher Vorentwurf," *Monatsschrift für Kriminalpsychologie und Strafrechtsreform* 8 (1911–1912): 29–30.

Feminist Responses

The common response of the mainstream women's movement was either to ignore or quietly to endorse §250. The report on the *Proposal* in the *Centralblatt des Bundes deutscher Frauenvereine (Central Publication of the League of German Women's Associations)* only briefly mentioned §250, noting that the Legal Commission of the League of German Women's Associations had, after debate, taken the stance that §175 was unjust because it contained an arbitrary inequality in favor of women. The report concluded that while the organization was surprised at the direction of the equality that §250 instituted, it nonetheless satisfied the league's "continuing love of justice."[29] The majority of the women's movement followed suit and did not contest the proposed §250.

Certain feminist groups did protest, however, albeit with qualifications. For example, Anna Pappritz, the chairperson of the German abolitionist movement, made clear that her organization's opposition to §250 did not imply a moral approbation of homosexuality, emphasizing that "the sin, when practiced by women, is just as reprehensible, unpleasant, and revolting as when it is committed by men."[30] If less vociferous than Pappritz, Helene Stöcker's protest of §250 also came with provisos. Even as she called on the League for the Protection of Mothers to protest the paragraph, she noted, "It is obvious and hardly needs here to be emphasized that we consider normal love, that is the love between man and woman, and parenthood, to be the highest and most desirable forms of love."[31]

Interestingly, however, these statements of disidentification coincided with opposition to antihomosexuality legislation, and in many cases the

29. Camilla Jellinek, "Der Vorentwurf zu einem Deutschen Strafgesetzbuch: Vom Standpunkte der Frauen aus betrachtet," *Centralblatt des Bundes deutscher Frauenvereine* 11, no. 21 (1910): 161. Several other paragraphs in the *Proposal* were debated—if less heatedly—by different factions of the women's movement: §361,6, revised as §305,4, which regulated prostitution; and §174, revised as §247, which prohibited *Kuppelei* in relations of dependency.

30. Anna Pappritz, "Zum §175," *Der Abolitionist* 10, no. 2 (1911): 9.

31. Helene Stöcker, "Die beabsichtigte Ausdehnung des §175 auf die Frau," *Die Neue Generation* 7, no. 3 (1911): 111. The League for the Protection of Mothers held a *Vortragsabend,* or discussion evening, to discuss §175/250 February 10, 1911, and a follow-up evening February 23, 1911. Reports are to be found in *Berlin Börsen-Courier* (1911); *Vorwärts* (14 February 1911); and *Die Wahrheit* (4 February 1911).

protesters within the women's movement allied themselves with the sexologists and jurists discussed above. The arguments of the two cooperating camps often overlapped, their differences being primarily a matter of emphasis: where the medical-juridical argument emphasized the *physical* indeterminacy of the female homosexual, the feminist argument tended to stress the problem of femininity as a *cultural* representation.

Like the sexologists and jurists, the feminists also began with the definitional complexity of *beischlafähnliche Handlungen*. But in this case the argument centered on the difficulty of distinguishing legally the *sexual* act from the *social* act, as the indeterminacy of *beischlafähnliche Handlungen* might be taken to include physical contact of any sort between two women. A standard argument was thus that the nature of femininity necessarily dissolved the sharp borders between the sexual and the social and between the legal and the criminal. As Elsbeth Krukenberg argued, "What is unnatural for men, what seems strangely 'feminine,'—conspicuously friendly, loving behavior between man and man, caresses, flattery, and the like—that is something completely natural for women of all ages." Fearing that these tendencies would border on the criminal because of the terminological uncertainty of §250, Krukenberg asked, "Should the woman have to give up all of that in order not to arouse false suspicion?"[32] She feared that women would have to become "men" in terms of their social interactions in order to avoid being suspect simply for *being women*.

Agreeing with Krukenberg on this matter, both Stöcker and Pappritz carried the discussion away from the innate characteristics of women and toward the historically specific circumstances in which women live. Drawing on a favorite theme of the League for the Protection of Mothers, the plight of the single woman, Stöcker reminded her readers of the celibacy and loneliness to which such women were often condemned, as well as of a common solution:

> Precisely women, with their stronger need for tenderness, when fate has denied them children and a husband, have the wish at least for an inner community, for a common home. The [solution] that recommends itself on economic grounds routinely involves a common bedroom for the same

---

32. Elsbeth Krukenberg, "§175," *Monatsschrift für Kriminalpsychologie und Strafrechtsreform* 7 (1910–1911): 612.

reason. Hundreds of thousands of our educated women, teachers, artists, and employees in other professions live calmly and peacefully with one another.

This economically and personally motivated choice to share a common bedroom, Stöcker argued, would be suspect under §250, such that these women would have criminal punishment imposed on top of the economic and personal hardship to which they were already condemned. Whether it is true or not that those women who chose to share a bedroom did so solely out of economic considerations and desire for platonic companionship, Stöcker was pointing primarily to the potential legal inability to distinguish between the social practices of homosexual and heterosexual women. The move was a turn away at once from the sexual question, as well as from the homosexual woman as object of concern. At one point Stöcker made the latter turn explicit, arguing that "the burden of this paragraph that wants to place women under the stigma of punishability affects not only those for whom friendship actually condenses into sexual acts, but rather also those for whom that is not the case."[33] Although the danger Stöcker perceived was that the paragraph would fail to differentiate between the heterosexual and homosexual woman, her own rhetoric successfully eliminated the homosexual woman from the discussion altogether. If less detailed, the same emphasis can be found in the arguments of Pappritz and Krukenberg, as well as in that of Käthe Schirmacher.

In coincidence with the abolitionist interest, Schirmacher made the question of prostitution the central concern in her criticism of §250. Due to social and economic hardships, she argued, women were driven into prostitution, where "sexual relations [between women] are common." Socially, these prostituted women are already condemned to a "civil death." Schirmacher pleaded: "Should these corpses be killed yet again, should sex with women also be punished? Then the prostitute has no quiet within her own four walls, and the reach of arbitrariness devours her last refuge." If Schirmacher here recognized actual sexual relations between women, it was only among deadened bodies. These women were not "naturally" homosexual but rather turned to one another "out of a disgust with men." In Schirmacher's view, female homosexuality was a problem to be overcome through economic and social reform, not through the law. With proper

33. Stöcker, "Die beabsichtigte Ausdehnung," 111–113.

reform, heterosexual women would not be driven to the "aberration." Schirmacher thus advocated not for the rights of the female homosexual subject but rather for the entity that had fallen out of the social.[34] The ultimate goal was to rectify the conditions that produced female homosexuality in the first place, not to protect the legal safety of homosexual women.

In agreement with Schirmacher on the issue of prostitution, Stöcker added that "now extortion, prison, and disgrace threaten them all."[35] And the issue of extortion brought the concerns of the feminists back in line with those of the medical doctors and legal scholars in a telling fashion. Rohleder had argued that the new paragraph would instigate first a new form of prostitution, namely, a female homosexual prostitution, which would in turn give rise to extortion with §250 as the threat. Without the paragraph, he claimed, "the social ostracism alone, with which the extortionist would then have to work, cannot possibly be as effective as the fear before imprisonment." Prostitution and extortion were intertwined, he averred, leaving the prostitute particularly well situated to identify homosexual women: "And if at first only gradually the prostitutes should become aware of the punishability of these offenses (should §250 of the *Proposal* become law), the desire for revenge on the part of these women from the lowest class would be given a large playing field for denunciation, and with that [access] to legal process." In other words, the law would establish conditions that would not only promote illegal female homosexual prostitution but also enable those prostitutes to identify their clients. In short, the law would first create a new female criminal figure, the extortionist; the extortionist would then identify and thereby produce the desiring female homosexual as a socially visible—albeit criminal—individual. Far from preventing her possibility, the law would enable her unequivocal social existence. "These are consequences," Rohleder concluded, "of which the lawmakers of §250 are perhaps not yet aware."[36]

---

34. Käthe Schirmacher, "§175 des Deutschen Strafgesetzes," *Der Abolitionist* 10, no. 1 (1911): 4. On the theme of the second death, see also Stöcker, "Die beabsichtigte Ausdehnung," 113.

35. Stöcker, "Die beabsichtigte Ausdehnung," 113.

36. Rohleder, "Paragraph 250," 74–75. For a similar argument, see also Dr. Franz Brück, "Homosexualität und Erpressertum," *Deutsche Medizinische Wochenschrift* 37, no. 15 (1911): 702. The response on the part of the Social Democratic women's movement also addressed the issue of extortion. Sarcastically, an article in *Die Gleichheit* remarked: "Yes, [the law] should be extended to the intercourse between women so that extortion can develop

The feminist and the legal-medical protests thus converged in a critique of the productivity of the law, or the idea that the law brings into being the very thing it claims to penalize. The legal-medical argument had begun with sexual orientation as an innate, bodily determined phenomenon. Under this model the homosexual woman as subject had dissolved in a morass of indeterminacy. The feminist position, by contrast, had begun with the *cultural* manifestations of the feminine. On the cultural level, that which would be uniquely and femininely homosexual could never be firmly established. Instead, the feminists claimed, if enacted the law would infringe on the innately *feminine*. In this picture the innately homosexual female subject was at once everywhere, and thereby nowhere.[37] Under the arguments of the feminists she receded into the infinite background. Although from seemingly opposite starting points, the protesters succeeded in their arguments precisely by vanishing the very individual their protests claimed to protect. While the legal-medical opponents did so in terms of legal identity, and the feminists through cultural identity, together they raised more generally the question of just what—if anything—constituted the origin or ground of the modern subject.

Ultimately, the controversy around §250 was short-lived. With the start of the war in 1914, discussion of the *Proposal* came to an abrupt halt and was not resuscitated at the war's end. The historical relevance of §250 thus does not reside in its legislative outcome. Rather, it is of interest solely for the content and conflicts of the debates themselves. The debates reflected a general contention around the moral basis of modern law and its relationship to formal and informal regulation of individuals. These concerns entailed assessing just what was taken to constitute both the moral individual and the social, and where the divide between the public and the private

---

even more opulently." Critical of what it considered to be bourgeois morality and law, however, the author of the *Gleichheit* article made a much stronger claim about the *Proposal* as a whole: "These samples may suffice to characterize summarily the *Proposal*. It is born out of the same anti-social spirit as the penal reform and the criminal legal amendment. Despite some modern reform patchwork, with which it shows off, it must be recognized by Social Democracy as intrinsically and thoroughly reactionary." In H. B., "Der Vorentwurf eines neuen Strafgesetzbuchs," *Die Gleichheit* 20, no. 6 (1909): 87.

37. For a surprisingly parallel argument about female homosexuality as both "everywhere" and "nowhere" in interwar France, see Carolyn Dean, *The Frail Social Body: Pornography, Homosexuality, and Other Fantasies in Interwar France* (Berkeley, Calif., 2000), 173–215.

might best be drawn in a world that wanted to think of itself as modern. The debates around §250 were forced to contend with the issues of both how sexuality contributed to individual identity and how that sexual identity was at once a public and a private matter.

Moreover, the *Proposal* provided an impetus for a public discussion about the character of female homosexuality. In this regard, the female homosexual proved to be a social entity particularly resistant to legal categorization in part because she represented a new public category. In terms of legal matters in Germany, she had for some time been of little public concern. When §250 resuscitated her for public discussion, both the authors of the *Proposal* and its protesters suddenly had to contend with a new category of public, sexual individual. If, as the sociologist Pierre Bourdieu has suggested, law has the power to instantiate categories that are meaningful to the individuals and social groups to which it pertains, the debates around §250 provide an instance in which the law did not work.[38] The social interests and juridical practices in this example refused to coalesce in a way that allowed the "female homosexual" to emerge as a product for regulation. What is striking about this is that all arguments about §250 tended to turn attention away from female homosexuality and toward more conventional figures of public dispute, that is, toward the homosexual man or the heterosexual woman. As a consequence, the moral clarity of those categories themselves came into question. The male homosexual might not be as "immoral" as the Criminal Code supposed, while the female heterosexual might be more morally suspect than anyone imagined. In this sense, the female homosexual was simultaneously marginal and exemplary:

38. In a sociological study of the juridical "field," Bourdieu portrayed law as the quintessential form of the symbolic power of naming that creates the things it names, individuals and social groups in particular. "It confers," Bourdieu wrote, "upon the reality which arises from its classificatory operations the maximum permanence that any social entity has the power to confer upon another, the permanence which we attribute to objects." Yet if Bourdieu granted legal language this privileged status, he nevertheless insisted that the operations of law are not sui generis. "It would not be excessive," he explained, "to say that [law] *creates* the social world, but only if we remember that it is this world which first creates the law." That is, categories can be consecrated by law only if they make sense to the historically constituted individuals and social world to which they pertain. "Law" and its pretense to universality happen at the negotiated (and often combative) intersection of juridical tradition and social interest. See Pierre Bourdieu, "The Force of Law: Toward a Sociology of the Juridical Field," trans. Richard Terdiman, *Hastings Law Journal* 38, no. 5 (1987): 838–839.

marginal as an easily overlooked or swept-aside figure, and exemplary in that she typified the mobility of sexual identities and their moral status at the fin de siècle. In like fashion, the seemingly marginal story of the 1909 debates about female homosexuality can be seen as exemplary in depicting the vitality and indeterminacy of the sexualized moral subject.

PART III

Resonances and Resistances

6

SOCIAL MATTERS

Social Democracy and the Ethics of Materialism

It is not the hope for a better beyond, but rather the insight into the conditions of a better here and now that will lead politics to subvert morality.

EDUARD BERNSTEIN

The ethics reformers whose efforts are described in the preceding chapters were largely bourgeois. Bracketed out of the story so far, however, is one of the most significant developments of the turn of the century, the growth of the workers' movement and the blossoming of the Social Democratic Party (SPD). Banned under antisocialist laws since 1878, the party returned with a vengeance when the laws lapsed after 1890.[1] While the emergence of worker culture and the organized party created alarm for many in bourgeois reform circles, some active ethics reformers saw it as an opportunity. It is thus

1. Literature on the history of Social Democracy in imperial Germany includes Susanne Miller and Heinrich Potthoff, *A History of German Social Democracy from 1848 to the Present,* trans. J. A. Underwood (New York, 1986); Günther Roth, *The Social Democrats in Imperial Germany: A Study in Working-Class Isolation and National Integration* (Totowa, N.J., 1963); Gerhard Ritter and Klaus Tenfelde, *Arbeiter im Deutschen Kaiserreich* (Bonn, 1992); Vernon Lidtke, *The Alternative Culture: Socialist Labor in Imperial Germany* (New York, 1985); and Franz Osterroth and Dieter Schuster, *Chronik der Deutschen Sozialdemokratie* (Hannover, 1963).

necessary now to go back to 1890, to the beginnings of ethics reform, in order to observe the movement's relationship to Social Democracy.

One would expect to find in Social Democracy little tolerance for ethics reform. In 1848, with the "Manifesto of the Communist Party," Marx and Engels had famously differentiated their work from the moralistic variants of bourgeois socialism.[2] Despite significant fluctuations in Marx's thought in the intervening decades, Engels had shored up the scientistic dimension of Marxist thought with his challenge to Eugen Dühring, a moralist socialist with a growing following in Germany. Engels's *Herrn Eugen Dührings Umwälzung der Wissenschaft (Anti-Dühring) (Anti-Dühring: Herr Eugen Dühring's Revolution in Science)* became the chief conduit for many young socialists in Europe to the Marxist project and thus helped to consolidate the more deterministic qualities of Marx's thought for late nineteenth-century Marxism.[3] Although both Marx and Engels over time fluctuated in their interpretation of consciousness, ideology, and the role of intellectual work in historical materialism, this most determinist brand that Engels's *Anti-Dühring* helped to popularize had no room for ethics, a mere symptom of bourgeois ideology.[4]

2. Karl Marx and Friedrich Engels, "Manifest der Kommunistischen Partei," in *Karl Marx, Friedrich Engels: Werke,* vol. 4, ed. Institut für Marxismus-Leninismus (Berlin, 1961–1974), 459–493. Hereafter references to this collection are cited as *ME Werke,* followed by volume and page numbers.

3. Friedrich Engels, *Herrn Eugen Dührings Umwälzung der Wissenschaft (Anti-Dühring),* in *ME Werke,* 20, 3–303. On the simplification and totalizing of the Marxist project by Engels, see Gareth Stedman Jones, "Engels and the End of Classical German Philosophy," *New Left Review* 79 (1973): 17–36.

4. An enormous literature exists on the place of consciousness, ideology, and intellectual work in Marxist thought. See, for example, Stanley Pierson, *Marxist Intellectuals and the Working-Class Mentality in Germany, 1887–1912* (Cambridge, Mass., 1993); Harold Mah, *The End of Philosophy and the Origins of "Ideology,"* (Berkeley, Calif., 1987); Jerrold Seigel, "Consciousness and Practice in the History of Marxism," *Comparative Studies in Society and History* 24, no. 1 (1982): 164–177; Schlomo Avineri, "Marx and the Intellectuals," *Journal of the History of Ideas* 28, no. 2 (1967): 269–278; and William Gleberzon, "Marxist Conceptions of the Intellectual," *Historical Reflections* 5, no. 1 (1978): 81–97. Philosophical and theoretical discussions of Marxism and ethics include Robert C. Tucker, *The Marxian Revolutionary Idea* (New York, 1969); and Allen Wood, "The Marxian Critique of Justice," *Philosophy and Public Affairs* 1, no. 3 (1972): 244–282. For a critique of Tucker and Wood, see Allen E. Buchanan, *Marx and Justice: The Radical Critique of Liberalism* (Totowa, N.J., 1982), esp. 50–85. See also Marshall Cohen, Thomas Nagel, and Thomas Scanlon, eds., *Marx, Justice, and History* (Princeton, N.J., 1980); Steven Lukes, *Marxism and Morality* (Oxford, 1985); Lawrence

At the outset, Social Democratic theorists were consequently the most outspoken critics of the ethics movement as a whole. Yet those same theorists were in constant dialogue with ethics reformers throughout the 1890s and 1900s. Furthermore, the most stringent and scientistic among the Social Democratic theorists searched for a language of ethics that would coincide with the historical materialist project. Their eventual embrace of ethics as a mode of critique took the potential of ethics reform to its limit: Social Democratic theorists redefined ethics, turned the considerations of ethics away from solely individual considerations, and insisted even more adamantly than the original ethics reformers on the necessary political valence of ethics as critique. Moreover, when the ethics discussions within Social Democracy turned to matters of gender and sexuality, the theorists again rejected ethics reform even as they carried its emphasis on rethinking the relation of public and private to new heights.

Social Democracy and the German Society for Ethical Culture

The newly resurgent SPD proved a significant source of contention among founders of the German Society for Ethical Culture (DGEK). Technically, the DGEK insisted on its autonomy from all political parties, whether bourgeois or proletariat. Yet some within the movement kept particular distance from all manifestations of socialism. Felix Adler and the New York Society for Ethical Culture, for instance, viewed socialism as a pressing danger of modernity and something that Ethical Culture must stridently counter. Several in the DGEK followed suit, including Friedrich Jodl, who feared an anti-Enlightenment tendency in Social Democracy.[5] Friedrich Wilhelm Foerster also grew increasingly hostile throughout the 1890s to the SPD's rhetoric of war and violence in the class fight.[6]

Wilde, *Ethical Marxism and Its Radical Critics* (New York, 1998); and Rodney G. Peffer, *Marxism, Morality, and Social Justice* (Princeton, N.J., 1990).

5. Friedrich Jodl, "Ethische Kultur und soziale Organisation," *Ethische Kultur* 2, nos. 14–15 (1894): 110–111, 118–119. On the conflict between Jodl and Gizycki over Social Democracy, see Gimpl, *Vernetzungen,* esp. 70–95.

6. See, for instance, Friedrich Wilhelm Foerster, "Sozialdemokratie und ethische Bewegung," *Ethische Kultur* 3, no. 18 (1895): 142–143. For autobiographical reflections, see Foerster, *Erlebte Weltgeschichte,* 89–95.

Yet many other early members of the DGEK sought a close relationship with Social Democracy. Georg von Gizycki, for instance, had
a long-standing interest in the workers' movement and envisioned an
intimate—albeit independent—relationship with the party. Writing in
Vorwärts (Forward), the Berlin-based political organ of the SPD, he clarified that while the DGEK must at all costs maintain its independence
from political parties, it shared with Social Democracy a fundamental
concern for equality and justice. The DGEK did "not want to hinder the
class fight," he explained. Rather, "it sought to ethicize it."[7] An anonymous contributor to *Ethische Kultur* was even more adamant on the implicit relationship of the DGEK to Social Democracy, claiming that the
success of the DGEK depended largely on the connection with the workers' movement. Without a substantial contingent of workers' voices to
counter implicit views of the "Manchesterites," the contributor claimed,
the DGEK stood no chance of revitalizing "public opinion."[8]

Ferdinand Tönnies defended the DGEK's project in *Die Neue Zeit (The
New Times)*, the chief theoretical periodical of the Social Democrats, clarifying what it meant to "ethicize" the class conflict. On the simplest level, he
explained, any real ethics reform must entail a critique of private property,
and in this regard it cannot help but be of interest to the workers' movement.
More defensively, he sought to dispel anxieties that ethics reform and its
attention to the private were tools of bourgeois ideology. He claimed that
contemporary society consists of both public and private realms, and that
the private realm cannot be left to its own. In order to criticize private
property and with it the particular manner in which the public is divided
from the private, one had to address not only the makeup of the public but
also that of the private. Such was the special facility of ethics reform.[9]

Tönnies's constant reiteration of a scientific ethics was also tied to his interest in the workers' movement. Unscientific, uninterrogated moral claims,
he maintained, run the risk of simply serving class aims. But with the rigor
of science, the field of ethics can move beyond arbitrary and class-based

7. Gizycki, "In Sachen der Deutschen Gesellschaft für ethische Kultur."
8. Ein Mitglied der D. G. E. K., "Die Deutsche Gesellschaft für ethische Kultur und die
Sozial Demokratie," *Ethische Kultur* 1, no. 17 (1893): 133–134.
9. Ferdinand Tönnies, "Noch einiges über Ethik," *Die Neue Zeit* 11, pt. 2, no. 31 (1893):
103–104. See also Tönnies, "Ethisches Scharmützel: Offener Brief an Herrn Dr. Franz
Mehring in Berlin," *Deutsche Worte* 13, no. 1 (1893): 47–57.

judgments to serve a critical social function. To be sure, he acknowledged, science itself can serve specific class interests, but the class-based dimension of science—including a science of ethics—is only accidental. What is essential in science—including a science of ethics—is its ability to transcend class in order to function as a critique of existing social conditions.[10]

The prosocialist forces in the DGEK were not enough to overcome the skeptics, however, and within just a few years, discussion of cooperation subsided almost altogether. When Gizycki died in 1895, the chief power within the DGEK for a socialist orientation disappeared. After his death, Gizycki's wife, Lily von Gizycki (later Lily Braun), briefly coedited *Ethische Kultur* with Friedrich Wilhelm Foerster, a short-lived cooperation that encapsulated the tensions in the DGEK around Social Democracy. Eventually, Gizycki retreated, renouncing her membership in the DGEK and joining the SPD. Foerster carried on as editor of *Ethische Kultur,* marking symbolically the definitive break of the DGEK from socialist collaboration.[11] Individual crossover continued, but the hopes by some that the DGEK might have a more intimate relationship with Social Democracy than with other organizations had died.

Yet if the overtures from the DGEK were not successful, they instigated a significant commentary from leading theorists in the SPD on ethics as a mode of critique. This response—which was overwhelmingly negative—must, however, be read against the background of developments in the SPD and the ongoing effort to consolidate a historical materialist line of argumentation. The party had in fact only recently adopted a solidly Marxist historical materialist program in 1891 at its first congress after the repeal of the antisocialist laws, but even then party activists and theorists were not unanimous.[12] Leading the Bavarian faction, Georg von Vollmar challenged the party to renounce its revolutionary stance and to embrace

---

10. Tönnies, "Noch einiges über Ethik," 103–104.

11. The first conflict between Foerster and Gizycki occurred in May 1895, already over the relationship of the DGEK to the SPD. See Lily von Gizycki, "Politik und ethische Bewegung," *Ethische Kultur* 3, no. 21 (1895): 164–165, and Foerster's rejoinder, "Politik und ethische Bewegung," *Ethische Kultur* 3, no. 21 (1895): 166–167. Gizycki (Braun) gives an account of her departure from the periodical in "An die Leser," *Ethische Kultur* 3, no. 42 (1895): 329.

12. On the program of 1891, see Karl Kautsky, *Das Erfurter Programm, in seinem grundsätzlichen Theil,* 3rd ed. (Stuttgart, 1892). See also Friedrich Engels, "Zur Kritik des sozialdemokratischen Programmentwurfs 1891," in *ME Werke,* 22, 227–240.

the parliamentarism that had in practice become its strongest trait.[13] Almost simultaneously, the so-called *Jungen Revolt* (youth revolt) began, a movement led largely by young intellectuals who wanted to call the party back to its revolutionary goals and to resist any tactics that aimed at mitigating the effects of capitalism. When members of the DGEK made overtures, Social Democratic leaders—including Friedrich Engels, August Bebel, and Karl Kautsky—thus already had their hands full in their effort to consolidate a unified party program that would integrate but not succumb fully to the SPD's parliamentary successes.[14] The mood among the orthodox was consequently not one of openness to outsiders.

With few exceptions, including some interest in the DGEK on the part of Conrad Schmidt, a leading figure of the *Jungen,* the dominant tendency within SPD leadership was to reject ethics reform altogether. The initial hope was that the party could simply ignore the DGEK, as leaders feared that significant resistance from Social Democracy would only help to legitimate the ethics reform project. Unfortunately for SPD theorists, the DGEK had already received too much attention in the press and did not seem about to disappear anytime soon. The party leadership found itself consequently forced to take a stand.[15]

Franz Mehring, a regular contributor to *Die Neue Zeit* after 1891, led the charge. Interestingly, his primary criticism echoed those from other quarters that were skeptical about the DGEK's insistence on the autonomy of ethics. Where Eugen Heinrich Schmitt and Ernst Haeckel had maintained that ethics remained necessarily dependent on religion, however, Mehring saw ethics as necessarily dependent on class difference. The "ethical perspectives of the individual," he explained, "are above all determined solely by their political position, or better said, by their social class." Moreover, he insisted, ethics is the language with which one class justifies its actions. The Junkers, for example, will always find their exploitation of the workers "ethical." So long as the DGEK failed to see the impossibility

13. Carl Schorske, *German Social Democracy, 1905–1917: The Development of the Great Schism* (Cambridge, Mass., 1955), 8; Pierson, *Marxist Intellectuals,* 33–34. On Vollmar, see Reinhard Jansen, *Georg von Vollmar* (Bonn, 1956).

14. On the *Jungen,* see Pierson, *Marxist Intellectuals,* 11–34; and Dirk Müller, *Idealismus und Revolution: Zur Opposition der Jungen gegen den sozialdemokratischen Parteivorstand, 1890–1894* (Berlin, 1975).

15. Franz Mehring, "Allerlei Ethik," *Die Neue Zeit* 11, pt. 1, no. 9 (1892): 265.

of a "common ethics," it necessarily failed also to address "the meaningful battles of the day."[16]

Yet Mehring did not exclude the language of ethics altogether from historical materialism. He simply demanded that ethics be understood as necessarily specific to an economic class. The proletariat, he explained, "lead themselves to their own morality."[17] Moreover, he conceded that Marx had exhibited a moral sentiment against capitalism and private property. But while Mehring applauded the intentions of Tönnies and Gizycki, he insisted that they naively conflated Marx's moral sentiment with his real insights, which were fundamentally scientific and excluded ethics. The mistaken premise by the DGEK that Marx's moral antagonism against capitalism was part and parcel of his scientific work led Tönnies and Gizycki to believe falsely that moral condemnation of capitalism alone might suffice to bring about cultural transformation. Mehring thus applauded the moral aim of the DGEK, that is, the idea of "justice and truth, humanity and mutual respect." But he thought the organization was trying to leap over the hard work of real material development to get there.[18]

At this point Karl Kautsky, the editor of *Die Neue Zeit,* jumped into the debate to reinforce Mehring's position and to bring even more scrutiny to the problematic relationship between ethics and science. Where Mehring had been willing to accept that science might transcend class differences, Kautsky was more skeptical. His objection relied on the uncertain difference between ethics (*Ethik*) as an abstract field of study and morality (*Sittlichkeit*) as historically contingent social norms. One could plausibly construct a science of ethics (*Ethik*), but clearly it made no sense to speak of a "scientific morality" (*wissenschaftliche Sittlichkeit*). Unfortunately, Kautsky charged, the two cannot be as easily separated from each other as members of the DGEK liked to believe. The scientific study of ethics takes historically specific moral codes as its object of inquiry but inadvertently conflates those with transhistorical principles of ethics. The problem becomes apparent, he charged, when some members of the DGEK speak of the

---

16. Ibid., 266.

17. Franz Mehring, "Ethik und Klassenkampf," *Die Neue Zeit* 11, pt. 2, no. 22 (1893): 700.

18. Members of the DGEK should read "the statutes of the International," Mehring explained, "if they really want to know how their ethical culture will actually be realized." Mehring, "Ethik und Klassenkampf," 700–702.

"eternal norms of moral behavior."[19] Yet Kautsky did not fully dismiss the idea of a scientific study of the laws of morality, so long as one included class conflict as part of the investigation.[20] Indeed, if one were truly attentive to the class dimensions of ethics, he maintained, one would recognize how the development of moral science actually works dialectically to overturn the idea of a scientific morality. That is, a truly scientific study of morality would reveal the class dimension that underlay the seemingly objective "science."[21] Kautsky thus repeated Mehring's general admiration of the aims of the DGEK but likewise found the methods simply false. "The offer sounds good," he concluded, "but I just don't buy it."[22]

Ethics in Social Democracy

The rejection of the DGEK by Social Democratic theorists rested largely on political grounds, because the ethics reformers situated their project outside party affiliation and failed to give adequate attention to class conflict. The mini-controversy thus caused little tension among the SPD leadership. It was a different story, however, when questions of ethics arose *within* the party, as the well-known controversy around Eduard Bernstein's revisionism illustrated. Bernstein's revision of Marxist theory, which in part aimed to reintroduce an ethics into socialism that would transcend the class divide, caused a real crisis for party leadership. Leaders had been able to rally their core to resist the DGEK project. In the case of Bernstein, however, the core itself was at stake, as he had long been one of the most reliable revolutionary members of the party. Like many German socialists, he had come to Marxism largely through Engels's book, *Anti-Dühring*. Living in exile under the threat of the antisocialist laws, he became the chief editor of *Der Sozialdemokrat (The Social Democrat)*, the primary periodical for German Social Democracy between 1881 and 1890. He had been in close correspondence for years with leading figures in the party such as Kautsky, Engels, and Bebel, when he began to question the party's

19. Karl Kautsky, "Noch einiges über Ethik," *Die Neue Zeit* 11, pt. 2, no. 31 (1893): 111.
20. Ibid., 113.
21. Ibid., 114.
22. Ibid., 115–116.

principles in the mid-1890s.[23] Like Mehring and Kautsky, he had sharply dismissed the DGEK at its inception, largely because the organization sought to keep ethics autonomous of party politics.[24] Perhaps hinting at his future turn, however, he praised a book published posthumously by Georg von Gizycki, *Vorlesungen über soziale Ethik (Lectures on Social Ethics)*, as an "unvarnished socialist" book.[25]

Despite—or because of—his long-term commitment to the SPD, Bernstein found himself compelled by the mid-1890s to call for a reconsideration of the party platform and to update historical materialist theory. His challenge took the form first of a series of articles in *Die Neue Zeit* which he synthesized in book form in 1899 as *Die Voraussetzungen des Sozialismus und die Aufgaben der Sozialdemokratie (The Presuppositions of Socialism and the Tasks of Social Democracy).*[26] In the articles and book, he set out to determine what aspects of Marxism needed to be reconsidered and, most significantly, questioned the necessity of revolution in socialism. He set himself up "against the view that we are to expect in the near future a collapse of bourgeois society, and that the tactics of social democracy should be determined by the expectation of such an imminent, great, social catastrophe."[27] In contrast to the historical materialist prediction that poverty would grow to include ever more of the population, Bernstein held up empirical observation to demonstrate that in fact an ever increasing percentage of the population was becoming wealthier. Further, he noted that "the surplus product is increasing everywhere, but the relation of its increase to the increase of wages-capital is today declining in advanced

23. On Bernstein's life and career, see Manfred Steger, *The Quest for Evolutionary Socialism: Eduard Bernstein and Social Democracy* (Cambridge, 1997); Bo Gustafsson, *Marxismus und Revisionismus: Eduard Bernsteins Kritik des Marxismus und ihre ideengeschichtlichen Voraussetzungen,* 2 vols. (Frankfurt am Main, 1972); Helga Grebing, *Der Revisionismus von Bernstein bis zum "Prager Frühling"* (Munich, 1977); and Helmut Hirsch, *Der "Fabier" Eduard Bernstein: Zur Entwicklungsgeschichte des Evolutionären Sozialismus* (Bonn, 1977).

24. Bernstein, "Moralische und unmoralische Spaziergänge," 4–9.

25. Eduard Bernstein, "Literarische Rundschau," *Die Neue Zeit* 14, pt. 1, no. 6 (1895): 218.

26. The major points of Bernstein's argument unfolded in a series called "Probleme des Sozialismus," in *Die Neue Zeit* 15, pt. 1, nos. 6, 7, 10, 25 (1896): 164–171, 204–213, 303–311, 772–783; 15, pt. 2, nos. 30, 31 (1897): 100–107, 138–143; 16, pt. 2, nos. 34, 39 (1897–1898): 225–232, 388–395. See also the collection of his essays from the period in Eduard Bernstein, *Zur Theorie und Geschichte des Sozialismus: Gesammelte Abhandlungen,* 4th ed. (Berlin, 1904).

27. Eduard Bernstein, *Die Voraussetzungen des Sozialismus und die Aufgaben der Sozialdemokratie* (Stuttgart, 1899), v.

countries."[28] In other words, the overall exploitation of the working class was on the decline. "The outlook for socialism depends not on the decline of social wealth," he thus concluded, "but rather on its increase."[29]

Though Bernstein called on Marx's own writings to support his position, he recognized that his observations placed him in direct opposition to the more determinist dimensions of historical materialism.[30] Speaking to these determinist presuppositions of Marxist theory, Bernstein charged that "the materialist is a Calvinist without God," adding, "If he does not believe in a predestination determined by a divinity, he believes nevertheless and must believe that, from any chosen point of time onward, all further events are determined in advance by the whole of existing matter and the relations of force between its parts."[31] Bernstein's most fundamental critique was thus that empirical observation revealed the science of Marxism to be in need of revision, as the "necessary" path of history had turned out to be more contingent than hitherto understood.

Writing in an era when reform-oriented socialisms were popping up across Europe, Bernstein too came to endorse a program of reform that was to lead gradually rather than inevitably and violently toward the acquisition of political power by the proletariat.[32] He noted that a primary tactic in Marxist thought is the acquisition of political power by the proletariat, and he argued therefore for "parliamentary struggle" through the "exploitation of the vote."[33] Democracy itself, taken as the real acquisition of political power on the part of the proletariat, he argued, would necessarily lend itself to ethical concerns. The right to vote generates a sense

28. Ibid., 43.

29. Ibid., 51.

30. Literature on Bernstein has often suggested that he was relying on recent "softening" in the determinist, revolutionary outlook by the older Marx and Engels. See, for instance, Manfred Steger, "Historical Materialism and Ethics: Eduard Bernstein's Revisionist Perspective," *History of European Ideas* 14, no. 5 (1992): 647–663. Dmitrij Owetschkin reminds us, however, that the projects of Marx and Engels oscillated frequently on the matter of conscious agency by historical actors, in "Die materialistische Geschichtsauffassung in der Interpretation E. Bernsteins," *Beiträge zur Geschichte der Arbeiterbewegung* 40, no. 1 (1998): 38–49.

31. Bernstein, *Die Voraussetzungen,* 4–5.

32. The influences on Bernstein are contested. Hirsch sought to prove the Fabian influence in his *Der "Fabier."* Gustafsson, *Marxismus und Revisionismus,* saw the influences in a much wider revisionist culture that included Georges Sorel, Benedetto Croce, Antonio Labriola, and Jean Jaurès.

33. Bernstein, *Die Voraussetzungen,* 87.

of social partnership and responsibility, and it is this responsibility that produces moral freedom. He concluded that "democracy is a condition of socialism to a much greater degree than is often assumed, i.e., it is a condition not only as means but also as substance. Without a certain amount of democratic institutions or traditions, the socialist doctrine of the present would not at all be possible."[34] In this regard, Bernstein was in some respects doing little more than providing a theoretical justification for many of the practices already used by the party. Universal (male) suffrage had been a tenet of the Lassallean platform from the beginning and had been retained with the founding of the SPD. Moreover, the antisocialist laws, which had allowed the SPD to maintain a presence in the Reichstag, had channeled the party's activities and interests toward parliamentarism, albeit an ambivalent one. This tendency had only increased with the renewed legalization of the party.[35]

In terms of ethics discussions, however, Bernstein's real intervention derived from his critique of materialism. First, like Tönnies, Bernstein saw in the older Marx and Engels a strong emphasis on moral considerations. Referring to Marx's *Capital,* Bernstein argued that it is marked by "a dualism that consists in this, that the work wants to be a scientific inquiry but also wants to prove a thesis set down long before its conception."[36] For Bernstein, however, this splitting was not a failure on Marx's part but rather an opening to the limits of materialist determinism altogether. Informed especially by the neo-Kantian thinker Friedrich Albert Lange, Bernstein argued that materialism was too flat and deterministic to provide a viable social politics.[37] According to Bernstein, it reduced thought and human action to nothing but mechanistic responses to material circumstances, and

34. Ibid., 140.
35. Vernon Lidtke, *The Outlawed Party: Social Democracy in Germany, 1878–1890* (Princeton, N.J., 1966), 153–154.
36. Bernstein, *Die Voraussetzungen,* 177. On this point, critics have suggested that Bernstein was focused largely on the older versions of both Marx and Engels as staid if grumpy bespectacled scholars rather than radical revolutionaries ready to take up arms in the street. See, for example, Sidney Hook, *Towards the Understanding of Karl Marx: A Revolutionary Interpretation* (New York, 1933), 43; Gillis J. Harp, "Determinism or Democracy? The Marxisms of Eduard Bernstein and Sidney Hook," *History of European Ideas* 25, no. 5 (1999): 243.
37. See especially Eduard Bernstein, "Das realistische und das ideologische Moment im Sozialismus: Probleme des Sozialismus, 2. Serie II," *Die Neue Zeit* 16, pt. 2, no. 34 (1897–1898): 225–232. Bernstein had in fact first become interested in Lange as early as 1892, when

disallowed any moral ideal by which social action could measure itself. He notoriously called for a "return to Kant" (*zurück auf Kant*) as a means to re-instill human agency and individual moral choice in the historical materialist framework.[38] For Bernstein, this return to Kant would revitalize the domain of human freedom and its ability to counter materialist determinism. Moral freedom was supposed to transcend the laws of causal necessity and was thus able to reflect on those laws. With this rallying cry, Bernstein quite consciously aimed to reintroduce a dualism into historical materialism, setting thought and moral freedom off from material phenomena and economic modes of production.

Efforts to Create an Historical Materialist Ethics

Bernstein found considerable support from the more moderate wing of the party, those who came to be labeled the "revisionists" or, even more derisively, the "ethicists." Indeed, Conrad Schmidt and Ludwig Woltmann were also calling from within the party for an adoption of neo-Kantian thought for socialist theory.[39] But Bernstein, whose position in the party was much more prominent and therefore crucial than that of Schmidt or Woltmann, endured the most scathing attacks from the more orthodox leaders such as Kautsky, Mehring, Rosa Luxemburg, and the Russian Georgi Plekhanov (Plechanow). Kautsky had held back while Bernstein published his series of articles in *Die Neue Zeit*.[40] By 1898, however, Kautsky was becoming alarmed and began to fear he could no

---

he wrote "Zur Würdigung F. A. Langes," *Die Neue Zeit* 10, pt. 2, nos. 29–31 (1892): 68–78, 101–109, 132–141. See also Willey, *Back to Kant,* 175.

38. Bernstein, "Das realistische und das ideologische Moment," 225–226.

39. See, for instance, Ludwig Woltmann, *System des Moralischen Bewusstseins mit besonderer Darlegung des Verhältnisses der kritischen Philosophie zu Darwinismus und Sozialismus* (Düsseldorf, 1898), reviewed as a "self-advertisement" in *Die Neue Zeit* 16, pt. 2, no. 29 (1898): 87–88; Conrad Schmidt, "Einige Bemerkungen über Plechanows letzten Artikel in der 'Neuen Zeit,'" *Die Neue Zeit* 17, pt. 1, no. 11 (1898): 324–334; and "Was ist Materialismus?" *Die Neue Zeit* 17, pt. 1, no. 22 (1899): 697–698. Schmidt's challenge did not go entirely unnoticed. For a critique, see Georgi Plechanow, "Konrad Schmidt gegen Karl Marx und Friedrich Engels," *Die Neue Zeit* 17, pt. 1, no. 5 (1898): 133–145; and Plechanow, "Materialismus oder Kantianismus," *Die Neue Zeit* 17, pt. 1, nos. 19–20 (1899): 589–596, 626–632.

40. Pierson, *Marxist Intellectuals,* 122.

longer work with Bernstein.[41] He confronted Bernstein's theses publicly at a party conference in Stuttgart and tried to persuade Bernstein to resign from his editorial post at *Die Neue Zeit,* a request Bernstein initially rejected but to which he ultimately had to capitulate.[42] Bernstein continued to publish there only to defend his project, but he turned to the increasingly revisionist *Sozialistische Monatshefte (Socialist Monthly)* for his further work.

While Bernstein found company in the reform-oriented wing of the party, the more orthodox members were confronted not only with the continued political challenge of the revisionists but also with the challenge of responding to the theoretical criticism Bernstein had issued. Especially significant in the context of ethics reform, and in contrast to the response to the DGEK, Bernstein's challenge did not induce his most orthodox critics to take an even harder line against a rhetoric of ethics. Rather, it prompted them to think more creatively about the possibilities of ethics *within* historical materialism. Four sustained efforts that articulated a materialist ethics within Social Democracy deserve special attention. The first two, the Spinozism of Jakob Stern and the neo-Kantianism of Franz Staudinger, stand out in part because they received official sanction from SPD leadership and in part because they had concrete ties to the DGEK. The other two, the neo-Kantianism of Max Adler and the evolutionary approach of Kautsky himself, bore strong similarities to the first two, though they showed no conscious sympathy for the ethics reform discussion. Together the four models covered the span of approaches to ethics within orthodox Social Democracy, delineating the traits that came to be necessary to any socialist

41. Kautsky's letters to Victor Adler throughout 1898 and 1899 depict his growing frustration with Bernstein. See especially Victor Adler, *Briefwechsel mit August Bebel und Karl Kautsky* (Vienna, 1954), 249. In their own correspondence, Kautsky and Bernstein sought to maintain civil relations. Kautsky's direct challenge to Bernstein came on October 23, 1898; see *Eduard Bernsteins Briefwechsel mit Karl Kautsky (1895–1905),* 2 vols., ed. Till Schelz-Brandenburg (Frankfurt am Main, 2003), 792–801.

42. On the discussion at Stuttgart, see H. Tudor and J. M. Tudor, eds. and trans., *Marxism and Social Democracy: The Revisionist Debate, 1896–1898* (Cambridge, 1988), 276–304. On Kautsky, see Ingrid Gilcher-Holtey, *Das Mandat des Intellektuellen: Karl Kautsky und die Sozialdemokratie* (Berlin, 1986); Gary P. Steenson, *Karl Kautsky, 1854–1938: Marxism in the Classical Years* (Pittsburgh, 1978); Dick Geary, *Karl Kautsky* (New York, 1987); and Walter Holzheuer, *Karl Kautskys Werk als Weltanschauung: Beitrag zur Ideologie der Sozialdemokratie vor dem ersten Weltkrieg* (Munich, 1972).

ethics that wanted to make the claim to "orthodoxy": immanence, political engagement, and redirection of ethics away from a focus on the individual.

Jakob Stern and Spinozist Ethics

The first effort to think about ethics within historical materialism in the 1890s came from Jakob Stern. Stern was a former rabbi from Württemberg who, after being driven from his profession in 1880 for suspected atheism, turned to Social Democracy and Spinozism. His book on Spinoza, *Die Philosophie Spinoza's: Erstmals gründlich aufgehellt und populär dargestellt (Spinoza's Philosophy: First Fundamentally Illuminated and Popularly Represented),* including two small appendixes on the contemporary political relevance of the seventeenth-century philosopher, was issued in 1894 by Dietz Verlag, the well-known publisher of socialist works. He had embarked as well on a major new translation of all of Spinoza's works, which was published by Dietz between 1886 and 1906.[43] Stern had already eagerly contributed to *Ethische Kultur* in its first year, making a case for a materialist ethics and pleading with the DGEK to embrace socialism.[44] He intervened in the Bernstein controversy as early as 1897, using the opportunity less to criticize revisionist efforts and more to demonstrate the importance of Spinoza's thought for Social Democracy.

In his intervention in *Die Neue Zeit,* Stern offered his own analysis of "economic and natural-philosophical materialism," fearing that a false or naive theory of materialism would leave Social Democracy without foundation.[45]

43. For a short biography of Stern, see Heiner Jestrabek's introduction in *Jakob Stern: Vom Rabbiner zum Atheisten; Ausgewählte religionskritische Schriften* (Aschaffenburg, 1997). Two helpful articles document his work on Spinoza: Manfred Lauermann, "Jakob Stern—Sozialist und Spinozist: Eine kleine Skizze zum 150. Geburtstag," in *Spinoza in der europäischen Geistesgeschichte,* ed. Hanna Delf, Julius H. Schoeps, and Manfred Walther (Berlin, 1994); and Ursula Goldenbaum, " 'Der alte Spinoza hatte ganz recht'? Zur Aneignung Spinozas in der deutschen Sozialdemokratie," in *Transformation der Metaphysik in die Moderne: Zur Gegenwärtigkeit der theoretischen und praktischen Philosophie Spinozas,* ed. Michael Czelinski, Thomas Kisser, Robert Schnepf, Marcel Senn, and Jürgen Stenzel (Würzburg, 2003), 239–266.

44. Jakob Stern, "Materialistische Geschichtstheorie und Ethik," *Ethische Kultur* 1, nos. 3–4 (1893), 19–20, 30–31; Stern, "Die sozialistische Bewegung eine ethische Bewegung," *Ethische Kultur* 1, no. 17 (1893): 131–133.

45. Jakob Stern, "Der ökonomische und der naturphilosophische Materialismus," *Die Neue Zeit* 15, pt. 2, no. 36 (1897): 301–302.

Recent theories of materialism—which Stern labeled "inadequate" and "superficial"—tended to treat matter as the absolute, "the eternal being."[46] All mental phenomena ("the psychical: sensation, feeling, willing, thinking"), Stern further explained, are understood simply as a product of matter, which itself is comprised of infinite energies that are in constant motion. As a consequence, all events, including mental events and human actions, are said to be governed by laws of physical causality. Although these theories derive from the best of modern sciences, Stern insisted, they nevertheless remain "in essence part of the old, obsolete metaphysical direction of philosophy."[47] He identified two problems of recent materialist theories. First, he claimed, they reproduce a dualism that they simultaneously deny: they assert a fundamental difference between mind and matter, even when they claim that all being is matter. As a consequence they wind up simply presupposing something they cannot explain, namely, mind. Second, these theories of materialism begin with what Stern called an "inadequate application of categories of causality." They want to say that somehow physical phenomena are absolutely different from mental, but they cannot locate the "part between material energy and psychical quality," or they cannot explain why matter bothers to produce mind at all.[48]

As an alternative to materialism, which Stern found woefully inadequate, he offered Spinozist monism. Spinozism shared with materialism the valuable quality, according to Stern, that it was directed against "churchly spiritualism" and "cartesian dualism." Moreover, it adhered rigidly to the laws of natural causality. But in opposition to crass materialism, Stern asserted, Spinozism did not deny the being of thought, nor did it view thought as a mere product of matter.[49] According to Stern's Spinozism, thought and extension, mind and matter, are not different substances ("as Cartesius had taught"). Rather, it assumes that there is only *one* substance, one "absolute," of which thought and extension are simply two attributes. "The psychical and the physical run parallel," he explained, adding that "every thing has a material and a mental side; even the inorganic

46. Ibid., 302.

47. Ibid., 304.

48. Ibid. For further elaboration by Stern on materialism and causality, see "Substanz- und Causalitätsidee," *Sozialistische Monatshefte* 8, pt. 2, no. 10 (1904): 824–828.

49. Stern, "Der ökonomische und der naturphilosophische Materialismus," 302.

has a psychical quality; every atom is 'spiritualized.'"[50] Mind is not a product of matter, but both mind and matter operate according to laws of causality and necessity.

In Stern's view, Spinozist monism not only provided a better foundation for socialism than did the crass theories of materialism but also pointed to a viable socialist ethics. Following Spinoza, Stern understood ethics not as a matter of *ought,* that is, as how one *ought* to live, but rather as an *is,* how life *is,* how one *must* live according to parallel-running intellectual and physical laws of causality. Stern thus began, again following Spinoza, with the assumption of the drive for self-preservation. The drive for self-preservation, he explained, is the strongest drive of the individual, and an ethics must work with it. Ethics thus must be based not on the premise of suppressing the affects but rather on nurturing the affects. The command, according to Spinoza, is to "seek your advantage."[51] In principle this drive is best served through intellectual contemplation, especially through the intellectual love of "God," which is also the intellectual love of nature, as God is nature or the totality of being. Only through such contemplation does one seek the true, rather than just the most immediate, advantage. The highest ethical law is, therefore, to love the neighbor—not, however, because one *should* love the neighbor. Rather, one loves the neighbor ethically because love for the neighbor is the most direct way to serve the drive for self-preservation. There are two seemingly opposed reasons for this. On the one hand, individuals come together in order to enhance their power, "because when, for example, two individuals of the same nature combine with one another, they create an entity that can do twice as much as the individualized individual."[52] On the other hand, in Spinoza's thought, all individual entities are only temporary instantiations of a permanently transforming nature. To truly seek one's own advantage is thus to be able to see beyond the self as a distinct entity and to recognize the self as part of that eternal nature in its eternally changing manifestations. As Stern wrote in his book on Spinoza, "the demise of the individual is in truth the closest

---

50. Ibid., 302.
51. Stern, "Materialistische Geschichtstheorie und Ethik," 30; Jakob Stern, *Die Philosophie Spinoza's: Erstmals gründlich aufgehellt und populär dargestellt,* 2nd ed. (Stuttgart, 1894), 147.
52. Ibid., 156.

thing to the ethical idea in its purest form."[53] One thus loves the neighbor ethically as another manifestation of the nature of which one's self is also a part. One loves the self in loving the neighbor, or in loving God as nature.

Class society, however, presents an obstacle to Spinozistic ethics. In class society, Stern explained, the individual person is alienated—from the self, from nature, and from the neighbor.[54] The competition for means of existence governs all human relationships, and the drive for self-preservation pursues only the logic of "earnings-based materialism" (*Erwerbs-Materialismus*).[55] This limitation on ethics and the drive for self-preservation, Stern explained, "is inseparable from the nature of the person in the class state, and can only disappear with the class state itself."[56]

In his critique of the class state, Stern had ventured far from Spinoza, as he himself recognized. Spinoza had proved the unavoidable causality of nature (both mind and matter), Stern claimed, but he had not considered the inevitable causality of history. The logic of historical development had to wait to be discovered first by Hegel, who uncovered the necessary law of the "permanent development from the less perfect to the more perfect," and then by Darwin, who brought to light the necessary evolution of "plants and animals." Marx was then the first to identify the necessary historical path of economic development. Only with Marx's insight, Stern explained, was it possible to see beyond "earnings-based materialism." And only then was it also possible to understand how the drive for self-preservation must lead necessarily to the socialist society and beyond the competition for the means of existence. The drive for self-preservation has no choice in this sense, as it is determined by nature, is part of nature, and is governed by the laws of nature. The ethics of socialism consist in understanding this necessary process intellectually and affirming its inevitability subjectively.[57]

Stern's plea for a Spinozist approach to historical materialism and to ethics stood in sharp contrast to Bernstein's call for a return to Kant. Where Bernstein had heralded ethics as outside nature, Stern's Spinozism

53. Ibid., 187.

54. Marx, "Ökonomisch-philsophische Manuskripte aus dem Jahre 1844," in *ME Werke*, Ergänzungsband, Part 1, 465–588, esp. 510–522, contains a strikingly similar conception of a threefold alienation; there is no indication that Stern had read this work, however.

55. Stern, "Materialistische Geschichtstheorie und Ethik," 30.

56. Ibid.

57. Stern, *Die Philosophie Spinoza's*, 180–182.

spoke to an immanent ethics. It was an ethics that was a part of nature and worked on nature in order to nurture nature.[58] Significantly, this immanent ethics was to be in the position to reflect on matter, but not without accompanying work *on* and *in* matter, that is, not without praxis. Thus Stern had already made it clear in his initial contributions to *Ethische Kultur* that ethics discussions must necessarily be political. A historical materialist ethics has no interest simply in reflecting on the world without also trying to work up or transform that world.[59]

Stern had not leveled his challenge directly at Bernstein, but rather had offered a critique of crass materialism just as Bernstein was launching his own attack on historical determinism. Bernstein understood Stern's intervention largely as a critique of materialism and as an appeal for the intervention of subjective factors in the historical process.[60] Stern himself did not correct Bernstein, but the Russian theorist Georgi Plekhanov, who had just completed his own weighty study of the history of materialism, stepped in to claim Stern's Spinozist monism for the side of revolutionary orthodoxy.[61] If neither Stern's nor Plekhanov's Spinozism became central to the evolving orthodoxy of German historical materialism, both Stern and the core of his ethical project did. Clara Zetkin, for instance, the defender of orthodoxy in the Social Democratic women's movement, hailed Stern on his death as a "real part of the fighting proletariat," and his Spinozism as completely consistent with the Marxist project.[62] More important in the

58. In his effort to depict the Spinozist heritage in "immanent philosophers," Yirmiahu Yovel argues that a similar logic infused Marx's early approach to nature, in which the human is a part of nature but sets itself over and against nature in order to work up or transform nature. Yovel, *Spinoza and Other Heretics: The Adventures of Immanence* (Princeton, N.J., 1989), 85–93.

59. Stern, "Die Sozialistische Bewegung," 131.

60. See Bernstein, "Das realistische und das ideologische," 228.

61. Georgi Plechanow, "Bernstein und der Materialismus," *Die Neue Zeit* 16, pt. 2, no. 44 (1897–1898): 545–555; Plechanow, *Beiträge zur Geschichte des Materialismus* (Stuttgart, 1896). For more recent theorizations of Marxism and Spinozism, see Louis Althusser, *Essays in Self-Criticism,* trans. Grahame Lock (Atlantic Heights, N.J., 1976); Pierre Macherey, *Hegel ou Spinoza* (Paris, 1979); Etienne Balibar, *Spinoza and Politics,* trans. Peter Snowdon (London, 1998); and Antonio Negri, *The Savage Anomaly: The Power of Spinoza's Metaphysics and Politics,* trans. Michael Hardt (Minneapolis, 1991).

62. Clara Zetkin, "Jakob Stern," *Die Neue Zeit* 29, pt. 2, no. 27 (1911): 56, 59. See also Karl Kautsky's fond remembrance of Stern in *Erinnerungen und Erörterungen,* ed. Benedikt Kautsky (The Hague, 1960), 542.

context of ethics discussions, Stern's approach to ethics illustrated especially well the constraints on all orthodox approaches—that is, that ethics must be understood as immanent and as part of, rather than in opposition to, historical necessity.

Franz Staudinger and Max Adler: The Kantian "New Critics"

Stern's intervention might easily have been overlooked not only because of its indirect approach but also because the full extent of the Bernstein controversy was yet to be felt in the party in 1897. Within a year, however, Kautsky and Bebel both grew alarmed at the threat. Kautsky began his full-scale rejoinder in 1898 but did not at this point address explicitly the question of ethics.[63] To deal with the question of ethics itself, he dispatched none other than Franz Staudinger from the DGEK. Not a party member, Staudinger published his critique of Bernstein in both *Ethische Kultur* and *Die Neue Zeit,* the latter, however, under the anagrammatic pseudonym Sadi Gunter.[64]

Like Stern, Staudinger worried about an ill-founded split between thought and matter. Also like Stern, Staudinger sought to find the basis for an immanent ethics that would correspond to laws of causality. Unlike Stern, however, Staudinger approached the matter from the angle of a very Marxist neo-Kantianism, and he aimed his argument directly against Bernstein's Kantian appeal to a transcendent freedom. According to Staudinger, Bernstein had erred when, finding historical materialism's reliance on notions of causality too fatalistic, he placed ethics *outside* the realm of materiality and causality. In doing so, Staudinger insisted, Bernstein had enacted a split between thought and matter that is inconsistent not only with historical materialism but also with sound philosophical principles. Bernstein was content to understand physicality as governed by laws of causality but nonetheless looked to ethics as that which transcended those laws.

63. For Kautsky's response to Bernstein in *Die Neue Zeit,* see especially "Bernstein und die materialistische Geschichtsauffassung," *Die Neue Zeit* 17, pt. 2, no. 27 (1899): 4–16; "Bernstein und die Dialektik," *Die Neue Zeit* 17, pt. 2, no. 28 (1899): 36–50; and "Bernstein über die Werttheorie," *Die Neue Zeit* 17, pt. 2, no. 29 (1899): 68–81. For his book-length response, see Kautsky, *Bernstein und das sozialdemokratische Programm: Eine Antikritik* (Stuttgart, 1899).

64. Pierson, *Marxist Intellectuals,* 133; Karl Vorländer, *Kant und Marx: Ein Beitrag zur Philosophie des Sozialismus* (Tübingen, 1911), 224.

Staudinger countered, however, that modern science recognizes the transcendent in a much more limited fashion than Kant had done, solely as that which is not yet perceivable or fully explainable through scientific methods. Accordingly, the seeming gap between mind and matter is greatly reduced. To be sure, Staudinger admitted, science has not yet been able to explain fully the relationship of consciousness to physicality. That does not imply, however, that one can assume that the realm of consciousness exceeds the laws of causality. Indeed, to forget that consciousness and ethics *both* obey the laws of causality, and thus must both be treated with sound scientific methods, is to throw caution to the wind and to retreat to superstition.[65]

Bernstein made this unfortunate leap, according to Staudinger, because he failed to understand two crucial points. First, Bernstein failed to grasp the central tenet of historical materialism, which assumes the intimate interaction of humanity and nature, thought and matter. His effort to distinguish a unique dimension for ethics and human freedom situated humanity and the human "soul" *outside* nature, as something that works on nature and may be affected by nature, but must be perceived as somehow fundamentally different from nature. This, Staudinger insisted, is the core danger that results when one seeks to understand thought as somehow reliant on its own laws that are not natural laws. Moreover, Staudinger continued, when Bernstein segregated humanity from nature, he removed the individual from the historical process. That is, Bernstein separated the individual from the natural and social world in which he or she arises.[66]

Finally, Staudinger claimed, Bernstein's forgetting of the interaction of humanity and nature, of humanity as part of nature, and the resulting isolation of the individual as a nonhistorical entity, coincided with his inability to understand the difference between "mechanism" and "inner determinism." According to Staudinger, mechanism refers to the mechanistic response of an object when affected by an external object. Determinism, in contrast, speaks to the inner necessity of an organism or a process, such as the inner necessity that a small child will grow to be an adult unless confronted mechanistically by external circumstances. To be sure, Bernstein lamented this image of the individual and of humanity as affected

65. Sadi Gunter [Franz Staudinger], "Bernstein und die Wissenschaft," *Die Neue Zeit* 17, pt. 2, no. 47 (1899): 646–647.

66. Ibid., 651.

mechanistically by external events, as if they had no means to react and interact. But with his justified refusal of a world in which nature works mechanistically on passive individuals and humanity, Staudinger asserted, Bernstein also tossed out the possibility of determinism as the inner necessity of development, or as the necessity that at once is a part of nature and changes nature historically.[67]

To counter Bernstein further, Staudinger articulated an alternative ethics of scientific socialism, an ethics that he held to be in correspondence with the laws of causality and historical materialism. Like Bernstein, Staudinger assumed that a socialist ethics begins with Kant and develops logically out of Kant's emphasis on human freedom, though it must remove the "metaphysical veil" that remained in Kant's thought. According to Staudinger, an ethics of socialism must assume at the outset that freedom implies a world in which the actions of equal individuals correspond with one another, and in which those individuals and that society do not impose limits on or annihilate one another. More precisely, freedom implies the elimination of contradictions.[68] The moral individual suffers when confronted with intellectual contradictions, and society suffers from social contradictions. Moreover, moral freedom, or the individual freedom from intellectual contradictions, is possible only in a social economy that is itself also free from contradictions. The two must work together, according to Staudinger, if human freedom is to be realized.[69]

The inner determination of the individual and of society thus works necessarily toward the elimination of moral and social contradictions. That is, the inner determination is to work toward individual and social freedom that cannot be realized independently of each other.[70] Bernstein was on the right track when he emphasized the importance of freedom in the socialist project, Staudinger noted, but he stopped short. He settled for a limited dimension of freedom, an individual freedom that he thought might be realized in an unfree society and an unfree economy. Unfortunately, according to Staudinger, Bernstein opened his thought to doctrinalism when he stopped short in this fashion, as the end point had no necessary

---

67. Ibid., 649.
68. Franz Staudinger, "Ed. Bernstein und die Ethik," *Ethische Kultur* 7, no. 16 (1899): 122.
69. Gunter [Staudinger], "Bernstein und die Wissenschaft," 652.
70. Ibid.

justification. It thus differed little from the doctrinalism of a party, a state, or a church. An ethics of freedom breaks from arbitrary doctrinalism, Staudinger concluded, only when it recognizes freedom as a product of causal necessity that demands the historical process continue to strive for *both* individual *and* social freedom.[71] The idea for Staudinger was thus not to "return to Kant" but rather to develop Kant's thought to its logical— and socialist—conclusion.

In his criticism of Bernstein, Staudinger took the neo-Kantian approach to socialism well beyond his peers. Staudinger was intellectually affiliated with Hermann Cohen's Marburg school, identified expressly by one of its leading members, Karl Vorländer, as "neocritical" (*neukritisch*) as opposed to neo-Kantian.[72] According to Vorländer, the neocritical school borrowed from Kant the focus on epistemological criticism (*Erkenntniskritik*) as opposed to merely academic epistemology (*Erkenntnistheorie*), and used it to purge philosophy—including legacies of Kantian philosophy—of all "metaphysical leftovers" (*metaphysische Überbleibsel*), especially the notorious "thing in itself" (*das Ding an sich*) that Kant had posited as inaccessible to human knowledge. Like Staudinger, this school emphasized the necessity of moral laws and thus worried about the loose, indeterminate quality of freedom that Bernstein associated with Kant and that seemed to recall a residue of the "thing in itself" as outside the laws of causality.[73] In this regard, Staudinger's project exemplified the overall critical leanings of his fellow pupils out of Marburg. Yet unlike Staudinger, other high-profile practitioners of that school—especially Rudolf Stammler and Paul Natorp—tended to insist nonetheless on the autonomy and indeed primacy of ethics over material dialectics. Staudinger, conversely, insisted on the necessary interaction of the material and the ethical, maintaining that they were in their inner deterministic fashion inseparable. In this way, according to Vorländer, Staudinger carried the neocritical impulse furthest in the direction of Marxist thought.[74]

71. Staudinger, "Ed. Bernstein und die Ethik," 122. Staudinger further developed these themes in his *Ethik und Politik* and *Wirtschaftliche Grundlagen der Moral* (Darmstadt, 1907).

72. Vorländer, *Kant und Marx*, iv. On the rise of neo-Kantianism, see especially Köhnke, *Rise of Neo-Kantianism*. On the socialist tendencies in the Marburg school, see Willey, *Back to Kant*, esp. 102–130, 170–178; and Steger, "Historical Materialism and Ethics," 656.

73. Vorländer, *Kant und Marx*, 118.

74. Ibid., 151.

At roughly the same time as Staudinger's intervention, a slightly different critical Kantian project emerged from the Austrian Social Democratic Party, an autonomous organization but one that maintained close correspondence with its German counterpart. Articulated by Max Adler, this project began also as a correction to the Bernsteinian interpretation of Kant's relevance for Marxism. Adler first appeared on the scene in 1901, when the Austrian Social Democrats set out to revise their 1899 party program (known as the Hainfeld program). He objected loudly to suggested changes to the program that seemed to quiet the revolutionary tone of the party. Identifying the revised program as too revisionist—too "Bernsteinian"—Adler quickly caught the approving eye of Kautsky.[75] In the next years Adler, along with Otto Bauer, Rudolf Hilferding, and Karl Renner, began articulating a distinctively Austrian Marxist project that emphasized the "systematic survey and study of the teachings of Karl Marx and Friedrich Engels."[76] In this context they founded *Marx-Studien (Marx Studies)* in 1904, a forum in which they published the majority of their theoretical works. Significantly, the project received considerable praise and recognition from the orthodox guard at *Die Neue Zeit.*[77] In 1907, they also founded *Der Kampf (The Struggle),* an Austrian counterpart to *Die Neue Zeit,* to foster discussion of both theoretical matters and practical politics. Adler's magnum opus, *Kausalität und Teleologie im Streite um die Wissenschaft (Causality and Teleology in the Conflict Regarding Science),* appeared in the first edition of *Marx-Studien* in 1904, asserting the importance of Kant's project for socialism and setting the parameters for Adler's own intervention in the debates on ethics.

In *Kausalität und Teleologie,* Adler identified Kantian thought as the basis for an ethics consistent with the scientific claims of orthodox Marxism. In contrast to Staudinger, however, Adler did so less by drawing on Kant's moral theory than by critically reshaping the philosopher's epistemology, especially his conception of the transcendental categories of experience.

75. For Max Adler's intervention in the discussions about revision, see especially his "Zur Revision des Parteiprogramms," *Arbeiter-Zeitung* 13 (October 22–24, 1901); Victor Adler, *Briefwechsel mit August Bebel und Karl Kautsky,* 374–375.

76. Max Adler and Rudolf Hilferding, "Vorwort," *Marx-Studien* 1 (1904): v. See also Vorländer, *Kant und Marx,* 250.

77. See articles from Max Zetterbaum, "Die Marx-Studien," *Die Neue Zeit* 23, pt. 1, nos. 7–8 (1904): 196–204, 242–247.

Just as Kant understood space and time as a priori categories of thought, or categories through which thought operates prior to experience, Adler asserted the social as an a priori category. Accordingly, all human experience, acts, and moral decisions take place in a *social* context that precedes the individual. Indeed, even the phenomenon of the self, or the "I," as Adler put it, is an illusion, a product of social consciousness. He thus explained that a person "is not a social being that feels driven to others out of inclination or instinct or reason; he lives socially with others not in consequence of habit or because of emergency: rather he is social and in direct proximity to his own kind because of the very circumstances that enable him to exist. The social character is already given in the condition of individual existence."[78] As Tom Bottomore explains, placing social association prior to experience enabled Adler to dismiss not on moral but rather on *methodological* grounds all individualistic forms of social theory or philosophy.[79]

In keeping with his overall focus on the social rather than the individual, Adler approached the problem of ethics as a fundamentally social problem. He began with the premise that social life and social consciousness presuppose some form of moral valuation, explaining that the (always social) individual "is in the first instance a practical, consummate, and goal-setting being."[80] As such, moral valuation cannot be removed from human existence without radically impoverishing that existence. The question for Adler was thus not *whether* ethics must play a role in social life but *which* role ethics should play. He insisted that Marxism could not simply assume that all aspects of human existence that do not correspond to laws of physical nature can be set off as the pure realm of ethics, and certainly not in the space of an arbitrary "freedom." Nor did he incline toward any moral ideals that would transcend historical circumstances. So what role did Adler give to ethics within Marxism?

The answer, for Adler, lay in his understanding of Marxism first and foremost as an empirical science of society. Marxism as social science, according to Adler, must understand social life as something other than a simple product of nature, and it must have techniques that differ from

---

78. Max Adler, *Kausalität und Teleologie im Streite um die Wissenschaft* (Vienna, 1904), 181.

79. Tom Bottomore, introduction to *Austro-Marxism,* ed. and trans. Bottomore and Patrick Goode (Oxford, 1978), 20.

80. Adler, *Kausalität und Teleologie,* 239.

those of the natural sciences. Nevertheless, in its empirical study of society Marxism cannot subordinate itself to what he called "teleological" thinking or norms, or a predetermined moral aim. If it does, it loses its claim to be a science. The challenge, Adler thus argued, was for Marxism as social science to observe the crucial distinction between objective observation and analysis on the one hand and moral valuation on the other, without forgoing moral consideration altogether. Scientific inquiry must be used as a "means for moral purposes, as a value to be realized," but its potential lay solely in its cold observation of actual social development.[81] In this role, Marxism as social science can serve social development by clarifying what the given social conditions are and then deducing what realistic and delimited possibilities of creating a different social order exist, that is, making clear what kind of practical action can be taken. Moreover, this connection to practical action as *product* of social science is what distinguishes Marxist critical science from bourgeois academic research. Adler thus understood this connection of rigorous social research together with subsequent moral action to derive directly from Marx's thought, referencing at the end of his own book Marx's famous line that "the philosophers have only interpreted the world; it is necessary, however, to change it."[82]

Karl Kautsky and Negative Idealism

These interventions by Stern, Staudinger, and Adler were by no means the only models that circulated in Social Democracy. The *Sozialistische Monatshefte,* to which Bernstein himself had retreated, continued to publish articles on ethics, including a follow-up contribution by Staudinger in which he claimed that the liberal ideas of Kant led necessarily to socialism.[83] Likewise, discussions about ethics and Marxism continued in the increasingly orthodox pages of *Die Neue Zeit* even after the standoff between Kautsky and Bernstein subsided.[84] But together the arguments from Stern,

81. Ibid. See also Vorländer, *Kant und Marx,* 257; and Bottomore, *Austro-Marxism,* 77.

82. Adler, *Kausalität und Teleologie,* 241.

83. Staudinger elaborated on this schema in "Kant und der Socialismus: Ein Gedenkwort zu Kants Todestage," *Sozialistische Monatshefte* 8, pt. 1, no. 2 (1904): 103–114.

84. See, for instance, Sadi Gunter [Franz Staudinger], "Antonio Labriola und die Ethik," *Die Neue Zeit* 18, pt. 2, nos. 45–46 (1900): 556–560, 586–591; Franz Mehring, "Karl Vorländer, die neukantische Bewegung im Sozialismus," *Die Neue Zeit* 20, pt. 2, no. 4

Staudinger, and Adler indicated the breadth of possibility and simultaneously the shared features of nonrevisionist historical materialist approaches
to ethics that even Kautsky himself would eventually embrace in his own
ethical turn: an insistence that ethics speaks not to individual comportment
but to social conditions; that ethics is an *immanent* phenomenon, and not
external to nature and material life; that ethics is consequently part and
parcel of praxis—or is *political.*

Kautsky's own journey in the matter of ethics reveals a dramatic shift
in orientation, aptly illustrating the productive ways in which intellectuals
actively learned to redefine ethics. As we have seen, Kautsky had joined
his fellow socialists to reject the DGEK in the early 1890s, fearing that an
appeal to ethics would "blunt the weapons" of the class fight.[85] In 1901,
however, he returned to the topic of ethics after provocation from another
member of the DGEK, Friedrich Wilhelm Foerster. Foerster had recently
published an article speaking to the English working class and the need for
that movement's ethicization.[86] In response Kautsky gave the earliest inclinations of his gradual shift toward articulating a more positive socialist
ethics, making a distinction between "ethical jargon" and ethical societies
on the one hand and "true ethics" on the other.[87] He criticized Foerster not
for the turn to ethics per se but for Foerster's continued insistence on ethics as a force outside material conditions. In this miniature tête-à-tête with
Foerster, Kautsky also began to hint that a "true ethics" must be seen as a
social phenomenon that necessarily exceeds the individual.[88]

Finally, in 1906, Kautsky published his own small book on ethics, the
culmination of his contributions to the ethics discussions that had unfolded
anew in *Die Neue Zeit* and in *Vorwärts*. This more substantial intervention

---

(1902): 123–124; Max Zetterbaum, "Internationalität und Ethik," *Die Neue Zeit* 20, pt. 2,
no. 4 (1902): 101–105; A. Joffe, "Zu Mandevilles Ethik und Kants 'Sozialismus,'" *Die Neue
Zeit* 24, pt. 2, no. 28 (1906): 45–50; Otto Bauer, "Marxismus und Ethik," *Die Neue Zeit* 24,
pt. 2, no. 41 (1906): 485–499; and Karl Kautsky, "Leben, Wissenschaft und Ethik," *Die
Neue Zeit* 24, pt. 2, no. 42 (1906): 516–529.

85. Kautsky, "Noch einiges über Ethik," 115.

86. Friedrich Wilhelm Foerster, "Soziale Demokratie und Ethik: Ein neues Kapitel aus
dem englischen Munizipalismus," *Soziale Praxis* 10, no. 4 (1900): 73–74.

87. Karl Kautsky, "Klassenkampf und Ethik," *Die Neue Zeit* 19, pt. 1, no. 8 (1900): 241–242.

88. Ibid., 240, 241. For follow-ups by both Foerster and Kautsky, see Friedrich Wilhelm
Foerster, "Klassenkampf und Ethik," *Die Neue Zeit* 19, pt. 1, no. 14 (1901): 438–441; Karl
Kautsky, "Nochmals Klassenkampf und Ethik," *Die Neue Zeit* 19, pt. 1, no. 14 (1901): 468–472.

was motivated by arguments with Kurt Eisner, then coeditor with Franz Mehring of *Vorwärts* and a reinvigorated voice for Kantian ethics in Social Democracy. The explicit controversy between Eisner and Kautsky in *Vorwärts* pertained to the use of the general strike in the party, a conversation instigated by the publication in 1905 of *Generalstreik und Sozialdemokratie (The General Strike and Social Democracy)* by the Dutch socialist Henriette Roland-Holst. At stake was the use of the general strike as a tactical maneuver, and in particular whether it would have valuable political impact or might conversely produce negative effects for workers. Yet these explicitly political concerns necessarily raised once again the theoretical questions of consciousness and intention in the evolution of history and progress toward a socialist revolution. And for Kautsky they brought up anew the role of the "ethical and aesthetical questions" in the party's program.[89]

In the standoff with Eisner, Kautsky stuck primarily to matters of political tactics. He published his subsequent reflections on ethics, however, in his book-length *Ethik und materialistische Geschichtsauffassung (Ethics and the Materialist Perspective on History)*. Here he sought to navigate between what he called the "materialists" and the "idealists" to articulate an approach to ethics that would coincide with historical materialism. He had to find a way to counter the materialist moralists, who, he claimed, rightly viewed moral codes as products of social necessity but who maintained that it was consequently impossible to criticize those moral codes. That is, according to Kautsky, the materialist moralists were stuck arguing that because moral codes are products of social necessity, they are inherently justified.[90] Conversely, though Kautsky wanted to insert space for critique in the materialist study of moral codes, he did not want to go so far as the moral idealists, who held out a transhistorical moral ideal against which

89. For Eisner's arguments, see Kurt Eisner, "Debatten über Wenn und Aber," *Vorwärts* 22, nos. 205–211 (September 2–9, 1905). For Kautsky's response in *Vorwärts,* see Karl Kautsky, "Die Fortsetzung einer unmöglichen Diskussion," *Vorwärts* 22, nos. 204, 208, 209 (September 1, 6, and 7, 1905); see also Kautsky, "Die Fortsetzung einer unmöglichen Diskussion," "Noch einmal die unmögliche Diskussion," and "Der mögliche Abschluss einer unmöglichen Diskussion," *Die Neue Zeit* 23, pt. 2, nos. 48–51 (1905): 681–692, 717–727, 776–785, 795–804. See also Kautsky, "Patriotismus, Krieg und Sozialdemokratie," *Die Neue Zeit* 23, pt. 2, no. 37 (1905): 343–348; Vorländer, *Kant und Marx,* 187, 220–221; and Willey, *Back to Kant,* 177–178.

90. Karl Kautsky, *Ethik und materialistische Geschichtsauffassung* (Stuttgart, 1906), 121–122.

to judge historically specific social codes as moral or immoral.[91] Kautsky's task was thus to find a non-idealist way to affirm the insights of the materialist moralists while articulating a means to criticize social mores and a social order of economic inequality.

In his effort to negotiate the terrain between the materialists and the ethical idealists, Kautsky found guidance not so much from Stern or Staudinger but rather from Joseph Dietzgen. Dietzgen, a self-educated tanner-turned-philosopher who had enjoyed considerable esteem from Marx, had in the 1870s set the precedent for thinking about ethics within materialism.[92] Most important, he had understood ethics as a material necessity of the inherently social existence of humanity. That is, he maintained that ethics derived from the fact that humans need and serve one another. He explained in his book, *Das Wesen der menschlichen Kopfarbeit (The Essence of Human Mental Work),* that "the individual finds himself lacking, insufficient, limited. He needs the other and society for his own completion, and thus in order to live, he must also let live. In a word morality refers to the consideration that grows out of this need."[93] Based on specific human needs, ethics accordingly vary with social eras, as material necessities of social life change. Unfortunately, ethicists tend to understand the forms that ethics take in specific historical eras as their essence or transhistorical truth, and in this they go awry. When they do so, they lose sight of ethics as a bodily instinct, or as a material component of human life, and they transform materially necessitated moral behaviors into transcendent truths. In time, as material conditions change, the reified ethics lose their relevance, as they no longer pertain to historically specific social and political conditions.[94] Such pretenses to unfounded absolutes, according to Dietzgen, form the foundation of intolerance and intellectual misguidance.[95]

91. Ibid., 133.

92. Eugen Dietzgen, "Joseph Dietzgen: A Sketch of His Life," trans. Ernest Untermann, in Joseph Dietzgen, *Some of the Philosophical Essays: Socialism and Science, Religion, Ethics, Critique-of-Reason and the World-at-Large,* ed. Eugen Dietzgen and Joseph Dietzgen Jr., trans. M. Beer and Th. Rothstein (Chicago, 1906), 7–33.

93. Joseph Dietzgen, "Das Wesen der menschlichen Kopfarbeit," in Joseph Dietzgen, *Schriften in Drei Bänden,* vol. 1 of 3 (Berlin, 1961), 117.

94. Joseph Dietzgen, "Die Religion der Sozialdemokratie," in Dietzgen, *Schriften in Drei Bänden,* 1:250–267.

95. Dietzgen, "Das Wesen der menschlichen Kopfarbeit," 112.

Although both Marx and Engels had held Dietzgen in high regard, his influence on socialist theory declined until the turn of the century, when, largely through the efforts of his son, Eugen Dietzgen, his work resurfaced. At this point the reception was generally enthusiastic in orthodox quarters, although interpretations of his importance varied.[96] The Dutch socialist Cornelie Huygens saw in Dietzgen a promising Spinozist challenge to Kant, while Vorländer, Eugen Dietzgen, and several others saw Dietzgen as working in a Kantian tradition while going beyond the limits of Kant's own thought.[97]

In his turn to ethics, Kautsky too echoed the newfound interest in Dietzgen, exhibiting less concern for the Spinozist or Kantian tradition he might be furthering and more for the attention to historically specific human needs that inform the moral sensibility. In his early dismissal of the DGEK, Kautsky had already taken a line very reminiscent of Dietzgen, hinting at a distinction between moral inclination or energy as the driving force of ethics on the one hand and moral codes on the other.[98] By 1906, he was ready to elaborate further on the relevance of the distinction for a historical materialist ethics. Now citing Dietzgen explicitly, he spoke of the social instinct, or the instinct to work socially with other human beings, as the transhistorical basis of ethics or as the moral force (*Kraft*) that makes ethics possible. Conversely, he further connected moral codes and rules to historically specific social needs, those that arise in conjunction with historically specific modes of production. Indeed, Kautsky remarked, the ability to create moral codes that hold force over the individual subject distinguishes the human moral capacity from the animal moral capacity. Both exhibit a social instinct and demand sacrifices from individuals, but only humans elaborate complex moral codes.[99]

96. Vorländer, *Kant und Marx,* 99.

97. Cornelie Huygens, "Dietzgens Philosophie," *Die Neue Zeit* 21, pt. 1, nos. 7–8 (1902): 197–207, 231–239; Eugen Dietzgen, "Der wissenschaftliche Sozialismus und J. Dietzgens Erkenntnistheorie" *Die Neue Zeit* 22, pt. 1, no. 8 (1903): 231–239; Otto Ehrlich, "Kant und Dietzgen," *Die Neue Zeit* 23, pt. 2, no. 30 (1905): 118–123. See also Bruno Wille, "Der Arbeiterphilosoph Josef Dietzgen," *Der sozialistische Akademiker* 2, no. 4 (1896): 206–215; Anton Pannekoek, "Historischer Materialismus und Religion," *Die Neue Zeit* 23, pt. 2, nos. 31–32 (1904): 133–142, 180–186; and Edward Belfort-Bax, "Die Geschichte und Philosophie des Sozialismus," *Die Neue Zeit* 23, pt. 1, no. 2 (1904): 48–51.

98. Kautsky, "Noch einiges über Ethik," 110–111.

99. Kautsky, *Ethik,* 134.

Like Dietzgen, Kautsky understood the conflict within ethics to arise when moral codes break free from historical and social necessity and take on a life of their own. When they lose direct contact with historical necessity, they threaten to lose their force, as they can no longer draw on the social instinct. They become purely logical phenomena and rely on a transcendent ideal from which moral codes are said to derive. In other words, the moral codes erect the transcendent ideal on which they themselves come to depend. Thus weakened, such moral codes come to rely on vast institutions, especially religion, for their survival and influence. Only in this condition, when moral codes can no longer demonstrate their obvious necessity for social existence, do they take on a conservative and coercive dimension. They become conservative because they no longer keep pace with social developments, and they become coercive because they no longer serve social needs.[100]

Yet Kautsky found a solution between the idealists and the materialists precisely in the contradictions that arise when the moral codes no longer correspond to social needs. When this happens, he claimed, the moral ideal appears as a *negative* power.[101] As a negative power, the materially based moral ideal confronts the outdated moral code with new social needs. It is, Kautsky insisted, a moral ideal that has nothing to do with philosophical idealism because it appeals to no eternal concepts such as "freedom, equality, fraternity, justice, humanity."[102] Rather, it is a moral ideal of indignation that always demands that the historically specific *content* of such moral concepts be both expressed and realized.

Practically speaking, Kautsky's moral idealism demanded "sober economic considerations."[103] Like the ethics of Stern's Spinozism, Kautsky's moral idealism recognized no "ought" but rather a "must"—the "must" of social necessity.[104] And much as Adler had emphasized Marxism as the practice of social science, Kautsky too claimed that science stands above ethics, in that scientific study reveals the contradictions between existing moral codes and social needs. Furthermore, science alone can indicate the

100. Ibid., 130–131.
101. Ibid., 140.
102. Ibid., 144.
103. Ibid.
104. Ibid., 141.

changes that are necessary in both social and moral organization to resolve those contradictions. To be sure, science cannot be guided by ethics, but it can be motivated by the moral ideal of indignation, or by the negative moral ideal. Thus motivated, science provides direction for necessary political work. Again, like Stern, Staudinger, and Adler, Kautsky came to see ethics, science, and politics as part and parcel of a common historical materialist praxis.

Kautsky's book did not lay the issue of ethics fully to rest in Social Democracy. But it marked the culmination of the orthodox appropriation of the rhetoric of ethics for a historical materialist praxis. Where Stern, Staudinger, and Adler had received the accolades of the party's faithful, Kautsky spoke as the one who determined orthodoxy. Where Kautsky had once feared ethics would weaken the class struggle, he now could articulate an immanent ethics of necessity as an integral part of the class struggle, indeed as a "special weapon for the special conditions of the class war."[105] Moreover, Kautsky's own reversal on the matter was a product of the very active public discussion that was taking place in and around Social Democracy, not just among the revisionists or so-called ethicists but also among the most revolutionary materialists. In this sense Kautsky's reversal marks better than almost any other individual's contributions the success of the ethics reform movement—not to create a new and modern ethics but rather to make the *discussion* of ethics and its contestation a vital necessity of public intellectual work.

Gender and Sexuality in Social Democratic Ethics

The SPD had struggled with issues of gender equality from its inception. Marx, Engels, and Bebel in particular had been some of the most outspoken theorists of late nineteenth-century Germany on the matter of women's economic and legal equality.[106] At the level of practice, however, the party's stance was a bit more modulated. The party was the first in Germany to

---

105. Ibid.

106. Marx and Engels, "Manifest"; Friedrich Engels, *Der Ursprung der Familie, des Privateigentums und des Staats,* in *ME Werke* 21, 27–173; August Bebel, *Die Frau und der Sozialismus* (Zurich, 1879).

include women's suffrage as part of its platform, but the measure had been hard to push through the ranks. Though Bebel and Wilhelm Liebknecht had advocated for female suffrage on the party platform at the Gotha unification congress of 1875, they were defeated.[107] Only in 1891 at the Erfurt congress did the party finally adopt a platform for universal suffrage regardless of sex.[108] Matters were equally sticky in the realm of labor. Marx and Engels had held female labor in the public realm to be both a necessary development of capitalism and a necessary step toward female emancipation. But in practice the matter was much thornier, as workers resisted the "feminization" of their trades.[109]

By the time of the ethics debates, the economic and political relevance of sexuality and gender difference remained a fairly open question in the SPD. Overall a fairly liberal attitude toward sexual practices ran through the orthodox-revisionist spectrum, along with a hostile attitude toward state-sponsored regulation of sexual morality.[110] For some, this tradition continued without change after the turn of the century. Clara Zetkin, for instance, the editor of the Social Democratic women's periodical *Die Gleichheit,* objected to the moral regulations implied in the Civil Code as a tool of capitalism, an opinion that was echoed by a colleague in reference to the *Proposal for a Criminal Code.*[111] Alongside this strain, however, appeared a growing tendency to appeal to transhistorical gender roles and gendered

107. "Protokoll des Vereinigungskongresses der Sozialdemokraten Deutschlands zu Gotha," quoted in Werner Thönnessen, *The Emancipation of Women: The Rise and Decline of the Women's Movement in German Social Democracy, 1863–1933,* trans. Joris de Bres (London, 1973), 32.

108. Ibid., 34.

109. Kathleen Canning, *Languages of Labor and Gender: Female Factory Work in Germany, 1850–1914* (Ithaca, N.Y., 1996), esp. 3, 50–51; Jean Quataert, "Social Insurance and the Family Work of Oberlausitz Home Weavers in the Late Nineteenth Century," in *German Women in the Nineteenth Century: A Social History,* ed. John Fout (New York, 1984), 280–295.

110. See, for instance, the discussion in *Der Sozialistische Akademiker:* Albert Martens, "Das sexuelle Leben und seine Vorbedingungen," *Der Sozialistische Akademiker* 2, no. 2 (1896): 94–105, followed by the collection of responses under "Weiteres zur Debatte über das sexuelle Problem" and "Rückblick auf die Sexualdebatte," *Der Sozialistische Akademiker* 2, no. 4 (1896): 225–231, and 2, no. 6 (1896): 365–373.

111. Clara Zetkin [Die Redaktion], "Ehe und Sittlichkeit, V," *Die Gleichheit* 16, no. 17 (1906): 114; H. B., "Der Vorentwurf eines neuen Strafgesetzbuchs," *Die Gleichheit* 20, no. 6 (1909): 87. Many of Zetkin's articles were listed in *Die Gleichheit* under the authorship of "Die Redaktion," or editorial staff. In such cases I attribute the article to Zetkin while noting "Die Redaktion" in brackets.

moral considerations that often dovetailed with appeals to the home as the proper place for women.[112] A concluding paragraph in Kautsky's book on ethics illustrates the ambivalence in the party on the matter, even among its orthodox core. Kautsky celebrated the fact that the modes of production had finally freed women from "the family hearth," or the "private household." Yet, he noted, the "natural" distinction of men from women would not disappear, nor would many of the distinctly gendered moral demands. Some would continue to exist, while others that had been buried by historical processes might even be revived. But the future evolution of society, he was sure, promises "not simply the abolition of the exploitation of one class by another, but also the abolition of the subjection of woman by man."[113] In other words: yes, men and women are equal but different, and somehow that difference might pertain to their moral roles, but it is hard to see exactly how from within capitalism.

If Kautsky's treatment of the topic was brief, its ambiguity pointed to the pressing questions on the table: how exactly does one understand gendered moral duties in the historical materialist framework? Are gendered moral roles transhistorical or determined by economic necessity? How do those gender-specific material necessities evolve? And does the sexual drive itself evolve? How does the reconfiguration of the public by the entry of women into work outside the home affect the understanding of moral roles? And how might Social Democracy, or the socialist society, understand equality in light of gendered moral considerations? Kautsky only touched on these problems, but two leading figures in the Social Democratic women's movement, Lily Braun (formerly Lily von Gizycki) and Clara Zetkin, gave these questions much more sustained attention.

Lily Braun and a Feminine Ethics beyond Economic Reform

Lily Braun had been associated with the prosocialist faction of the DGEK until her fallout with Friedrich Wilhelm Foerster. In 1899, after she had left the DGEK and joined the SPD, she and Foerster faced off again, this

---

112. A controversial contribution on this point was Edmund Fischer, "Die Frauenfrage," *Sozialistische Monatshefte* 9, pt. 1, no. 3 (1905): 258–266. For Clara Zetkin's direct response to Fischer, see "Aus Krähwinkel," *Die Gleichheit* 15, no. 6 (1905): 31–32; and "Aus Krähwinkel, II," *Die Gleichheit* 15, no. 7 (1905): 37–38.

113. Kautsky, *Ethik,* 143.

time over the relationship of the bourgeois to the proletariat women's movements. Foerster understood the two to share an ethical goal of emancipating women from outdated moral expectations.[114] Braun's own stance on the matter vacillated over time. While working with the DGEK, she had supported cooperation between the two groups.[115] But now she adamantly opposed such cooperation, noting the naiveté of Foerster's view that women's emancipation required a moral rather than an economic solution. The truth is, she asserted, "that economic emancipation is the presupposition that makes possible all general and deep moral education and elevation of a people."[116] Braun spent the next several years negotiating a position somewhere between these two. As a committed socialist, albeit gradually more closely allied with the revisionist camp, she demanded attention first and foremost to economic considerations and cast skepticism on all variants of ethics reform. Simultaneously, however, her attention to femininity and feminine sexuality caused her to reopen the door just a little to the place of ethics in socialist activism.[117]

Braun began to articulate a new position with her 1901 book, *Die Frauenfrage (The Woman Question),* in which she initiated a retreat from the hard-line stance she had taken against Foerster and ethics reform. A weighty study, *Die Frauenfrage* combined a historical account of women's social status with substantial empirical information regarding the economic situation of women in Europe at the end of the nineteenth century. Braun suggested that law, ethics, and religion all derive originally from a matriarchal protection of the mother-child relationship. "The task of the blood-related family and the origin of the marital clan ... does not derive from a higher moral knowledge," she explained, "but rather from the primal drives of nature: hunger and love. Out of these originate mores

114. Friedrich Wilhelm Foerster, "Zur 'Ethik des Kampfes': Eine Entgegnung," *Die Gleichheit* 9, no. 22 (1899): 173–174.

115. Jean Quataert, *Reluctant Feminists in German Social Democracy, 1885–1917* (Princeton, N.J., 1979), 125.

116. Lily Braun, "Herrn Foerster zur Erwiderung," *Die Gleichheit* 9, no. 22 (1899): 174. Braun was responding to Friedrich Wilhelm Foerster, "Proletarische und bürgerliche Frauenbewegung," *Centralblatt des Bundes deutscher Frauenvereine* 1, no. 11 (1899): 81–83, and 1, no. 23 (1899): 89–91.

117. For general accounts of Lily Braun, see Ute Lischke, *Lily Braun, 1865–1916: German Writer, Feminist, Socialist* (Rochester, N.Y., 2000); Alfred Meyer, *The Feminism and Socialism of Lily Braun* (Bloomington, Ind., 1985); and Quataert, *Reluctant Feminists,* 77–80, 107–133.

and out of mores the morality of a period."[118] Like Kautsky and Dietzgen, Braun thus saw the rise of ethics and law as a natural product of primal human relationships and needs. As a consequence she came to accept at least the limited potential of legal and ethical reform for socialist purposes, although not without significant trepidation, reminding her readers that at bottom, "social-political legislation is powerless before problems" that are at the base of the class conflict.[119]

This focus on maternity as the basis of ethics led Braun to explore two competing directions regarding the constitution of femininity and its meaning for ethics. On the one hand, she emphasized the historical composition of femininity, pointing to how seemingly feminine traits such as "servility" and "voluntary subordination" were purely historical. They may have served a use when economic circumstances kept the women in the home, she asserted, but were becoming irrelevant as women were achieving economic independence.[120] To the extent that those traits embody femininity, she suggested, the term itself must be seen to denote "not a sum of living character traits but a number of virtues fossilized into tradition."[121] On the other hand, reaching back to her assertion that ethics derive from the needs of the mother-child relationship, she presented motherhood and "kindness and compassion" as eternal qualities of femininity and as the basis of a distinctively feminine ethics. Braun thus maintained a twofold approach to ethics that bore a striking resemblance to the claims by Dietzgen and Kautsky that social needs require ethics but that moral codes—or, in this case, moral traits—tend to detach themselves from historical circumstances and crystallize into seemingly eternal laws.

Yet as Braun continued to explore the transhistorical dimensions of femininity, she came up against the problem that moral aspects of femininity might not be accounted for solely through economic considerations. That is, her focus on the mother-child relation as the basis of ethics led her to emphasize a moral right to feminine sexuality, which she equated with maternity. She echoed Helene Stöcker and the New Ethics reformers, whose League for the Protection of Mothers Braun supported from the outset, when she

118. Braun, *Die Frauenfrage*, 5.
119. Ibid., 556.
120. Ibid., 415.
121. Ibid., 416.

suggested that "the right to work, the right to public activity means little for the liberation of the woman and for the full flourishing of her personality as long as she has not fought for the right to love."[122] Here, vaguely echoing Bernstein's Kantian move, she seemed to be pointing to a moral freedom that exists independent of historical and economic developments—although in Braun's case, that freedom was placed in the "right to love."

Nevertheless, Braun was not tempted to switch camps and endorse wholeheartedly the project of the New Ethicists. Indeed, writing in *Die Neue Gesellschaft (The New Society)*, a periodical that she and her husband founded and that was intended as an independent socialist production— "independent not from the program and principles of Social Democracy, grounds on which it stands steadfast, but rather independent from the authority of the official party channels"[123]—Braun began to express serious skepticism about any unidimensional project of either reform or revolution. The advocates of the New Ethic in particular, she maintained, invested too much in sexual liberation itself, conflating the sexual instinct with ethics and with "intellectual understanding."[124] While Braun supported the New Ethic, especially in its celebration of feminine sexuality and maternity, she found it meaningless "as a solution to the sexual problem" insofar as its ethical-legal emphasis precluded serious consideration of the economic circumstances that modern women confront.[125]

Braun did not limit her skepticism to the New Ethic and sexual liberation, however. On the one hand, she extended it to all variants of sexual-ethics reform—moderate, radical, and conservative alike—insofar as they all identify the problem of modern gender relations and the associated moral difficulties in the loss of religion, a depletion of traditional mores, the physical degeneration of modernity, or the strains of economic relations.[126] "We however," she explained, emphasizing her opposition to these one-dimensional critiques, "believe [the problem] to have developed through the joint effect of economic relations and religious-moral influences."[127] Braun thus held the socialists equally limited in their belief in

122. Lily Braun, "Die Entthronung der Liebe," *Die Neue Gesellschaft* 1, no. 20 (1905): 238.
123. "An die Leser," *Die Neue Gesellschaft* 5, no. 18 (1907): 545.
124. Lily Braun, "Das Problem der Ehe," *Die Neue Gesellschaft* 1, no. 10 (1905): 115.
125. Lily Braun, "Die Befreiung der Liebe," *Die Neue Gesellschaft* 1, no. 22 (1905): 261.
126. Ibid., 260.
127. Ibid.

a singular solution to the complex social problem of ethics, sexual relations, and society. Still siding firmly with the socialist approach, she nevertheless wrote: "The overcoming of necessity is the most important step toward the liberation of love, and finally it is here that socialism has a world-liberating task to fulfill ... but regarding the most interior dimensions of problems affecting people, it would be mistaken to expect everything from purely economic reforms."[128]

In short, Braun's attention to femininity opened up a space for ethics in her socialist thought, as she had discerned the origin of ethics not in the regulation of oppressed classes but rather in the social needs of the primal mother-child relationship. She consequently did not propose a transcendent ethics, or a transhistorical moral law. Instead, she grounded ethics in the human condition, that is, in the caring and nurturing that she saw as intimately tied to the reproductive processes. Yet for Braun, understanding ethics did not require attention solely to the modes of production. It required attention to feminine sexuality and to the modes of reproduction. But this very attention to feminine sexuality that was at once historical and transhistorical—even if deeply social—made social reform at large exceedingly difficult. An approach to an ethics of feminine sexuality required attention to both economics *and* ethics reform, even if the two seemed intrinsically at odds.

Clara Zetkin and the History of Sexual Morality

Braun's harshest critic was her fellow Social Democrat, Clara Zetkin, who had been a rising star in the Social Democratic women's movement since her public debut at the 1889 Second International in Paris. She had become involved in the workers' movement in Leipzig by way of association with emigré Russian socialists and joined her intimate friend, Ossip Zetkin, in exile in Paris in the wake of the antisocialist laws. In 1891, she took over the editorship of the periodical *Die Gleichheit (Equality),* the successor to the short-lived *Die Arbeiterin (The Woman Worker),* which quickly became the primary periodical for the Social Democratic women's movement.[129]

---

128. Ibid., 263.
129. On Zetkin's work and life, see, for example, Quataert, *Reluctant Feminists,* 65–76, 107–133; Karen Honeycutt, "Clara Zetkin: A Left-Wing Socialist and Feminist in Wilhelmian Germany" (Ph.D. diss., Columbia University, 1975); Luise Dornemann, *Clara Zetkin: Ein*

Zetkin approached the topics of sexuality and ethics somewhat indirectly through a 1906 series of articles on marriage and morality in *Die Gleichheit*. In this series Zetkin was responding as much to the bourgeois ethics reform movements as to the tendency in her own party to identify a transhistorical feminine moral role. Where Kautsky, for instance, left the definition of this role open and Braun understood it primarily in terms of sexuality and maternity, others such as Edmund Fischer had recently pushed for a reassertion of the intimate relation of the feminine and the domestic, advocating a Social Democratic platform that would support returning women to the house.[130] Zetkin's own response was to radically historicize ethics, femininity, and sexuality in one sweeping gesture.

To do so she traced the long history of monogamous marriage, around which so many of the bourgeois sexual-ethics debates—and lately those in her own party—had come to concentrate. Indebted to the arguments of Engels, Bebel, and Julius Lippert, Zetkin's account meandered from early matriarchy to contemporary bourgeois marriage, calling into question especially the latter's moral status.[131] She found in ancient Greece a monogamous marriage that rested not on moral but rather on purely economic grounds. She also found there the origins of the simultaneous sexualization and privatization of women. As slavery evolved and disparities in wealth grew, Zetkin maintained, women performed less labor, lost social prestige, and came to be "valued exclusively as sexual apparatus for the generation of legitimate heirs."[132] Thus the seemingly transhistorical moral role of

---

Lebensbild (Berlin, 1957); and Gilbert Badia, *Clara Zetkin: Eine neue Biographie,* trans. from the French by Florence Hervé and Ingeborg Nödinger (Berlin, 1994). For analyses of Zetkin on ethics or sexuality, see Tânia Ünlüdag, "Bourgeois Mentality and Socialist Ideology as Exemplified by Clara Zetkin's Constructs of Femininity," *International Review of Social History* 47, no. 1 (2002): 33–58; Richard J. Evans, "Theory and Practice in German Social Democracy, 1880–1914: Clara Zetkin and the Socialist Theory of Women's Emancipation," *History of Political Thought* 3, no. 2 (1982): 285–304; and Keith Allen, "Toward a Socialist Morality of Sexuality: An Examination of Aleksandra Kollontai's and Clara Zetkin's View of Working-Class Women's Reproduction," *Voenno-Istoricheskii Zhurnal* 10 (1992): 68–81.

130. Fischer, "Die Frauenfrage," 258–266. For Zetkin's direct response to Fischer, see in particular her articles "Aus Krähwinkel," 31, and "Aus Krähwinkel, II," 37.

131. Clara Zetkin [Die Redaktion], "Ehe und Sittlichkeit, II," *Die Gleichheit* 16, no. 10 (1906): 64.

132. Ibid., 72.

women as mothers and sexual beings, according to Zetkin, arose solely in response to division of labor and inequalities in wealth.

Only during the Renaissance and Reformation was morality welded to monogamous marriage, though not without producing serious internal contradictions. This period, which itself was inaugurated by a shift from a "natural economy" to a "money economy" and which was thus marked by a new wealth in Europe, saw a world of "remodeled spiritual and moral values" for the economic elite.[133] With the newfound celebration of the "individual character" came a valorization of individual sexuality and the idea that the sexual drive is "one of the strongest human expressions of life."[134] In this era, sexuality came to be understood as an expression of freedom and as such to be attached to the individual will and individual morality. It also came into conflict with the practice of monogamous marriage.

The Reformation took up where the Renaissance left off. Where the sexual liberations associated with the Renaissance remained confined to the economic elite, the marriage reforms of the Reformation in principle affected the entirety of society. These reforms, Zetkin informed her readers, began as protest against "the celibacy of the spiritual." Yet deriving from this original protest were demands for marriage reform that "proclaimed the freedom of the individual will over and against the church dogma."[135] In these efforts, Zetkin claimed, the Reformation not only transformed the relationship to God into a free contract and "introduced into the domain of religious life free testing and decision as moral duty." It also brought "the theoretical recognition of love as the natural-moral basis of marriage."[136] That is, where the Renaissance had valorized sexual individuality, the Reformation coupled sexual with moral individuality and reinstated both in monogamous marriage. Furthermore, the Reformation insisted on individualized moral sexuality "as equal for man and woman. The right that was declared was a human right, not merely a man's right."[137]

133. Clara Zetkin [Die Redaktion], "Ehe und Sittlichkeit, IV," *Die Gleichheit* 16, no. 14 (1906): 91.

134. Ibid., 92.

135. Clara Zetkin [Die Redaktion], "Ehe und Sittlichkeit, IV," *Die Gleichheit* 16, no. 15 (1906): 99. Note that two articles were referred to as part IV.

136. Ibid.

137. Ibid, 99–100.

When Zetkin turned to the era of capitalism, she began to echo implicitly Staudinger's ethics of noncontradiction and Kautsky's negative idealism. The bourgeoisie, she maintained, has inherited from the Renaissance the ideal of sexualized individualism and from the Reformation the ideal of love within marriage. Yet insofar as bourgeois marriage remains a product of capitalism, she claimed, it represents little more than a contract of "sale and convenience" that functions according to the logic of private property.[138] Spousal relations amount to little more than the exchange of property for sexual rights. The "prostitution of man and woman in marriage," Zetkin claimed, is now "sanctioned by the state, blessed by the church."[139] Not recognizing the extent to which marriage has come to be determined by private property, Zetkin claimed, the bourgeoisie adheres to the ideal of love within marriage, an ideal she held to be fundamentally impossible within capitalism. And the contradiction played out with special ferocity on the woman. The era invested its moral ideals in the woman, even as it defined her ever more as nothing but a sexual being. In keeping with this contradiction, it glorified the banishment of the bourgeois woman to the home even as the move depleted her subjecthood. Conversely, the era abjected the proletarian woman, who had to sell her body in the factory. The resulting contradictions between practice and ideal in the bourgeois framework necessitated a dialectical—or "negative ideal"—resolution. In a metaphor all too obvious for its reproductive materiality, Zetkin insisted that "capitalism is due."[140]

Like Kautsky, Zetkin looked for a new moral ideal growing out of real economic conditions. This she found in the proletariat, not so much because the proletariat are intrinsically moral, but because economic circumstances compel them to live in a fashion that has nothing to do with bourgeois morality and that does not correspond to the public/private divide that defines both private property and bourgeois sexual morality. Because the proletariat possess no private property, they are "not in general led to one another's arms through the allure of earning and maintaining property."[141]

138. Ibid., 100.
139. Clara Zetkin [Die Redaktion], "Ehe und Sittlichkeit, V," *Die Gleichheit* 16, no. 17 (1906): 114.
140. Ibid., 105.
141. Clara Zetkin [Die Redaktion], "Ehe und Sittlichkeit, V," *Die Gleichheit* 18, no. 16 (1906): 119. Note that two other articles were also listed as part V.

Consequently, and "in dialectical nature," the proletariat's role is not solely to eliminate bourgeois norms. Rather, in the realm of marriage in particular, the proletariat "establishes simultaneously the meaningful characteristics of a higher bond of man and woman."[142] Again, the proletariat are not in a position to *choose* an intrinsically more moral form of human relations. Rather, their material circumstances *compel* them to live a form of human relations that resolve the intrinsic contradictions of bourgeois ethics.

Always One Step Further

In her comprehensive study of the Social Democratic women's movement, Jean Quataert correctly characterizes the political activist stances of Braun and Zetkin as a replay of the revisionism/orthodoxy split in the Social Democratic Party.[143] Intellectually, however, their two stances also did a different kind of work. Braun, who was allied politically with the revisionists, articulated an ethics reminiscent of the immanent models of her more orthodox counterparts. She didn't resort to anything like Bernstein's transcendent ideal of freedom but rather found the kernel of ethics in the social needs that arise in the mother-child relationship. Moreover, while she understood sexuality as a force that cannot be fully accounted for by economic conditions, she nevertheless understood it and any ethics that derive from it as very material phenomena. Likewise, Zetkin was in many ways more orthodox than her counterparts at *Die Neue Zeit* in her radical historicization of ethics, sexuality, and femininity, when even Kautsky had relented and suggested that transhistorical gender roles might exist. For her, femininity and its connotations of the private and the maternal were born of slavery, and sexuality as a defining feature of the individual will was born of a market economy. Moreover, though Zetkin hinted that a "true ethics" might emerge in a classless state, she recognized absolutely no transhistorical basis for it—not even the social needs or maternal instinct that Kautsky and Braun respectively identified.

Just as Braun and Zetkin seemed to take the critical engagement with ethics one step beyond their male counterparts, Social Democracy as

142. Ibid.
143. Quataert, *Reluctant Feminists,* 123.

a whole took the discussion of ethics one step beyond the bourgeois re-formers. The orthodox theorists insisted with even more force than their bourgeois counterparts on two of the central tenets of ethics reform: that discussions of ethics must be a contestation of "morality" as unquestioned norms, and that any meaningful discussion of ethics must have political import. Even more striking, however, was the socialist theorists' greater emphasis on the reconsideration of the public. On this front, the socialist theorists were much less interested in the work of the private in reshaping the public, and instead, coinciding with their broader critique of private property, challenged the very distinction between the private and the public. For Zetkin and Braun, the challenge held an added, gendered dimension, as they sought to dissociate a feminine ethics from the private.

The contributions from Braun and Zetkin were especially poignant in light of their responses to the discourse on the sexualization of ethics. Braun partially accepted the intersection of ethics and sexuality, but she saw that intersection as a necessary obstacle to utopian reform projects. Zetkin went even further. Although she did not sever ethics from sexuality entirely, she presented their intersection as fundamentally contingent on historical developments. Sexuality remained for her an important example in the discussion of ethics—perhaps even the most important example because it *seemed* for so many of her contemporaries to be a "natural" phe-nomenon. Yet precisely because sexuality could appear so natural—and to have a natural relationship to ethics—it proved to be the most incorrigible moment of ideology. It was thus all the more important for her to push it and its regulation into the realm of historical development, and to dem-onstrate in the process how the materiality of humanity moves together with thought about it. In historicizing the idea that sexuality bears *any* relationship to ethics, Zetkin distinguished her thought not only from that of bourgeois reformers such as Helene Stöcker and Ellen Key, and not only from the Social Democratic revisionism represented by Braun. She also demonstrated her thought to be more orthodox in its approach to historical materialism, more "negatively idealist" than even her most orthodox col-league, Kautsky. In her approach to ethics, the human experience in every aspect of its mental and its physical composition evolved with economic conditions.

At the broader level, developments in Social Democracy indicate the power that ethics as a critical language came to have in the decades before

World War I. The Social Democrats had been the sharpest critics of early ethics reform. And though they never joined the club, a clear consensus emerged between 1890 and 1905 among theorists—not only the revisionists but, more important, the orthodox thinkers—that ethics must somehow be engaged within socialist theory. The Social Democratic case illustrates especially well how both ubiquitous and diffuse the language of ethics became in public intellectual culture at the turn of the century. Participants demonstrated that a reference to ethics by no means implied a return to Kant or to a transcendent ideal of justice or the good. Moreover, whether discussants used ethics to refer to the *ought* or the *is,* to the direction in which society *should* go or the direction in which society *will* develop, they found it increasingly necessary to employ the language of ethics in its mobile and critical potential as a mechanism to explain social action. Indeed, as the Social Democratic discussions suggest, it was precisely in the diversity of form that the rhetoric of ethics reached beyond science, religion, or politics as an explanatory mechanism for social reform or, in this instance, revolution. If the success of the ethics movement should be measured not by the determination of the best school of ethics for social reform, but rather by the aim the DGEK had initially set of prompting critical public discussion about ethics and the presuppositions behind moral claims, then the evolution of socialist theory on the subject and the diversity of approaches that arose *within* Marxist orthodoxy earns the ethics movement a high mark.

7

LOSSES AND UNLIKELY LEGACIES

Psychoanalysis and Femininity

> It is well known that the cannibal remains at this point; he consumes
> his enemies with love, and he refrains from consuming those
> whom he cannot somehow lovingly behold.
>
> SIGMUND FREUD, *Group Psychology and the Analysis of the Ego*

As it did for so many things, World War I brought a sudden end to the
vitality of the ethics discussions. Although the ethics organizations did not
die, their optimism that ethics was a means to reform society was simply
overwhelmed by the unforeseen violence of the war. Before August 1914,
few in the ethics debates had contended with insurmountable problems
of violence and aggressivity. In her memoirs, written mostly in exile in
the 1930s, Helene Stöcker summed up the impact of World War I: "for
people of our time, the Rousseauean belief in the original good of human
nature had been fundamentally driven out."[1] Likewise, Gertrud Bäumer,
who had always been more of a critic than an advocate of ethics reform,
argued that the "conflict of powers" that was in fact well under way in

---

Significant portions of this chapter appeared as an article in *Seminar: A Journal of
Germanic Studies* 36, no. 1 (February 2000): 5–21.

1. Stöcker, "Psychoanalyse 1911/1912," in the Swarthmore Peace Collection, DG 035
Box 1, Folder 5. See also Hermanns, "Stöckers autobiographisches fragment."

latent form before the war and that materialized in extraordinary violence between 1914 and 1918 was on such a large scale and so entrenched in "developments of necessity" that "no moral ideal can help us to resolve them."[2] For Bäumer, politics and the industrial and military developments that produced the war superseded the matter of ethics, including both the individual conscience and the individual sexual life.

Bäumer's comments arose as part of a small series of articles in *Die Frau* *(The Woman)* titled "Between Two Laws" ("Zwischen zwei Gesetze"), in which she and others reflected on competing moral demands presented by the war: between the civil duty to love and honor the nation on the one hand and the "Christian" demand to love the neighbor, including the enemy, on the other. Whether reformers opted for the former or the latter, the majority accepted the set of incompatible options as a difficult but inevitable one. To be sure, complicated moral choices still remained, but the fluidity of their movement—the ways in which ethics reformers could mobilize ethics creatively in multiple directions—declined. If ethics reformers did not renounce the ethics movement altogether (and they by no means did), they often echoed Bäumer's claim that politics and material necessities first of the war and then of building democracy simply overtook ethics as organizational categories for social reform.

In the face of the war itself, the ethics movement thus underwent extreme polarization. As we have seen, individuals such as Helene Stöcker and Friedrich Wilhelm Foerster opted for internationalist pacifism. Rudolf Penzig, conversely, called on the German Society for Ethical Culture (DGEK) not to accept the idea that politics crushes ethics, but rather to turn ethical attention to support of the nation at war.[3] Franz Staudinger, who had once lamented the nationalist feeling that arose in the Franco-Prussian War, greeted World War I as a tragic necessity that one could support ethically only by making it the last war, the "desert" one must cross before arriving at "Canaan."[4] For Staudinger, political necessity trumped ethics in the short run, in the hopes of a moral payoff in the future. To

---

2. Gertrud Bäumer, "Zwischen zwei Gesetzen," *Die Frau* 23, no. 1 (1915): 41.

3. Rudolf Penzig, "Was soll uns jetzt 'Ethische Kultur'?" *Ethische Kultur* 22, no. 16 (1914): 121–122.

4. Franz Staudinger, "Wie müssen wir heute stehen?" *Ethische Kultur* 22, no. 18 (1914): 138–140.

be sure, this was not an embrace of chauvinist nationalism. Moreover, if leaders of the DGEK tended to rally to support the nation, *Ethische Kultur* remained committed to its general practice of open debate, sponsoring a forum to discuss the "morality of the war" and allowing space for pacifist voices.[5] The Social Democrats were equally divided. Those in the Reichstag famously endorsed war credits and sided with Germany in the war, and Lily Braun advocated vocally for national loyalty. On the other side, more radical party leaders such as Clara Zetkin vehemently condemned the war as a project of imperialist capitalism, a position that the revisionist Eduard Bernstein eventually adopted as well.[6]

After the war, leaders of the ethics movement took stock, assessing the effects of the war and the subsequent revolutions on ethics reform and mapping possibilities for the movement's future. In an article of 1920, Penzig reflected on the past and future of the DGEK, acknowledging honestly that the original justification for the organization no longer existed. He did not know whether to place blame on a "mistaken formation of the society" or on the "reorientation of youth from 1890 to 1920," but he had no choice but to admit "the simple fact that the high times of the Ethical Culture movement seem to be past." The war itself had not brought an end to the movement, he noted, though it had stretched the organization thin, bringing its finances to the point of collapse even as it struggled to make its periodical affordable to members during and after the conflict. But the war and the subsequent revolutions had changed the social context, eliminating the need for the ethical movement in its prewar formation. As it was founded in the 1890s, he explained, the ethical movement had been largely a critical movement, or an "opposition party," that fought to preserve the basic rights of individuals and especially the freedom of

5. See the series "Sittlichkeits-probleme im Krieg," *Ethische Kultur* 22, nos. 16–17, 19 (1914): 125–126, 133, 148–149. See also Prof. Schücking, "Der Weltkrieg und der Pazifismus," *Ethische Kultur* 22, no. 20 (1914): 156–157.

6. On developments in the Social Democratic Women's movement in the face of the war, see Quataert, *Reluctant Feminists,* 209–227. On the effects of the war on the SPD, see Eric Weitz, *Creating German Communism, 1890–1990* (Princeton, N.J., 1996), 62–99; David W. Morgan, *The Socialist Left and the German Revolution: A History of the German Independent Social Democratic Party, 1917–1922* (Ithaca, N.Y., 1975), 19–52; Schorske, *German Social Democracy,* 285–321; Abraham Joseph Berlau, *The German Social Democratic Party, 1914–1921* (New York, 1949).

conscience of confessional minorities. With the collapse of the monarchy, however, and the advent of a new era, the times called less for critique, or "negative work," than for the positive, constructive work entailed in building up a new society. As Penzig wrote, "In Germany, in light of the terrible destruction of our moral world, the idea now circulates everywhere that building up is more valuable than tearing down." Nevertheless, the ethical movement would not die, Penzig insisted. Indeed, it lived on as a way both for individuals to pursue moral lives and for groups to determine the course of action, all the more important in an era when society needed to be built anew. But as an organization intended primarily to interrogate categories of ethics, it was obsolete.[7]

Stöcker provided a complementary statement on the reorientation of the New Ethic in the wake of the war and its aftermath. On the one hand, she acknowledged that many of the aims of the New Ethic in its prewar formation had been met: women had just acquired the vote and the right to participate in parliamentary politics; they had entered the work force during the war in unprecedented numbers; and although the pronatalist policies of the war era had banned women's contraception, those same pronatalist policies had also led to increased support for mothers, whether married or single. Accordingly, the New Ethic could afford to move on to new pursuits. At the same time, however, the war had made it clear that the former focus on matters of "life reform"—on the part of the New Ethic as well as other life-reform movements—could no longer suffice without attention to what she called *real* life reform in the sense of preserving life: "One cannot create a higher generation so long as the life of the living generation that is supposed to create the higher one is not yet certain."[8] To be sure, Stöcker remained committed to an ethics of love as the source of reform, just as she remained committed to the critique of stagnant beliefs that block intellectual and social reform. But with the turn of the New Ethic to pacifism and political mobilization against militarism in Europe, she shifted her focus away from the importance of subjectivity and the individual moral outlook and toward politics proper, to the "fundamental

7. Rudolf Penzig, "Die Zukunft der ethischen Bewegung in Deutschland," *Ethische Kultur* 28, no. 6 (1920): 41–44.

8. Stöcker, "Mutterschutz und Pazifismus!" 63.

bases of our governmental lives."[9] Stöcker did not renounce ethics reform, but in fusing the New Ethic with politics, she moved away from a key component of her earlier stance, from the insistence on the separation of ethics and politics, or from the insistence on ethics as a mechanism with which to reflect on and critique the limits of the political.

The shifts that Penzig and Stöcker identified were by no means shifts of resignation but rather calls to a new kind of action, a new kind of reform, informed by but no longer pursuing the intellectual dimension of ethics reform from the preceding decades. And in this shift to concrete politics in the name of ethics, both Ethical Culture and the New Ethic were in good company. For instance, after the war, and after women in both Austria and Germany had acquired the vote, Anita Augspurg and Lida Gustava Heymann began a new periodical, *Die Frau im Staat (Woman in the State)*. It was devoted to mobilizing the newly acquired suffrage toward a pacifist and feminist project of political change based on the "essential connection between women's politics, international understanding, and enduring peace."[10] Echoing the prewar debates about whether a distinctively feminine ethics exists, Augspurg and Heymann now assumed that a feminine ethics did in fact exist and that it could be mobilized for a specific feminization of politics that would include international cooperation between formerly warring states. Yet the two women expressed little interest in furthering the prewar debates, instead concentrating on mobilizing a particular conception of feminine ethics for democratic politics.

From a different angle, two other periodicals that appeared in the 1920s, *Ethik, Pädagogik und Hygiene des Geschlechtslebens (Ethics, Pedagogy and Hygiene for the Sexual Life)* beginning in April 1922 and *Ethik: Sexual- und Gesellschafts-Ethik (Ethics: Sexual and Societal Ethics)* beginning in January 1926, also demonstrate the fusion of ethics with political aims. These periodicals were both devoted to matters of sexuality and hygiene, reaching back to shared concerns with groups such as the League for the Protection of Mothers. Likewise, they both exhibited an interest in moral pedagogy, seeming to take a page right out of the DGEK's book. But unlike their prewar precursors, these newer efforts did not combine their more regulatory tendencies with intellectual interrogations into the meaning of ethics,

---

9. Ibid., 67.
10. Augspurg and Heymann, "Was will 'Die Frau im Staat?'" 1.

the makeup of the moral subject, or the constitution of the community of moral consideration. When these postwar periodicals mentioned the "education of the people"[11] or the need to educate each individual "to place all of his powers and special gifts in the service of the whole,"[12] they did so without asking what kind of moral command undergirded such projects. They took the moral obligation of the individual to the nation as a starting point and sought simply the best means of realizing that moral obligation.

In short, ethics reform had a powerful legacy in the Weimar era, as the proliferation of ethics discussions of the prewar era was channeled into democratic practice after the war. Yet if we remember how central was the mobilization of *Ethik* against *Sittlichkeit* in ethics reform and its intellectual interrogation of moral norms, the periodicals *Ethik* and *Ethik, Pädagogik und Hygiene des Geschlechtslebens* symbolize also the decline of the *intellectual* dynamism of the movement and its vigilant mobilization of ethics as a critical intellectual category. That is, the Weimar era demanded that the language of ethics be mobilized in concrete projects and not further interrogated in public intellectual discussion. And if ethics reform as a movement is to be understood first and foremost as the public *discussion* of subcategories of ethics—the makeup of the moral subject and of the community of moral consideration, the origin of moral sentiment and of the individual conscience—then Penzig was right: the ethics reform movement was over.

Just as the ethics reform movement became thoroughly politicized, however, the critical interrogation of ethics found new life in an intellectual movement that had long been in dialogue with ethics reform: the psychoanalytic movement. Indeed, while reformers began to turn away from ethics as the central category of investigation, the psychoanalytic movement began to explore with ever more intensity questions of ethics and the makeup of the moral subject. Yet like Social Democracy, psychoanalysis represented only a partial inheritance of ethics reform: where Social Democracy insisted on the full politicization of ethics, psychoanalysis would seem at least initially to represent its complete depoliticization. We have already seen how Freud himself had begun to suspect ambivalence and

11. "Zur Einführung," *Ethik: Sexual- und Gesellschafts-Ethik* 2, no. 1 (1926): 1.
12. Emil Abderhalden, "Einführung," *Ethik, Pädagogik und Hygiene des Geschlechtslebens* 1, no. 1 (1922): 1.

hostility as an unacknowledged dimension of the moral subject. In the wake of the war, themes of violence and destructive drives became ever more prominent in the psychoanalytic movement, only furthering Freud's skepticism about the possibilities of ethics as a category of social reform. At the same time, however, participants in the movement in the 1920s began to investigate the specifically gendered formation of the moral subject and its relevance for the ambivalence Freud had identified: they began to ask whether Freud's story about ethics changed when they took into account the gendering process that occurs in conjunction with the formation of the moral subject. In doing so, they found precisely in the gendering of the moral subject the grounds on which to think ethics anew, that is, to take the specifically feminine moral subject as a means to rethink the dilemma of ethics Freud had identified.

The partial legacy of ethics reform was nowhere more obvious than in the psychoanalytic work of Lou Andreas-Salomé, who grappled more continuously and creatively than any other in the psychoanalytic context with the relevance of a gendered ethics for the problem of ambivalence. Her work thus forms the focus of this chapter. Her interest in the question drew on her autodidactic intellectual development as well as her casual but sustained dialogue with reformers such as Ellen Key and Helene Stöcker. She had corresponded for years with Key about both personal and intellectual matters and had spent significant amounts of time socially with Stöcker.[13] She also contributed regularly to Stöcker's *Neue Generation*.[14] Intellectually, she was, also like Key and Stöcker, drawn to an ethics of self-stylization. In the 1880s, she had famously befriended Nietzsche, with whom she shared an immediate intellectual affinity, especially in the critique of ascetic

---

13. Brev till Ellen Key, at the Kungliga Biblioteket, National Library of Sweden, L 41a:1, L 41:63:1; Rudolf Binion, *Frau Lou: Nietzsche's Wayward Disciple* (Princeton, N.J., 1968), 309, 312, 321, 323, 447; Cordula Koepcke, *Lou Andreas-Salomé: Leben, Persönlichkeit, Werk* (Frankfurt am Main, 1986), 247–249. On Salomé's always ambivalent relationship to feminism, see Caroline Kreide, *Lou Andreas-Salomé: Feministin oder Antifeministin? Eine Standortsbestimmung zur wilhelminischen Frauenbewegung* (New York, 1996).

14. For examples of Salomé's articles in *Die Neue Generation,* see "Der Lebensbund," 6, no. 10 (1910): 391–406; "Von Paul zu Pedro," 8, no. 10 (1912): 529–533; "Die Russin," 13, nos. 7–8 (1917): 314–318; "Zum Thema vom Weibe," 15, no. 3 (1919): 148–150. Although Andreas-Salomé was the writer's married name, most scholars use her more famous family name of Salomé, and I follow suit.

morality.[15] In 1894, after Nietzsche's decline, she published one of the first book-length studies of his work.[16] Also important for Salomé, however, especially as she approached psychoanalysis, was the thought of Spinoza, in whom she saw "the philosophical extension beyond Freud."[17] As Ursula Welsch and Michaela Wiesner note, Salomé found in Spinoza a thinker who helped her explore "how body, mind, life, and death are related to one another."[18] Both Nietzsche and Spinoza represented for her alternatives to what she took to be the unnecessary delineations between mind and matter in philosophy and ethics. In her psychoanalytic work, she drew heavily on the ethics of self-stylization or self-articulation inaugurated by Spinoza and developed further by Nietzsche—and "feminized" by Stöcker—as she sought to articulate an ethics that was not built on the premise of sacrifice. Moreover, through her manipulation of psychoanalytic terminology, she echoed the reformers when she also called on sexual difference as a way to pose her challenge to the Freudian psychoanalytic means of thinking about ethics. Yet she also used her psychoanalytic intervention as a means of commentary on the politicization of ethics after the war.

A quick note on style is necessary. Although in dialogue with reform, Salomé's thought engaged the psychoanalytic context and not the reform context. It thus marks a considerable break in style from those whose project she carried forth. She redefined and redeployed dense psychoanalytic terminology through the use of a deeply literary style. To grasp the relevance of her intervention, it is necessary to wade through that literary-psychoanalytic terminology. Doing so patiently should allow her intervention in psychoanalysis and her continuation of—and ultimately mourning for—the intellectual project of ethics reform to emerge clearly.

15. Of Salomé, Nietzsche had remarked to his friend Peter Gast that she was "most markedly prepared for my way of thinking and my ideas." Quoted in Biddy Martin, *Woman and Modernity: The (Life) Styles of Lou Andreas-Salomé* (Ithaca, N.Y., 1991), 79. Also available in Ernst Pfeiffer, ed., *Friedrich Nietzsche, Paul Rée, Lou von Salomé: Die Dokumente ihrer Begegnung* (Frankfurt am Main, 1970), 159.

16. Lou Andreas-Salomé, *Friedrich Nietzsche in seinen Werken* (Frankfurt am Main, 1983); in English as *Nietzsche*, ed. and trans. Siegfried Mandel (Redding Ridge, Conn., 1988).

17. Lou Andreas-Salomé, *In der Schule bei Freud: Tagebuch eines Jahres 1912/1913* (Zurich, 1958), 68–69.

18. Ursula Welsch and Michaela Wiesner, *Lou Andreas-Salomé: Vom "Lebensurgrund" zur Psychoanalyse* (Munich, 1988), 124.

Violence, Ambivalence, and the "Death Drive"

Salomé's own approach to ethics and ambivalence addressed ongoing discussions within the psychoanalytic movement that were increasingly interested in violence and aggressivity, or destructive drives. Sabina Spielrein had made some of the first stabs in this direction. Spielrein was a young Russian medical student and former patient and student of Carl Jung at the Burghölzli Institute in Switzerland who had found her way to the Freudian school of psychoanalysis after a personal conflict with Jung and the almost simultaneous fallout between Jung and Freud.[19] At a 1911 meeting of the Vienna Psychoanalytic Society, Spielrein presented perhaps the earliest theory of a destructive instinct as a constitutive element of subjectivity.[20] Later published in the *Jahrbuch für psychoanalytische und psychopathologische Forschungen* (*Yearbook for Psychoanalytic and Psychopathological Research*) as "Die Destruktion als Ursprung des Werdens" ("Destruction as the Origin of Becoming"), Spielrein's article maintained that a destructive drive, or a violent drive to destroy, always accompanies the sexual drive, and that both the sexual and destructive drives exhibit creative potential.[21] Subjectivity, she argued, arises out of a cyclical pattern of sacrifice wherein a destructive drive that accompanies the sexual drive at once disrupts the status quo even as it opens up possibilities for new articulations of the subject. According to this view, destruction is a necessary condition of human existence and hence is ethically neutral. On her presentation, Spielrein endured considerable criticism from the Vienna audience, but eventually even Freud—initially her sharpest critic, in large part because of the proximity to Jung he sensed in her words—acknowledged her thesis as a foreshadowing of his own thoughts on violent drives.[22]

19. On Spielrein and her relationship to psychoanalysis, see Aldo Carotenuto, *A Secret Symmetry: Sabina Spielrein between Freud and Jung,* trans. Arno Pomerans, John Shepley, and Krishna Winston (New York, 1982); and John Kerr, *A Most Dangerous Method: The Story of Jung, Freud, and Sabina Spielrein* (New York, 1994).

20. *Minutes of the Vienna Psychoanalytic Society,* 3:329–335; Kerr, *Most Dangerous Method,* 367–372.

21. "Die Destruktion als Ursprung des Werdens," *Jahrbuch für psychoanalytische und psychopathologische Forschungen* 4 (1912): 465–503; reprinted in Sabina Spielrein, *Sämtliche Schriften,* ed. Barbara Hermann (Freiburg, 1987), 98–143.

22. Sigmund Freud, "Jenseits des Lustprinzips," in *GW* 13, 59. For a discussion of the presentation, see Kerr, *Most Dangerous Method,* 367–372.

If Spielrein displayed an early and acute interest in the work of destruction, she was hardly the only one among the early psychoanalysts exploring
in depth the functions of violence and aggressivity in the human psyche.
Many were especially quick to follow in this direction after the outbreak
of the war and the emergence of the shell-shocked soldier as a widespread
phenomenon. Viktor Tausk, a young doctor and former lawyer from
Slovenia and an intimate friend of Salomé, had already found matters of
violence and subjectivity compelling when his own military service made
them ever more pressing. Confronted by the urgent problem of war neurosis and the apparent solace or escape that pathology seemed to offer soldiers in the face of violent warfare, Tausk anticipated aspects of Freud's
own thought on melancholia and attachment to painful associations.[23] The
Berlin-based analyst Ernst Simmel also made war neurosis his primary
focus during the war.[24] Approaching the problem of violence from another
angle, the Polish-born Helene Deutsch began to theorize in the 1920s the
innately masochistic character of feminine sexuality, wherein the feminine
self is supposed to emerge through various phases of sexual development
that are experienced and endured as violent attacks.[25] At roughly the same
time, Melanie Klein's explorations in child analysis revealed the role of
aggressivity in the child's first steps toward self-formation.[26]

Freud had been significantly more hesitant than his colleagues to recognize the primacy of aggressivity or destructive drives in the formation

23. Viktor Tausk, "Diagnostic Considerations Concerning the Symptomatology of the
So-Called War Psychoses," in *Sexuality, War, and Schizophrenia: Collected Psychoanalytic Papers,* ed. Paul Roazen, trans. Eric Mosbacher and others (New Brunswick, N.J., 1991), 141–
165. For an earlier piece by Tausk in which he dwelled on the problem of internalized guilt
very similar to Freud's later superego, see his contributions to *Die Onanie: Vierzehn Beiträge
zu einer Diskussion der Wiener Psychoanalytische Vereinigung,* ed. Wiener Psychoanalytische
Vereinigung (Wiesbaden, 1912), 48–68.

24. See especially Ernst Simmel, ed., *Kriegsneurose und psychisches Trauma: Ihre gegenseitige Beziehungen dargestellt auf Grund psychoanalytischer, hypnotischer Studien* (Munich, 1918).

25. For her earliest explication of the masochistic woman, see Helene Deutsch, *Psychoanalysis of the Sexual Functions of Women,* ed. Paul Roazen, trans. Eric Mosbacher (New
York, 1991), originally published in German in 1925. For a biographical account, see Paul
Roazen, *Helene Deutsch: A Psychoanalyst's Life* (Garden City, N.Y., 1985); Lisa Appignanesi
and John Forrester, *Freud's Women* (New York, 1992), 307–328; and Deutsch's autobiography, *Confrontations with Myself: An Epilogue* (New York, 1973).

26. See especially Melanie Klein, "The Development of a Child" (1921), in *Love, Guilt
and Reparation, and Other Works, 1921–1945* (New York, 1975), 1–53.

of the subject. Even before the war, as we saw in chapter 4, he had reluctantly explored the patricidal origins of both culture and the self in his work on totemism and narcissism, respectively. During the war, as he was immersed in his so-called metapsychological papers and the revision of his theory of the mind from a dynamic to a structural model, he began to reflect on the work of mourning and melancholia. He was puzzled in particular by the mechanisms of the mind that allow it to adhere to painful losses and memories.[27] In addition, he too began to engage the phenomenon of war neurosis, seeking initially to find in it a sexual kernel, perhaps even an originary sexual trauma or fantasy that a soldier's war experiences rekindled.[28] Eventually, however, war neurosis led him in another direction.

In *Beyond the Pleasure Principle,* Freud puzzled over the fact that those suffering from traumatic neurosis routinely experience dreams that take them back to the original traumatic event. This habit of repeatedly returning to the psychic danger most obviously contradicted Freud's notion of the "pleasure principle," or the individual tendency to pursue pleasure and avoid pain. It also, however, defied explanation according to the "reality principle," or the condition wherein objective obstacles to pleasure cause the individual ego to renounce its immediate pursuit of pleasure in order to preserve itself. Revisiting the traumatic incident in a dream could not provide pleasure; neither, however, did it result from any literal physical threat. Why then, Freud had to ask himself, would a traumatized patient repeatedly recall the unpleasant memory? To sort out this mystery, Freud was compelled to introduce a new category of drives into the language of psychoanalysis, namely, the "death drives," which compel the individual to return to an inanimate state.[29] These reveal themselves quintessentially in

---

27. Sigmund Freud, "Trauer und Melancholie," in *GW* 10, 428–446.

28. Sigmund Freud, "Einleitung zur Psychoanalyse und Kriegsneurose," in *GW* 12, 321–324.

29. In its treatment of ethics, the Lacanian school has been in the forefront of thematizing the problem of the death drive, deriving primarily from Jacques Lacan, "Kant with Sade," trans. James B. Swenson Jr., *October* 51 (1989): 55–104, which claims the insurmountable paradox of ethics in social existence. According to Lacan, the possibility of a death drive induces the categorical imperative to give way to the logic of the Marquis de Sade, causing "the ancient axis of ethics to slip, by an imperceptible fracture, for everyone" (71). In Kantian logic, the moral agent could never affirm a universal maxim that might lead to enslavement or self-destruction, as this would negate the necessary freedom of the ethical subject. Lacan counters that if one considers the irrationality of the death drive, that is, "the freedom

the traumatic "compulsion to repeat" that the shell-shocked soldiers and melancholics exhibited, but they might also take the form of a primary masochism or related violent fantasy structures.[30] When, just three years later, Freud presented his fully structural theory of the mind in *The Ego and the Id,* he portrayed the potentially excessive tendencies of the superego (the *Über-ich*) as exhibiting sadistic desires that may indeed derive from these newly postulated death drives.[31] If Freud's turn to aggressivity was not completely original, it institutionally legitimated the area of research in the psychoanalytic movement.

Love Thy Neighbor?

Salomé developed an interest in psychoanalysis just as the questions of violence and aggressivity were gaining sway in the movement. She made her first formal acquaintance with the discipline when she attended the 1911 international congress on psychoanalysis in Weimar. Shortly thereafter, Salomé contacted Freud about the possibility of visiting Vienna for several months to immerse herself in the study of psychoanalysis and to take part in the Wednesday evening meetings of the Vienna Psychoanalytic Society. Freud greeted the request from the already renowned author with enthusiasm, and the two soon embarked on a lifelong correspondence of mutual respect and admiration.[32] Soon thereafter Salomé began

---

to die" (69), then this ethical safety valve no longer holds. The subject who may affirm pain, violence, even death, could no longer be taken as the guarantor of rational action or decision. In other words, the bracketing of self-interest or of the pursuit of the pleasure principle on the part of the moral agent does not preserve the sanctity of the law against the *morbidity* of desire.

30. Freud, "Jenseits," 37–45. Theorists interested in trauma have tended to focus more on the ethical implications of the repetition compulsion as the most elementary manifestation of the death drive. For example, see Cathy Caruth, *Unclaimed Experience: Trauma, Narrative, and History* (Baltimore, 1996); for a critical analysis of Caruth, see Dominick LaCapra, *Writing History, Writing Trauma* (Baltimore, 2001), 181–185.

31. Sigmund Freud, "Das Ich und das Es," in *GW* 13, 235–289.

32. See Ernst Pfeiffer, ed., *Sigmund Freud and Lou Andreas-Salomé: Letters,* trans. William Robson-Scott and Elaine Robson-Scott (New York, 1972), 7; also cited in Martin, *Woman and Modernity,* 191–193. On Salomé's relationship to psychoanalysis, see Martin, *Woman and Modernity,* esp. 191–229; and Inge Weber and Brigitte Rempp, "Einleitung," in Lou Andreas-Salomé, *Das "Zweideutige" Lächeln der Erotik,* ed. Weber and Rempp (Freiburg, 1990).

practicing analysis at her home in Göttingen and publishing psychoanalytically informed articles in *Imago,* the journal devoted to psychoanalytic explorations of culture.

In her own critical approach to aggressivity and ethics, Salomé did not contend with the death drive in the way Freud had articulated it. Rather, she went back to his reflections on narcissism, in which he had first struggled to understand the mechanism by which the individual becomes a self-reflective subject. Following Freud, Salomé became interested in the phenomenon of narcissism before the war, exchanging letters with Freud on the topic and voicing to others her concerns about his ideas.[33] Yet she held off on publishing her thoughts until after the war and after Freud's work on the death drive. In the resulting article, "Narzißmus als Doppelrichtung" ("Narcissism as Dual Orientation"), which appeared in *Imago* in 1921, Salomé did not dwell on the death drive in its most technical sense, that is, as a primary masochism or as a traumatic repetition compulsion. But she confronted the unconscious proclivities to violence and destruction that are part of the self Freud had described, and she explored the implications of that observation for ethics.

Salomé presented her argument by returning to a distinction that had been central to Freud's theory of narcissism, the distinction between narcissistic love and object love.[34] Freud had defined narcissistic love as love that takes itself as its object, and object love as love that is aimed at another. He had not only privileged object love as a more mature form of love than its narcissistic opposite; he had also tended to align it with the subject's moral development on the premise that the ability to love another enabled a moral concern for the other.[35] Yet Salomé wanted to ask whether object love is really so opposed to narcissistic love. Moreover, much as Freud would later do, she also questioned whether object love really provides a safe ground for ethics. In *Civilization and Its Discontents* (1930), Freud

---

33. See, for instance, her entry from March 5, 1913, titled "Narzissmus," in *In der Schule bei Freud,* esp. 112–116; letter from Salomé to Freud from January 1915, in Pfeiffer, *Letters,* 22–26.

34. On Salomé and narcissism, see Martin, *Woman and Modernity,* 191–229; Sarah Kofman, "The Narcissistic Woman: Freud and Girard," *Diacritics* 10 (1980): 36–45; for a comparison between Salomé on narcissism and Julia Kristeva, see Karla Schultz, "In Defense of Narcissus: Lou Andreas-Salomé and Julia Kristeva," *German Quarterly* 67 (1994): 185–196.

35. Martin, *Woman and Modernity,* 215–219; Kofman, "Narcissistic Woman," 40–41.

began to ponder whether it is ethical to love the other who may not be worthy of love, hinting that one ought morally to honor one's own love and desire.[36] Salomé took a different tack. She began to wonder if love for the other might be dangerous not to the self but to that loved other.

In his own study of narcissism, Freud had struggled to discern how and why the small child who begins seeking pleasure for itself and initially loves only those things that bring it pleasure ultimately learns to redirect its love onto another, or to exhibit object love. He had answered his query by deciding that object love begins because the individual psyche contains an excess that seeks an object to receive its overflow. If the psyche does not find an object, he insisted, it will become sick (while, conversely, sickness itself tends to prevent the individual psyche from investing in another object).[37]

Salomé simply took this observation one step further. She speculated that the very excess that enables and motivates object love produces as well the need to idealize and shower an *excess* of love on an other. That is, it produces what Freud had called idealization, or the overinvestment of libido in the object. Assuming a utilitarian ethics of self-interest, the reverence for the object would motivate the individual to want to preserve the loved object and would thus generate responsibility to that object. Salomé saw in idealization "the grounds and motivations for ethics."[38] Clearly, an ethics of idealization could not be seen as Kantian, because idealization in Salomé's sense derives from—indeed is inconceivable without—self-interest. Nevertheless, such an ethics would be one that recognizes the coincidence between love of an other and responsibility toward that other, much like the above-mentioned Freudian ethics of object love. It also coincided conceptually with Helene Stöcker's New Ethic, insofar as it assumed that love for the self enables, or is the prerequisite for, love for the other. To this point, Salomé had simply translated this logic into psychoanalytic terms.

Yet Salomé did not stop here in complicity either with Freud or with the reformers. Instead, she pushed the logic of idealization one step further to

---

36. Sigmund Freud, "Das Unbehagen in der Kultur," in *GW* 14, 461.

37. Sigmund Freud, "Zur Einführung des Narzissmus," in *GW* 10, 151–152.

38. Lou Andreas-Salomé, "Narzissmus als Doppelrichtung," in *Das "Zweideutige" Lächeln der Erotik,* 208. The translations of Salomé's passages are my own. However, in reference to her essay on narcissism, I have benefitted greatly from the translation of Stanley Leavey, which appeared as "The Dual Orientation of Narcissism," *Psychoanalytic Quarterly* 31 (1962): 1–30.

the point of its ethical inversion, maintaining that in its effort to preserve the loved object, the excess of idealization threatens simultaneously to crush it, to destroy the object's existence as a finite object. She introduced this step of her argument by rewriting Freud's story of the evolution of the self, producing a narrative that looked nothing like the Oedipal story Freud had told.

According to Salomé's narrative, the process of idealization as response to a primary excess of libido originates in the trauma of birth. She articulated this phenomenon most lucidly in her autobiographical notes, in which she wrote, "Just before [birth] we were everything, undifferentiated, indivisibly part of some kind of being—only to be pressed into being born."[39] This shock results, she claimed elsewhere, in "our shared primal hurt [*Urkränkung*]."[40] What remains, according to her account, after "the loss of that which isn't anymore," is a "residual knowledge, a certainty, that it *should* still exist."[41] Taking her own experience as exemplary, she maintained that the healthy child must construct a divine figure to guarantee the contiguity of the world in order to satisfy the demands of that residual awareness of perceived intimacy. Regardless of its form, which would vary culturally and individually, this construction of a divinity prevents a situation in which the child might "take revenge against a sobering reality through imaginative exaggeration" and subsequently abandon "objective standards."[42] That is, far from leading the child into delusional patterns, the comfort provided by this construction should ease the child's gradual adaptation to the reality principle, or to external limitations on the child's fantasies. Functioning as mediation, this imaginary deity bridges the perceived divide between child and object. Further, although the presence of the imaginary deity fades as the child adapts to the reality principle, its very imaginary character means that it need never disappear entirely. In other words, its imaginary character grants it more flexibility than a really-existing—and therefore really-disappearing—deity would have. In the realm of imagination, the deity endures despite dramatic shifts and breaks in the child's development.

39. Lou Andreas-Salomé, *Lebensrückblick: Grundriss einiger Lebenserinnerungen,* ed. Ernst Pfeiffer (Frankfurt am Main, 1968), 9.

40. Andreas-Salomé, "Narzissmus," 194.

41. Andreas-Salomé, *Lebensrückblick,* 9.

42. Ibid.

The role of the imaginary divinity functioned for Salomé's reconsideration of narcissism in two ways. First, it helped her to tie together stages of development that Freud had distinguished, namely, primary and secondary narcissism. Freud had understood primary narcissism as an infantile stage that individuals overcome when they accomplish object love. Secondary narcissism, on the other hand, he understood as a regression that occurs after the mind is mature enough for object love but takes the self nevertheless as its object. Salomé, conversely, wanted to see narcissism in the singular, as a continuum throughout life. Narcissism is thus "not something that is limited to a single stage of the libido," she argued, but rather "a piece of our love of self that accompanies all stages. [It is] not merely a primitive starting point of development, but rather remains as a fundamental continuity that extends to all later object attachments of the libido."[43] In this regard, the imaginary deity functioned as the mechanism of continuity for individual development. Moreover, the imaginary deity served as Salomé's means to contest the rigid distinction of narcissistic love from object love. For her, this imaginary deity—that which provides contiguity in the world of distinct objects—connected the self to other objects, serving as a fantasmatic unification of self and world.

Significant is the fact that the child produces *divine* protection, an inherently *excessive* construction. As the child enters the world of objects and finite individuals, he or she does not abandon the divine figure, the source of narcissistic security. Rather, he or she takes the relation to the excessive and divine figure as a model for relations to other love objects. The child has invested the divine construction with the representation of the totality of being that is not the self. Adhering to that pattern, he or she will next seek to project the same value onto the chosen love object. According to this model, object love will always strive toward idealization, seeking to replace the divine construction. Just as the constructed god figure functions as a bridging mechanism, first establishing a fantasmatic unification of self and world, it later provides a model for that very unification sought through relationships between self and other. One thus seeks in the object the promise of individuation overcome, a desire that enhances reverence for the object and thereby inaugurates idealization.

43. Salomé, "Narzissmus," 191.

Yet Salomé's understanding of idealization remained decisively ambivalent in terms of ethics. On the one hand, she saw in idealization the impetus toward ethics, as reverence for the object serves self-interest. On the other hand, due to its excessive source, this motivation toward an ethics of the other threatens simultaneously to destroy the other. Salomé warned: "Narcissism [i.e., that which enables idealization] instead endangers the object; its enduring intervention is guilty that its persistent interference ultimately annihilates the object. Since it had been admitted from the outset only as a type of substitute [*Stellvertreterschaft*], the object in reality disappears in its possession all the more as it is celebrated."[44] That is, the narcissistic process of idealization, in seeking and revering totality in the object, fails to recognize the specificity of the *finite* object. This danger pertains not only to the idealized object but rather to every object, as "in the end every object serves representatively as—understood literally in the strict psychoanalytic sense—a 'symbol' for that otherwise inexpressible abundance [*Fülle*] of the unconscious associated with it."[45] The object thus finds itself in a logic of replacement, substitution, and misrecognition.

With respect to the question of ethics, one might consider the sacrificial language of substitution used in this context. The operation whereby the sacred finds representation in the figure of the specific individual has been designated by multiple schools of thought the premise or the logic of sacrifice. According to Jacques Derrida, "sacrifice supposes the putting to death of the unique in terms of its being unique, irreplaceable, and most precious." Simultaneously, however, and this is the paradoxical structure of sacrifice, it "also therefore refers to the impossibility of substitution, the unsubstitutable."[46] That is, the movement of the sacred in sacrificial logic requires that to be worthy of sacrifice, to be a loss, the victim transcend all other individuals and individuation. It must be unique. Yet the victim acquires this status even as it always only *represents* the sacred; it must be replaceable after its destruction if the sacred is to survive. Salomé described the process of idealization in just these terms: "By overvaluation the

44. Ibid., 202–203.

45. Ibid., 199.

46. Jacques Derrida, *The Gift of Death,* trans. David Wills (Chicago, 1995), 58. See also Georges Bataille, "Hegel, Death, and Sacrifice," trans. Jonathan Strauss, *Yale French Studies* 78 (1990): 9–28, esp. 11–19; and Adorno and Horkheimer, *Dialektik der Aufklärung,* 55–63.

substitute returns as it were to the essential content itself and replaces that content in spirit."[47] Conversely, as sacred, the object weighs too powerfully, too heavily, and thereby threatens to crush precisely those who have conferred on it its sacred status. This threat then motivates anxiety toward and subsequent destruction of the object. Herein lies the paradox of an ethics of the other according to Salomé's logic: if left uncountered, love for the other overshoots itself to the point of idealizing the other, to a desire to see "all" in the other. The responsibility to the loved object that arises from a desire to preserve the object always entails as well the danger of irresponsibility in the form of excess if the finitude of the object is not recognized. Thus the tendency to love the other, which enables responsibility to that other, is logically inseparable from—because it produces—the countertendency to annihilate the other in its specificity.

This dilemma of object love or idealization prompted Salomé's dismissal of an ethics of love for an other as adequate grounds for an ethics of responsibility. It also indicated Salomé's partial break from an ethics of love as hinted at by Freud or as outlined more explicitly by Stöcker. Rather than see love as a safe phenomenon and as an alternative to an ethics of self-denial, Salomé drew attention to its excessive and—at least symbolically—violent potential. Yet Salomé did not give up entirely on love as a premise of ethics. Instead, she wanted to establish what other kind of ethical work love could do when it is not aimed directly at an other but rather is conceived as the basis for an ethics of self-stylization. In place of the idea of sexual rights that Stöcker had emphasized, Salomé's ethics of self-stylization looked more to love as the basis of creative pursuits or, in the psychoanalytic terms she used, as an ethics of sublimation.[48]

In neither Freud's nor Salomé's work was sublimation a straightforward term.[49] Sublimation could be defined provisionally, albeit crudely,

---

47. Andreas-Salomé, "Narzissmus," 205.

48. With the idea of an "ethics of sublimation," Salomé anticipated at least partially the argument of the Lacanian theorist Joan Copjec in "Sex and the Euthanasia of Reason," in *Supposing the Subject,* ed. Copjec (New York, 1994), 16–44; and more comprehensively in *Imagine There's No Woman: Ethics and Sublimation* (Cambridge, Mass., 2002).

49. On the incorrigibility of the term, see the entry in Jean Laplanche and J.-B. Pontalis, *The Language of Psychoanalysis,* trans. Donald Nicholson-Smith (New York, 1973), 432–433: "In the psycho-analytic literature the concept of sublimation is frequently called upon; the idea indeed answers a basic need of the Freudian doctrine and it is hard to see how it could

as the displacement of unconscious libidinal energy into intellectual and creative pursuits. As in the case of idealization, Salomé derived her understanding of sublimation from Freud, claiming to adhere to his terminological guidelines. In his "Introduction to Narcissism," Freud differentiated between sublimation and idealization as libidinal processes, explaining that whereas idealization concentrates on and aggrandizes the object, sublimation diverts its aim away from the object and away from direct sexual satisfaction. Freud added in no uncertain terms that the two processes should be assiduously differentiated.[50] As she had done with both object and narcissistic love, as well as with primary and secondary narcissism, Salomé again questioned the distinction Freud made. Referring to the "two clearly differentiated processes, against whose confusion with one another Freud has rightly warned," she also wrote of "the symbolic act of idealizing the object" as "already accompanied by sublimatory elaboration of the drive."[51] This idea that sublimation and idealization should *accompany* each other followed logically from Salomé's redefinition of narcissism. Indeed, she saw both idealization and sublimation as functions of a primary and persistent narcissism that does not oppose itself to object love. Yet if she could not keep the terms as clearly separate as Freud had suggested, she nonetheless saw ethical reasons for their analytical distinction. That is, she agreed on their analytical distinction but wanted to highlight their common origin in order to understand their *ethical* difference.

In Salomé's work, sublimation must be seen to share with idealization the origin that made idealization the basis or motivation for ethics: they both participate in the process of value formation, or the evaluation of the world and of objects in it. They both participate as well in the parallel process, both conscious and unconscious, of labeling *specific* objects to be of significant worth. Moving toward an elaboration of the ethical potential of sublimation, Salomé thus described the more generalized value-formation process:

> The libidinal attachment of narcissism that is forced to remain at that point successfully captivates the judgment which had become ever more adapted

---

be dispensed with. The lack of a coherent theory of sublimation remains one of the lacunae in psycho-analytic thought."

50. Freud, "Zur Einführung des Narzissmus," 161.

51. Salomé, "Narzissmus," 206.

to reality and settles with it on a compromise, according to which "value" stands symbolically for the essential thing, the "one-and-all." The problem of value in general is always a problem of the libido; only with the help of the libidinal condition is it possible for an object to emerge from *seclusion*. All values strive toward overevaluation and away from the relativity of individual particularity.[52]

In other words, all acts of value construction, of designating objects as having "worth"—positive or negative—work against object individuation. Moreover, since she suggests that all libidinally driven constructions of value aim for overevaluation, the processes of idealization and sublimation can be described as pursuits of the sacred, if the sacred is considered that which contests intellectual perceptions of limitations and finitude in the world. Like idealization, sublimation as the process of value formation also serves the desire to overcome the perceived individuation of the self that Salomé labeled the basis of ethics. It strives for the divine, that is, for precisely what she found in idealization had *motivated* ethics.

Yet if Salomé presented idealization and sublimation as sharing the pursuit of the divine through value formation, she posited sublimation as the limitation to idealization and its dangerous excesses. Sublimation in Salomé's work, in contrast to idealization, thus took the form of the *negotiation* between two tendencies: on the one hand, it relates to the idea that "life is only complete in its exaggerations in both directions, in its too absolute overevaluations."[53] This, in short, is the path of idealization. On the other hand, she claimed, sublimation strives for "creativity, while seeking law, rule, the ought."[54] Where idealization projects unlimited value onto the specific object, sublimation projects specific, limited values into the unlimited world. This reversal occurs because, unlike idealization, sublimation does not take an explicit object.

Biddy Martin identifies Salomé's emphasis on the lack of a specific object as "objectless love," a concept Salomé shared with another close confidant, Rainer Maria Rilke.[55] For Salomé, this mechanism of objectless love

52. Ibid., 205.
53. Ibid., 206.
54. Ibid., 212.
55. Martin, *Woman and Modernity,* 32, 44. My argument is clearly deeply indebted to Martin's explication of "objectless love," and builds on it in my own assessment of the term's ethical implications.

or of sublimation enabled the excesses of the libido to be transformed into creative navigation and redefinition of the objective world and its possible articulations via production of and respect for limits and finite specificity: "Through the friction within such a contradiction—through the unconditionality that realizes itself only 'from case to case,' that is, only in the living instance—is *the* creative activity par excellence fulfilled [or ethical sublimation], performing that which 'nowhere and never comes to pass.'"[56] Alternatively phrased, sublimation is the ever-renewed creative production and reproduction of forms. In its movement beyond the individuated self, it shares the ethical *motivation* of idealization, while departing from its object-oriented, and object-crushing, telos.

To clarify why sublimation might be termed ethical, we must recognize its libidinal narcissistic source. Neither Salomé nor Freud understood sublimation as repression but rather saw it as a *redirection* of libidinal energy. Or rather, like idealization, sublimation responds to the excesses of unconscious desire. For Salomé, the excess of unconscious desire results in the aggressivity of idealization. For its part, sublimation does not "overcome" those aggressive excesses but may, with its emphasis on production of form and limit, diffuse the destructive potential. It violently creates new forms in the symbolic world but, in doing so, protects individual loved objects from its wrath.

Furthermore, for Salomé, sublimation's redirection of desire occurs in response to the inaccessibility of the desired object, that is, to the intervention of the social and moral law that establishes prohibitions. Thus the invocation of sublimation necessarily returns a discussion of ethics to the moral law, albeit again not in a Kantian, disinterested form. Rather, this socially oriented moral law merges with the *desirous* superego, where the superego is the partially conscious and partially unconscious aspect of the self that derives pleasure from the assertion of its power to enforce moral and cultural prohibitions. If left unchecked, even Freud had suggested, the superego may exhaust the subject in its insatiable appetite for ever stricter obedience.[57] In order not to be consumed by superegoic moral restriction, sublimation must establish its own limits and their contours. In so doing,

---

56. Salomé, "Narzissmus," 212–213.
57. Freud, "Das Ich und das Es," esp. 256–276.

it creatively articulates a self-world relation, thereby responding to and reorienting the outline and potential of both:

> All real ethics, all ethical autonomy, creates undoubtedly a compromise be-
> tween command and desire, while attempting, in principle, to avoid just
> that compromise. That which is desired is out of reach because of the ideal
> strictness of values, but the imperatives are grounded in the primal dream
> of an all-encompassing, all-supporting Being. This character of compromise
> betrays itself clearly even in the most rigid valuations—yes, especially in
> them—by revealing those subterranean connections between obligation and
> desire, or, otherwise named: between ethics and religion.[58]

The movement of sublimation toward the transcendent thus stops short of delusion only via creative self-articulation of limits. Salomé's ethics of sublimation consists in the process through which the subject expresses itself and its desires in and through the world, while working with, challenging, resurrecting, and restructuring the given limits of that social and material world.

Two points in reference to an ethics of sublimation should be stressed. First, neither the limits nor the imperatives themselves constituted for Salomé the ethical as such. Because the ethical consists in the *process* of creation, one may in fact neither accept nor construct hypostatized principles or laws. The second point logically follows from Salomé's understanding of narcissism: the creative articulation of ethics is by no means sui generis but rather always social, always informed by but not limited to available social articulations. Salomé's depiction of the artist as the ethical exemplar illustrates this condition:

> Without necessarily wanting it, the artist has his public within himself, with
> himself, and all the more so, the more completely he is accustomed to look
> elsewhere, consumed as he is in the creative process itself. It is impressive,
> in my opinion, how much the universal, as in the last instance the ethical,
> needs the "case to case" to realize itself, and that it is in this seemingly par-
> adoxical manner that the special creative significance of ethics first becomes
> apparent. It is a surprising fact that the artist's involvement in his work,

---

58. Salomé, "Narzissmus," 209.

which is so fully personal, also fully comprehends the universal, in order for once to be truly realized as a work. What seems to be the most subjective comes to be the crux of objective validity.[59]

One might say that the poet who has the "public within" and whose work leads to "objective validity" operates narcissistically and ethically in tandem with the reality principle. That is, he or she acts with and against the socially and materially given.

Consequently, Salomé's version of an ethics of self-articulation remained preeminently socially concerned, in reverence—albeit critical—of the possibilities immanent in the social, if the social is understood not simply as interpersonal relations but rather also as the linguistic and aesthetic media of those relations. And while the emphasis of her ethics fell to the realm of the social at large, it is the necessary function of the reality principle that guides a return to the concern for the individual other. This return occurred in Salomé's argument through the recognition of the other as disappointment, as finite. Such recognition propels the movement toward self-awareness of the narcissistic investments behind exultation of the other: "And in fact: it is *we* who disappoint or displease ourselves. The one who disappoints and the one who is convinced of his ideal value remain inseparably united within us, such that the narcissistic source of love does not get exhausted."[60] This return to the other in the manner of disappointment corresponds to the movement of sublimation in the projection of value limited by the imposition of form. As an ethical mode of relating to the other, disappointment operates not as responsibility per se but rather as a check against annihilation. Nevertheless, non-annihilation never falls to the position of mere ethical by-product precisely because ethics as possibility *begins* with the capacity for idealization, a fundamentally social gesture. In order to be ethical in Salomé's sense—that is, in order to construct a self-world relation in narcissistic, creative, ethical fashion—one requires the enduring presence of the other.

Here it is worth noting provisionally some of the parallels to and departures from earlier arguments in ethics reform. Salomé's emphasis on the creative negotiation of values resonates with Stöcker's insistence on the eternal becoming of values as opposed to reinforcement of given norms.

59. Ibid., 216.
60. Ibid., 208–209.

Salomé's affirmation of the social as part and parcel of love for the self also echoes Stöcker's romantic- and Nietzsche-influenced argument that love of self is the foundation for love of the other. Of course, in her concern that love for the other might ultimately invert itself to become destruction of the other, Salomé departed from Stöcker's New Ethic. It is necessary to turn to the femininity debates in psychoanalysis, however, to see how Salomé's own gendering of the problem of ethics at once continued to echo Stöcker, the New Ethic, and ethics reform, even as it contained a critical commentary on the recent politicization of a gendered ethics.

Femininity Debates

In her study of narcissism, Salomé did not dwell explicitly on matters of gender, though she hinted that the full power of sublimation is realized only in cases where "it has not been pushed so far into the realm of the ego as to be 'masculinized.'"[61] Here she again differentiated her thought sharply from Freud, who had continuously argued that women are less capable of sublimation than men.[62] Salomé's own sustained consideration of the role of gender in the formation of the moral subject, however, awaited the further developments of the 1920s, when the psychoanalytic movement became embroiled in debates about the constitution of "femininity."

Before the war, psychoanalysis had only rarely treated femininity as an explicit object of inquiry. Freud and his colleague Josef Breuer had, of course, discovered psychoanalysis largely through the study of female hysterics. These studies, however, were concerned primarily with the workings of the unconscious and the role of sexuality in the development of neuroses rather than with femininity per se. When in the 1920s and early 1930s the debates around femininity (conventionally referred to as the "Freud-Jones controversy") took off, they contended more directly with the issue of how the individual comes into being *as a particular kind of being*—as a sexed being—within a social context. Historians have tended to view the discussion as splitting into two camps over the problem of biologism (or the biologistic determination of a gendered psyche), and consequently as

---

61. Ibid., 200.
62. See, for example, Sigmund Freud, "Die 'kulturelle' Sexualmoral und die moderne Nervosität," in *GW* 7, 158, 162; and "Das Unbehagen in der Kultur," in *GW* 14, 462–463.

determining the lines of Freudian orthodoxy as decidedly nonbiologistic.[63] Yet insofar as the debates followed Freud in understanding the formation of a sexual subject as a moral subject, they exhibited theoretical parallels to the prewar ethics debates, especially to the discussions about the "moral destiny of woman." And no intervention built on that tradition more so than Salomé's.

Initiated by a 1922 article from Karl Abraham, the Berlin psychoanalyst and close confidant of Freud, the femininity debates circled around the notorious psychoanalytical notion of penis envy. In his article, Abraham asserted that both male and female children undergo a "castration complex." Whereas boys are said to fear castration as a result of their illicit desires, Abraham argued, girls experience their lack of a penis as the sign that they have already been punished. Menstruation and defloration, he further claimed, are experienced as verification of the primal wound. In the course of the argument, he emphasized the necessary assumption that girls wish they could be male and possess a penis. The persistence of this desire into womanhood, he concluded, incites both resentment toward men who have what they do not and fantasies of avenging the loss.[64]

Abraham's article found in Freud its greatest defender. Bolstering Abraham's thesis about the different processes by which boys come to be boys and girls come to be girls, Freud published in 1924 "The Dissolution of the Oedipus Complex," in which he worked out the origin of a *moral* discrepancy arising from two different paths for negotiating the Oedipal scenario.[65] Following Abraham, he argued that the little boy verifies his fear of castration when he witnesses the girl's lack of a penis, a lack he construes to be a result of castration. Only this "validated" fear of castration induces the boy to renounce his quest to have the mother. As a result, according

63. See, for instance, Juliet Mitchell, "Introduction I," in *Jacques Lacan: Feminine Sexuality,* ed. Mitchell and Jacquelyn Rose, trans. Rose (New York, 1982), 1–26. Mitchell discusses the divide between the two positions as one of "form" versus "content." She suggests that where Horney, Jones, and others discerned in femininity a distinctive content deriving from reproductive traits and held this up against the distinctive content accorded to masculinity and its privileged access to the phallus, Freud and his followers understood sexual difference to be one of *form,* wherein the masculine and the feminine represented distinctive means of relating to the phallus.

64. Karl Abraham, "Manifestations of the Female Castration Complex," *International Journal of Psycho-Analysis* 3, no. 1 (1922): 1–29.

65. Sigmund Freud, "Der Untergang des Ödipuskomplexes," in *GW* 13, 393–402.

to Freud, the boy identifies with the father and, in so doing, introjects the father's authority in the form of the nascent superego. In other words, the boy's fear of punishment that results from his guilty desires for his mother induce him to renounce his desire and to incorporate a moral sensibility: the sense that not all actions are legitimate actions, and not all desires can be pursued. The girl, in contrast, realizes she has "come off short" when she learns that the boy has a penis and she does not. As a consequence of this apparently insuperable fact, however, the female Oedipus complex itself is far simpler, as it does not have to contend with a looming threat. The girl must merely convert her desire for the mother to an identification with the mother, subsequently adopting the mother's attitude toward the father and desiring a child from him as compensation for the "missing" penis. Insofar as the girl does not identify with the father, however, "there falls away a powerful motive for the formation of the superego," or the moral agent of the psyche.[66]

In a 1925 follow-up essay, "Some Psychical Consequences of the Anatomical Distinction between the Sexes," Freud elaborated on the same theme. Here he surmised the consequence that he hesitated to express: that "the level of what is morally normal for the woman is other [than that for the man]. The superego is never so demanding, so impersonal, so independent from its affective origins as we expect from the man's."[67] The ambiguous language of Freud's statement is noticeable. He did not necessarily diminish the moral capacity of women; he simply described women's relationship to morality as "different" from that of men. Indeed, only one of his feminist protegés, Helene Deutsch, who had been active in the Polish women's and nationalist movements before her move to Munich and eventually Vienna, made the argument that women literally have a *weaker* moral sense than men because of the fact that their relationship to the superego derives from the father, a figure whom they desire but not with whom they identify.[68] In either case, whether articulating a "different" or a weaker relationship to morality, this Freudian "orthodox" line of development within the femininity debates agreed on the basic premise

66. Ibid., 401.
67. Sigmund Freud, "Einige psychische Folgen des anatomischen Geschlechtsunterschieds," in *GW,* 14, 29.
68. Deutsch, *Psychoanalysis of the Sexual Functions of Women.*

that women experience a relationship to morality distinct from that experienced by men, and that the paths by which they come to occupy these different positions will determine their "sex."

The counterargument was led most vociferously by Karen Horney, another Berlin psychoanalyst and in fact a student of Karl Abraham. In the 1923 article "On the Genesis of the Castration Complex in Women," Horney accepted Abraham's terms of argument, namely, the castration complex and penis envy.[69] Like Freud's assumption that the moral individual arises out of a primary sexual desire and the process of renouncing that desire, Horney's response depended on the notion of sexual pleasure as a moral freedom. The boy, she suggested, quite literally enjoys a privilege due to the existence of the penis. In what she labeled the "scopophilic" dimension, the boy experiences the pleasure of seeing his genitals and of being able to comfort himself as to their existence and function. Of crucial importance to the small child is the pleasure associated with urination. Unlike the girl in this practice, the boy enjoys the right to touch his genitals in the act of urination. This socially sanctioned freedom, Horney claimed, grants the boy an access to an onanistic pleasure unavailable to the girl. In this difference lies a primary moral distinction between the boy and the girl: insofar as moral autonomy depends on the freedom to act and the capability to decide whether or not to do so, the boy is placed within the moral realm in a manner unavailable to the disadvantaged girl. The presuppositions behind Horney's argument were, however, more Kantian than the utilitarian assumption of Freud's ethics. Where Freud stuck to an ethics that derived from and honored the pursuit of pleasure or happiness, Horney's conception of moral freedom equated freedom with the physical ability to pursue pleasure and the moral ability to deny it.

Ernest Jones, a London psychoanalyst and close friend of Freud, carried this dimension of Horney's argument one step further. In a 1927 article titled "The Early Development of Female Sexuality," he explored directly the moral implications of the female who is impoverished in terms

---

69. Karen Horney, "On the Genesis of the Castration Complex in Women," in Horney, *Feminine Psychology,* ed. Harold Kelman (New York, 1967), 37–53; originally published as "Zur Genese des weiblichen Kastrationskomplexes," *Internationale Zeitschrift für Psychoanalyse* 9 (1923): 12–26, and reprinted in *International Journal of Psycho-Analysis* 5, no. 1 (1924): 50–65.

of the right to sexual enjoyment. "For obvious physiological reasons," he remarked, she is more dependent on a partner for sexual pleasure than is the male.[70] As a consequence, her access to morality is always mediated by an other. In other words, unlike the male's autonomous (onanistic) relationship to morality, the female relationship to morality necessarily takes place within the bounds of social ties and through relationships to individual others.

In one of her own follow-up essays, Horney had gone on to counter the idea that masculinity bore any privileged relationship to morality, maintaining that the intellectual framework that denoted such a privileged relationship had itself derived from a uniquely masculine perspective. Because the question of sexual difference had been "measured by masculine standards," she argued, it failed "to present quite accurately the real nature of women."[71] Most explicitly, she claimed, the perspective heralded by Freud and Abraham, among others, failed to account for the pleasures of motherhood and the privileged connection women have to the reproductive process.[72] This privileged connection, she further claimed, amounted to a sexual pleasure unique to the female sex. According to the psychoanalytic logic of sexual enjoyment as the basis of moral freedom (in either of its forms of pursuing and honoring or being able to resist pleasure), Horney's argument suggested that women had access to *another kind* of morality, one defined by a distinctively feminine sexual capacity. The historian Mari Jo Buhle has noted the resemblance between the platforms of the fin-de-siècle feminists and Horney's argument, both of which emphasized maternity as the distinguishing characteristic of femininity.[73] In this context, Horney's inversion of the language of envy might suggest another line of continuity between prewar feminism and her own psychoanalytic project. In a language reminiscent of the Nietzschean feminists from a generation earlier, she invoked a logic of *ressentiment,* claiming that men

70. Ernest Jones, "The Early Development of Female Sexuality," *International Journal of Psycho-Analysis* 8 (1927): 459–472.

71. Karen Horney, "The Flight from Womanhood," in *Feminine Psychology,* 57; originally published as "Flucht aus der Weiblichkeit," *Internationale Zeitschrift für Psychoanalyse* 12 (1926): 360–374.

72. Horney, "Flight from Womanhood," 60.

73. Mari Jo Buhle, *Feminism and Its Discontents: A Century of Struggle with Psychoanalysis* (Cambridge, Mass., 1998), 80.

are more productive in the world precisely because they have a greater envy to conquer and deny.[74] Like some strains of fin-de-siècle feminism, Horney thus countered devaluations of feminine morality by inverting the masculine-feminine dyad while retaining the underlying premise of ethics as sexually differentiated.

Although the terms of the argument aligned Horney with Jones on one side and Freud with Abraham and Deutsch on the other, the debates also helped to consolidate the premise that, one way or another, sexuality and sexual difference were constitutive of the moral subject. In this point of agreement, the debates echoed uncannily those of the prewar reformers. Moreover, if the psychoanalytic theorists were not looking to reform society per se, they were asking how those moral identities contributed to or detracted from the shaping of public and political action.

Patricide Averted

Salomé is not usually treated as a participant in the femininity debates. Yet a contribution of hers to *Imago* in 1928 must be seen in the context in which the psychoanalytic movement was trying to consolidate its understanding of the formation of sexualized moral identities. Salomé took the occasion of the controversy, however, less to influence those debates than to think about their relevance for her own question about the dangers of an ethics of love.

In an essay more literary than scientific in style, Salomé played with Freud's narrative of *Totem and Taboo,* speculating, as she titled her essay, on the "consequences of the fact, that it was not the woman who killed the father" ("Was daraus folgt, daß es nicht die Frau gewesen ist, die den Vater totgeschlagen hat").[75] In this literary play, she focused as much on the cultural narrative Freud had offered as on the individual reenactment that each child undergoes in the process of identity formation. In doing so, she

74. Horney, "Flight from Womanhood," 61.

75. Lou Andreas-Salomé, "Was daraus folgt, daß es nicht die Frau gewesen ist, die den Vater totgeschlagen hat," in her *Das zweideutige Lächeln der Erotik,* ed. Inge Weber and Brigitte Rempp (Freiburg, 1990), 237–242. The translation of the title is from Martin, *Woman and Modernity,* 216.

painted the ethically troubling phenomenon of idealization as a product of Freud's model of a specifically masculine process of identity formation. And she asked whether another model, perhaps one closer to sublimation, might be open to the feminine process.

As with her work on narcissism, Salomé borrowed heavily from Freud in this essay, while posing subtle questions that challenged his overall framework. Like Freud, she proceeded to outline the patricidal narrative of masculinization in relation to law and guilt. In Salomé's narrative, as in Freud's, masculine idealization and deification of the father coincide with murderous tendencies toward him, culminating in the onset of guilt. According to Salomé, however, guilt ensues owing to self-sacrifice as the truth of patricidal desire: "Emotionally guilt is first an awareness that one is not 'all.' One must first suffer this guilt in order to become something."[76] That is, while the father's presence counters the child's fantasmatic claim to omnipotence, the consequent desire to remove the father functions intrinsically as admission of self-limitation because, through identification, the son has made of the father his "own future image."[77] Desire to eliminate the father therefore amounts to elimination of part of the self. The quest for omnipotence and its renunciation establish a pattern of sacrificial schisms within the self, as "the claim to be all" can no longer sustain itself. Furthermore, the claim to be all "transforms itself in the demand to exert itself; the infantile desires become the masculine action in life."[78] As a result, the explicitly masculine contest between idealization and patricide founds an either/or relation not only to the father but also to his law: "the man [stands] between guilt and desire, between a natural rebelliousness which wants to liberate itself from anything in its path, as if from an enemy [the father], and the impulse to turn one's own values into a punitive other in order to pull oneself up from one level to the next."[79] The male child either *is* the father and sets the law, or he *obeys* the father and observes his law. Though both options always remain available, the child must always renounce one or the other at any given moment or in any given deed. Significantly, not hate but love and admiration for the father propels the son's

76. Andreas-Salomé, "Was daraus folgt," 238–239.
77. Ibid., 238.
78. Ibid., 239.
79. Ibid., 240.

murderous inclinations—inclinations to be, to replace, and thus to destroy the loved object. In an only slightly oblique reference, Salomé hinted that this sacrificial logic not only defined individual relations but culturally also made up the core of Kantian ethics and its categorical imperative, noting that the son's subsequent "standard of value preserves that excess restriction that can only express itself imperatively and categorically."[80]

Accepting temporarily the exclusion of women in the Freudian narrative, Salomé proceeded to trace the logically resulting implications and alternatives of the narrative for feminine identity construction and its relation to the moral law. As in the case of the masculine, she suggested, the feminine model may also tend to idealize the father. Yet in the feminine alternative, this idealization need not pursue patricidal directions, as the idealization itself "occurs without conflict."[81] In feminine idealization, Salomé explained: "the object-deifying excitation refines itself only to the utmost point of the intellectual; it never loses altogether that last touch of intoxication, as it were, that is still being fed out of the primal bodily bond, out of the paternal (=divine=) inheritance [*Vater (=Gotes=) Kindschaft*] which realizes itself in that intoxication."[82] In other words, the daughter need not sever the tie to the father so finally or dramatically but rather may uphold and survive a love for the father. The language of sublimation speaks strongly here, as sublimation prevents the intoxication behind idealization from settling exclusively on the father. Rather, in accordance with the work of sublimation, that intoxication diffuses multidirectionally into the world, seeking expansion and expression of self in the world, interested in and motivated by, while not bound to or limited by, the specific object.

Nevertheless, the intoxication itself as that which corresponds to the ethical *potential* of idealization endures. It remains in its physicality, in its "primal bodily bond," as the surplus of intellectuality and as that which moves the subject toward the other. The diffused, expanded relation to the father logically concludes with a correspondingly sublimated—now understood as ethical—position with respect to cultural law: "However big or small be the reach of the feminine, it is in any case not unjust to say

80. Ibid.
81. Ibid., 239.
82. Ibid.

the entire sex remains free from a real sense of strictness of conscience and lawfulness, for that which is externally determined, for the imperative, as if she had a kind of sobriety that the more sensitively reacting man lacks: her law and order are elsewhere."[83] The fact that the law and order are "elsewhere" for the feminine could appear either anarchic or utopian if one does not read it as corresponding to the work of sublimation, work that always operates interactively within negotiable limits of social and material contexts. In Salomé's argument, the woman is exempt neither from lawfulness nor from conscience, but only from the *strictness* ("Strenge") of the *external,* superegoic imposition. In terms of ethics, Salomé's female character retains a commitment to creative expression and exploration of law, but not to the masculine law governed by (self-)sacrifice, patricide, and obedience—not to the categorical imperative behind which both she and Freud had found ambivalence and hostility.

This notion of the daughter's relatively nonconflictual attachment to the father led Salomé ultimately to her most dramatic departure from the Freudian narrative, as well as to its undoing. The woman's relationship to the father, she suggested, is one "through which then freely nothing more is missing from universally realized 'Incest!'"[84] Simply put, she remains in love with the father without idealizing him. Her relationship to the father stands in opposition to that of the son who had idealized the father, and who had consequently overevaluated and desired him to the point of annihilation. With the renunciation of the incest taboo—with the renunciation of the primary law underpinning culture in the narrative of *Totem and Taboo*—Salomé returned to the fundamental premise of Freud's account: the male child confronted his own limitation precisely through the father's instigation of the incest taboo and the prohibition against having the mother. In Salomé's narrative, the disablement of the incest taboo appeared as the necessary outcome of the extrapolation of the Oedipal narrative to the woman. Consequently, articulation of the feminine would seem to undo the most basic law of culture and its corresponding cultural narrative, a narrative that had led Freud to view women as perhaps less moral than men and that Salomé turned on its head.

83. Ibid., 239–240.
84. Ibid., 242.

Political Reflections: Ethics and Entry into the Law

The participants in the psychoanalytic femininity debates did not understand themselves as continuing the ethics reform discussions. Yet the parallels between the two movements and their discussions of ethics are striking,
especially in their presupposition about the sexually differentiated nature of the moral subject. Finding the premises of Freudian ethics—or its
critique—flawed, Salomé in particular reached back to the intellectual orientation that had originally drawn her to Spinoza and Nietzsche, and in
so doing responded to Freud's work with an ethics of self-articulation very
resonant with Helene Stöcker's New Ethic. Much as Stöcker had found in
the feminine subject of ethics an alternative to asceticism and *ressentiment,*
Salomé found in the feminine a type of ethics that is not bound by the ambivalence that Freud had identified in the moral subject.

If the psychoanalytic inquiries into the presuppositions of ethics bore
a striking resemblance to their prewar predecessors, the seeming absence
of an explicit political valence in the psychoanalytic project stands out all
the more. Yet here the legacy of ethics reform compels one to ask if the
participants in the psychoanalytic debates were really as disinterested in
the potential political implications of their discussions as it might seem on
the surface. If one thing stood out in ethics reform, it was the noted discrepancy between the ethical and the political. Indeed, the ability to mobilize the feminine ethical subject as a model of critique, as a moral stance
from outside the law, relied on the clear distinction between the political
and the ethical—on the de facto exclusion of the feminine ethical subject
from specific political and legal rights. The question is whether a similar
dynamic persisted into the psychoanalytic discussions. To be sure, as the
psychoanalytic movement sorted out its interpretation of femininity and
the moral subject, it did not pursue a direct political project. But does this
mean that it fully bracketed the relationship of ethics to citizenship and
political and legal rights? Or did it simply pose a different kind of question
about that relationship?

Important for any consideration of this question is the fact that women
had just received the vote in most of Central Europe when the psychoanalytic movement embarked on its femininity debates. In her own contribution, Salomé gave a nod to this new development in women's history
through a slight temporal shift in her narrative. The transition occurred

toward the end of her essay when she slid almost imperceptibly from the nonhistorical mythic tone with which she treated the woman whose law is elsewhere to a distinctly historical tone to mark the historical entry of women into the law:

> With the possibility of enslavement by humans, a quest for equality must have arisen ("penis envy"), a competition for rights; [as an option] that the woman may also choose, remaining only clearly conscious that when she does make this choice, unavoidably, her most intimate sources dry up; that she then crosses over the border to the drought and suffering of conflict, that in rebellious ambition and guilt she alienates herself, in short: that she begins to kill the father.[85]

Like the women of Central Europe who gained suffrage after the war, Salomé's daughter-figure here enters into a new relationship to the law when she takes on a subject position indistinguishable from that of the man. Interestingly, Salomé did not immediately celebrate this moment but rather seemed to find it unbecoming. In fact, her presentation of "penis envy" did not differ significantly from those of Abraham and Freud, equating it with women's jealousy and resentment of men's privileged social role.

Yet Salomé seemed less concerned with the positive appearance of jealousy or resentment and much more so with the losses that women undergo in the entry into the law. She painted the movement as a dry, deserted process, quite in contrast to the overflowing creativity of the woman whose law had been elsewhere. The description of the historical moment may have been a simple antifeminist statement on Salomé's part, and to be sure Salomé had never joined forces wholeheartedly with strict advocates for women's legal and political rights. But she had also not been strictly antifeminist. And the passage seems to lament less the inevitable entry of women into the law than the possible consequences for women whose law was once elsewhere and who now no longer occupied that differentiated position. A subject position of alterity that Salomé wanted to celebrate seems to have been lost.

In this sense, the passage from Salomé seems to be less an antifeminist statement than a lament, or a work of mourning for a lost difference. Much

85. Ibid., 241.

like the reformers who had preceded her, she had found a critical voice in the feminine whose moral subject position could not be conflated with a legal subject position. And she seemed to be worried that such a critical voice might be lost. Indeed, when one considers that ethics reform as a critical phenomenon died under the weight of politics, or rather became conflated with politics, Salomé's lament could be seen to be for the whole of ethics reform, or for the public insistence on an ethics that can stand over and against the political. At the same time, Salomé seems to be asking whether the distinction between the moral and the political subject might be maintained analytically. By emphasizing that the woman can choose her path—that the movement of women into the law was at once an inevitable one, and one that she "may also choose"—Salomé seemed to be suggesting that not *all* was lost and barren. Just as she had emphasized that the woman can idealize the father *and* sublimate those feelings, she seems in this passage to be asking women to choose both rights *and* a subject position that continues to stand in another relationship to the moral law. That is, the passage is a plea to the reader not to lose the analytic distinction between the political subject of rights and the feminine subject of ethics, but to hold onto the alterity of ethics even when politics seems to crush its relevance. It is in this sense that Salomé inherited and kept alive within the language of psychoanalysis the most critical dimension of ethics reform.[86]

86. Salomé here also anticipates a tradition, growing in and out of French psychoanalysis, that placed an emphasis on, in the words of Luce Irigaray, an "ethics of sexual difference." See especially Irigaray, *An Ethics of Sexual Difference,* trans. Carolyn Burke and Gillian C. Gill (Ithaca, N.Y., 1993). Also relevant are Irigaray, *Thinking the Difference: For a Peaceful Revolution,* trans. Karin Montin (New York, 1994); and Tina Chanter, *Ethics of Eros: Irigaray's Rewriting of the Philosophers* (New York, 1995).

Afterword: Moral Citizenship, or Ethics beyond the Law

By way of conclusion I return to the themes of particularism and universalism that were a constant part of the ethics reform debates but that also point beyond them. In this regard, a brief look at the reading by political theorist Slavoj Žižek of Otto Weininger's *Sex and Character* provides a useful starting point for reflecting on the implications of ethics reform and its sexualization. In chapter 2 we saw how Weininger had argued that "woman does not exist" because she lacks the capacity to transcend her physicality. Made up solely of a sexual essence, he charged, woman has only one ambition as a living being: to mate. In other words, her desire for the other determines exclusively her entire life. In reference to this depiction of an entity defined solely by its insatiable desire for something outside itself, Žižek draws a parallel to the Hegelian model of subjectivity. According to—Žižek's reading of—Hegelian subjectivity, the foundation for the self does not exist in itself; rather, the individual subject always seeks support or anchor for itself in the other or in the world around it. From the Hegelian-Žižekian perspective, Weininger's depiction of the female entity who seeks grounding in another should be understood not as the abominable exception to human existence but rather as the image of the subject par excellence: the model of the subject-as-void as opposed to the fantasy of a centered, rational, autonomous agent. According to Žižek's reading, Weininger thus feared the woman not because she is a failed subject but because she is an all too visible case of the universal condition of subject formation.[1]

Although Žižek's argument is clearly indebted to developments in mid and late twentieth-century thought on subjectivity, it nevertheless raises a question quite germane to the turn-of-the-century ethics debates that were so often troubled by the feminine ethical subject: namely, did femininity represent a *particular* challenge, or did it function rather as an especially freighted example of a more *general* concern? Indeed, despite the fact that many of the foregoing chapters have concentrated on the vicissitudes of femininity, it may be apt to suggest that femininity served largely as synecdoche for the broader uncertainty in the modern era about concepts such as the "individual," the "citizen," and the "social." Take, for instance, the discussion of female homosexuality and the law in chapter 4. There we saw reformers explicitly cite the feminine case as exemplary of the general. If reformers took as transparent the impossibility of conclusively attaching something known as "homosexual acts" to a feminine individual or "character," they argued that the same pertained to the male individual. The broken connection between "acts" and "character" in the masculine case was simply less obvious.

On closer inspection, it becomes clear that this pattern ran throughout the reform debates. Although Stöcker launched her critique of bourgeois sexual ethics largely to liberate women from the moral double standard, she argued explicitly that both men and women were confounded by a "slave morality." The plight of women was simply more visible than that of men. Indeed, Stöcker's own trajectory from feminism to pacifism, with a shift in emphasis from women's rights to human rights, lends credence to the claim that the New Ethic always took the feminine as nothing more than an exemplary case of the human. Likewise, when the DGEK debated the "moral destiny of woman," not all were content to accept the

---

1. Slavoj Žižek, *The Metastases of Enjoyment: Six Essays on Woman and Causality* (New York, 1994), esp. 144–145.

question, some maintaining rather that one could only ask about the moral destiny of the person—beyond gender. In the case of Social Democracy, the depiction of woman as segmented under the forces of capital only illustrated with particular ferocity the divisive work of private property and the need to reshape the public for an international community. And finally, the femininity debates in psychoanalysis suggest that the feminine case stood out in the ethics debates in large part because, in Salomé's words, her law is "elsewhere"—that is, because woman's moral and legal positions did not coincide. Moreover, as Salomé suggests, something might even be lost when her citizenship status comes to stand in for the moral possibilities of alterity that the feminine ethical subject promised.

Yet whereas Weininger perceived a crisis in the universal relevance of feminine subjectivity, ethics reformers viewed it as an opportunity. Indeed, while a vulnerability attended women's limited access to legal and political rights, that limited access allowed ethics reformers a means to highlight the difference between law and ethics, an especially important tactic in an era when they feared that legal and political concerns threatened to subsume the moral ones.

It is not surprising in this context, then, that reformers zeroed in on the issue of sexual difference in the construction of the moral subject at the fin de siècle, when European nationalism was reaching its zenith but also when global empires were making internationalist activism among intellectuals possible. As we saw in chapter 4, the heightened public intellectual concern with the interiority of the moral subject coincided explicitly with early intuitions of and efforts toward a global civil society.[2] It seems that reformers understood the interiority of a subject and the international community to be complementary ways of challenging the moral monopoly of nation-states and official citizenship. While some commentators such as

---

2. On the emergence of global civil society in the late nineteenth century, see John Boli and George M. Thomas, eds., *Constructing World Culture: International Nongovernmental Organizations since 1875* (Palo Alto, Calif., 1999); Akira Iriye, *Cultural Internationalism and World Order* (Baltimore, 1997); and Iriye, *Global Community: The Role of International Organizations in the Making of the Contemporary World* (Berkeley, Calif., 2002). On global civil society as a more recent concept for political and sociological theory, see, for example, Mary Kaldor, *Global Civil Society: An Answer to War* (Cambridge, 2003), esp. 6–10, where Kaldor clarifies how global civil society differs from conventional, nationally based forms of civil society.

Stöcker and Salomé emphasized the dimensions of the moral subject that eluded the definition of the national citizen, others such as the spokespersons for the German Society for Ethical Culture focused on those aspects of the moral subject that related first and foremost to the universal.

In this regard, the fin-de-siècle ethics movement speaks presciently to the present turn of the century. The nascent global civil society that reformers intuited at the fin de siècle has in some senses become a reality in the twenty-first century, and questions of universalism, difference, and morality beyond the law have returned with a new force. Indeed, the global context makes it all the more obvious that the interiority of the moral subject is constructed not only through national and local institutions but also through global conversations and relations. Through human migration and high-speed means of communication, individuals' intimacies and loyalties routinely stretch across the globe. The rise in scholarly and activist interest in cosmopolitanism and world citizenship is just one manifestation of these developments, as intellectuals and activists try to sort out the implications of the affective and moral allegiances individuals have to both local and transnational concerns, allegiances that might overlap with but are not necessarily coterminous with their legal rights and obligations.[3]

The contemporary relevance of the distinction between moral citizenship and legal and political standing that informed the ethics debates becomes obvious when we consider the conceptual "citizen of the world" that informs much discussion of both cosmopolitanism and global civil society.[4] To ethics reformers, the legal and political point of reference remained the nation-state, with a moral stance that lay in critical relationship to it. To the contemporary "citizen of the world," however, there exists no comparable political entity as the legal referent: there is no world government to which such moral citizenship relates, or of which this moral citizen could also claim simultaneously to be a legal entity. This moral citizenship of

3. A sampling of the literature includes Cheah and Robbins, *Cosmopolitics;* Kwame Anthony Appiah, *Cosmopolitanism: Ethics in a World of Strangers* (New York, 2006); Carol A. Breckenridge, Sheldon Pollock, Homi K. Bhabha, and Dipesh Chakrabarty, eds., *Cosmopolitanism* (Durham, N.C., 2002); and Steven Vertovec and Robin Cohen, eds., *Conceiving Cosmopolitanism: Theory, Context, and Practice* (Oxford, 2002).

4. For just one example, see Martha Nussbaum, "Patriotism and Cosmopolitanism," and responses, in *For Love of Country: Debating the Limits of Patriotism,* ed. Joshua Cohen (Boston, 1996).

the world is thus necessarily stateless. It is also simply the most general example of a phenomenon that can take more urgent form, as in the case of political and economic refugees, individuals who must renounce or are renounced by a state and can appeal to another primarily in the name of morality, albeit with the aid of international treaties.

In reference to the global consideration of world citizenship, the ethics movement is doubly provocative. On the one hand, through its focus on women in particular—and through the tendency of the feminine to stand in for the universal—it drew attention to the vulnerability of those who are situated outside or in a compromised relation to the law. On the other hand, that very attention to those in that outside or compromised position served as a mechanism through which to raise questions about the limited and potentially nonmoral status of the law itself. In other words, the feminine acted as a constant reminder of the space that exists between the law and ethics. In the globalized world, that attention must be transferred to the space between the work of nation-states and the moral citizens that inhabit the globe. The logic remains comparable, however, in that both instances compel a critical but engaged moral relationship to the law.

Thus from within psychoanalysis and even from within sexual liberation, we have the challenge and promise to hear the voices that speak from beyond the law, from outside the specific delineations of political citizenship. From Social Democracy, we hear the command at once to beware the political effects of moral rhetoric and to be open to human needs, needs that exceed or are not met by a rhetoric of human rights. And from the German Society for Ethical Culture, we hear the call to a vigilance about public discussion: a vigilant awareness of the slipperiness and openness of moral claims and arguments, and a vigilant attunement to the difference between political and legal rights and duties on the one hand and moral citizenship of the world on the other. More so than any one approach to ethics, then, it is this insistence on public discussion about both the constitution of the moral subject and the reach of the community of moral consideration—the refusal to accept a final definition of either—that remains the most enduring challenge of the fin-de-siècle ethics reform movement.

BIBLIOGRAPHY

Primary Sources

Abderhalden, Emil. "Einführung." *Ethik, Pädagogik und Hygiene des Geschlechtslebens* 1, no. 1 (1922): 1.

Abraham, Karl. "Manifestations of the Female Castration Complex." *International Journal of Psycho-Analysis* 3, no. 1 (1922): 1–29.

Adler, Felix. "The International Ethical Congress." *Ethical Addresses* 3 (1896).

——. "Rede, gehalten in einer Versammlung im Victoria-Lyceum zu Berlin am 7. Mai 1892." In *Die ethische Bewegung in Deutschland: Vorbereitende Mitteilungen eines Kreises Gleichgesinnter Männer und Frauen zu Berlin*. Berlin: Ferd. Dümmlers, 1892.

Adler, Max. *Kausalität und Teleologie im Streite um die Wissenschaft*. Vienna: Wiener Volksbuchhandlung Ignaz Brand, 1904.

——. "Zur Revision des Parteiprogramms." *Arbeiter-Zeitung* 13 (October 22–24, 1901).

Adler, Victor. *Victor Adler: Briefwechsel mit August Bebel und Karl Kautsky*. Edited by the Parteivorstand der Sozialistischen Partei Österreichs. Vienna: Wiener Volksbuchhandlung, 1954.

Andreas-Salomé, Lou. *Friedrich Nietzsche in seinen Werken*. Reprint. Frankfurt am Main: Insel, 1983.

———. *In der Schule bei Freud: Tagebuch eines Jahres 1912/1913.* Zurich: Max Niehans, 1958.

———. *Lebensrückblick: Grundriss einiger Lebenserinnerungen.* Edited by Ernst Pfeiffer. Frankfurt am Main: Insel, 1968.

———. *Das zweideutige Lächeln der Erotik.* Edited by Inge Weber and Brigitte Rempp. Freiburg: Kore, Verlag Traute Hensch, 1990.

Augspurg, Anita, and Lida Gustava Heymann. "Was will 'Die Frau im Staat?'" *Die Frau im Staat: Eine Monatsschrift* 1, no. 1 (1919): 1–2.

Baader, Ottilie. "Die sittliche Bestimmung der Frau." *Ethische Kultur* 2, no. 19 (1894): 148–149.

Bauer, Otto. "Marxismus und Ethik." *Die Neue Zeit* 24, pt. 2, no. 41 (1906): 485–499.

Bäumer, Gertrud. *Der Krieg und die Frau.* Stuttgart: Deutsche Verlags-Anstalt, 1914.

———. *Lebensweg durch eine Zeitenwende.* Tübingen: Rainer Wunderlich, 1933.

———. "Mutterschutz und Mutterschaftsversicherung." *Die Frau* 16, no. 4 (1909): 193–203.

———. "Zwischen zwei Gesetzen." *Die Frau* 23, no. 1 (1915): 37–42.

Bäumer, Gertrud, et al., eds. *Frauenbewegung und Sexualethik: Beiträge zur modernen Ehekritik.* Heilbronn: Eugen Salzer, 1909.

Bebel, August. *Die Frau und der Sozialismus.* Zurich: Hottingen Volksbuchhandlung, 1879.

Belfort-Bax, Edward. "Die Geschichtstheorie und Philosophie des Sozialismus." *Die Neue Zeit* 23, pt. 1, no. 2 (1904): 48–51.

Bernstein, Eduard. *Eduard Bernsteins Briefwechsel mit Karl Kautsky (1895–1905).* 2 vols. Edited by Till Schelz-Brandenburg. Frankfurt am Main: Campus, 2003.

———. "Literarische Rundschau." *Die Neue Zeit* 14, pt. 1, no. 6 (1895): 218.

———. "Moralische und unmoralische Spaziergänge." *Die Neue Zeit* 1, pt. 1, nos. 1 and 12–13 (1893): 4–9, 357–361, 396–402.

———. "Probleme des Sozialismus." *Die Neue Zeit* 15, pt. 1, nos. 6, 7, 10, 25 (1896): 164–171, 204–213, 303–311, 772–783; 15, pt. 2, nos. 30, 31 (1897): 100–107, 138–143; 16, pt. 2, nos. 34, 39 (1897–1898): 225–232, 388–395.

———. *Die Voraussetzungen des Sozialismus und die Aufgaben der Sozialdemokratie.* Stuttgart: Dietz, 1899.

———. *Zur Theorie und Geschichte des Socialismus: Gesammelte Abhandlungen.* 4th ed. Berlin: Ferd. Dümmlers, 1904.

———. "Zur Würdigung F. A. Langes." *Die Neue Zeit* 10, pt. 2, nos. 29–31 (1892): 68–78, 101–109, 132–141.

Bohn, P. Lic. "Unsere Forderungen zum Vorentwurf des neuen Strafgesetzbuches." *Zeit- und Streitschriften zur Sittlichkeitsfrage* 5 (1910): 1–11.

Börner, Wilhelm. *Die ethische Bewegung in Deutschland.* Gautsch bei Leipzig: Felix Dietrich, 1912.

———. *Friedrich Jodl: Eine Studie.* Stuttgart: Cotta, 1911.

Bousset, Wilhelm. "Die Gesellschaften für ethische Kultur." *Die Christliche Welt* 6 (1895): 6–10, 30–35, 56–59, 80–85.

Braun, Lily. "An die Leser." *Ethische Kultur* 3, no. 42 (1895): 369–370.

———. "Die Befreiung der Liebe." *Die Neue Gesellschaft* 1, no. 22 (1905): 260–263.

——. "Die Entthronung der Liebe." *Die Neue Gesellschaft* 1, no. 20 (1905): 237–239.

——. *Die Frauenfrage, ihre geschichtliche Entwicklung und wirtschaftliche Seite.* Leipzig: S. Hirzel, 1901.

——. "Herrn Foerster zur Erwiderung." *Die Gleichheit* 9, no. 22 (1899): 174.

——. "Das Problem der Ehe." *Die Neue Gesellschaft* 1, no. 10 (1905): 114–116.

—— "Weiblichkeit." *Die Zukunft* 21, no. 11 (1902): 413–419.

Brück, Franz. "Homosexualität und Erpressertum." *Deutsche Medizinische Wochenschrift* 37, no. 15 (1911): 702.

Büchner, Ludwig. *Kraft und Stoff: Empirisch-naturphilosophische Studien.* Leipzig: Theodor Thomas, 1855.

Cauer, Minna. *Die Frau im 19. Jahrhundert.* Berlin: S. Cronback, 1898.

de Tocqueville, Alexis. *Democracy in America.* Translated by George Lawrence. New York: Perennial, 1988.

Deutsch, Helene. *Confrontations with Myself: An Epilogue.* New York: Norton, 1973.

——. *Psychoanalysis of the Sexual Functions of Women.* Translated by Eric Mosbacher. Edited by Paul Roazen. New York: Karnac Books, 1991.

Dietzgen, Eugen. "Der wissenschaftliche Sozialismus und J. Dietzgens Erkenntnistheorie." *Die Neue Zeit* 22, pt. 1, no. 8 (1903): 231–239.

Dietzgen, Joseph. *Joseph Dietzgen: Some of the Philosophical Essays on Socialism and Science, Religion, Ethics, Critique-of-Reason and the World-at-Large.* Translated by M. Beer and Th. Rothstein. Edited by Eugene Dietzgen and Joseph Dietzgen Jr. Chicago: Charles H. Kerr, 1906.

——. *Schriften in Drei Bänden.* 3 vols. Edited by the Arbeitsgruppe für Philsophie an der Deutschen Akademie der Wissenschaft zu Berlin. Berlin: Akademie, 1961.

Dohm, Hedwig. "Nietzsche und die Frauen." *Die Zukunft* 6, no. 25 (1898): 534–543.

——. *Wie Frauen werden—Werde, die du bist!* Breslau: Schles, Buch dr., Kunst—u. Verlag Aust., 1894.

Durkheim, Émile. *Elementary Forms of Religious Life.* Translated by Karen E. Fields. New York: Free Press, 1995.

Ehe? Zur Reform der sexuellen Moral. Berlin: Internation. Verlag-Aust., 1911.

Ehrenfels, Christian von. "Die aufsteigende Entwicklung des Menschen." *Politisch-Anthropologische Revue* 2 (1903): 45–59.

——. "Berichtigung zur Monogamie der Germanen." *Politisch-Anthropologische Revue* 2 (1903): 243–246.

——. "'Doppelte' und differenzierte Moral." *Sexual-Probleme* 4 (1908): 66–82.

——. "Die Ehe nach Mutterrecht." *Politisch-Anthropologische Revue* 4 (1905): 633–647.

——. "Entwicklungsmoral." *Politisch-Anthropologische Revue* 2 (1903): 214–226.

——. "The Ethical Theory of Value." *International Journal of Ethics* 6, no. 3 (1896): 371–384.

——. "Die gelbe Gefahr." *Sexual-Probleme* 4 (1908): 185–205.

——. *Grundbegriffe der Ethik.* Wiesbaden: J. F. Bergmann, 1907.

——. "Die konstitutive Verderblichkeit der Monogamie und die Untentbehrlichkeit einer Sexualreform." *Archiv für Rassen- und Gesellschafts-Biologie* 4 (1907): 615–617.

——. "Monogame und polygyne Sozialpolitik." *Politisch-Anthropologische Revue* 7 (1909): 536–550.

———. "Monogamische Entwicklungsaussichten." *Politisch-Anthropologische Revue* 2 (1903): 706–718.

———. "Das Mutterheim." *Politisch-Anthropologische Revue* 4 (1906): 633–647.

———. *Philosophische Schriften.* 3 vols. Edited by Reinhard Fabian. Munich: Philosophia, 1982.

———. "Die Postulate des Lebens." *Sexual-Probleme* 4 (1908): 614–635.

———. "Die sadistischen Liebesopfer des Abend- und des Morgenlandes." *Sexual-Probleme* 1 (1908): 299–320.

———. *Sexualethik.* Wiesbaden: J. F. Bergmann, 1907.

———. "Sexual Reformvorschläge." *Politisch-Anthropologische Revue* 4 (1905): 425–443.

———. "Die Sexuale Reform." *Politisch-Anthropologische Revue* 2 (1903): 970–993.

———. "Werdende Moralität." *Freie Bühne für den Entwicklungskampf der Zeit* 3 (1892): 1049–1060.

Ehrlich, Otto. "Kant und Dietzgen." *Die Neue Zeit* 23, pt. 2, no. 30 (1905): 118–123.

Eisler, Rudolf. *Wörterbuch der Philosophischen Begriffe.* 3rd ed. Berlin: Ernst Siegfried Mittler und Sohn, 1910.

Eisner, Kurt. "Debatten über Wenn und Aber." *Vorwärts: Berliner Volksblatt,* September 2–9, 1905.

Ellis, Havelock. "The Woman Question." *Fortnightly Review* 80 (1906): 123–134.

Die ethische Bewegung in Deutschland: Vorbereitende Mitteilungen eines Kreises gleichgesinnter Männer und Frauen zu Berlin. Berlin: Ferd. Dümmlers, 1892.

Eulenburg, August. "Homosexualität und neuer Strafgesetzentwurf." *Deutsche Montags-Zeitung* 1, no. 13 (1910): 1–2.

Feuerbach, Ludwig. *Das Wesen des Christentums.* Leipzig: O. Wigand, 1841.

Fischer, Edmund. "Die Frauenfrage." *Sozialistische Monatshefte* 9, pt. 1, no. 3 (1905): 258–266.

Foerster, Friedrich Wilhelm. "Bemerkungen zu Ellen Keys 'Lebensglauben.'" *Die Frau* 14, no. 2 (1906): 65–73.

———. "Einige nachträgliche Bemerkungen zu den letzten Sittlichkeitskongressen." *Ethische Kultur* 12, no. 23 (1904): 178–179.

———. *Der Entwicklungsgang der Kantischen Ethik bis zur Kritik der reinen Vernunft.* Berlin: Mayer & Müller, 1893.

———. "Erklärung." *Ethische Kultur* 13, no. 12 (1905): 94.

———. *Erlebte Weltgeschichte, 1869–1953: Memoiren.* Nürnberg: Glock & Lutz, 1953.

———. "Die Genossenschaftsbewegung der englischen Arbeiter in ihrer sozial-ethischen Bedeutung." *Ethische Kultur* 3, nos. 30–34 (1895): 236–238, 243–245, 252–254, 262–263, 269–271.

———. "Die Grenzen des bloßen Verstandes in Fragen des Lebens und Menschenkenntnis." *Ethische Kultur* 13, no. 1 (1905): 3–4.

———. *Jugendlehre: Ein Buch für Eltern, Lehrer und Geistliche.* Berlin: G. Reimer, 1904.

———. "Der Kaiser und die Sozialdemokratie." *Ethische Kultur* 3, no. 37 (1895): 289–290.

———. "Klassenkampf und Ethik." *Die Neue Zeit* 19, pt. 1, no. 14 (1901): 438–441.

———. "Leben wir in einem Rechtsstaat?" *Ethische Kultur* 12, no. 13 (1904): 97–98.

———. "Politik und ethische Bewegung." *Ethische Kultur* 3, no. 21 (1895): 166–167.

——. "Proletarische und bürgerliche Frauenbewegung." *Centralblatt des Bundes Deutscher Frauenvereine* 1, nos. 11 and 23 (1899): 81–83 and 89–91.

——. *Sexualethik und Sexualpädagogik: Eine Auseinandersetzung mit den Modernen.* Kempten: Jos. Kösel'schen Buchhandlung, 1907.

——. "Sozialdemokratie und ethische Bewegung." *Ethische Kultur* 3, no. 18 (1895): 142–143.

——. "Soziale Demokratie und Ethik: Ein neues Kapitel aus dem englischen Munizipalismus." *Soziale Praxis* 10, no. 4 (1900): 73–74.

——. "Sprechsaal." *Ethische Kultur* 13, no. 6 (1905): 47.

——. "Sprechsaal: Zur Erkenntnistheorie der Ethik." *Ethische Kultur* 13, no. 3 (1905): 22–23.

——. "Zur 'Ethik des Kampfes': Eine Entgegnung." *Die Gleichheit* 9, no. 22 (1899): 173–174.

——, ed. *Einführung in die Grundgedanken der ethischen Bewegung: Zur Ausbreitung des Wirkens der Deutschen Gesellschaft für ethische Kultur.* Berlin: Verlag der Deutschen Gesellschaft für ethische Kultur, 1894.

Foerster, Wilhelm. *Die Begründung einer Gesellschaft für ethische Kultur: Einleitungs-Rede gehalten am 18. October 1892 zu Berlin.* Berlin: Ferd. Dümmlers, 1892.

——. *Lebensfragen und Lebensbilder: Socialethischer Betrachtungen.* Berlin: Edelheim, 1902.

——. "Sexual-Ethik und Frauen-Befreiung." *Ethische Kultur* 4, no. 17 (1896): 132–133.

——. *Zur Ethik des Nationalismus und der Judenfrage: Vortrag Gehalten am 23. November 1892 zu Berlin in der Deutschen Gesellschaft für ethische Kultur.* Berlin: Ferd. Dümmlers, 1893.

Forel, Auguste. *Die Sexuelle Frage: Eine naturwissenschaftliche, psychologische, hygienische und soziologische Studie für Gebildete.* Munich: S. Reinhardt, 1905.

——. *Ueber die Zurechnungsfähigkeit des normalen Menschen: Ein Vortrag gehalten in der Schweizerischen Gesellschaft für ethische Kultur in Zürich.* 4th ed. Munich: Ernst Reinhard, 1902.

Freud, Sigmund. *Gesammelte Werke, Chronologisch Geordnet.* Edited by Anna Freud, Edward Bibring, Willi Hoffer, Ernst Kris, and Otto Isakower. 18 vols. London: Imago, 1940–1952.

Fürth, Henriette. "Mutterschaft und Ehe." *Mutterschutz: Zeitschrift zur Reform der sexuellen Ethik* 1, no. 7 (1905): 265–269.

Furtmüller, Carl. *Psychoanalyse und Ethik: Eine Untersuchung.* Munich: Ernst Reinhardt, 1912.

Gizycki, Georg von. "Einleitung." *Ethische Kultur* 1, no. 1 (1893): 1–2.

——. "Ethik und Vegetarismus." *Ethische Kultur* 2, no. 39 (1894): 306–307.

——. "In Sachen der Deutschen Gesellschaft für ethische Kultur." *Vorwärts: Berliner Volksblatt,* October 5, 1892.

——. "Materialismus und Ethik." *Ethische Kultur* 1, no. 19 (1893): 151–152.

——. *Moralphilosophie gemeinverständlich dargestellt.* Leipzig: Friedrich, 1888.

——. *Vorlesungen über soziale Ethik.* Berlin: Ferd. Dümmlers, 1895.

Gizycki, Lily von. "Politik und ethische Bewegung." *Ethische Kultur* 3, no. 21 (1895): 164–165.

H., R. G. "Kultur der Zeit." *Ethische Kultur* 41, no. 8 (1933): 123–125.

Haeckel, Ernst. "Ethik und Weltanschauung." *Die Zukunft* 1 (1892): 309–315.

——. *History of Creation, or the Development of the Earth and Its Inhabitants by the Action of Natural Causes: A Popular Exposition of the Doctrine of Evolution in General, and That of Darwin, Goethe, and Lamarck in Particular.* New York: Appleton, 1876.

——. "Die Weltanschauung der monistischen Wissenschaft." *Freie Bühne für den Entwickelungskampf der Zeit* 3, nos. 3–4 (1892): 1155–1169.

——. "Zellseelen und Seelenzellen." *Deutsche Rundschau* 16 (1878): 40–59.

Hegel, G. W. F. *Werke.* 20 vols. Edited by Eva Moldenhauer and Karl Markus Michel. Frankfurt am Main: Suhrkamp, 1969–1971.

Henning, Max. *Handbuch der freigeistigen Bewegung Deutschlands, Österreichs und der Schweiz (Jahrbuch des Weimarer Kartells: 1914).* Frankfurt am Main: Neuer Frankfurter, 1914.

Hiller, Kurt. "Homosexualismus und Deutscher Vorentwurf." *Monatsschrift für Kriminalpsychologie und Strafrechtsreform* 8 (1911–1912): 28–38.

Hirschfeld, Magnus. "Kritik des §250 und seiner Motive im Vorentuwrf zu einem Deutschen Strafgesetzbuch." *Archiv für Kriminal-Anthropologie und Kriminalistik* 38 (1910): 89–119.

Horney, Karen. *Feminine Psychology.* Edited by Harold Kelman. New York: Norton, 1967.

——. "Flucht aus der Weiblichkeit." *Internationale Zeitschrift für Psychoanalyse* 12 (1926): 360–374.

——. "Zur Genese des weiblichen Kastrationskomplexes." *Internationale Zeitschrift für Psychoanalyse* 9 (1923): 12–26.

Huygens, Cornelie. "Dietzgens Philosophie." *Die Neue Zeit* 21, pt. 1, nos. 7–8 (1902): 197–207, 231–239.

Jastrow, Hermann. *Das Recht der Frau nach dem bürgerlichen Gesetzbuch: Dargestellt für Frauen.* Berlin: O. Liebmann, 1897.

Jellinek, Camilla. "Der Vorentwurf zu einem Deutschen Strafgesetzbuch: Vom Standpunkte der Frauen aus Betrachtet." *Centralblatt des Bundes deutscher Frauenvereine* 11, nos. 20–22 (1910): 153–155, 161–162, 170–171.

Joachimsen-Böhm, Marg. "Mitteilung des Bund für Mutterschutz: Gründung der Ortsgruppe München." *Mutterschutz: Zeitschrift zur Reform der sexuellen Ethik* 1, no. 2 (1905): 89–90.

Jodl, Friedrich. "Die ethische Bewegung in Deutschland." *Neue freie Presse,* August 23, 1893.

——. "Ethische Kultur und soziale Organisation." *Ethische Kultur* 2, nos. 14–15 (1894): 110–111, 118–119.

——. "Was heißt ethische Kultur?" *Ethische Kultur* 1, no. 1 (1893): 2–3.

——. *Wesen und Ziele der ethischen Bewegung in Deutschland.* Frankfurt am Main: Gebrüder Knauer, 1893.

Jodl, Margarete. *Friedrich Jodl: Sein Leben und Wirken.* Stuttgart: Cotta, 1920.

Joffe, A. "Zu Mandevilles Ethik und Kants 'Sozialismus.'" *Die Neue Zeit* 24, pt. 2, no. 28 (1906): 45–50.

Jones, Ernest. "The Early Development of Female Sexuality." *International Journal of Psycho-Analysis* 8 (1927): 459–472.

Juliusburger, Otto. "Die Homosexualität im Vorentwurf zu einem Deutschen Strafgesetzbuch." *Allgemeine Zeitschrift für Psychiatrie und psychisch-gerichtliche Medizin* 68, no. 5 (1911): 674–691.

Kant, Immanuel. "An Answer to the Question: 'What Is Enlightenment?'" In *Kant: Political Writings,* edited by Hans Reiss and translated by H. B. Nisbet. Cambridge: Cambridge University Press, 1970.

———. *Critique of Practical Reason.* Translated and edited by Mary Gregor. Cambridge: Cambridge University Press, 1997.

———. *Kant: Gesammelte Schriften.* Edited by Königlich Preußische Akademie der Wissenschaften. 24 vols. Berlin: Georg Reimer, 1913.

———. *Religion within the Boundaries of Mere Reason.* Translated and edited by Allen Wood and George Di Giovanni. Cambridge: Cambridge University Press, 1998.

Kautsky, Karl. "Bernstein über die Werttheorie." *Die Neue Zeit* 17, pt. 2, no. 29 (1899): 68–81.

———. *Bernstein und das sozialdemokratische Programm: Eine Antikritik.* Stuttgart: Dietz, 1899.

———. "Bernstein und die Dialektik." *Die Neue Zeit* 17, pt. 2, no. 28 (1899): 36–50.

———. "Bernstein und die materialistische Geschichtsauffassung." *Die Neue Zeit* 17, pt. 2, no. 27 (1899): 4–16.

———. *Das Erfurter Programm, in seinem grundsätzlichen Theil.* 3rd ed. Stuttgart: Dietz, 1892.

———. *Erinnerungen und Erörterungen.* The Hague: Mouton, 1960.

———. *Ethik und materialistische Geschichtsauffassung.* Stuttgart: Dietz, 1906.

———. "Die Fortsetzung einer unmöglichen Diskussion" (parts 1 and 2), "Noch einmal die unmögliche Diskussion," and "Der mögliche Abschluss einer unmöglichen Diskussion." *Die Neue Zeit* 23, pt. 2, nos. 48–51 (1905): 681–692, 717–727, 776–785, 795–804.

———. "Die Fortsetzung einer unmöglichen Diskussion." *Vorwärts: Berliner Volksblatt,* September 1–7, 1905.

———. "Klassenkampf und Ethik." *Die Neue Zeit* 19, pt. 1, no. 8 (1900): 233–242.

———. "Leben, Wissenschaft und Ethik." *Die Neue Zeit* 24, pt. 2, no. 42 (1906): 516–529.

———. "Noch einiges über Ethik." *Die Neue Zeit* 11, pt. 2, no. 31 (1893): 109–116.

———. "Nochmals Klassenkampf und Ethik." *Die Neue Zeit* 19, pt. 1, no. 14 (1901): 468–472.

———. "Patriotismus, Krieg und Sozialdemokratie." *Die Neue Zeit* 23, pt. 2, no. 37 (1905): 343–348.

Kempin, Emilie. *Die Stellung der Frau nach den zur Zeit in Deutschland gültigen Gesetzesbestimmung sowie nach dem Entwurf eines bürgerlichen Gesetzbuches für das deutsche Reich.* Leipzig: Schäfer, 1892.

Key, Ellen. "Die Frauen und das Wahlrecht." *Sozialistische Monatshefte* 6, pt. 1, no. 7 (1902): 528–531.

———. *Das Jahrhundert des Kindes: Studien.* Translated by Francis Maro. Berlin: S. Fischer, 1902.

———. *Liebe und Ethik.* Translated by Francis Maro. Berlin: Pan-Verl., 1905.

———. *Love and Marriage.* Translated by Arthur G. Chater. Introduction by Havelock Ellis. New York: Knickerbocker Press, 1912.

———. *Über Liebe und Ehe.* Translated by Francis Maro. Berlin: S. Fischer, 1905.

Klein, Melanie. *Love, Guilt and Reparation, and Other Works, 1921–1945.* Edited by R. E. Money-Kyrle. New York: Dell, 1975.

Kohlcr, Josef. "Der deutsche und der österreichische Vorentwurf eines Strafgesetzbuchs." *Archiv für Strafrecht und Strafprozess* 56 (1909): 285–312.

Konfessionelle oder Weltliche Schule? 3 Ansprachen in der Deutschen Gesellschaft f. ethische Kultur (Abt. Berlin) 14. Okt. 1904. Berlin: Verlag für ethische Kultur, 1904.

Krukenberg, Elsbeth. "§175." *Monatsschrift für Kriminalpsychologie und Strafrechtsreform* 7 (1910–1911): 612.

Lange, Helene. "Die Frauenbewegung und das 'Recht auf die Mutterschaft.'" *Die Frau* 11, no. 4 (1904): 193–197.

Lange, Helene, and Gertrud Bäumer. *Handbuch der Frauenbewegung.* Berlin: S. W. Moser, 1901–1902.

Leo, Victor. "Zur neuen Ethik." *Die Frau* 16, no. 1 (1908): 39–47.

Lüders, Else. *Der "Linke Flügel": Ein Blatt aus der Geschichte der Deutschen Frauenbewegung.* Berlin: W. & S. Loewenthal, 1904.

Luschan, Felix von. "Rassen-Anthropologie." *Die Umschau: Übersicht über die Fortschritte und Bewegungen auf dem Gesamtgebiet der Wissenschaft und Technik* 36, no. 2 (1911): 733–737.

———. "Der Rassen-Kongreß in London 1911." *Koloniale Rundschau* 3 (1911): 597–623.

Marcuse, Max. "Mitteilungen des Bundes für Mutterschutz." *Mutterschutz: Zeitschrift zur Reform der sexuellen Ethik* 1, no. 1 (1905): 45–47.

———. "'Sexual-Probleme': Ein Wort zur Einführung." *Sexual-Probleme: Der Zeitschrift "Mutterschutz" neue Folge* 4, no. 1 (1908): 1–5.

Martens, Albert. "Das Sexuelle Leben und seine Vorbedingungen." *Der sozialistische Akademiker* 2, no. 2 (1896): 94–105.

Marx, Karl, and Friedrich Engels. *Karl Marx, Friedrich Engels: Werke.* 41 vols. Edited by Institut für Marxismus-Leninismus. Berlin: Dietz, 1956–.

Mehring, Franz. "Allerlei Ethik." *Die Neue Zeit* 11, pt. 1, no. 9 (1892): 265–270.

———. "Ethik und kein Ende." *Die Neue Zeit* 11, pt. 2, no. 31 (1893): 106–109.

———. "Ethik und Klassenkampf." *Die Neue Zeit* 11, pt. 2, no. 22 (1893): 700–702.

———. "Karl Vorländer, die neukantische Bewegung im Sozialismus." *Die Neue Zeit* 20, pt. 2, no. 4 (1902): 123–124.

Meisel-Hess, Grete. *Weiberhass und Weiberverachtung: Eine Erwiderung auf die in Dr. Otto Weiningers Buche "Geschlecht und Charakter" geäußerten Anschauungen über "Die Frau und ihre Frage."* 2nd ed. Vienna: Verlag "Die Wage," 1904.

Menger, Carl. *Collected Works.* Edited by F. A. Hayek. London: London School of Economics, 1933.

Meyer, Bruno. "Der Aufstand des Gefühls gegen die Vernunft." *Ethische Kultur* 13, no. 12 (1905): 90–93.

———. "Zur Psychologie der Geschlechtsmoral." *Mutterschutz: Zeitschrift zur Reform der sexuellen Ethik* 1, no. 1 (1905): 12–32.

Mill, John Stuart. *On Liberty.* Indianapolis, Ind.: Hackett, 1978.

Mitteilungen der Deutschen Gesellschaft für Ethische Kultur. Vols. 1–4. Berlin: Ferd. Dümmlers, 1892–1896.

Mueller, Paula. "Der Bund für Mutterschutz und die 'Neue Ethik.'" *Evangelische Frauenzeitung* 6, no. 1 (1905): 3–5.

———. *Die "Neue Ethik" und ihre Gefahr.* Berlin: Edwin Runge, 1908.

Nietzsche, Friedrich. *Friedrich Nietzsche Werke: Kritische Gesamtausgabe.* 25 vols. Edited by Giorgio Colli and Mazzino Montinari. Berlin: Walter de Gruyter, 1967.

Nunberg, Herman, and Ernst Federn, eds. and trans. *Minutes of the Vienna Psychoanalytic Society.* 4 vols. New York: International Universities Press, 1962–1975.

Pannekoek, Anton. "Historischer Materialismus und Religion." *Die Neue Zeit* 22, pt. 2, nos. 31–32 (1904): 133–142, 180–186.

Pappritz, Anna. "Die Strafrechtsreform." *Der Abolitionist* 9, no. 1 (1910): 1–6.

———. "Zum §175." *Der Abolitionist* 10, no. 2 (1911): 9–11.

Paulsen, Friedrich. "Die sittliche Bestimmung der Frau." *Ethische Kultur* 2, no. 12 (1894): 90–91.

———. "Die unabhängige Moral und ihre kirchlichen Richter—Thesen über Religion und Moral." *Ethische Kultur* 1, no. 1 (1893): 4–5.

Penzig, Rudolf. "Was haben wir getan?" "Die Wirkung des bisherigen Arbeit," and "Was muss zunaechst getan werden?" *Deutsche Liga für weltliche Schule und Moralunterricht* 1, no. 1 (1906): 1–4.

———. "Was soll uns jetzt 'Ethische Kultur'?" *Ethische Kultur* 22, no. 16 (1914): 121–122.

———. "Die Zukunft der ethischen Bewegung in Deutschland." *Ethische Kultur* 28, no. 6 (1920): 41–44.

Pfeiffer, Ernst, ed. *Friedrich Nietzsche, Paul Rée, Lou von Salomé: Die Dokumente ihrer Begegnung.* Frankfurt am Main: Insel, 1970.

———. *Sigmund Freud and Lou Andreas-Salomé: Letters.* Translated by William Robson-Scott and Elaine Robson-Scott. New York: Harcourt Brace Jovanovich, 1972.

Planck, G. *Die rechtliche Stellung der Frau nach dem bürgerlichen Gesetzbuche.* Göttingen: Vandenhoeck & Ruprecht, 1899.

Platter, J. "Ein ethisches Problem." *Ethische Kultur* 4, no. 17 (1896): 129–132.

Plechanow [Plekhanov], Georgi. *Beiträge zur Geschichte des Materialismus.* Stuttgart: Dietz, 1896.

———. "Bernstein und der Materialismus." *Die Neue Zeit* 16, pt. 2, no. 44 (1898): 545–555.

———. "Konrad Schmidt gegen Karl Marx und Friedrich Engels." *Die Neue Zeit* 17, pt. 1, no. 5 (1898): 133–145.

———. "Materialismus oder Kantianismus." *Die Neue Zeit* 17, pt. 1, nos. 19–20 (1899): 589–596, 626–632.

Ploetz, Alfred. "First Universal Races Congress." *Archiv für Rassen- und Gesellschafts-Biologie* 8, no. 3 (1911): 412–413.

Proelß, Sera, and Marie Raschke. *Die Frau im neuen bürgerlichen Gesetzbuches: Eine Beleuchtung und Gegenübersetzung der Paragraphen des Entwurfs eines bürgerlichen Gesetzbuchs für das deutsche Reich (2. Lesung) nebst Vorschlägen zur Änderung derselben im Interesse der Frauen.* Berlin: Dümmler, 1895.

Protokoll des ... ordentlichen Gesellschaftstages der Deutschen Gesellschaft für ethische Kultur. Vols. 1–7. Berlin: Siebenmark, 1897–1903.

Record of the Proceedings of the First Universal Races Congress, Held at the University of London, July 26–29, 1911. London: P. S. King, 1911.

Rohleder, Hermann. "Paragraph 250, der Ersatz des Paragraph 175, in seinen eventuellen Folgen für das weibliche Geschlecht." *Reichs-Medizinal-Anzeiger* 36, no. 3 (1911): 67–76.

Rüling, Anna. "Welches Interesse hat die Frauenbewegung an der Lösung des homosexuellen Problems?" *Jahrbuch für sexuelle Zwischenstufen* 7, no. 1 (1905): 131–151.

Salter, William Mackintire. *Die Religion der Moral: Vorträge, Gehalten in der Gesellschaft für moralische Kultur, in Chicago.* Translated by Georg von Gizycki. Leipzig: Friedrich, 1885.

Scheven, Katharina. "Die Behandlung der Geschlechtlichen Delikte im Gegenentwurf zum Vorentwurf eines Deutschen Strafgesetzbuchs." *Der Abolitionist* 11, no. 3 (1912): 21–27.

Schirmacher, Käthe. "§175 des Deutschen Strafgesetzes." *Der Abolitionist* 10, no. 1 (1911): 3–5.

Schleiermacher, Friedrich. *Vertraute Briefe über die Lucinde.* Lübeck: Friedrich Bohn, 1800.

Schmidt, Conrad. "Einige Bemerkungen über Plechanows letzten Artikel in der 'Neuen Zeit.'" *Die Neue Zeit* 17, pt. 1, no. 11 (1898): 324–334.

———. "Was ist Materialismus?" *Die Neue Zeit* 17, pt. 1, no. 22 (1899): 697–698.

Schmitt, Eugen Heinrich. *Die Gnosis: Grundlagen der Weltanschauung einer edleren Kultur.* 2 vols. Leipzig: Diederichs, 1903–1907.

———. *Warum ist eine religiöse Bewegung Notwendigkeit? Ein Wort an die "Gesellschaften für ethische Kultur."* Leipzig: Alfred Janssen, 1894.

Schreiber, Adele, ed. *Mutterschaft: Ein Sammelwerk für die Probleme des Weibes als Mutter.* Munich: Albert Langen, 1912.

Schücking, Prof. "Der Weltkrieg und der Pazifismus." *Ethische Kultur* 22, no. 20 (1914): 156–157.

Simmel, Ernst, ed. *Kriegsneurose und psychisches Trauma: Ihre gegenseitige Beziehungen dargestellt auf Grund psychoanalytischer, hypnotischer Studien.* Munich, 1918.

Spielrein, Sabina. "Die Destruktion als Ursprung des Werdens." *Jahrbuch für psychoanalytische und psychopathologische Forschungen* 4 (1912): 465–503.

———. *Sämtliche Schriften.* Edited by Barbara Hermann. Freiburg: Kore, Verlag Traute Hensch, 1987.

Spiller, Gustav. *The Ethical Movement in Great Britain: A Documentary History.* London: Farleigh Press, 1934.

———, ed. *Papers on Inter-racial Problems Communicated to the First Universal Races Congress Held at the University of London July 26–29, 1911.* London: P. S. King & Son, 1911.

Spinoza, Baruch. *The Ethics and Selected Letters.* Translated by Samuel Shirley. Indianapolis, Ind.: Hackett, 1982.

Staudinger, Franz. *Beiträge zur Volkspädogogik.* Bern: Steiger, 1897.

———. "Ed. Bernstein und die Ethik." *Ethische Kultur* 7, no. 16 (1899): 121–122.

———. *Ethik und Politik.* Berlin: Ferd. Dümmler, 1899.

——. "Das Gemüt und die Wahrheit." *Ethische Kultur* 12, no. 22 (1904): 171–172.

——. *Die Gesetze der Freiheit.* Darmstadt: Brill, 1887.

——. "Kant und der Socialismus: Ein Gedenkwort zu Kants Todestage." *Sozialistische Monatshefte* 8, pt. 1, no. 2 (1904): 103–114.

——. "Sprechsaal: Die Grenzen des Verstandes in Fragen der Lebens- und Menschenkenntnis." *Ethische Kultur* 13, no. 2 (1905): 15.

——. "Sprechsaal: Wer setzt die Autorität fest?" *Ethische Kultur* 13, no. 4 (1905): 30.

——. *Sprüche der Freiheit: Wider Nietzsche's und anderer Herrenmoral.* Darmstadt: Eduard Roether, 1904.

——. "Wie müssen wir heute stehen?" *Ethische Kultur* 22, no. 18 (1914): 138–140.

——. *Wirtschaftliche Grundlagen der Moral.* Darmstadt: Roether, 1907.

——. *Die zehn Gebote im Lichte moderner Ethik.* Darmstadt: Saeng, 1902.

Staudinger, Franz (Sadi Gunter). "Antonio Labriola und die Ethik." *Die Neue Zeit* 18, pt. 2, nos. 45–46 (1900): 556–560, 586–591.

——. "Bernstein und die Wissenschaft." *Die Neue Zeit* 17, pt. 2, no. 47 (1899): 646–652.

Steiner, Rudolf. "Eine Gesellschaft für ethische Kultur." *Die Zukunft* 1 (1892): 216–220.

Stern, Jakob. "Materialistische Geschichtstheorie und Ethik." *Ethische Kultur* 1, nos. 3–4 (1893): 19–20, 30–31.

——. "Der ökonomische und der naturphilosophische Materialismus." *Die Neue Zeit* 15, pt. 2, no. 36 (1897): 301–302.

——. *Die Philosophie Spinoza's: Erstmals gründlich aufgehellt und populär dargestellt.* 2nd ed. Stuttgart: Dietz, 1894.

——. "Die sozialistische Bewegung eine ethische Bewegung." *Ethische Kultur* 1, no. 17 (1893): 131–133.

——. "Substanz- und Causalitätsidee." *Sozialistische Monatshefte* 8, pt. 2, no. 10 (1904): 824–828.

Stöcker, Adolf. "Die Aufgaben der Frau in der Gegenwart." *Evangelische Frauenzeitung* 5, no. 5 (1905): 39–40.

——. *Reden im Reichstag: Amtlicher Vorlaut.* Ed. Reinhard Mumm. Schwerin: Friedrich Dahn, 1914.

——. "Vereine und Kongresse." *Deutsche Evangelische Kirchenzeitung* 6, no. 44 (1892): 428–429.

——. "Das Volksschulgesetz und die Generalsynode." *Deutsche Evangelische Kirchenzeitung* 6, no. 5 (1892): 45.

——. "Das Volksschulgesetz und seine Gegner." *Deutsche Evangelische Kirchenzeitung* 6, no. 7 (1892): 61–62.

Stöcker, Helene. "Abarten der Liebe." *Die Neue Generation* 10, no. 7 (1914): 375–387.

——. "Die beabsichtigte Ausdehnung des §175 auf die Frau." *Die Neue Generation* 7, no. 3 (1911): 110–123.

——. "Lex-Heinze Moral." *Mutterschutz: Zeitschrift zur Reform der sexuellen Ethik* 1, no. 2 (1905): 49–51.

——. *Die Liebe und die Frauen.* Minden: J. C. C. Bruns', 1906.

——. "Mutterschutz und Pazifismus!" *Die Neue Generation* 15, no. 2 (1919): 61–68.

——. "Neue Ethik in der Kunst." *Mutterschutz: Zeitschrift zur Reform der sexuellen Ethik* 1, no. 8 (1905): 301–306.

——. "Psychoanalyse 1911/1912." *Luzifer-Amor* 4, no. 8 (1991): 181–186.

——. "Von neuer Ethik." *Mutterschutz: Zeitschrift zur Reform der sexuellen Ethik* 2, no. 1 (1906): 5–11.

——. "Zum Titel- und Verlagswechsel der Zeitschrift." *Die Neue Generation* 4, no. 1 (1908): 39.

——. *Zur Kunstanschauung des XVIII. Jahrhunderts.* Berlin: Mayer, 1904.

——. "Zur Reform der sexuellen Ethik." *Mutterschutz: Zeitschrift zur Reform der sexuellen Ethik* 1, no. 1 (1905): 3–12.

Strafgesetzbuch für das Deutsche Reich. 22nd ed. Berlin: J. Guttentag, 1907.

Suttner, Bertha von. "Groß-Wien." *Ethische Kultur* 1, no. 1 (1893): 2–3.

——. "Die sittliche Bestimmung der Frau." *Ethische Kultur* 2, no. 12 (1894): 93–94.

Tausk, Viktor. "Diagnostic Considerations Concerning the Symptomatology of the So-Called War Psychoses." In *Sexuality, War, and Schizophrenia: Collected Psychoanalytic Papers,* edited by Paul Roazen, translated by Eric Mosbacher et al. New Brunswick: Transaction, 1991.

Tille, Alexander. *Von Darwin bis Nietzsche: Ein Buch Entwicklungsethik.* Leipzig: Naumann, 1895.

Tönnies, Ferdinand. *"Ethische Cultur" und ihr Geleite: 1) Nietzsche-Narren [in der "Zukunft" und in Der "Gegenwart"]; und 2) Wölfe in Fuchspelzen.* Berlin: Ferd. Dümmlers, 1893.

——. "Ethisches Scharmützel: Offener Brief an Herrn Dr. Franz Mehring in Berlin." *Deutsche Worte* 13, no. 1 (1893): 47–57.

——. *Gemeinschaft und Gesellschaft: Abhandlung des Communismus und des Socialismus als empirischer Culturformen.* Leipzig: Fues, 1887.

——. *Kritik der öffentlichen Meinung.* Berlin: Julius Springer, 1922.

——. "Nachreden des Rassenkongresses." *Ethische Kultur* 20, no. 12 (1912): 89–90.

——. "Noch Einiges über Ethik." *Die Neue Zeit* 11, pt. 2, no. 31 (1893): 103–106.

——. "Die sittliche Bestimmung der Frau." *Ethische Kultur* 3, no. 4 (1895): 25–27.

v. den Eken, Anna. *Mannweiber—Weibmänner und der §175: Eine Schrift für denkende Frauen.* Leipzig: Max Spohr, 1906.

von Bolberitz, Georgina. "Die sittliche Bestimmung der Frau." *Ethische Kultur* 2, no. 44 (1894): 346–348.

von Bunsen, Georg. "Die Sittliche Bestimmung der Frau." *Ethische Kultur* 2, no. 12 (1894): 90–91.

Vorentwurf zu einem Deutschen Strafgesetzbuch. Berlin: J. Guttentag, 1909.

Vorentwurf zu einem Österreichischen Strafgesetzbuch. Berlin: J. Guttentag, 1909.

Vorländer, Karl. *Kant und Marx: Ein Beitrag zur Philosophie des Sozialismus.* Tübingen: J. C. B. Mohr, 1911.

Weber, Marianne. *Ehefrau und Mutter in der Rechtsentwicklung: Eine Einführung.* Tübingen: J. C. B. Mohr (Paul Siebeck), 1907.

——. *Frauenfragen und Frauengedanken: Gesammelte Aufsätze.* Tübingen: J. C. B. Mohr (Paul Siebeck), 1919.

——. *Die Frauen und die Liebe.* Freiburg: Karl Robert Langewiesche, 1950.

——. *Lebenserinnerungen.* Bremen: Storm, 1948.

Weber, Max. "Science as a Vocation." In *From Max Weber: Essays in Sociology,* edited by H. H. Gerth and C. Wright Mills, 129–156. New York: Oxford University Press, 1946.

Weininger, Otto. *Geschlecht und Charakter: Eine prinzipielle Untersuchung.* Vienna: Wilhelm Braumüller, 1903.

Wiener Psychoanalytische Vereinigung, ed. *Die Onanie: Vierzehn Beiträge zu einer Diskussion der Wiener Psychoanalytische Vereinigung.* Wiesbaden: J. F. Bergmann, 1912.

Wille, Bruno. "Der Arbeiterphilosoph Josef Dietzgen." *Der sozialistische Akademiker 2,* no. 4 (1896): 206–215.

Winzer, F. Heinrich. *Der neue §175 RStGB! §250 des "Vorentwurfs zu einem Deutschen Strafgesetzbuch": Kritik und Vorschläge.* Leipzig: Max Spohr, 1910.

Woltmann, Ludwig. *System des Moralischen Bewusstseins mit besonderer Darlegung des Verhältnisses der kritischen Philosophie zu Darwinismus und Sozialismus.* Düsseldorf: Hermann Michels, 1898.

Wundt, Wilhelm. *Elemente der Völkerpsychologie: Grundlinien einer psychologischen Entwicklungsgeschichte der Menschheit.* Leipzig: Barth, 1912.

——. *Ethik: Eine Untersuchung der Tatsachen und Gesetze des sittlichen Lebens.* Stuttgart: Ferdinand Enke, 1886.

——. *Grundzüge der physiologischen Psychology.* 2 vols. Leipzig: Engelmann, 1873–1874.

——. *Völkerpsychologie: Eine Untersuchung der Entwicklungsgesetze von Sprache, Mythus und Sitte.* 10 vols. Leipzig: Barth, 1911–1920.

Zetkin, Clara. "Aus Krähwinkel." *Die Gleichheit* 15, nos. 6–7 (1905): 31–32, 37–38.

——. "Ehe und Sittlichkeit." *Die Gleichheit* 16, nos. 8, 10–11, 14–18 (1906): 49–50, 64, 71–72, 91–92, 99–100, 105–106, 113–114, 119–120.

——. "Jakob Stern." *Die Neue Zeit* 29, pt. 2, no. 27 (1911): 56–59.

——. *Zur Geschichte der proletarischen Frauenbewegung Deutschlands.* 3rd ed. Frankfurt am Main: Marxist. Blätter, 1984.

Zetterbaum, Max. "Internationalität und Ethik." *Die Neue Zeit* 20, pt. 2, no. 4 (1902): 101–105.

——. "Die Marx-Studien." *Die Neue Zeit* 23, pt. 1, nos. 7–8 (1904): 196–204, 242–247.

Zur Psychoanalyse der Kriegsneurosen. Leipzig: Internationaler Psychoanalytischer, 1919.

Secondary Literature

Abrams, Lynn. "Companionship and Conflict: The Negotiation of Marriage Relations in the Nineteenth Century." In *Gender Relations in German History: Power, Agency and Experience from the Sixteenth to the Twentieth Century,* edited by Lynn Abrams and Elizabeth Harvey. London: UCL Press, 1996.

——. "Prostitutes in Imperial Germany, 1870–1918: Working Girls or Social Outcasts?" In *The German Underworld: Deviants and Outcasts in German History,* edited by Richard J. Evans. New York: Routledge, 1988.

Accampo, Elinor A., Rachel G. Fuchs, and Mary Lynn Stewart, eds. *Gender and the Politics of Social Reform in France, 1870–1914.* Baltimore: Johns Hopkins University Press, 1995.

Adorno, Theodor, and Max Horkheimer. *Dialektik der Aufklärung: Philosophische Fragmente.* Amsterdam: Querido, 1947.

Albisetti, James. "The Feminization of Teaching in the Nineteenth Century: A Comparative Perspective." *History of Education* 22, no. 3 (1993): 235–263.

———. *Schooling German Girls and Women: Secondary and Higher Education in the Nineteenth Century.* Princeton, N.J.: Princeton University Press, 1988.

Alderman, Hans. *Nietzsche's Gift.* Athens: Ohio University Press, 1977.

Allen, Ann Taylor. "Feminism and Eugenics in Germany and Britain, 1900–1940: A Comparative Perspective." *German Studies Review* 23, no. 3 (2000): 477–505.

———. *Feminism and Motherhood in Germany, 1800–1914.* New Brunswick, N.J.: Rutgers University Press, 1991.

———. "Feminism, Venereal Diseases and the State in Germany, 1890–1918." *Journal of the History of Sexuality* 4, no. 1 (1993): 27–50.

———. "German Radical Feminism and Eugenics, 1900–1908." *German Studies Review* 11, no. 1 (1988): 31–56.

———. "Mothers of the New Generation: Adele Schreiber, Helene Stöcker, and the Evolution of a German Idea of Motherhood." *Signs* 10, no. 3 (1985): 418–438.

Allen, Keith. "Toward a Socialist Morality of Sexuality: An Examination of Aleksandra Kollontai's and Clara Zetkin's View of Working-Class Women's Reproduction." *Voenno-Istoricheskii Zhurnal* 10 (1992): 68–81.

Althusser, Louis. *Essays in Self-Criticism.* Translated by Grahame Lock. Atlantic Heights, N.J.: Humanities Press, 1976.

Anderson, Harriet. *Utopian Feminism: Women's Movements in Fin-de-Siècle Vienna.* New Haven, Conn.: Yale University Press, 1992.

Anderson, Margaret Lavinia. "The Limits of Secularization: On the Problem of Catholic Revival in Nineteenth-Century Germany." *Historical Journal* 38, no. 3 (1995): 647–670.

Appiah, Kwame Anthony. *Cosmopolitanism: Ethics in a World of Strangers.* New York: Norton, 2006.

Appignanesi, Lisa, and John Forrester. *Freud's Women.* New York: Basic Books, 1992.

Asad, Talal. *Formations of the Secular: Christianity, Islam, Modernity.* Palo Alto, Calif.: Stanford University Press, 2003.

Aschheim, Steven. *The Nietzsche Legacy in Germany, 1890–1990.* Berkeley: University of California Press, 1992.

Ash, Mitchell. *Gestalt Psychology in German Culture, 1890–1967: Holism and the Quest for Objectivity.* Cambridge: Cambridge University Press, 1995.

Avineri, Schlomo. "Marx and the Intellectuals." *Journal of the History of Ideas* 28, no. 2 (1967): 269–278.

Badia, Gilbert. *Clara Zetkin: Eine neue Biographie.* Translated from the French by Florence Hervé and Ingeborg Nödinger. Berlin: Dietz, 1994.

Bajohr, Frank, Werner Johe, and Uwe Lohalm, eds. *Zivilisation und Barbarei: Die widersprüchlichen Potentiale der Moderne.* Hamburg: Christians, 1991.

Balibar, Etienne. *Spinoza and Politics.* Translated by Peter Snowdon. London: Verso, 1998.

Barlösius, Eva. *Naturgemässe Lebensführung: Zur Geschichte der Lebensreform um die Jahrhundertwende.* Frankfurt am Main: Campus, 1997.

Bataille, Georges. "Hegel, Death, and Sacrifice." Translated by Jonathan Strauss. *Yale French Studies* 78 (1990): 9–28.

Berger, Peter. *The Sacred Canopy: Elements of a Sociological Theory of Religion.* New York: Anchor, 1967.

Berlau, Abraham Joseph A. *The German Social Democratic Party, 1914–1921.* New York: Columbia University Press, 1949.

Berlin Museum, ed. *Eldorado: Homosexuelle Frauen und Männer in Berlin, 1850–1950: Geschichte, Alltag und Kultur.* Berlin: Fröhlich & Kaufmann, 1984.

Bhargava, Rajeev, ed. *Secularism and Its Critics.* New York: Oxford University Press, 1998.

Biddiss, Michael. "The Universal Races Congress of 1911." *Race* 13, no. 1 (1971): 37–46.

Binion, Rudolph. *Frau Lou: Nietzsche's Wayward Disciple.* Princeton, N.J.: Princeton University Press, 1968.

Blackbourn, David. *The Long Nineteenth Century: A History of Germany, 1780–1918.* Oxford: Oxford University Press, 1998.

———. *Marpingen: Apparitions of the Virgin Mary in Nineteenth-Century Germany.* New York: Knopf, 1994.

Blackbourn, David, and Geoff Eley. *The Peculiarities of German History: Bourgeois Society and Politics in Nineteenth-Century Germany.* New York: Oxford University Press, 1984.

Blaschke, Olaf. "Das 19. Jahrhundert: Ein Zweites Konfessionelles Zeitalter?" *Geschichte und Gesellschaft* 26 (2000): 38–75.

Blasius, Dirk. *Ehescheidung in Deutschland, 1794–1945: Scheidung und Scheidungsrecht in historischer Perspektive.* Göttingen: Vandenhoeck & Ruprecht, 1987.

Bleibtreu-Ehrenberg, Gisela. *Tabu Homosexualität: Die Geschichte eines Vorurteils.* Frankfurt am Main: S. Fischer, 1978.

Blue, Gregory. "China and Western Social Thought in the Modern Period." In *China and Historical Capitalism: Genealogies of Sinological Knowledge,* edited by Timothy Brook and Gregory Blue. Cambridge: Cambridge University Press, 1999.

Blumenberg, Hans. *The Legitimacy of the Modern Age.* Translated by Robert M. Wallace. Cambridge, Mass.: MIT Press, 1983.

Boli, John, and George M. Thomas, eds. *Constructing World Culture: International Nongovernmental Organizations since 1875.* Palo Alto, Calif.: Stanford University Press, 1999.

Bonakdarian, Mansour. "Negotiating Universal Values and Cultural and National Parameters at the First Universal Races Congress." *Radical History Review* 92 (2005): 118–132.

Bottomore, Tom, and Patrick Goode, eds. *Austro-Marxism.* Oxford: Oxford University Press, 1978.

Bourdieu, Pierre. "The Force of Law: Toward a Sociology of the Juridical Field." Translated by Richard Terdiman. *Hastings Law Journal* 38, no. 5 (1987): 805–854.

Brakelmann, Günter, Martin Greschat, and Werner Jochmann, eds. *Protestantismus und Politik: Werk und Wirkung Adolf Stöckers.* Hamburg: Christians, 1982.

Brantz, Dorothee. "Stunning Bodies: Animal Slaughter, Judaism, and the Meaning of Humanity in Imperial Germany." *Central European History* 35, no. 2 (2002): 167–194.

Breckenridge, Carol A., Sheldon Pollock, Homi K. Bhabha, and Dipesh Chakrabarty, eds. *Cosmopolitanism.* Durham, N.C.: Duke University Press, 2002.

Bruch, Rüdiger vom, ed. *Weder Kommunismus noch Kapitalismus: Bürgerliche Sozialreform in Deutschland in Vormärz bis zur Ära Adenauer.* Munich: C. H. Beck, 1985.

Buchanan, Allen E. *Marx and Justice: The Radical Critique of Liberalism.* Totowa, N.J.: Rowman & Littlefield, 1982.

Buhle, Mari Jo. *Feminism and Its Discontents: A Century of Struggle with Psychoanalysis.* Cambridge, Mass.: Harvard University Press, 1998.

Burrow, J. W. *The Crisis of Reason: European Thought, 1848–1914.* New Haven, Conn.: Yale University Press, 2000.

Butler, Judith. *The Psychic Life of Power: Theories in Subjection.* Palo Alto, Calif.: Stanford University Press, 1997.

Canning, Kathleen. "Class vs. Citizenship: Keywords in German Gender History." *Central European History* 37, no. 2 (2004): 225–244.

———. *Languages of Labor and Gender: Female Factory Work in Germany, 1850–1914.* Ithaca: Cornell University Press, 1997.

Canning, Kathleen, and Sonja Rose, eds. *Gender, Citizenships, and Subjectivities.* Ames, Iowa: Blackwell, 2002.

Carotenuto, Aldo. *A Secret Symmetry: Sabina Spielrein between Freud and Jung.* Translated by Arno Pomerans, John Shepley, and Krishna Winston. New York: Pantheon Books, 1982.

Caruth, Cathy. *Unclaimed Experience: Trauma, Narrative, and History.* Baltimore: Johns Hopkins University Press, 1996.

Chadwick, Owen. *The Secularization of the European Mind in the 19th Century.* Cambridge: Cambridge University Press, 1975.

Chanter, Tina. *Ethics of Eros: Irigaray's Rewriting of the Philosophers.* New York: Routledge, 1995.

Cheah, Pheng, and Bruce Robbins, eds. *Cosmopolitics: Thinking and Feeling beyond the Nation.* Minneapolis: University of Minnesota Press, 1998.

Clark, Christopher, and Wolfram Kaiser, eds. *Culture Wars: Secular-Catholic Conflict in Nineteenth-Century Europe.* Cambridge: Cambridge University Press, 2003.

Coale, Ansley. "The Decline of Fertility in Europe, 1789–1940." In *Fertility and Family Planning: A World View,* edited by S. J. Behrman, Leslie Gorba Jr., and Ronald Freeman. Ann Arbor: University of Michigan Press, 1969.

Cohen, Marshall, Thomas Nagel, and Thomas Scanlon, eds. *Marx, Justice, and History.* Princeton, N.J.: Princeton University Press, 1980.

Copjec, Joan. *Imagine There's No Woman: Ethics and Sublimation.* Cambridge, Mass.: MIT Press, 2002.

———. *Read My Desire: Lacan against the Historicists.* Cambridge, Mass.: MIT Press, 1994.

———. "Sex and the Euthanasia of Reason." In *Supposing the Subject,* edited by Joan Copjec. New York: Verso, 1994.

Crompton, Louis. "The Myth of Lesbian Impunity: Capital Laws from 1270 to 1791." In *Historical Perspectives on Homosexuality,* edited by Salvatore J. Licata and Robert P. Petersen. New York: Hayward Press, 1981.

Dampier, William Cecil. *A History of Science and Its Relations with Philosophy and Religion.* 4th revised ed. New York: Macmillan, 1949.

Daum, Andreas. *Wissenschaftspopularisierung im 19. Jahrhundert: Bürgerliche Kultur, naturwissenschaftliche Bildung und die deutsche Öffentlichkeit, 1848–1914.* Munich: R. Oldenbourg, 2002.

Dean, Carolyn. *The Frail Social Body: Pornography, Homosexuality, and Other Fantasies in Interwar France.* Berkeley: University of California Press, 2000.

de Lauretis, Teresa. *The Practice of Love: Lesbian Sexuality and Perverse Desire.* Bloomington: Indiana University Press, 1994.

Derrida, Jacques. *The Gift of Death.* Translated by David Wills. Chicago: University of Chicago Press, 1995.

Dickinson, Edward Ross. "Biopolitics, Fascism, Democracy: Reflections on Our Discourse Concerning 'Modernity.'" *Central European History* 37, no. 1 (2004): 1–48.

——. "Reflections on Feminism and Monism in the Kaiserreich, 1900–1913." *Central European History* 34, no. 2 (2001): 191–230.

——. "Sex, Masculinity, and the 'Yellow Peril': Christian Von Ehrenfels' Program for a Revision of the European Social Order." *German Studies Review* 25, no. 2 (2002): 255–284.

Diethe, Carol. *Nietzsche's Women: Beyond the Whip.* Berlin: W. De Gruyter, 1996.

Dornemann, Luise. *Clara Zetkin: Ein Lebensbild.* Berlin: Dietz, 1957.

Eaton, Howard O. *The Austrian Philosophy of Values.* Norman: University of Oklahoma Press, 1930.

Eley, Geoff. *From Unification to Nazism: Reinterpreting the German Past.* Boston: Allen & Unwin, 1986.

Eley, Geoff, and James Retallack, eds. *Wilhelminism and Its Legacies: German Modernities, Imperialism, and the Meanings of Reform, 1890–1930.* New York: Berghahn Books, 2003.

Etkind, Alexander. *Eros of the Impossible: The History of Psychoanalysis in Russia.* Translated by Noah Rubins and Maria Rubins. Boulder, Colo.: Westview Press, 1997.

Evans, Richard J. *Comrades and Sisters: Feminism, Socialism and Pacifism in Europe, 1870–1945.* New York: St. Martin's Press, 1987.

——. *The Feminist Movement in Germany.* Beverly Hills, Calif.: Sage, 1976.

——. "Politics and the Family: Social Democracy and the Working-Class Family in Theory and Practice before 1914." In *The German Family: Essays on the Social History of the Family in Nineteenth- and Twentieth-Century Germany,* edited by Richard J. Evans and W. R. Lee. Totowa, N.J.: Croom Helm, 1981.

——. "Prostitution, State, and Society in Imperial Germany." *Past and Present* 70 (1976): 106–129.

——. *Tales from the German Underworld: Crime and Punishment in the Nineteenth Century.* New Haven, Conn.: Yale University Press, 1998.

——. "Theory and Practice in German Social Democracy, 1880–1914: Clara Zetkin and the Socialist Theory of Women's Emancipation." *History of Political Thought* 3, no. 2 (1982): 285–304.

Fabian, Reinhard. "Leben und Wirken von Christian V. Ehrenfels: Ein Beitrag zur intellektuellen Biographie." In *Christian Von Ehrenfels: Leben und Werk,* edited by R. Fabian. Amsterdam: Rodopi, 1986.

Fabian, Reinhard, and P. M. Simons. "The Second Austrian School of Value Theory." In *Austrian Economics: Historical and Philosophical Background,* edited by Wolfgang Grassl and Barry Smith. London: Croom Helm, 1986.

Faderman, Lillian, and Brigitte Eriksson, eds. *Lesbians in Germany, 1890's–1920's.* Tallahassee, Fla.: Naiad Press, 1990.

Fanon, Frantz. *Black Skin, White Masks.* Translated by Charles Lam Markmann. New York: Grove Press, 1967.

Fletcher, Roger. *Revisionism and Empire: Socialist Imperialism in Germany, 1897–1914.* London: G. Allen and Unwin, 1984.

Foucault, Michel. "An Aesthetics of Existence" and "The Art of Telling the Truth." In *Michel Foucault: Politics, Philosophy, Culture; Interviews and Other Writings, 1977–1984.* Edited by Lawrence Kritzman. Translated by Alan Sheridan. New York: Routledge, 1990.

———. *Discipline and Punish: The Birth of the Prison.* Translated by Alan Sheridan. New York: Vintage, 1979.

———. "Ethic of Care for the Self as a Practice of Freedom." Translated by J. D. Gauthier. *Philosophy and Social Criticism* 2 (1987): 112–131.

———. *The History of Sexuality.* 3 vols. Translated by Robert Hurley. New York: Vintage, 1990.

Fout, John. "Adolf Stöcker's Rationale for Anti-Semitism." *Journal of Church and State* 17, no. 1 (1975): 47–63.

———. "The Moral Purity Movement in Wilhelmine Germany and the Attempt to Regulate Male Behavior." *Journal of Men's Studies* 1 (1992): 5–27.

———. "Policing Gender: Moral Purity Movements in Pre-Nazi Germany and Contemporary America." In *Redeeming Men: Religion and Masculinities,* edited by Stephen Boyd, W. Merle Longwood, and Mark Muesse. Louisville, Ky.: Westminster John Knox Press, 1996.

———. "Sexual Politics in Wilhelmine Germany: The Male Gender Crisis, Moral Purity and Homophobia." *Journal of the History of Sexuality* 2, no. 3 (1992): 388–421.

———, ed. *Forbidden History: The State, Society, and the Regulation of Sexuality in Modern Europe.* Chicago: University of Chicago Press, 1990.

Freunde eines Schwulen-Museum in Berlin e.V., ed. *Die Geschichte des §175: Strafrecht gegen Homosexuelle.* Berlin: Rosa Winkel, 1990.

Frevert, Ute. *Women in German History: From Bourgeois Emancipation to Sexual Liberation.* Translated by Stuart McKinnon-Evans. Oxford: Berg, 1989.

Friess, Horace. *Felix Adler and Ethical Culture: Memories and Studies.* Edited by Fannia Weingartner. New York: Columbia University Press, 1981.

Fritzen, Florentine. *Gesünder Leben: Die Lebensreformbewegung im 20. Jahrhundert.* Stuttgart: Steiner, 2006.

Fromm, Erich. *Psychoanalyse und Ethik.* Frankfurt am Main: Ullstein, 1978.

Fuss, Diana. *Identification Papers.* New York: Routledge, 1995.

Gasman, Daniel. *Haeckel's Monism and the Birth of Fascist Ideology.* New York: Peter Lang, 1998.

———. *The Scientific Origins of National Socialism.* Rev. ed. New Brunswick, N.J.: Transaction, 2004.

Gay, Peter. *The Dilemma of Democratic Socialism: Eduard Bernstein's Challenge to Marx.* New York: Collier Books, 1962.

———. *Freud: A Life for Our Time.* New York: Doubleday, 1988

Geary, Dick. *Karl Kautsky.* New York: St. Martin's Press, 1987.

Gerhard, Ute. *Unerhört: Die Geschichte der Deutschen Frauenbewegung.* Reinbek bei Hamburg: Rowohlt, 1990.

――. *Verhältnisse und Verhinderungen: Frauenarbeit, Familie und Rechte der Frauen im 19. Jahrhundert, mit Dokumenten.* Frankfurt am Main: Suhrkamp, 1978.

――, ed. *Frauen in der Geschichte des Rechts: Von der frühen Neuzeit bis zur Gegenwart.* Munich: C. H. Beck, 1997.

Geyer, Michael, and Hartmut Lehmann, eds. *Religion und Nation, Nation und Religion: Beiträge zu einer unbewältigten Geschichte.* Göttingen: Wallstein, 2004.

Gilcher-Holtey, Ingrid. *Das Mandat des Intellektuellen: Karl Kautsky und die Sozialdemokratie.* Berlin: Siedler, 1986.

Gilman, Sander. *Freud, Race, and Gender.* Princeton, N.J.: Princeton University Press, 1993.

Gimpl, Georg. *Vernetzungen: Friedrich Jodl und sein Kampf um die Aufklärung.* Oulu: Historischer Institut der Universität Oulu, 1990.

――, ed. *Ego und Alterego: Wilhelm Bolin und Friedrich Jodl im Kampf um die Aufklärung.* Frankfurt am Main: Peter Lang, 1996.

Gleberzon, William. "Marxist Conceptions of the Intellectual." *Historical Reflections* 5, no. 1 (1978): 81–97.

Glick, Thomas. *The Comparative Reception of Darwinism.* Chicago: University of Chicago Press, 1988.

Goldenbaum, Ursula. "'Der alte Spinoza hatte ganz recht'? Zur Aneignung Spinozas in der deutschen Sozialdemokratie." In *Transformation der Metaphysik in die Moderne: Zur Gegenwärtigkeit der theoretischen und praktischen Philosophie Spinozas,* edited by Michael Czelinski, Thomas Kisser, Robert Schnepf, Marcel Senn, and Jürgen Stenzel. Würzburg: Königshausen & Neumann, 2003.

Gollwitzer, Heinz. *Die gelbe Gefahr: Geschichte eines Schlagworts.* Göttingen: Vandenhoeck & Ruprecht, 1962.

Götschl, Johann, and Christoph Klauser. *Der sozialdemokratische Intellektuelle.* Vienna: Literas, 1983.

Graf, Friedrich Wilhelm. "'Dechristianisierung': Zur Problemgeschichte eines kulturpolitischen Topos." In *Säkularisierung, Dechristianisierung, Rechristianisierung im neuzeitlichen Europa,* edited by Hartmut Lehmann. Göttingen: Vandenhoeck & Ruprecht, 1997.

Graf, Friedrich Wilhelm, and Hans Martin Müller, eds. *Der Deutsche Protestantismus um 1900.* Gütersloh: Chr. Kaiser, 1996.

Grebing, Helga. *Der Revisionismus von Bernstein bis zum "Prager Frühling."* Munich: C. H. Beck, 1977.

Gregory, Frederick. *Scientific Materialism in Nineteenth Century Germany.* Dordrecht: D. Reidel, 1977.

Greven-Aschoff, Barbara. *Die bürgerliche Frauenbewegung in Deutschland, 1894–1933.* Göttingen: Vandenhoeck & Ruprecht, 1981.

Gröll, Johannes. *Das moralische bürgerliche Subjekt: Kant, Hegel, Marx, Freud, Rousseau, Adorno.* Münster: Westfälisches Dampfboot, 1991.

Groschopp, Horst. *Dissidenten: Freidenkerei und Kultur in Deutschland.* Berlin: Dietz, 1997.

Gross, Michael. "Kulturkampf and Unification: German Liberalism and the War against the Jesuits." *Central European History* 30, no. 4 (1997): 545–566.

———. *The War against Catholicism: Liberalism and the Anti-Catholic Imagination in Nineteenth-Century Germany.* Ann Arbor: University of Michigan Press, 2004.

Grossman, Atina. *Reforming Sex: The German Movement for Birth Control and Abortion Reform, 1920–1950.* New York: Oxford University Press, 1995.

Gustafsson, Bo. *Marxismus und Revisionismus: Eduard Bernsteins Kritik des Marxismus und ihre ideengeschichtlichen Voraussetzungen.* 2 vols. Frankfurt am Main: Europäische Verlagsanstalt, 1972.

Habermas, Jürgen. *Strukturwandel der Öffentlichkeit: Untersuchungen zu einer Kategorie der bürgerlichen Gesellschaft.* Neuwied: Luchterhand, 1962.

———. "Technology and Science as 'Ideology.'" In *Toward a Rational Society: Student Protest, Science, and Politics.* Translated by Jeremy J. Shapiro. Boston: Beacon Press, 1968.

Hacker, Hanna. *Frauen und Freundinnen: Studien zur weiblichen Homosexualität am Beispiel Österreich, 1870–1938.* Weinheim: Beltz, 1987.

Hackett, Amy. "Helene Stöcker: Left-Wing Intellectual and Sex Reformer." In *When Biology Became Destiny: Women in Weimar and Nazi Germany,* edited by Renate Bridenthal, Atina Grossman, and Marion Kaplan. New York: Monthly Review Press, 1984.

Hamelmann, Gudrun. *Helene Stöcker, der "Bund für Mutterschutz" und "Die neue Generation."* Frankfurt am Main: Haag & Herchen, 1992.

Harp, Gillis J. "Determinism or Democracy? The Marxisms of Eduard Bernstein and Sidney Hook." *History of European Ideas* 25, no. 5 (1999): 243–250.

Harrington, Anne. *Re-enchanted Science: Holism in German Culture from Wilhelm II to Hitler.* Princeton, N.J.: Princeton University Press, 1996.

Harrowitz, Nancy, and Barbara Hyams, eds. *Jews and Gender: Responses to Otto Weininger.* Philadelphia: Temple University Press, 1995.

Hau, Michael. *The Cult of Health and Beauty in Germany: A Social History, 1890–1930.* Chicago: University of Chicago Press, 2003.

Hemleben, Johannes. *Rudolf Steiner: An Illustrated Biography.* London: Sophia Books, 2000.

Hergemöller, Bernd-Ulrich. *Einführung in die Historiographie der Homosexualitäten.* Tübingen: Edition Diskord, 1999.

Hermanns, Ludger M. "Helene Stöckers autobiographisches Fragment zur Psychoanalyse." *Luzifer-Amor* 4, no. 8 (1991): 177–180.

Herzog, Dagmar. *Intimacy and Exclusion: Religious Politics in Pre-revolutionary Baden.* Princeton, N.J.: Princeton University Press, 1996.

Hett, Benjamin. *Death in the Tiergarten: Murder and Criminal Justice in the Kaiser's Berlin.* Cambridge, Mass.: Harvard University Press, 2004.

Heymann, Lida Gustava, and Anita Augspurg. *Erlebtes—Erschautes: Deutsche Frauen kämpfen für Freiheit, Recht und Frieden, 1850–1940.* New ed. Edited by Margrit Twellmann. Frankfurt am Main: Ulrike Helmer, 1992.

Hirsch, Helmut. *Der "Fabier" Eduard Bernstein: Zur Entwicklungsgeschichte des evolutionären Sozialismus.* Bonn: Dietz, 1977.

Hölscher, Lucian, ed. *Datenatlas zur religiösen Geographie im protestantischen Deutschland von der Mitte des 19. Jahrhunderts bis zum Zweiten Weltkrieg.* 4 vols. Berlin: Walter de Gruyter, 2001.

Holt, Niles R. "Ernst Haeckel's Monistic Religion." *Journal of the History of Ideas* 32, no. 2 (1971): 265–280.

Holton, Robert John. "Cosmopolitanism or Cosmopolitanisms? The Universal Races Congress of 1911." *Global Networks* 2, no. 2 (2002): 153–170.

Holzheuer, Walter. *Karl Kautskys Werk als Weltanschauung: Beitrag zur Ideologie der Sozialdemokratie vor dem ersten Weltkrieg.* Munich: C. H. Beck, 1972.

Homans, Peter. *The Ability to Mourn: Disillusionment and the Social Origins of Psychoanalysis.* Chicago: University of Chicago Press, 1989.

Honeycutt, Karen. "Clara Zetkin: A Left-Wing Socialist and Feminist in Wilhelmian Germany." Ph.D. dissertation, Columbia University, 1975.

Hook, Sidney. *Towards the Understanding of Karl Marx: A Revolutionary Interpretation.* New York: J. Day, 1933.

Hornback, James. "The Philosophic Sources and Sanctions of the Founders of Ethical Culture." Ph.D. dissertation, Columbia University, 1983.

Huber, Ernst. *Deutsche Verfassungsgeschichte seit 1789.* 8 vols. Stuttgart: Kohlhammer, 1969.

Hübinger, Gangolf. *Kulturprotestantismus und Politik: Zum Verhältnis von Liberalismus und Protestantismus im wilhelminischen Deutschland.* Tübingen: J. C. B. Mohr, 1994.

Hull, Isabel. *The Entourage of Kaiser Wilhelm II, 1888–1918.* New York: Cambridge University Press, 1982.

———. *Sexuality, State, and Civil Society in Germany, 1700–1815.* Ithaca: Cornell University Press, 1996.

Hunt, Alan. *Governing Morals: A Social History of Moral Regulation.* New York: Cambridge University Press, 1999.

Hutter, Jörg. *Die gesellschaftliche Kontrolle des homosexuellen Begehrens: Medizinische Definitionen und juristische Sanktionen im 19. Jahrhundert.* Frankfurt am Main: Campus, 1992.

Irigaray, Luce. *An Ethics of Sexual Difference.* Translated by Carolyn Burke and Gillian C. Gill. Ithaca: Cornell University Press, 1993.

———. *Thinking the Difference: For a Peaceful Revolution.* Translated by Karin Montin. New York: Routledge, 1994.

Iriye, Akira. *Cultural Internationalism and World Order.* Baltimore: Johns Hopkins University Press, 1997.

———. *Global Community: The Role of International Organizations in the Making of the Contemporary World.* Berkeley: University of California Press, 2002.

Jansen, Reinhard. *Georg von Vollmar.* Bonn: Droste, 1956.

Janssen-Jurreit, Marie-Luise. "Nationalbiologie, Sexualreform und Gebürtenrückgang—Über die Zusammenhänge von Bevölkerungspolitik und Frauenbewegung um die Jahrhundertwende." In *Die Überwindung der Sprachlosigkeit,* edited by Gabriele Dietz. Darmstad: Luchterhand, 1978.

Jarausch, Konrad. *Students, Society, and Politics in Imperial Germany: The Rise of Academic Illiberalism.* Princeton, N.J.: Princeton University Press, 1982.

Jefferies, Matthew. *Imperial Culture in Germany, 1871–1918.* New York: Palgrave, 2003.

Jestrabek, Heiner. "Einleitung." In *Jakob Stern: Vom Rabbiner zum Atheisten; Ausgewählte religionskritische Schriften.* Aschaffenburg: IBDK, 1997.

Joest, Mechthild, and Martina Nieswandt. "Das Lehrerinnen-Zölibat im Deutschen Kaiserreich: Die rechtliche Situation der unverheirateten Lehrerinnen in Preußen und die Stellungnahmen der Frauenbewegung zur Zölibatsklausel." In *Die ungeschriebene Geschichte: Historische Forschung; Dokumentation des 5. Historikerinnentreffens in Wien, 16. Bis 19. April 1984,* edited by Beatrix Bechtel. Himberg bei Vienna: Wiener Frauenverlag, 1984.

John, Michael. *Politics and the Law in Late Nineteenth-Century Germany: The Origins of the Civil Code.* Oxford: Clarendon Press, 1989.

Jones, Gareth Stedman. "Engels and the End of Classical German Philosophy." *New Left Review* 79 (1973): 17–36.

Jones, James. *"We of the Third Sex": Literary Representations of Homosexuality in Wilhelmine Germany.* New York: Peter Lang, 1990.

Jordan, Jane. *Josephine Butler: A Biography.* London: John Murray, 2001.

Judd, Robin. *Contested Rituals: Circumcision, Kosher Butchering, and Jewish Political Life in Germany, 1843–1933.* Ithaca: Cornell University Press, 2007.

Kaldor, Mary. *Global Civil Society: An Answer to War.* Cambridge: Cambridge University Press, 2003.

Kavka, Misha. "The 'Alluring Abyss of Nothingness': Misogyny and (Male) Hysteria in Otto Weininger." *New German Critique* 22, no. 66 (1995): 123–145.

Kelly, Alfred. *The Descent of Darwin: The Popularization of Darwinism in Germany, 1860–1914.* Chapel Hill: University of North Carolina Press, 1981.

Kerbs, Diethart, and Jürgen Reulecke, eds. *Handbuch der Deutschen Reformbewegungen, 1880–1933.* Wuppertal: Hammer, 1998.

Kerr, John. *A Most Dangerous Method: The Story of Jung, Freud, and Sabina Spielrein.* New York: Vintage, 1994.

Khanna, Ranjana. *Dark Continents: Psychoanalysis and Colonialism.* Durham, N.C.: Duke University Press, 2003.

Knodel, John. *The Decline of Fertility in Germany, 1871–1939.* Princeton, N.J.: Princeton University Press, 1974.

Koepcke, Cordula. *Lou Andreas-Salomé: Leben, Persönlichkeit, Werk.* Frankfurt am Main: Insel, 1986.

Kofman, Sarah. "The Narcissistic Woman: Freud and Girard." *Diacritics* 10 (1980): 36–45.

Köhnke, Klaus Christian. *The Rise of Neo-Kantianism: German Academic Philosophy between Idealism and Positivism.* Translated by R. J. Hollingdale. New York: Cambridge University Press, 1991.

Krabbe, Wolfgang. *Gesellschaftsveränderung durch Lebensreform.* Göttingen: Vandenhoeck & Ruprecht, 1974.

Kraft, Sibylla. *Zucht und Unzucht: Prostitution und Sittenpolizei im München der Jahrhundertwende.* Munich: Hugendubel, 1996.

Kraut, Benny. *From Reform Judaism to Ethical Culture: The Religious Evolution of Felix Adler.* Cincinnati: Hebrew Union College Press, 1979.

Kreide, Caroline. *Lou Andreas-Salomé: Feministin oder Antifeministin? Eine Standortbestimmung der wilhelminischen Frauenbewegung.* New York: Peter Lang, 1996.

Lacan, Jacques. *The Ethics of Psychoanalysis, 1959–1960: The Seminar of Jacques Lacan, Book 7.* Translated by Dennis Porter. Edited by Jacques-Alain Miller. New York: Norton, 1992.

——. "Kant with Sade." Translated by James B. Swenson Jr. *October* 51 (1989): 55–104.

——. *On Feminine Sexuality: The Limits of Love and Knowledge (Encore 1972–1973).* Translated by Bruce Fink. New York: Norton, 1998.

LaCapra, Dominick. *Writing History, Writing Trauma.* Baltimore: Johns Hopkins University Press, 2001.

Lamberti, Marjorie. *Jewish Activism in Imperial Germany.* New Haven, Conn.: Yale University Press, 1978.

——. *State, Society, and the Elementary School in Imperial Germany.* New York: Oxford University Press, 1989.

Landes, Joan, ed. *Feminism, the Public and the Private.* Oxford: Oxford University Press, 1998.

Lane, Christopher, ed. *The Psychoanalysis of Race.* New York: Columbia University Press, 1998.

Laplanche, Jean, and J.-B. Pontalis. *The Language of Psychoanalysis.* Translated by Donald Nicholson-Smith. New York: Norton, 1973.

Laqueur, Thomas. *Making Sex: Gender and the Body from Aristotle to Freud.* Cambridge, Mass.: Harvard University Press, 1990.

Lauermann, Manfred. "Jakob Stern—Sozialist und Spinozist: Eine kleine Skizze zum 150. Geburtstag." In *Spinoza in der europäischen Geistesgeschichte,* edited by Hanna Delf, Julius H. Schoeps, and Manfred Walther. Berlin: Edition Hentrich, 1994.

Lautmann, Rüdiger. *Seminar: Gesellschaft und Homosexualität.* Frankfurt am Main: Suhrkamp, 1977.

Lees, Andrew. *Cities Perceived: Urban Society in European and American Thought, 1820–1940.* Manchester: Manchester University Press, 1985.

——. *Cities, Sin, and Social Reform in Imperial Germany.* Ann Arbor: University of Michigan Press, 2002.

——. "Deviant Sexuality and Other 'Sins': The Views of Protestant Conservatives in Imperial Germany." *German Studies Review* 23, no. 3 (2000): 453–476.

Lehmann, Hartmut, ed. *Säkularisierung, Dechristianisierung, Rechristianisierung im neuzeitlichen Europa.* Göttingen: Vandenhoeck & Ruprecht, 1997.

Lenman, R. J. V. "Art, Society, and the Law in Wilhelmine Germany: The Lex Heinze." *Oxford German Studies* 8 (1973): 86–113.

Le Rider, Jacques. *Der Fall Otto Weininger: Wurzeln des Antifeminismus und Antisemitismus.* Vienna: Löcker, 1985.

"A Lesbian Execution in Germany, 1721: The Trial Records." Translated by Brigitte Eriksson. In *Historical Perspectives on Homosexuality,* edited by Salvatore J. Licata and Robert P. Petersen. New York: Hayward Press, 1981.

Lidtke, Vernon. *The Alternative Culture: Socialist Labor in Imperial Germany.* New York: Oxford University Press, 1985.

——. *The Outlawed Party: Social Democracy in Germany, 1878–1890.* Princeton, N.J.: Princeton University Press, 1966.

Lisberg-Haag, Isabell. *"Die Unzucht—das Grab der Völker": Die evangelische Sittlichkeitsbewegung und die "sexuelle Moderne," 1870–1918.* Münster: Lit, 1999.

Lischke, Ute. *Lily Braun, 1865–1916: German Writer, Feminist, Socialist.* Rochester, N.Y.: Camden House, 2000.

Livingstone, Angela. *Lou Andreas-Salomé: Her Life and Work.* Mt. Kisco, N.Y.: Moyer, Bell, 1984.

Lübbe, Hermann. *Säkularisierung: Geschichte eines ideenpolitischen Begriffs.* Freiburg: K. Alber, 1965.

Luft, David. *Eros and Inwardness in Vienna: Weininger, Musil, Doderer.* Chicago: University of Chicago Press, 2003.

Lukes, Steven. *Marxism and Morality.* Oxford: Clarendon Press, 1985.

Lybeck, Marti. "Gender, Sexuality, and Belonging: Female Homosexuality in Germany, 1890–1933." Ph.D. dissertation, University of Michigan, 2007.

Macherey, Pierre. *Hegel ou Spinoza.* Paris: F. Maspero, 1979.

MacKillop, Ian Duncan. *The British Ethical Societies.* Cambridge: Cambridge University Press, 1986.

Mah, Harold. *The End of Philosophy and the Origins of "Ideology."* Berkeley: University of California Press, 1987.

Mannoni, Octave. *Prospero and Caliban: The Psychology of Colonisation.* Translated by Pamela Powesland. New York: Praeger, 1964.

Marshall, T. H., and Tom Bottomore. *Citizenship and Social Class, and Other Essays.* London: Pluto Press, 1992.

Martin, Biddy. *Femininity Played Straight: The Significance of Being Lesbian.* New York: Routledge, 1996.

———. "Feminism, Criticism, and Foucault." In *Knowing Women: Feminism and Knowledge,* edited by Helen Crowley and Susan Himmelweit. Cambridge, Mass.: Polity Press, 1992.

———. *Woman and Modernity: The (Life) Styles of Lou Andreas-Salomé.* Ithaca: Cornell University Press, 1991.

Massin, Benoit. "From Virchow to Fischer: Physical Anthropology and 'Modern Race Theories' in Wilhelmine Germany." In *Volksgeist as Method and Ethic,* edited by George Stocking. Madison: University of Wisconsin Press, 1996.

Matysik, Tracie. "Internationalist Activism at the Height of Nationalism: The Universal Races Congress of 1911." In *Global History: Interactions between the Universal and the Local,* edited by A. G. Hopkins. New York: Palgrave, 2006.

Mazón, Patricia. *Gender and the Modern Research University: The Admission of Women to German Higher Education, 1865–1914.* Palo Alto, Calif.: Stanford University Press, 2003.

McClintock, Anne. *Imperial Leather: Race, Gender, and Sexuality in the Colonial Contest.* New York: Routledge, 1995.

McDonald, Christie, ed. *The Ear of the Other: Otobiography, Transference, Translation; Texts and Discussion with Jacques Derrida.* Lincoln: University of Nebraska Press, 1985.

McGrath, William. *Dionysian Art and Populist Politics in Austria.* New Haven, Conn.: Yale University Press, 1974.

McGuire, Kristin. "Activism, Intimacy, and the Politics of Selfhood: The Gendered Terms of Citizenship in Poland and Germany, 1890–1919." Ph.D. dissertation, University of Michigan, 2004.

Meisenheim, Anton Hain, ed. *100 Jahre philosophische Nietzsche-Rezeption.* Frankfurt am Main: Anton Hain Meisenheim, 1991.

Melander, Ellinor. "Toward the Sexual and Economic Emancipation of Women: The Philosophy of Grete Meisel-Hess." *History of European Ideas* 14, no. 5 (1992): 695–713.

Meyer, Alfred. *The Feminism and Socialism of Lily Braun.* Bloomington: Indiana University Press, 1985.

Miller, Susanne, and Heinrich Potthoff. *A History of German Social Democracy from 1848 to the Present.* Translated by J. A. Underwood. New York: Berg, 1986.

Mitchell, Juliet. "Introduction I." In *Jacques Lacan: Feminine Sexuality,* edited by Juliet Mitchell and Jacquelyn Rose. New York: Norton, 1982.

Morgan, David W. *The Socialist Left and the German Revolution: A History of the German Independent Social Democratic Party, 1917–1922.* Ithaca: Cornell University Press, 1975.

Mosse, George. *The Crisis of German Ideology: Intellectual Origins of the Third Reich.* New York: Grosset & Dunlap, 1964.

———. *Nationalism and Sexuality: Respectability and Abnormal Sexuality in Modern Europe.* New York: Fertig, 1985.

Müller, Dirk. *Idealismus und Revolution: Zur Opposition der Jungen gegen den sozialdemokratischen Parteivorstand, 1890–1894.* Berlin: Colloquium, 1975.

Nandy, Ashis. *The Savage Freud, and Other Essays on Possible and Retrievable Selves.* Princeton, N.J.: Princeton University Press, 1995.

Negri, Antonio. *The Savage Anomaly: The Power of Spinoza's Metaphysics and Politics.* Translated by Michael Hardt. Minneapolis: University of Minnesota Press, 1991.

Neuman, R. P. "The Sexual Question and Social Democracy in Imperial Germany." *Journal of Social History* 7, no. 3 (1974): 271–286.

———. "Working Class Birth Control in Wilhelmine Germany." *Comparative Studies in Society and History* 20, no. 3 (1978): 408–428.

Nipperdey, Thomas. *Deutsche Geschichte, 1866–1918.* Munich: C. H. Beck, 1990.

———. *Religion im Umbruch: Deutschland, 1870–1918.* Munich: C. H. Beck, 1988.

———. "Religion und Gesellschaft: Deutschland um 1900." *Historische Zeitschrift* 246, no. 3 (1988): 591–615.

Nowacki, Bernd. *Der Bund für Mutterschutz (1905–1933).* Husum: Matthiesen, 1983.

Nussbaum, Martha. "Patriotism and Cosmopolitanism." In *For Love of Country: Debating the Limits of Patriotism,* edited by Joshua Cohen. Boston: Beacon Press, 1996.

O'Leary, Timothy. *Foucault: The Art of Ethics.* London: Continuum, 2002.

Oliver, Kelly. *Womanizing Nietzsche: Philosophy's Relation to the Feminine.* New York: Routledge, 1995.

Oliver, Kelly, and Marilyn Pearsall, eds. *Feminist Interpretations of Friedrich Nietzsche.* University Park: Pennsylvania State University Press, 1998.

Ong, Aihwa. *Flexible Citizenship: The Cultural Logics of Transnationality.* Durham, N.C.: Duke University Press, 1999.

Oosterhuis, Harry. *Stepchildren of Nature: Krafft-Ebing, Psychiatry, and the Making of Sexual Identity.* Chicago: University of Chicago Press, 2000.

Osterroth, Franz, and Dieter Schuster. *Chronik der Deutschen Sozialdemokratie.* Hannover: Dietz, 1963.

Owetschkin, Dmitrij. "Die materialistische Geschichtsauffassung in der Interpretation E. Bernsteins." *Beiträge zur Geschichte der Arbeiterbewegung* 40, no. 1 (1998): 38–49.

Peffer, Rodney G. *Marxism, Morality, and Social Justice.* Princeton, N.J.: Princeton University Press, 1990.

Pennybacker, Susan. "The Universal Races Congress, London Political Culture, and Imperial Dissent, 1900–1939." *Radical History Review* 92 (2005): 103–117.

Peters, H. F. *My Sister, My Spouse: A Biography of Lou Andreas-Salomé.* New York: Norton, 1962.

Peukert, Detlev. "The Genesis of the 'Final Solution' from the Spirit of Science." In *Reevaluating the Third Reich,* edited by Thomas Childers and Jane Caplan. New York: Holmes & Meier, 1993.

———. *Grenzen der Sozialdisziplinierung: Aufstieg und Krise der Jugendfürsorge von 1878 bis 1932.* Cologne: Bund, 1986.

Pierson, Stanley. *Marxist Intellectuals and the Working-Class Mentality in Germany, 1887–1912.* Cambridge, Mass.: Harvard University Press, 1993.

Planert, Ute. *Antifeminismus im Kaiserreich: Diskurs, soziale Formation und politische Mentalität.* Göttingen: Vandenhoeck & Ruprecht, 1998.

Porter, Roy, and Mikuláš Teich, eds. *Sexual Knowledge, Sexual Science: The History of Attitudes to Sexuality.* Cambridge: Cambridge University Press, 1994.

Proctor, Robert. *Racial Hygiene: Medicine under the Nazis.* Cambridge, Mass.: Harvard University Press, 1988.

Prüfer, Sebastian. *Sozialismus statt Religion: Die Deutsche Sozialdemokratie vor der religiösen Frage, 1863–1890.* Göttingen: Vandenhoeck & Ruprecht, 2002.

Pulzer, Peter. *The Rise of Political Anti-Semitism in Germany and Austria.* Rev. ed. Cambridge, Mass.: Harvard University Press, 1988.

Puschner, Uwe, Walter Schmitz, and Justus Ulbricht, eds. *Handbuch zur "völkischen Bewegung," 1871–1918.* Munich: K. G. Saur, 1996.

Quataert, Jean. *Reluctant Feminists in German Social Democracy, 1885–1917.* Princeton, N.J.: Princeton University Press, 1979.

———. "Social Insurance and the Family Work of Oberlausitz Home Weavers in the Late Nineteenth Century." In *German Women in the Nineteenth Century: A Social History,* edited by John Fout. New York: Holmes & Meier, 1984.

Radest, Howard B. *Felix Adler: An Ethical Culture.* New York: Peter Lang, 1998.

Ramazanoğlu, Caroline, ed. *Up against Foucault: Explorations of Some Tensions between Foucault and Feminism.* New York: Routledge, 1993.

Rantzsch, Petra. *Helene Stöcker (1869–1943): Zwischen Pazifismus und Revolution.* Berlin: Buchverlag der Morgen, 1994.

Rauscher, Anton, ed. *Probleme des Konfessionalismus in Deutschland seit 1800.* Paderborn: Ferdinand Schöningh, 1984.

Reagin, Nancy. *A German Women's Movement: Class and Gender in Hannover, 1880–1933.* Chapel Hill: University of North Carolina Press, 1995.

———. "A True Woman Can Take Care of Herself: The Debate over Prostitution in Hanover, 1906." *Central European History* 24, no. 4 (1991): 347–380.

Reinhard, Kenneth, Eric Santner, and Slavoj Žižek. *The Neighbor: Three Inquiries in Political Theology.* Chicago: University of Chicago Press, 2006.

Repp, Kevin. *Reformers, Critics, and the Paths of German Modernity: Anti-Politics and the Search for Alternatives, 1890–1914.* Cambridge, Mass.: Harvard University Press, 2000.

Rich, Paul. "'The Baptism of a New Order': The 1911 Universal Races Congress and the Liberal Ideology of Race." *Ethnic and Racial Studies* 7, no. 4 (1984): 534–550.

———. *Race and Empire in British Politics.* Cambridge: Cambridge University Press, 1990.

Rieff, Philip. *Freud: The Mind of the Moralist.* Garden City, N.Y.: Doubleday, 1961.

Ringer, Fritz. *The Decline of the German Mandarins: The German Academic Community, 1890–1933.* Cambridge, Mass.: Harvard University Press, 1969.

Ritter, Gerhard. *Die Arbeiterbewegung im Wilhelminischen Reich.* Berlin: Colloquium, 1959.

Ritter, Gerhard, and Klaus Tenfelde. *Arbeiter im Deutschen Kaiserreich.* Bonn: Dietz, 1992.

Roazen, Paul. *Helene Deutsch: A Psychoanalyst's Life.* Garden City, N.Y.: Doubleday, 1985.

Roth, Günther. *The Social Democrats in Imperial Germany: A Study in Working-Class Isolation and National Integration.* Totowa, N.J.: Bedminster Press, 1963.

Rudwick, Elliott M. "W. E. B. Dubois and the Universal Races Congress of 1911." *Phylon Quarterly* 20, no. 4 (1959): 372–378.

Sachs, Wulf. *Black Hamlet.* Introduction by Saul Dubow and Jacqueline Rose. Baltimore: Johns Hopkins University Press, 1996.

Santner, Eric. *On the Psychotheology of Everyday Life.* Chicago: University of Chicago Press, 2001.

Sarasin, Philipp. *Reizbare Maschinen: Eine Geschichte des Körpers, 1765–1914.* Frankfurt am Main: Suhrkamp, 2001.

Sartre, Jean-Paul. *Black Orpheus.* Translated by S. W. Allen. Paris: Présence Africaine, 1963.

Satris, Steven A. "The Theory of Value and the Rise of Ethical Emotivism." *Journal of the History of Ideas* 43, no. 1 (1982): 109–128.

Sauerteig, Lutz. *Krankheit, Sexualität, Gesellschaft: Geschlechtskrankheit und Gesundheitspolitik in Deutschland im 19. und frühen 20. Jahrhundert.* Stuttgart: Steiner, 1999.

Sawicki, Jana. *Disciplining Foucault: Feminism, Power, and the Body.* New York: Routledge, 1991.

Schirbel, Gabriele. *Strukturen des Internationalismus: First Universal Races Congress, London, 1911.* 2 vols. Münster: Lit, 1991.

Schluppman, Heide. "Die Radikalisierung der Philosophie: Die Nietzsche-Rezeption und die sexualpolitische Publizistik Helene Stöcker's." *Feministische Studien* 3 (1984): 10–38.

Schochet, Elijah. *Animal Life in Jewish Tradition: Attitudes and Relationships.* New York: Kvat, 1994.

Schoppmann, Claudia. *Der Skorpion: Frauenliebe in der Weimarer Republik.* Hamburg: Libertäre Assoziation, 1985.

———. *Verbotene Verhältnisse: Frauenliebe, 1938–1945.* Berlin: Quer, 1999.

Schorske, Carl. *Fin-de-Siècle Vienna: Politics and Culture.* New York: Vintage, 1981.

Schorske, Carl. *German Social Democracy, 1905–1917: The Development of the Great Schism.* Cambridge, Mass.: Harvard University Press, 1955.

Schott, Robin. *Cognition and Eros: A Critique of the Kantian Paradigm.* Boston: Beacon Press, 1988.

——, ed. *Feminist Interpretations of Immanuel Kant.* University Park: Pennsylvania State University Press, 1997.

Schröder, Iris. *Arbeiten für eine bessere Welt: Frauenbewegung und Sozialreform, 1890–1914.* Frankfurt am Main: Campus, 2001.

Schulte, Regine. *Sperrbezirke: Tugendhaftigkeit und Prostitution in der bürgerlichen Welt.* Frankfurt am Main: Syndikat, 1984.

Schultz, Karla. "In Defense of Narcissus: Lou Andreas-Salomé and Julia Kristeva." *German Quarterly* 67 (1994): 185–196.

Schumann, Rosemarie. "Helene Stöcker: Verkünderin und Verwirklicherin." In *Alternativen: Schicksale Deutsche Bürger,* edited by Olaf Graf. Berlin: Verlag der Nation, 1987.

Schwartz, Agatha. "Austrian *Fin-de-Siècle* Gender Heteroglossia: The Dialogism of Misogyny, Feminism, and Viriphobia." *German Studies Review* 28, no. 2 (2005): 347–366.

Seigel, Jerrold. "Consciousness and Practice in the History of Marxism." *Comparative Studies in Society and History* 24, no. 1 (1982): 164–177.

——. *The Idea of the Self: Thought and Experience in Western Europe since the Seventeenth Century.* Cambridge: Cambridge University Press, 2005.

Sengoopta, Chandak. *Otto Weininger: Sex, Science, and Self in Imperial Vienna.* Chicago: University of Chicago Press, 2000.

Simon-Ritz, Frank. *Die Organisation einer Weltanschauung: Die freigeistige Bewegung im wilhelminischen Deutschland.* Gütersloh: Chr. Kaiser/Gütersloher Verlagshaus, 1997.

Smith, Barry. *Austrian Philosophy: The Legacy of Franz Brentano.* Chicago: Open Court, 1994.

——, ed. *Foundations of Gestalt Theory.* Munich: Philosophia, 1988.

Smith, Helmut Walser. *German Nationalism and Religious Conflict: Culture, Ideology, Politics, 1870–1914.* Princeton, N.J.: Princeton University Press, 1995.

——, ed. *Protestants, Catholics, and Jews in Germany, 1800–1914.* New York: Berg, 2001.

Smith, Jill Suzanne. "Reading the Red Light: Literary, Cultural, and Social Discourses on Prostitution in Berlin, 1880–1933." Ph.D. dissertation, Indiana University, 2004.

Smith, John David. "W. E. B. Dubois, Felix von Luschan, and Racial Reform at the *Fin de Siècle.*" *Amerikastudien* 47, no. 1 (2002): 23–38.

Smith, Woodruff D. *Politics and the Sciences of Culture in Germany, 1840–1920.* New York: Oxford University Press, 1991.

Sperber, Jonathan. *Popular Catholicism in Nineteenth-Century Germany.* Princeton, N.J.: Princeton University Press, 1984.

Stark, Gary. "Pornography, Society, and the Law in Imperial Germany." *Central European History* 14, no. 3 (1981): 200–229.

Steakley, James P. *The Homosexual Emancipation Movement in Germany.* New York: Arno Press, 1975.

Steenson, Gary. *Karl Kautsky, 1854–1938: Marxism in the Classical Years.* Pittsburgh: University of Pittsburgh Press, 1978.

Steger, Manfred. "Historical Materialism and Ethics: Eduard Bernstein's Revisionist Perspective." *History of European Ideas* 14, no. 5 (1992): 647–663.

——. *The Quest for Evolutionary Socialism: Eduard Bernstein and Social Democracy.* Cambridge: Cambridge University Press, 1997.

Steinbrügge, Lieselotte. *The Moral Sex: Woman's Nature in the French Enlightenment.* Translated by Pamela Selwyn. New York: Oxford University Press, 1995.

Stepan, Nancy. "Biological Degeneration: Races and Proper Places." In *Degeneration: The Dark Side of Progress,* edited by J. Edward Chamberlin and Sander L. Gilman. New York: Columbia University Press, 1985.

Stephan, Inge. *Die Gründerinnen der Psychoanalyse: Eine Entmythologisierung Sigmund Freuds in zwölf Frauenporträts.* Stuttgart: Kreuz, 1992.

Stern, Fritz. *The Politics of Cultural Despair: A Study in the Rise of the Germanic Ideology.* Berkeley: University of California Press, 1961.

Stoler, Ann Laura. *Race and the Education of Desire: Foucault's History of Sexuality and the Colonial Order of Things.* Durham, N.C.: Duke University Press, 1995.

Stolleis, Michael. *Konstitution und Intervention: Studien zur Geschichte des öffentlichen Rechts im 19. Jahrhundert.* Frankfurt am Main: Suhrkamp, 2001.

Stümke, Hans-Georg. *Homosexuelle in Deutschland: Eine politische Geschichte.* Munich: C. H. Beck, 1989.

Sumser, Robert. "Rational Occultism in Fin de Siècle Germany: Rudolf Steiner's Modernism." *History of European Ideas* 18, no. 4 (1994): 497–511.

Surkis, Judith. *Sexing the Citizen: Morality and Masculinity in France, 1870–1920.* Ithaca: Cornell University Press, 2006.

Taylor, Charles. *Sources of the Self: The Making of Modern Identity.* Cambridge, Mass.: Harvard University Press, 1989.

Taylor, Dianna, and Karen Vintges, eds. *Feminism and the Final Foucault.* Urbana: University of Illinois Press, 2004.

Telman, D. A. Jeremy. "Adolf Stöcker: Anti-Semite with a Christian Mission." *Jewish History* 9, no. 2 (1995): 93–112.

Thomas, R. Hinton. *Nietzsche in German Politics and Society, 1890–1918.* Manchester: Manchester University Press, 1983.

Thompson, R. A. *The Yellow Peril, 1890–1924.* New York: Arno Press, 1978.

Thönnessen, Werner. *The Emancipation of Women: The Rise and Decline of the Women's Movement in German Social Democracy, 1863–1933.* Translated by Joris de Bres. London: Pluto Press, 1973.

Toews, John. "Refashioning the Masculine Subject in Early Modernism: Narratives of Self-dissolution and Self-construction in Psychoanalysis and Literature, 1900–1914." *Modernism/Modernity* 4, no. 1 (1997): 31–67.

Treitel, Corinna. *A Science for the Soul: Occultism and the Genesis of the German Modern.* Baltimore: Johns Hopkins University Press, 2004.

Tucker, Robert C. *The Marxian Revolutionary Idea.* New York: Norton, 1969.

Tudor, H., and J. M. Tudor, eds. *Marxism and Social Democracy: The Revisionist Debate, 1896–1898.* Cambridge: Cambridge University Press, 1988.

Turner, Bryan S., ed. *Citizenship and Social Theory*. London: Sage, 1993.

Ünlüdag, Tânia. "Bourgeois Mentality and Socialist Ideology as Exemplified by Clara Zetkin's Constructs of Femininity." *International Review of Social History* 47, no. 1 (2002): 33–58.

Usborne, Cornelia. *The Politics of the Body in Weimar Germany: Women's Reproductive Rights and Duties*. Ann Arbor: University of Michigan Press, 1992.

Vertovec, Steven, and Robin Cohen, eds. *Conceiving Cosmopolitanism: Theory, Context, and Practice*. Oxford: Oxford University Press, 2002.

von Bockel, Rolf. *Philosophin einer "neuen Ethik": Helene Stöcker (1869–1943)*. Hamburg: Ed. Hamburg Borman & von Bockel, 1991.

Waite, Geoff. *Nietzsche's Corps/e: Aesthetics, Politics, Prophecy, or the Spectacular Techno-culture of Everyday Life*. Durham, N.C.: Duke University Press, 1996.

Walkowitz, Judith R. *Prostitution and Victorian Society: Women, Class, and the State*. Cambridge: Cambridge University Press, 1980.

Wallwork, Ernest. *Psychoanalysis and Ethics*. New Haven, Conn.: Yale University Press, 1991.

Weeks, Jeffrey. *Sex, Politics and Society: The Regulation of Sexuality since 1800*. London: Longman, 1981.

Wehler, Hans-Ulrich. *The German Empire, 1871–1918*. Translated by Kim Traynor. Providence, R.I.: Berg, 1993.

Weikart, Richard. *From Darwin to Hitler: Evolutionary Ethics, Eugenics, and Racism in Germany*. New York: Palgrave, 2004.

——. *Socialist Darwinism: Evolution in German Socialist Thought from Marx to Bernstein*. San Francisco: International Scholars, 1998.

Weindling, Paul. *Darwinism and Social Darwinism in Imperial Germany: The Contribution of the Cell Biologist Oscar Hertwig, 1844–1922*. Stuttgart: G. Fischer, 1991.

——. *Health, Race, and German Politics between National Unification and Nazism, 1870–1945*. New York: Cambridge University Press, 1989.

Weindling, Paul, and Pietro Corsi. "Darwinism in Germany, France, and Italy." In *The Darwinian Heritage*, edited by David Kohn. Princeton, N.J.: Princeton University Press, 1985.

Weingart, Peter. "The Rationalization of Sexual Behavior: The Institutionalization of Eugenic Thought in Germany." *Journal of the History of Biology* 20, no. 2 (1987): 159–193.

Weir, Todd. "The Fourth Confession: Atheism, Monism, and Politics in the Freigeistig Movement in Berlin, 1859–1924." Ph.D. dissertation, Columbia University, 2005.

Weiss, Sheila Faith. *Race, Hygiene, and National Efficiency: The Eugenics of Wilhelm Schallmayer*. Berkeley: University of California Press, 1987.

Weitz, Eric. *Creating German Communism, 1890–1990*. Princeton, N.J.: Princeton University Press, 1996.

Welsch, Ursula, and Michaela Wiesner. *Lou Andreas-Salomé: Vom "Lebensurgrund" zur Psychoanalyse*. Munich: Internationale Psychoanalyse, 1988.

Werbner, Pnina, and Nira Yuval-Davis, eds. *Women, Citizenship and Difference*. London: Zed Books, 1999.

Wetzell, Richard. *Inventing the Criminal: A History of German Criminology, 1880–1945.* Chapel Hill: University of North Carolina Press, 2000.

Wickert, Christl. *Helene Stöcker, 1869–1943: Frauenrechtlerin, Sexualreformerin und Pazifistin; Eine Biographie.* Bonn: Dietz Nachf., 1991.

Wilde, Lawrence. *Ethical Marxism and Its Radical Critics.* New York: St. Martin's Press, 1998.

Willey, Thomas E. *Back to Kant: The Revival of Kantianism in German Social and Historical Thought, 1860–1914.* Detroit: Wayne State University Press, 1978.

Wood, Allen. "The Marxian Critique of Justice." *Philosophy and Public Affairs* 1, no. 3 (1972): 244–282.

Woycke, James. *Birth Control in Germany, 1871–1933.* New York: Routledge, 1988.

Yovel, Yirmiahu. *Spinoza and Other Heretics: The Adventures of Immanence.* Princeton, N.J.: Princeton University Press, 1989.

Zantop, Susanne. *Colonial Fantasies: Conquest, Family, and Nation in Precolonial Germany, 1770–1870.* Durham, N.C.: Duke University Press, 1997.

Zerbel, Miriam. *Tierschutz im Kaiserreich: Ein Beitrag zur Geschichte des Vereinswesens.* Frankfurt am Main: Peter Lang, 1993.

———. "Tierschutzbewegung." In *Handbuch zur "völksichen Bewegung," 1871–1918,* edited by Uwe Puschner, Walter Schmitz, and Justus Ulbricht. Munich: K. G. Saur, 1996.

Žižek, Slavoj. *The Metastases of Enjoyment: Six Essays on Woman and Causality.* New York: Verso, 1994.

INDEX